Off Stage/On Display

Off Stage / On Display

Intimacy and Ethnography
in the Age of Public Culture

Edited by
ANDREW SHRYOCK

Stanford University Press
Stanford, California
2004

Stanford University Press

Stanford, California

© 2004 by the Board of Trustees of the Leland Stanford Junior University.
All rights reserved.

Printed in the United States of America on acid-free, archival-quality paper.

Library of Congress Cataloging-in-Publication Data

Off stage/on display : intimacy and ethnography in the age of public culture / edited
by Andrew Shryock.

    p. cm.

  Includes bibliographical references and index.

   ISBN 0-8047-5006-8 (cloth : alk. paper)—ISBN 0-8047-5007-6 (pbk. : alk. paper)

   1. Ethnology—Congresses.   2. Intimacy (Psychology)—Congresses.
3. Privacy—Congresses.   4. Mass media and culture—Congresses.   5. Group
identity—Congresses.   6. Popular culture—Congresses.   I. Shryock, Andrew.

GN320.O35 2004

306.4—dc22   2004006387

Original Printing 2004

Last figure below indicates year of this printing:

13   12   11   10   09   08   07   06   05   04

Typeset by G&S Typesetters, Inc., in 10.5/12 Bembo

Contents

vi   *Contents*

Illustrations

Acknowledgments

THIS PROJECT BEGAN as a panel organized for the 2001 meeting of the American Anthropological Association, entitled "Cultural Intimacy and Mass Mediation: Articulating New Grounds for Ethnography between Public and Private Spheres." When I first invited colleagues to participate in the panel, I knew most of them only through their published work. My previous labors as an editor were "community-based," relying on long acquaintance and proximity, around which ideas developed. I have greatly enjoyed, this time around, building relationships on the topical affinities and theoretical resonances one finds in books. To the contributors I already considered friends, and to those who (often through the medium of email) have become close and reliable allies, I can happily point to yet another proof of the formative links between intimacy and mass mediation. Most of the panel's participants have carried their ideas through to the pages of this book, and those who joined later helped us amplify and expand the volume's central themes. I thank all the contributors for their enduring interest in the project and for the pleasure (a rare and not strictly editorial one) of reading their manuscripts over and over again, a task that has equipped me to think and argue differently and, in the process, to alter some old intellectual habits.

The essays "on display" in this volume have their own "off stage" areas of production. They have benefited greatly from the attention of many readers, not all of whom I can acknowledge personally, so I second the thanks offered elsewhere by individual contributors. Kay Warren, who read several of the papers in early drafts, encouraged me with her strong enthusiasm for the project, and Michael Herzfeld, whose ideas figure centrally in the volume, offered a judicious (and transformative) blend of criticism and support. It is safe to say the volume would never have materialized without his efforts, or his inspiration. The participants in "Cultural Intimacy and Mass Mediation," a seminar I taught at the University of Michigan in 2002, were a rich source of insight as well; many of my ideas made complete sense to me only after they had been tossed around by these sometimes skeptical, always creative students.

Two anonymous reviewers at Stanford University Press gave us fascinating commentary and lobbied for changes in ways that suggested a true appreciation for the project. Several essays changed radically (and for the better) in response to these readers. Our editors at the press, Pat Katayama and Carmen Borbón-Wu, brought the manuscript through its many stages of production, deftly and efficiently. Finally, I would like to thank my colleagues at the Center for Advanced Study in the Behavioral Sciences, especially members of the Identity and Difference reading group, whose discussions of their own work and mine supplied the perfect backdrop against which to write and edit this book. My year at CASBS (2002–2003) was generously supported by the Andrew W. Mellon Foundation (Grant # 29800639).

Contributors

WALTER ARMBRUST is a lecturer at St. Antony's College, Oxford, where he holds the Albert Hourani Chair in Middle East Studies. His research focuses on popular and mass culture, modernity, film studies, and Egyptian society. He is the author of *Mass Culture and Modernism in Egypt* (1996) and editor of *Mass Mediations: New Approaches to Popular Culture in the Middle East and Beyond* (2000).

KELLY M. ASKEW is an associate professor in the Department of Anthropology and Center for Afro-American and African Studies at the University of Michigan. She is the author of *Performing the Nation: Swahili Music and Cultural Politics in Tanzania* (2002) and editor, with Richard Wilk, of *The Anthropology of Media: A Reader* (2002). Askew was also an associate producer and editor for the documentary series *Rhythms from Africa*. She works in East Africa and among Swahili diaspora communities in the Middle East. Her most recent research "Zanzibar Revelations: Remembered Futures, Dismembered Pasts" traces the global circulation of memories and interpretations of the 1964 Zanzibar Revolution.

JOHN F. COLLINS is an assistant professor of anthropology at Queens College, City University of New York. He received his Ph.D. in Ethnology from the University of Michigan in 2003. His dissertation, *The Revolt of the Saints: Popular Memory, National Culture, and Urban Space in the Twilight of Brazilian Racial Democracy*, examines the making of a heritage center in the city of Salvador, Bahia, with particular attention to how state authorities and residents of the historical neighborhood negotiate concepts of culture, history, and personhood.

ANDREAS GLAESER is an assistant professor in the Department of Sociology at the University of Chicago. He is the author of *Divided in Unity: Identity, Germany and the Berlin Police* (1999) and "Placed Selves: The Role of Space in Identity Formation Processes of Eastern and Western Berlin Police Officers after German Unification," *Social Identities*, 1998. Glaeser is currently exploring how the meaning of Germany as a corporate entity is negotiated in the context of the government's move from Bonn to Berlin. He is also considering how organizational forms, ideologies, and personal desires interact in processes of reality construction among officers of the former secret police of the GDR.

MICHAEL HERZFELD is a professor of social anthropology in the Department of Anthropology at Harvard University. He is interested in social theory, history and anthropology, social poetics, the politics of history, Europe (especially Greece and Italy), and Thailand. He is the author of numerous books, including *Anthropology Through the Looking Glass* (1987), *A Place in History* (1991), *Cultural Intimacy* (1997), and *Anthropology: Theoretical Practice in Culture and Society* (2001).

RICHARD MADDOX is a professor in the Department of History at Carnegie Mellon University. He has done fieldwork in Ecuador and Spain. He is the author of *El Castillo: The Politics of Tradition in an Andalusian Town* (1993), winner of the President's Book Award of the Social Science History Association and the Robert E. Park Award of the American Sociological Association. His current research focuses on the state and public culture in contemporary Europe, and his latest book, *The Best of All Possible Islands: Seville's Universal Exposition, the "New Spain," and the "New Europe,"* is forthcoming.

J. LORAND MATORY is the Hugh K. Foster Professor of Anthropology and of Afro-American Studies at Harvard University. His research interests include the anthropology of religions, spirit possession, gender, ethnicity, and transnationalism. He has done fieldwork in West Africa and in the African diasporas of the Americas. Matory is the author of *Sex and the Empire That Is No More: Gender and the Politics of Metaphor in Oyo Yoruba Religion* (1994).

ROSALIND MORRIS is an associate professor of anthropology and director of the Institute for Research on Women and Gender at Columbia University. She has conducted fieldwork in Thailand, on questions of modernity, mass media, spirit possession, gender, and sexuality; and in South Africa, on mining, value, and languages of violence. Morris is the author of *In the Place of Origins: Modernity and Its Mediums in Northern Thailand* (2000). Her recent essays include "Theses on the Questions of War: History, Media, Terror" (*Social Text* 2002) and "Failures of Domestication: Speculations on Globality, Economy, and the Sex of Excess in Thailand" (*differences* 2002).

ESRA ÖZYÜREK is an assistant professor in the Department of Anthropology at the University of California, San Diego. Her interests include secularism and Islam, ideologies of the state, citizenship, alternative modernities, memory, nationalism, and gender. Özyürek is the author of *Remembering in Forgetting: Social Memory in Turkey* (2001), and her latest writing project is *Nostalgia for the Modern: Privatization of State Ideology in Turkey*, a monograph based on her dissertation.

ANDREW SHRYOCK is an associate professor of anthropology at the University of Michigan. He has done ethnographic fieldwork in Yemen, Jordan, and among Arab immigrant and ethnic communities in Detroit. His recent work has dealt with the politics of hospitality and the creation of cultural mainstreams. He is the author of *Nationalism and the Genealogical Imagination: Oral History and Textual Authority in Tribal Jordan* (1997) and editor, with Nabeel Abraham, of *Arab Detroit: From Margin to Mainstream* (2000).

Introduction

CHAPTER 1

Other Conscious/Self Aware

FIRST THOUGHTS ON CULTURAL
INTIMACY AND MASS MEDIATION

Andrew Shryock

THIS VOLUME IS a collective response to a range of problems—some theoretical, others practical, all of them political—that shape the work of anthropologists who study and take part in the making of social identities intended for display in the domain we now call "public culture." A simple contradiction generates these problems. The production of identities meant to be public, that have publicity as part of their function, will create, of necessity, a special terrain of things, relations, and activities that cannot themselves be public but are essential aspects of whatever reality and value public things might possess. This terrain is the "off stage" area in which the explicitly public is made, even staged, before it is shown. Though not universally "private"—it can include entire national communities, ethnoracial minorities, socioeconomic classes, religious movements, and global diasporas of almost any kind—this terrain can never be fully transparent, and it is often a site of social intimacy. The gaps and screens that set this terrain apart from contexts of public display make it hard to represent, ethnographically, aesthetically, and politically, despite the essential role it plays in the creation of public culture.

The contributors to this volume locate their work in the heart of this awkward terrain. We study the mass mediation of social identities and cultural forms, yet we are equally intrigued by the zones of intimacy mass mediation seems inevitably to require and (most interesting of all) to obscure. Our approaches to this analytical situation are as diverse as the geographical regions and theoretical traditions in which our ethnography is rooted. What we share, however, is a growing sense that crucial dimensions of the relationship between intimacy and mass mediation are being neglected in contemporary cultural analysis, with the sad result that our understandings of both are made thinner and less insightful. It is important to determine how and why this is so, and I will try to address these issues in the pages that follow. It is also important to realize that the pressure to look away from intimate zones of cultural production, to give attention instead to the "finished products" that circulate beyond them, is strong. Moreover, the very constitution of public culture as a sociopolitical sphere endows this pressure with the legitimacy (I am tempted to say "the sacredness") that so regularly exempts it from scrutiny. Still, in the face of political crisis, cultural difference, and historical change—settings in which much of our scholarship unfolds—the inner workings of public culture are exposed in all their fragility and power. As I was writing the early drafts of this introduction, a catastrophic turn of events gave unusual clarity to these issues and convinced me that they should be addressed in new, more challenging ways.

Meet the Press

On September 11, 2001, two commercial airliners slammed into the World Trade Center, a third hit the Pentagon, and a fourth crashed in the Pennsylvania countryside. Over three thousand people were killed. The men who hijacked these planes, it soon became evident, could be described using identity labels I had desperately hoped would not apply to them: they were Arab and Muslim. As an anthropologist who studies Arab communities in both the Middle East and the United States, I realized that the people I work with and write about—and with whom I identify personally in ways too complex to describe—were entering dangerous times. I knew also that I would be expected to play a public role in controlling the climate of fear that would quickly envelop all contexts, from the intimate to the impersonal, in which Arab and Muslim identities (and Arab Muslim persons) might be represented as legitimately "American" and therefore entitled to respect, protection, and equal treatment under U.S. law. A diverse array of ethnoreligious communities, whose place in American society was decidedly marginal before the events of 9/11, would now be glaringly on display. The American public would have to be "made aware" of Arabs and Muslims, especially the five million (or so) living in the United States, whose political loyalties were suddenly a matter of "national security." I braced myself for difficult work, hoping I would attract only passing attention from the mainstream press, whose coverage of Middle Eastern and Muslim issues is suffused by polemical discourses I had no desire to perpetuate.

   The calls began on September 13, 2001. Feature writers and fact checkers from the *Economist*, the *New York Times*, and the *New Yorker*; circumspect freelancers; journalists from local print and electronic media—it took them just two days to find me. Our encounters were predictable from the start. Except for a few strange calls, during which I was expected to interpret verses from the Qur'an (to elucidate how they might be used to plan future attacks), or asked to provide lists of Arab American groups that sponsor terrorism (as if I kept such things in my desk drawer), most of these journalists wanted information about Arabs in Detroit and how they were reacting to the events of 9/11. Several were preparing to travel, or send production crews, to Dearborn, and they wanted names of people they could talk to. Others were looking for angles and narratives. My job, more or less, was to tell them if their stories made sense and, if not, to help them develop more appropriate ones.

Media attention is something I seldom contend with, and the novelty of the situation triggered an ethnographer's response: I began to see patterns. Almost all of the reporters had located me on a Web site, where I was identified as someone who studies Arab Americans. They knew I was coeditor of a book called *Arab Detroit: From Margin to Mainstream* (2000). Nabeel Abraham, my collaborator on that project, has the good fortune of a surname that begins with the first two letters of the English alphabet; in bibliographies of "suggested readings" on Arab Americans, a genre of public education now rampant on the Web, our book nearly always appears at the top of the list. For the first wave of reporters who contacted me, I was a name on a screen, author of a mass-mediated artifact advertised on a global network of screens; using numbers provided on Web sites, I could be made to materialize as a voice on a telephone. To date, I have met only two of my reporters face-to-face. More puzzling still, hardly any of these reporters were referred to me by a colleague or, indeed, by anyone I knew personally.

The world I prepare journalists to enter is already formatted to receive and instruct them. Arab Detroit is filled with ready spokespeople, background data neatly packaged, reliable sound bites, and dozens of activist organizations willing to facilitate mass mediation. The people I encourage reporters to talk to include fellow academics who teach in Dearborn and Detroit; members of Detroit's Arab American press; and, most important of all, a long list of names associated with ACCESS, the Arab Community Center for Economic and Social Services, where I did volunteer work as a cultural arts programmer and grant writer in the 1990s. The voices and faces that appear in media accounts of Dearborn are disproportionately ACCESS officials, staff, former employees, their friends, relatives, and clients. In Detroit, ACCESS is the key purveyor of images and information about Arabs. It is also an elaborate buffer zone in which "outsiders"—journalists, certainly, but also academics, government officials, and anyone with business interests —can be told what they "need to know" about Arab Americans and, at the same time, be kept from straying into parts of the Arab immigrant community believed, by many Arabs in Detroit, to be "old country," exceedingly Other, and a potential embarrassment when exposed to the uncomprehending eye of the American mainstream. The inhabitants of this stigmatized terrain are called, in local slang, "boaters": newly arrived, socially conservative immigrants. As an ethnographer, I know and write about "boaters." I do not find them anything to be ashamed of; in fact, years of residence in Jordan and Yemen have made them very familiar to me, and I to them. But my willingness to engage with "boaters" and explain their position in a larger, Americanized politics of cultural display is often a source of consternation for those who police the boundaries between Arab Detroit and the larger society.

When faced with journalists who know nothing about Arab Detroit, however, and whose intentions I cannot accurately gauge, I find that my immediate response is not different from that of Arab Detroit's principal spokespeople. I do my best to make sure reporters do not talk to women like Fatma, who believes Israelis (or, more to the point, "the Jews") were behind the 9/11 attacks. "Arabs," she says, "cannot do anything that organized." I never mention my conversations with men like Ziyad, who urged me to inform the FBI that the next attack will come in the form of disease-laden pigeons. The plan is revealed in the Qur'an, which Ziyad reads as a key to the mind of Osama bin Laden. "I am an Arab," he says. "I know how he thinks." I do my best to keep reporters in the dark about internal politics at one of the local mosques, where the Imam was forbidden to preach because his sermons were "too pro-American," and where many of the "boaters" in attendance have opinions they are not artful enough to conceal. I steer reporters away from certain leaders of Detroit's Arabic-speaking Chaldean and Maronite Catholic communities, who cannot resist the urge—understandable under the circumstances—to distance themselves from Arab Muslims or make disparaging remarks about Islam, linking it to the persecution of Middle Eastern Christians, who are "not involved in terrorism."

The very mention of these things is problematic for me. In stating them so plainly, I cannot help but feel that I am revealing something I should keep secret. But why? The things I have told you are common knowledge in Arab Detroit. They proliferate in forwarded emails, on Arabic call-in talk shows, in the pages of the Muslim American press, and even in memoranda circulated to members of the U.S. Congress. Still, I do not share this kind of information with mainstream journalists and their wider publics. I fear that in doing so I would be abusing my familiarity with a community that has taken me into its confidence; that I would be giving "outsiders" the ability to divide the community (along Christian and Muslim lines) and disparage it (for its apparent addiction to rumor, conspiracy theory, and magical thinking). I *share* these sensitivities with Arab Americans in relation to external observers whom I, and they, imagine to be non-Arab and unsympathetic.

Yet this awareness has not stopped me from telling you things I normally conceal from others, nor has it kept me from assuming that you, my imagined reader, can be trusted with these revelations whereas others, who are perfectly real, cannot be. By writing this way, I place you in a category beyond Arab and non-Arab, beyond insider and outsider, and I realize that this placement is ultimately a projection of the interpretive space I occupy as an ethnographer. Identification and fellow feeling are clearly possible in this imaginary (and now public) space, but less congenial postures can never be ruled out, just as they cannot be factored out of the everyday worlds ethnography hopes to represent. My decisions to tell and not to tell, distributed so as to shape the new publics in which Arab Muslims must inevitably figure, have been made at a time of extreme vulnerability and risk. Yet because ethnographers are routinely drawn to forms of knowledge and aspects of identity that are neither entirely "off stage" nor fully "on display," I suspect that no other example I offer here could better encapsulate the tension between intimacy and mass mediation this volume intends to explore.

Immediacy/Publics/Zones of Trespass

The problems we grapple with in this book are characterized not only by moral ambiguity but also by an expanding imprecision of master narratives and their essential terms. Intimacy, mass mediation, public and private spheres: these concepts are now part of global discourses that pervade cultural criticism, public policy, models of citizenship, and the theory and practice of commerce. Whether one is talking about the reunification of Germany, tensions between Pentecostals and practitioners of Candomblé in Brazil, or museum exhibits designed to celebrate Turkish modernity, this array of concepts can rather quickly become indispensable. At the same time, it grows ever more difficult to say, in ways that are useful and not merely pedantic, exactly what intimacy, mass mediation, public, and private mean when they mean *something* in settings that differ from each other so dramatically. If we are to say anything new here, we will have to build on this odd foundation of incommensurability and common reference, since it is the conceptual space—the "area between"—in which new grounds for ethnography might be identified and brought together in anthropological projects that more effectively expose the limits and the potential of our work.

Part of this exposure would certainly include a reassessment of the language we use to tell ourselves what is interesting and important about ethnography. It has become habit, for instance, to stress the novelty of mass mediation and to treat the study of public culture as an enterprise contrary to what fieldwork has traditionally been about. A new kind of ethnography is called for, the story goes, when human communities are connected and transgressed by telecommunication networks, financial and commodity markets, (trans)national identities, and heavy flows (local and global) of print materials, movies, TV shows, music, and other forms of "expressive culture." Nodding one's agreement requires almost no effort. The claim is "good to think," and it gets better to think all the time. In the post–Cold War period, the global spread of neoliberal modernity and its ruling motifs —the downsizing nation-state, the expanding market, consumerism, electoral reform, democratization, civil society, transparency, sustainable development, universal human rights, and pluralism—has meant that metropolitan (some would say Eurocentric) understandings of private and public spheres are being imposed on, avidly embraced, and vigorously rejected by communities that do not always recognize these spheres, or who understand them differently, or who cannot agree on what belongs in "public" or "private" domains. These zones of categorical confusion, expansionist by design, have enveloped every human community ethnographers might hope to study; as a result, the community of ethnographers is being similarly restructured by these categories and the states of confusion that attend them.

Recent controversies over human subjects research, Internal Review Boards, governmental oversight of fieldwork, and ethnocentric or impractical notions of "informed consent" show rather starkly that ethnographers are caught up in delicate renegotiations of things public and private. The procedures university bureaucrats impose in order to control the gathering of data and the production of knowledge have, in ways no one predicted, ethically transcended (and morally trumped) our most belabored musings on reflexivity and positionality. Transparency of method was not quite what some of us had in mind when we cloaked ourselves in the language of subjectivity, political engagement, and social responsibility. We all have a private domain built into our work, a space of secrets, and our subjects must often come to terms with the harsh realization that written accounts of fieldwork invest more in protecting what is dear to us than what is dear to those who befriended or antagonized us (see Abu-Lughod 2000; Scheper-Hughes 2000). Ethnography is a form of publicity—not all of it good—and this has been the case from the very beginning.

The ethnographic monograph and the academic culture that produces it evolved in contexts of mass mediation, and the audience for anthropology has always been organized as a kind of public sphere, even a marketplace of ideas, with hierarchies of specialization and access built into it. From Mead and Benedict to Turner and Sponsel, ethnologists have correctly assumed that their findings will be of interest to a wider audience and will affect public opinion, and even public policy. Yet the "publics" anthropologists hoped to address in the past—and this remains the case today, as several observers of the latest Yanomami scandal have noted (Coronil et al. 2001)—were decidedly EuroAmerican and globally dominant. Anthropology evolved, and still functions, as one variant in a constellation of modern, Western, imperial discourses used to organize and govern human difference. It is one means— a fairly unimportant one, and one prone to counterhegemonic positions— by which a metropolitan public can be told, and can tell itself, what being modern and Western signify.

Ethnographic fieldwork, by contrast, was for many decades an activity understood to take place beyond the reach of mass media, outside modernity and the West, and beyond the publics for which ethnographic representations were produced. That the natives might actually read our monographs, see our films, or even hear our lectures once seemed a remote possibility to most ethnographers, and it was hardly cause for concern. Ironically, this attitude was the ex post facto reinstatement of a social distance fieldwork practice was designed to overcome. The methods ethnographers perfected on the margins of the world system were slanted toward face-to-face interaction, seeing and talking, imitation and repetition, bodily engagement, the retraining of tongues, the rethinking of thoughts, and other forms of immediate, highly localized, often traumatic experience. If the natives were literate, ethnographers usually were not (or were only marginally so); by default, "culture" was identified with the local, the embodied, the implicit, the quotidian. It accumulated in the zones of incompatibility that separated ethnographers from the societies they encountered; it could be rendered intelligible and explicit only through personal interaction. Ethnographers, especially those who work in postcolonial settings, can hardly pretend that this way of constructing Otherness is distinctive. It is not parochial misperception, but accumulated historical insight—and, more often than we care to admit, "admiration"—that prompts our subjects to compare us to colonial officers, spies, missionaries, (ad)venture capitalists, and other predecessors famed for their ability to speak the language, eat properly, show good manners, master the political system, and otherwise "infiltrate" local society. Ethnographers fit nicely in this fellowship of intrusive, intelligence-gathering social types: we enter alien terrain (or make familiar terrain alien); we change our spots, cross and pass, develop odd affinities and indescribable loyalties, then report on our activities and train others to do likewise.

Today, although zones of cultural incompatibility are supposedly shrinking, expressions of cultural difference flourish. The "infiltrations" continue, but it is harder now to determine who is crossing, and in what directions. Ethnographic subjects watch TV, read magazines, travel abroad, and partake in the anonymous communion of nationhood—just as ethnographers do— but these activities have done little to alter the terrain of intersubjective difference on which the "old" ethnographic methods were effective. If anything, that terrain is expanding. Contexts of intimacy and mass mediation now routinely overlap and constitute each other in the field, creating new publics in relation to which ethnography can (and cannot) be written. Culture is increasingly public, yet much of it is now off limits. Whether ethnography occurs on the set of a Hollywood film shot in South Africa featuring Kenyan pastoralists (imported, along with tall grass and lions, just for the occasion), or among municipal bureaucrats who must organize an exposition that will showcase Seville and "the new Spain" to millions of visitors from around the world, the challenge of contemporary fieldwork lies not in our inability to "enclose" these situations in structures of immediate experience. Rather, the challenge lies in the need to interpret immediacy (and the sense of enclosure it so often entails) in relation to larger, often global frameworks of cultural display in which ethnographers, and now their subjects, are self-consciously located.

Self-aware/Other-conscious

The advent of global self-consciousness has already shaped anthropological practice more than we realize, and an awareness of this effect is materializing in new analytical concepts designed, as it were, to problematize and treat this condition. Michael Herzfeld, for instance, has located much of his recent work in contexts of "cultural intimacy," which he defines as "the recognition of those aspects of cultural identity that are considered a source of external embarrassment but which nevertheless provide insiders with their assurance of common sociality" (1997: 3). Note that this concept of intimacy internalizes and renders essential the presence of an outside observer whose disapproval matters, whose judgments can be predicted, and (most important of all) whose opinion is vital in determining what value "common sociality" can have.

The deft example Herzfeld offers to explain this concept is the Greek government's attempt to ban the breaking of plates in restaurants frequented by tourists; not only is the practice "not Greek," despite all evidence to the contrary, but it is humiliating for some Greeks to realize that tourists—Northern European ones especially—see this custom as quintessentially Greek. Plate smashing becomes a site of "cultural intimacy" for Greeks in relation to German observers, and what Germans think about plate smashing is important because they are assumed to "look down" on Greeks for engaging in a practice Germans, representing the more modern of the two national communities, would never be "guilty" of. Whether Germans really do look down on Greeks for smashing plates does not matter; the intimacy that emerges in this context of self-recognition is decidedly Greek, as is the embarrassment that comes with the realization that cultural difference, yet again, upholds a larger system of ranking in which Greece is not quite modern, not quite Europe.

"Cultural intimacy," as Herzfeld describes it, makes immediate sense, but it remains a highly complex emotional reaction, and the emphasis on "embarrassment" might seem peculiar. Why not extend the concept to moments of self-recognition that trigger a feeling of pride or superiority? Are those German tourists, just as the Greek bureaucrats suspect, experiencing their own moment of smug cultural superiority as they watch hot-blooded Greeks break plates? The question quickly turns on itself, however, if we follow up by asking: would Germans feel embarrassed if we were to dwell publicly on this moment of gawking elitism, and (turning the question once again) could they feel proud of their ability to recognize and criticize their own feelings of superiority? This exercise could go on ad nauseam, but the factor that brings each permutation in line with its predecessor is the existence of an external observer whose opinion is imagined *and imagined to matter.* Today, cultural intimacy makes sense only when (only because) it appears in relation to "global stages," which, as Richard Wilk notes, "put diversity in a common frame, and scale it along a limited number of dimensions, celebrating some kinds of difference and submerging others" (1995:111).

Global stages, wherever they are successfully in place, foster structures and sentiments akin to the Habermasian notion of "intimacy oriented toward a public," the subjective condition that, in eighteenth-century Europe, enabled members of the newly emergent bourgeoisie to address each other as a community using indirect media of conversation: newspapers, journals, novels, essays, and personal diaries and letters fit for publication. The problem with this formulation for any anthropologist—indeed, for anyone whose understanding of "modernity" is transregional—is the assumption of cultural sameness on which Habermas based his model. He writes,

> For the experiences about which a public passionately concerned with itself sought agreement and enlightenment through the rational-critical public debate of private persons with one another flowed from the wellspring of a specific subjectivity. The latter had its home, literally, in the sphere of the patriarchal conjugal family. As is well known, this family type—emerging in changes of family structure for which centuries of transformations toward capitalism paved the way—consolidated itself as the dominant type within the bourgeois strata (1989:43–44).

It is more the case today, and it was probably always so, that intimacy does not "flow" out of a familial space, but is perceived against a backdrop that accentuates the experience of difference (in and beyond domestic spaces) and orients that experience toward the task of ranking, comparing, accommodating, impressing, persuading, or excluding an "audience" of real and imaginary onlookers. The advent of intimate zones protected from (or hidden from) contexts of ranking and comparison is the necessary correlate of regimes in which intimacy is not shared, but public frames of reference might be. The multicultural pluralism espoused in elite sectors of the world system is an obvious and influential case, since it everywhere generates "minoritized publics" that, as Lauren Berlant observes, "resist or are denied universalist collective intimacy expectations, [a condition that] has much complicated the possibility of (and even the ethics of the desire for) a general mass-critical public sphere deemed to be culturally and politically intimate with itself" (2000:4). These marginalized social spaces have the potential to become "counterpublics," complete with their own newspapers, TV programs, radio stations, and markets (Warner 2002). Yet insofar as these spaces continue to be stigmatized, their emergence as publics, even counterpublics, will cast "shadows" over aspects of identity that make inclusion in majoritized publics both difficult and undesirable. The content of shadow zones tends to be richer (and more sensitive) than material that circulates in counterpublics; academics need only consider the difference between corridor talk and critical theory. The area of shadows, ironically enough, is often used to initiate and entice. Outsiders are not automatically excluded from it. Unlike the counterpublic that helps shape it, however, the shadow zone is *not* meant to be broadly seen. Instead it provides relief from, alternatives to, and staging grounds for the representation of a fairly narrow spectrum of cultural materials and practices that, in an age of identity politics, must inevitably be shown.

Neither public nor private, these zones of intimacy are the sites in which most ethnography is now done. The identities that flourish in these spaces, away from (but alert to) the gaze of external observers, are frequently at odds with the types of cultural representation that predominate in more self-consciously (and comparatively) public formats. This is especially true when public identity displays are designed to foster unified national identities that aspire to modernity and progress, or when public presentations of self and community are explicitly intended to undermine metropolitan (or Euro-centric) depictions of Others. When a Yemeni government official tells me, with a straight face, "there are no tribes in Yemen today," though I spent the afternoon chewing qat with men of the Murad tribe, and when Arab immigrants in Detroit, after viewing my slides and hearing my accounts of Bedouin hospitality, state with confidence that "no one lives like that anymore," though I spent two years of my life living like that, each is attempting to evade accusations of "backwardness." When I tell my colleagues that tribal identity in Jordan is an alternative form of modernity, or that nearly all the Muslim women I know who wear head scarves do so as a matter of choice, or that honor killings are exceedingly rare and hardly deserve the sensationalized treatment they receive in Western media, I too am performing on a global stage. I am acutely aware that my stance is out of synch with many Arab progressives, for whom tribalism is a political curse (or a creation of the colonial state), hijabs are sartorial proof of sexism and patriarchy, and vociferous opposition to honor killings is solid evidence of moral advancement. Across this entire spectrum of "positions," the anthropologist figures as a trafficker in embarrassing and impolitic knowledge; he is, by turns, an apologist, a dupe, a spy, a defamer, an intellectual colonizer, a moral relativist. The fieldworker who has never been saddled with these labels has either avoided the hard labor of "participant observation" or, more likely still, has never ventured far from home.

I would suggest that the awkwardness and embarrassment (and, very often, the risks) that accompany ethnographic knowledge are rooted in the contradictory demands of intimacy and mass mediation that define ethnography as a genre. Insofar as ethnography is committed to the public scrutiny of intimate social worlds, it will draw attention to the complex discontinuity between identities made in realms of intimacy, those made for more general display, and the tactics people use to fix or shift the (imaginary) boundaries that distinguish these domains. As a result, ethnographers will continue to produce knowledge that is easily construed as irrelevant or antithetical to the transnational, postcolonial, and resistance-oriented agendas that animate the most compelling approaches to public culture. The latter have mostly thrown in their lot with mass mediation and either refuse to give sustained attention to intimacy (opting instead for the abstractions of theory) or insinuate that engagement with the intimate worlds of Others leads to voyeurism, political mischief, and epistemological blunders. With her uncanny ability to spot trends, Ortner (1995) has dubbed this tendency "ethnographic refusal," equating it with a reluctance to engage closely with the particulars of everyday life and an eagerness to engage, simultaneously and as a substitute, in critiques of an external, impinging power (the state, the empire, the West) and its gaze.

Unfortunately, "ethnographic refusal" was destined, though perhaps not intended, to become a term of abuse; it is now something one is accused of doing, or not doing, when there is a more profound sense in which all of us, to the extent that we are still in fact doing ethnography, will be caught up in elaborate patterns of refusal—moral, political, aesthetic, and temperamental. The issues at stake are clearly laid out by Appadurai, who assures us that "the fluidities of transnational communication" (1996:44) have radically altered the subject matter of ethnography.

[T]his is a world in which points of arrival and points of departure are in cultural flux, and thus the search for steady points of reference, as critical life choices are made, can be very difficult. It is in this atmosphere that the invention of tradition (and of ethnicity, kinship, and other identity markers) can become slippery. . . . As group pasts become increasingly parts of museums, exhibits, and collections, both in national and transnational spectacles, culture becomes less what Pierre Bourdieu would have called a habitus (a tacit realm of reproducible practices and dispositions) and more an arena for conscious choice, justification, and representation, the latter often to multiple and spatially dislocated audiences (1996:44).

I doubt that Appadurai believes people have less need of habitual practices or tacit dispositions now that a small number of specialists can showcase "group pasts" in museums and ethnic festivals; that would be far-fetched. It is precisely the cultural materials that cannot be easily displayed in public formats that take on exaggerated significance in situations of pervasive multicultural contact: distinctive models of time and space, ways of holding the body, methods of sexual approach, ideas about authority, reckonings of kinship, styles of talking, notions of clean and unclean. These things are still with us, still real and significant, and the fact that migration and mass media spread these things everywhere does not make them less important, only more so. Appadurai's vision is convincing because it appeals to a growing sense that certain kinds of difference—those that are *merely* habitual, for instance, and those that can be used to stereotype and stigmatize—should be politely ignored. This sentiment corresponds, in the world of cultural theory and politics, to a growing distaste for close scrutiny of the aspects of identity one cannot freely choose, justify, commodify, or represent to multiple and spatially dislocated audiences.

In short, whenever "culture" is not the kind of thing one can showcase, in a generically positive way, in mass-mediated forms, then odds are good that, like Greeks smashing plates, it is the sort of thing Others should not be allowed to see. To invoke Wilk's formulation once again: "public culture" is the kind of difference we celebrate and use to organize a community, "habitus" is increasingly the kind of difference we submerge unless, of course, it can be celebrated and put to use in a larger sphere of representational politics. Obviously, "we" is a pronoun that now includes both ethnographers and the people ethnographers write about, film, and place on exhibition; "we" are all engaged in self-aware and Other-conscious manipulations of what Appadurai calls "the cultural": "the process of mobilizing certain differences and linking them to group identity" (1996:14). Herein, intimacy is oriented toward an audience, and "ethnographic refusal" is part of a relentless struggle to define the terms, the very ground, on which showings and viewings will take place.

Backdrops/Sensitivities/Representations

"All the world's a stage." The words were said (and made perfect sense) in circumstances that were hardly modern—how else could one describe a time when global capital, empire, and industrialization were not yet England's?

Nonetheless, the idea of a stage that envelops the world, thus transforming it into a platform for artifice and representation, has recently become a dominant characterization of "modernity" as a distinctively European, colonial project. Timothy Mitchell, building on the work of Said, Derrida, and Foucault, has argued that nineteenth-century Egypt "refused to present itself like an exhibit, and so appeared orderless and without meaning. The colonizing process was to introduce the kind of order now found lacking—the effect of structure that was to provide not only a new disciplinary power but also the novel ontology of representation" (1991:xv). The manner in which Egyptians might have constituted their realities otherwise before colonization can only be discussed in language that is "deliberately fragmentary and incomplete," Mitchell assures us; anything more precise might risk "representing" this past.

What of the present? The reader is left to assume that ethnographers who treat cultural difference (and similarity?) as ordered and meaningful—no matter how improvised and contestable that order might be—will merely be reproducing "white mythology" and expressing the modern, Eurocentric urge to represent in order to control. True, one might contemplate "the possibility of thinking about language, meaning, and political order in ways that are not governed by the metaphysic of representation" (1991:xvi), but it is prudent to do so only in the interest of criticizing a political logic whose world-making power, ironically enough, the critic must endlessly reassert in order to destabilize it. The argument is closed and, in its own terms, incontestably correct.

Like so many attempts to subdue imperial monsters, *Colonizing Egypt* is animated by a strong, analytically suggestive blend of relevance and irrelevance. Whatever the case in 1830, the plain fact today is that Egypt does represent itself, and it does so using devices and designs that are widely shared and dominated by structures that, regardless of what Egyptians say or think, the anti-Orientalist can only portray as Western. "Insofar as one can allow a sweeping generalization," Said famously argued, "the felt tendencies of contemporary culture in the Near East are guided by European and American models" (1978:323). It follows logically that whatever is not guided by these models is not "contemporary" culture; attempts to engage with it would, in effect, be attempts to deny "coevalness" (Fabian 1983). The idea that other times and spaces might coexist with, or circulate within, European and American models—that people might strive constantly, and sometimes with success, to maintain these Other times and spaces as part of their own modernizing projects—is seldom taken up as a possibility. I have argued elsewhere (1996, 2000a) that, as the world's postcolonial and marginal populations are increasingly caught up in metropolitan social forms, anthropology is changing from an Otherizing discipline to a mainstreaming one. The people ethnographers study, even in peripheral settings, are incorporated in nation-states, multinational firms, and international markets; or they are attempting —sometimes warily; sometimes eagerly—to find a secure status for themselves in these globalizing structures.

Yet even when cultural difference is represented on global stages located firmly in the present, in contexts of mass mediation that can function *only* if cultural content is mainstreamed, very little attention is paid to the delicate representational politics that determine how Otherness is acknowledged and suppressed in the act of showing. In my career as a culture worker in Arab Detroit, I took part in numerous multicultural displays intended for "mainstream audiences" (as well as the Arab American audiences embedded within them). At the behest of my colleagues at ACCESS and the granting agencies that funded our work, these displays were designed to correct popular American (mis)conceptions about Arabs and Muslims. Given the heavy weight of prejudice that presses down on Arab Americans in Detroit, the fact that the sensibilities of an imaginary—but always hegemonically white, Christian, and English-speaking—mainstream were allowed to define both the key misconceptions about Arabs and the tactics used to correct them was not deemed troublesome in itself. At ACCESS, I quickly learned that the quality of cultural representations is judged not by how effectively they enable non-Arabs to "understand" what is peculiar or distinctive about Arabs in America. Instead, an effective representation is one that, in the simplest terms, "our community can be proud of." This agenda is a kind of self-conscious image making, animated by a desire to connect Arab Detroit to America—and to shelter the community from harm—and each strategy is developed in reaction to attitudes presumed to be dominant in the larger society.

As a scholar who had lived in the Arab world, was familiar with it, and was also a non-Arab, it was my special role to ensure that ACCESS cultural programs were "sensitive" to the concerns of multiple audiences. In the construction of museum exhibits, films, books, public readings, art shows, and other media, I was asked to recognize (without explicitly revealing) the zones of cultural intimacy that public Arabness, like the public face of other ethnic and racial communities in the United States, is specifically designed to protect. In representing Arab family life, for instance, I was compelled to tack imaginatively between the sensitivities of, say, an Iraqi Shi'a "boater," who believes Americans are promiscuous, neglectful of their children, inhospitable, and irreligious; a "middle-class American," who sees "the Arabs" as sexist, clannish, and fanatical in their religious practice; and a second generation, "Americanized" Arab who feels trapped between both sets of assumptions, in which she perceives a disconcerting mix of fact and fiction.

The typical response at ACCESS, given the impossibility of publicizing and normalizing all three points of view, was (1) to suppress viewpoints associated with "boaters"—thus, nowhere in ACCESS exhibits will one be told that many "boaters" think American women will sleep with almost anyone, that American men have no sexual jealousy because they eat pig meat, or that, in a recent survey of two hundred ACCESS clients, "a majority of Arabic men and women approved of physical abuse if a woman ignored what her partner told her, if she hit him first or if she was unfaithful to him" (Anstett 2001); (2) to correct the stereotypical thinking of "non-Arab Americans"—thus, ACCESS is careful to stress the respect given to women in Arab American homes and the adaptive qualities of close, supportive family networks; and (3) to construct texts and images that politically active, ethnically conscious Arab Americans find useful in pursuit of the first two agendas—thus, the following museum text, which appears in "Family Life," one of several displays that make up *Creating a New Arab World*, a permanent exhibit now standing at ACCESS.

FAMILY LIFE

Arab immigrants are bound to each other by strong family ties, and most want to live and work close to kin. Over the past century, entire villages in Lebanon, Palestine, and Iraq have relocated to greater Detroit one relative at a time. New immigrants bring with them the clan structure and family traditions that prevail "back home." Their Americanized kin help the new arrivals adapt to life in Detroit.

Historically, Arab families place a heavy emphasis on the sexual modesty of women, respect for elders, marriage, child-rearing, and individual sacrifice on behalf of the group. These traditional values help Arab immigrants adapt successfully to the demands of a fast-paced, highly competitive society. They also insulate Arab families from a broad range of social problems: teen pregnancy, high divorce rates, single parenthood, and poverty in old age.

Arab families tend to be large by American standards, and they enjoy spending time together. In Detroit, Arab families can often be seen sitting on the front porch, smoking water pipes, and sharing the latest news. Exchanging home visits and sharing lavish meals with kin are both a pleasure and an obligation. The demands of Arab family life are intense—one must attend dozens of weddings, baptisms, funerals, graduation parties, and weekend picnics each year—but time spent with family reinforces Arab identity and instills a genuine respect for hospitality.

Note, aside from the generic tone of endorsement, how family life is described in its more "traditional" immigrant manifestations, whereas many Arabs in Detroit are second- or third-generation Americans. The families of these "ethnic" Arab Americans, the text implies, do not need special explanatory treatment, except when they resemble those of immigrants. Very few readers, Arab or non-Arab, find anything offensive in the text. It is assumed to describe Detroit's immigrant Arabs accurately, more or less, and the home life on display is one ethnic Arabs (and non-Arabs) are frequently nostalgic for: namely, the mythical "big, warm, close, and stable" family that Americans are apt to believe existed in the past and, regrettably, no longer does (see Shryock 2000b).

A hegemonic model of "American culture," unmarked and unquestioned, serves as the backdrop against which displays such as these take place. More than any "inherent" aspect of "Arab culture," this backdrop also shapes the kind of culturally intimate material ACCESS does not reveal. In Detroit, when Arab immigrant families are "explained" to public school teachers, Islam is "interpreted" for hospital staff, the Arab-Israeli conflict is "placed in historical context" for businessmen who want to invest in the Middle East, or Arab music is played at multiethnic festivals, both the culture presenters and the audience to be educated are "wise" to the ritual contexts that encapsulate them. The point is to undermine stereotypes, celebrate diversity, foster tolerance, give institutional support to pluralism, and suppress any form of difference (cultural, religious, or political) whose display would make these representational goals more difficult to achieve. In these settings, "ethnographic refusal" (extreme, yet inclusive and polite) is the order of the day. It is as if the logic of representation necessarily creates the zones of "meaning and social order" that Mitchell argues, quite convincingly, are possible but inaccessible to the logic and method of representation. That logic and method lend reality to times, spaces, and forms of interaction that ought to stand apart from a world of stages and apart from which the world of stages would be insignificant and crumble under its own weight.

Public Secrets/Abominations

The problem I have been struggling to elucidate is both an impasse (to method) and an opening (to theory). Public stages of identity display cannot be constructed, nor can they be understood, without reference to zones of cultural intimacy; yet the very publicness of these representational contexts tends to obscure such references and understandings. This state of affairs makes it hard to engage critically with patterns of in-group recognition, stigma avoidance and projection, veiled assumptions of superiority or inferiority, and the persistent manifestations of "incorrigible Otherness" that coalesce alongside (and give an obviously strategic dimension to) representations that flourish in contexts of regional, national, and global display. Yet, as the contributors to this volume will demonstrate, ethnographic insight grows out of familiarity with precisely these forms of self-recognition, which are already marked by a strong tendency toward self-criticism and, stranger still, often constitute the "lesson book" from which the ethnographer was taught to interact and interpret in appropriate ways. One can hide the lesson book, publish an abridged version of it, or use it as indirect commentary on something grander, but seldom is it wise to reveal exactly how the lesson book is used; that knowledge must remain partially invisible, to preserve its power to mark (and constantly realign) the boundary between belonging and being external to a social scene. Taussig writes,

Wherever there is power, there is secrecy, except it is not only secrecy that lies at the core of power, but public secrecy. And there is a distinct possibility of falling into error here. To put it bluntly, there is no such thing as a secret. It is an invention that comes out of the public secret, a limit-case, a supposition, a great "as if," without which the public secret would evaporate. To see the secret as secret is to take it at face value, which is what the tension of defacement requires. . . . [T]his tension is where the fetishization of the secret as a hidden and momentous thing, made by persons but transcendent over them, verges on explosive self-destruction capable of dragging us all down. . . . But against this apocalyptic dread, I regard the public secret as fated to maintain the verge where the secret is not destroyed through exposure, but subject to a revelation that does justice to it (1999:7−8).

The "public secret" emerges unscathed from the telling of lesser secrets, is even enhanced by these revelations, but what of the tellers themselves? It would seem that the ethnographer's fate, as zones of intimacy and mass mediation overlap in a dizzying array of contexts, is to do justice to public secrets by revealing their power. This work is done best, to use Taussig's imagery, at "the verge" or just beyond it. Locating ethnography at the limits of social space only intensifies the ethnographer's traditional status as an "abomination," as a person who confounds categories, who is neither here nor there, but whose marginality is apt to be perceived as inauthentic wherever it appears. The ethnographer is a "strangely marked" creature and likely to be accused, for that reason, of cross-dressing, ventriloquism, privateering on behalf of foreign principalities and powers, and (even worse) of enhancing the Self by collecting, curating, and incarcerating the Other. More alarming still has been the shock of realizing—and now the compulsive urge to admit—that these accusations are true. They are true in the obvious and most negative sense, but they are also true in a positive sense both accuser and accused are ill-equipped to discern. In short, they are part of the "public secret" whose power is upheld and enhanced by the revelation of failed ethnographic practice.

Ethnography/The Ordinary/The Intolerable

Perhaps this is why ethnography continues to tantalize, just as secrets do. Its current appeal among nonanthropologists, who preach its virtues to young practitioners of media and cultural studies, history, sociology, even political science, is based on more than an appetite for raw, empirical data (see Willis 2000). Very often, this appeal is based on a desire for intimacy and the insights it might produce; very often, this desire can cause anthropologists to blush, since its romantic, populist underpinnings are too brazenly announced—our tastes have matured, after all—and the formula for repeating old mistakes is factored into the rapprochement. Literary critics, Peck rather graciously admits (1996:19), are apt to see in anthropology a chance to "get their hands dirty in the field," to do work with "public and political policy implications," to mix it up with "the oppressed, the displaced, and the less fortunate," not just "the urban, the corporate, and the well-to-do."

Of course, these well-established habits (which are now being broken) make ethnographers suspicious to a certain breed of critical theorist, who is drawn nonetheless to the *idea* of ethnography because doing it will amount to a "taking back" of analytical powers anthropologists—exoticizers, connoisseurs of the primitive—have woefully abused. Quite predictably, these scholars assume that "cultural intimacy" should not be available to everyone, only to "insiders" and "allies." For better and for worse, these new practitioners of ethnography gradually discover (and perhaps they blush) that ethnography turns them into "outsiders." In *Listening to Salsa* (1998), a study that prides itself on a fairly modest deployment of ethnographic method, Frances Aparicio is forced to ponder, and criticize, her distance from the people who produce and consume the cultural forms she analyzes.

Given the tools of ethnography, it is no longer sufficient to speak about popular culture without including the voices and knowledge of others. Too many of us think of ourselves as democratic, socialist, or even radical scholars, yet we speak only from written interventions that privilege our own voices and those of other "experts" to the exclusion of nonacademic perspectives. Moreover, how radical can this scholarship be when theorizing is still protected as the exclusive power of those formally "educated"?

We are, yet again, in the genre of "getting one's hands dirty," or at least we are being told that we should be ashamed that our hands are not dirty yet. As Aparicio extends her observations, she amplifies this faux populist trope, leaving little doubt that "intimacy" with rank-and-file consumers of salsa and the destabilizations of theory and practice that might result from this close acquaintance are not what she has in mind.

While I am fully aware that this book, as it is now written for an academic audience, may not necessarily be accessible to those outside our well-guarded territory, we must continue to strive toward expanding the dialogue beyond academic settings, thus reaching via radio, journals, television, and newspapers, the very communities that constitute popular culture. If we continue to speak to each other implosively, like a concentric force that rejects any "outside" element, then our work will fail to truly radicalize the production of knowledge that has kept popular culture outside the canon.

As is so often the case among advocates of cultural studies, the sphere of mass mediation is posed as a link to "the people," who must be instructed and led. There is no real interest in the everyday aspects of "plebian" worlds. Theory, after all, is what counts, and it comes from some other place, from a discourse of "education" and "books." Instead, there is a desire to engage with "the people" pedagogically, from a subject position that is matter-of-factly vanguardist. To the extent that Aparicio, through the medium of personal interviews, decides to "listen to the listeners" of salsa, her work leaves its "well-guarded territory" and begins, genuinely, to travel. The result is a productive sense of alienation and a desire for further contact with "the popular sectors."

The immediacy Aparicio yearns for can be realized most profoundly, Amitava Kumar suggests, when the analyst is willing to be in "a place away from home, or from that which could be called the familiar. To be where one is not, or where one is not expected to be, and sometimes not even welcome . . . to travel to that place and write about it becomes the credo of the postcolonial writer" (2000:11). This has been the credo of the ethnographer since Malinowski and Boas—both of whom, like Kumar, were immigrant intellectuals. One detects, in Kumar's subtle formulations, an openness to the realization (another secret worth hiding and telling) that ethnographers and postcolonial critics are now traveling over shared terrain, occasionally giving each other bad directions because we know, all too well, where the Other wants to go: to the time/space in which "our" identities, "our" public secrets are made, privileged, and can be unmade or held securely in place.

"The argument for such border crossings," Kumar notes, "lies ultimately in the reality of people's lives . . . [which can] restore a certain weight of experience, a stubborn density, a *life* to what we encounter in newspaper columns as abstract, often faceless figures without histories" (2000:xi). This reclamation of immediacy has limits, but they tend not to be limits defined by essentialized notions Self and Other, or by the "official" identities authorized by states. Whatever anthropologists and postcolonial writers fancy themselves to be when leaving home—halfies, cosmopolitans, Orientalists, super- or pseudo-natives, critical critics, unreconstructed members of the Western, or Eastern, bourgeoisie—it is often the case that, upon their (refusal to) return, they possess identity dimensions that cannot be neatly situated on existing identity grids, that cannot be conveniently displayed on global stages, that undermine popular ways of imagining human community simply by rendering these explicit and suggesting, in the process, that alternatives are possible. This sensibility is based on access to, and constant movement through, *multiple* zones of cultural intimacy, and there is much in current regimes of identity and power that renders this kind of activity ordinary, yet intolerable. The anxiety ethnographic knowledge provokes, among sub-

alterns and overlords alike, is proof that something potentially transformative is being done when ethnographic knowledge is created.

The contributors to this volume harness this transformative potential and
direct it toward the task of developing new kinds of cultural analysis. We
proceed on the shared assumption that increasingly vexed relationships between ethnography, intimacy, and mass mediation are inevitable and can, in
fact, be intellectually productive. We explore situations in which the global
spread of public spheres and mass-mediated identities is producing backstage
terrain that is localizing, distinctive, inwardly oriented, and acutely aware
both of cultural difference and of the meanings difference might acquire in
the minds of "external observers." Whether they occur in the planning
committees for Egyptian and Arab world film festivals, in nationally tele-
vised footage of Thai magnates and politicos at home with family, or in disputes over the meaning of certain (homo)sexual practices in the Yoruba trans-
nation, these tense interplays of intimacy and mass mediation are rarely based
on, and seldom produce, a neat opposition of public and private spheres.
Rather, they generate arenas in which things public and private transect,
mutually constitute, polarize, and infiltrate each other.

This unstable ground, filled with moral ambiguities and methodological
hazards, is the ground on which we live and work today, a bit stubbornly,
Kumar reminds us, and relying on the weight of our own experience. We
will question, from this vantage, how identity and writing about identity
might change if the mutual infiltrations of public and private spheres were
more explicitly traced. We will ponder the consequences of publicizing and
privatizing the "same" identities differently. We will study social spaces—
from party vanguards and secret police forces, to nation-states and ethnic
communities—in which collectively shared intimacy is hardly possible and
no proof of belonging is entirely reliable. Finally, we will suggest several
ways in which ethnographers, in collaboration with our subjects and newfound allies, can create spaces for cultural expression that do justice not only
to our "public secrets" but to the contexts of telling that, now more than
ever, we share.

The Cast, in Order of Appearance

The eight chapters that follow are divided into four sections, each featuring
two papers that address related themes. In "Staging and Screening," Kelly
Askew chronicles her involvement in the production of a major Hollywood
film, set (fictively) in Kenya, and Walter Armbrust explores how products
of the Egyptian film industry are displayed (and concealed) in international
film festivals, where they will inevitably be judged as representations of
Egypt. Both authors deal with the conflicting demands of realism and arti-

fice—mainstays of ethnographic writing—and each gives a frank account of the representational compromises ethnographers must make when they serve as promoters, expert consultants, and cultural guides. In "Exhibition-ism," Richard Maddox and Esra Özyürek take apart complex attempts to display, in the first case, notions of Spanishness and Seville, and in the second, domestic modernity and secularization in Turkey. Their essays demonstrate how central *not* showing is to the task of public display; they also lay out, with admirable precision, what have rapidly become the ground rules of exhibition in neoliberal public spheres.

In "Sex, Food, and Spirits," James Matory and John Collins chart the delicate paths by which Bahia is racialized and exoticized in the interests of Brazilian nationalism and in collusion with elite, cosmopolitan models of feminism, Africa, folk religion, and global blackness. Their findings lead them to consider how popular resistance to these processes is manifest in the everyday practice of Candomblé and in Pentecostal rejections of what Candomblé now stands for in Brazil and beyond. In "Fault Lines," Rosalind Morris, writing of Thailand, and Andreas Glaeser, writing of the former East Germany, turn our attention to failed and forced intimacies, to settings in which the structures of mass mediation, and the models of national belonging they carry, give rise to structural paranoia (of the sort that animated the policing strategies of Stasi) or to mandatory (and doomed) appeals for "transparency" in a political culture that locates certain varieties of power in unseen realms and certain forms of intimacy in domestic spaces that, even when nationalized, can never be fully visible.

In a final section, "Overly Familiar," I explore settings in which different, often oppositional, intimacies overlap, both in the person of the ethnographer and in the terms of which identity is itself made and mediated on a mass scale. The problem of terminological overlap, which most readers have encountered in the form of "hyphenated" ethnoracial identities—for instance, Chinese-American, French-Canadian, Palestinian-Jordanian, Japanese-Brazilian—is analyzed in relation to my own work in Arab Detroit, which has compelled me to write against and through powerful notions of "superiority" and "backwardness." Because issues of (invidious) distinction are a troubling presence in all the papers featured in this volume, I try in my final essay to amplify the theoretical and methodological innovations my colleagues have made in response to this troubling presence, hoping my amplifications will serve as an effective substitute for the more conventional summing up of themes this volume cannot pretend to accomplish.

Certain themes do, however, accumulate in these essays, and it is worth singling out the more interesting and unexpected ones. In several pieces, much of the "off stage" terrain on which intimacy flourishes is deeply historical, and this history is not directly available to ethnographic scrutiny in the present. If Armbrust must walk us through the development of the Egyptian cinema so carefully; if Askew must jump back and forth between nineteenth- and twentieth-century encounters between Africans, Europeans, and Americans; if the historicity and mythology of Atatürk pervade Özyürek's analysis of contemporary exhibit work in Istanbul, this is because, in each case, the identities put on display are shaped by events, persons, and genres that only a properly historicized analysis, conducted as a kind of genealogy of intimate expression, can detect. It is also clear that the relationship between intimacy and mass mediation is structurally tense for all the contributors to this volume. Attempts to understand this tension immediately place the analyst at the edge of comfortable sociability, at the interface of insider and outsider perspectives, where sociability in fact begins (and, if the analyst is cavalier, where it might also come to an end). The observations drawn by Maddox (about Spain) and Collins (about Brazil) touch very raw nerves; indeed, the politics of intimacy and suspicion explored by Glaeser is so delicate, so repressive that it became fully available to scrutiny, ethnographic and historical, only after the German Democratic Republic collapsed. The security apparatus Glaeser describes was unusual in its coercive power and attention to detail, but the sense of trespass (or, at the very least, the mood of controversy) that colors these essays is proof that even in regimes that are not "totalitarian," structures of intimacy are easily politicized. As social facts, they silence some people and stigmatize others, in part by shoring up the "official" ideologies that determine what kinds of sociability, and what types of ethnography, are appropriate to the public sphere.

   The power of nationalism and the nation-state to constitute public and private identities emerges dramatically in these essays, but one of the striking uniformities of these papers is the extent to which national belonging, in both its most intimate and mass-mediated forms, is thoroughly cross-cut—and made even more particular—by diasporic, regional, and global frames of reference. Matory's essay, located at the convergence of Brazilian, Bahian, Yorùbán, metropolitan feminist, West African, and black Atlantic worlds, shows how hopeless a task it is to understand national identity in a purely national context; the framework is now resolutely global, but the *frames of reference* are not always so, with the result that conflicting notions of intimacy can be built into a single cultural location. I would suggest, as a final observation, that the problem of how to locate intimacy ethnographically is perhaps the most puzzling of the many issues these essays explore. The "off stage" areas of identity formation in Arab Detroit, where people can find relief from the stereotypical demands of ethnicity, or the impromptu Reggae concerts that Bahian Pentecostals stage in the face of government officials who police Brazilian heritage, already belong to a kind of semiautonomous terrain that develops out of the endless collision of intimacy and public cultural display. Such locations cannot be understood (and perhaps should not be judged) in relation to places or times in which family life is "real," or social identities are "authentic." The real and the authentic are social constructions, yes, but that is now an easy (and very orthodox) claim to make. The contributors to this volume show, instead, that the affective content of Egyptian national identity, Africanness, Turkish patriarchy, and civic pride in Spain are artifacts of intensely personal interactions and sentiments *that can be perceived as such* only because they now stand in historically specific, formative, refracted, and often highly contrastive relationships to mass-mediated versions of themselves, which in turn provoke feelings of pride and shame.

If what have long been considered the best virtues of ethnography— close engagement, face-to-face exchange, a sense of immediacy, and the "imponderabilia of everyday life"—seem to be missing from these essays, it is due to the strange, analytic alchemy that occurs when ethnography is done in zones where intimacy and publicity merge to create both public culture and its representational shadows. These locations are filled with imponderabilia that are no less daily, no less real, and it is urgent business for ethnographers to find new ways to represent them "as they are" without taking them, as Armbrust warns, "at face value." We should not forget that the life we can restore to cultural simulacra and identitarian stagecraft, or the nuance we can bring to reductive, simplified, and coercive portrayals of people and social types, are representational qualities that will themselves be conveyed in mass media (if we are lucky), and their effectiveness will be measured against other ways of constructing and broadcasting the real. Making sense of social worlds that are immediate and mediated, virtual and empirical, will be the standard task of future ethnography. These essays point to multiple ways in which that work should, and perhaps should not, be done.

Epilogue

On October 17, 2001, a month after the 9/11 attacks, I received the following inquiry via email. Hundreds of people received it, pondered it, and forwarded it to others in moods ranging from dread to excitement.

Dear _____,

I'm writing you from the Casting Department of MTV's Real World and Road Rules. Feeling that Arab students are underrepresented in these two shows, I'm writing to ask if you could think of 5–10 Arab students in your student organization who might be good candidates for either one of these shows.

Please respond to this email or call me at _____ with questions and with the names and phone numbers or email addresses of anyone you think of.

Thank you for your help. I greatly appreciate it.

Very truly yours,

_____
Casting Associate
Bunim/Murray Productions

These are highly popular "reality" television shows, each dedicated to the display of intimacy before the horrified, titillated eyes of millions of teenage and twenty-something viewers. I have returned to the province of computer screens, where media people tend to find me, but now I am being asked to serve up a private person to the anonymous viewing public, who will come to know the weaknesses, personality quirks, charms, and perhaps (a reliable boost to ratings) the sexual idiosyncrasies of a real, live Arab American. It is everything "bad ethnography" was supposed to be: intrusive, staged, gawking, shamelessly oblivious to its own artifice. This is not cultural representation, as I know it; it is pure showbiz. And it *is* the real world. Having a member of your community—Latino, gay, African American, disabled, Southern white male, Asian—on *Real World* means you have been recognized as a viable and valid category of humanity.

All across America, Arab students weighed the options, and so did I. Who would make "us" proud? Who would make "us" look bad? A young woman in *hijab*? A young woman uncovered? Perhaps a Christian Arab, instead? A new immigrant, or a second-generation American? Each imagined persona, set in relation to imagined others, evokes "aspects of cultural identity that are considered a source of external embarrassment but which nevertheless provide insiders with their assurance of common sociality" (Herzfeld 1997). Cultural intimacy, yet again; the promise of inclusion; the threat of mass-mediated humiliation; exposure. These possibilities are the price of belonging to America now, in ways as public as they are private. Those Arab Americans who are willing to pay the price—college students, middle class (or aspiring to it), already adjusted to mainstream institutions and cultural expectations—will stand in for the rest, especially the "boaters," who seldom want to show themselves in this way, and for whom revelation might only bring ridicule and disgrace. I remember my days as a culture worker in Arab Detroit; I recognize the familiar rhythms of multicultural representation; and I am embarrassed (but pleasantly so) by this evidence of my own complicity in a larger, Americanizing project, the context in which my Arab American friends and I find assurance of our common sociality, acutely aware of what keeps us together and sets us apart, somewhere along the "underrepresented" edge of the nation.

References Cited

Abraham, Nabeel, and Andrew Shryock, eds. 2000. *Arab Detroit: From Margin to Mainstream*. Detroit: Wayne State University Press.

Abu-Lughod, Lila. 2000. "Preface to the Second Edition." Pp. xi–xxx in *Veiled Sentiments: Honor and Poetry in a Bedouin Society*. Berkeley: University of California Press.

Anstett, Patricia. 2001. "No Excuse for Abuse: Arabic Group Tackles Cultural and Religious Beliefs That Are Barriers to Treating Domestic Violence." *Detroit Free Press*, 27 March.

Aparicio, Frances. 1998. *Listening to Salsa: Gender, Latin Popular Music, and Puerto Rican Cultures*. Middletown, Conn.: Wesleyan University Press.

Appadurai, Arjun. 1996. *Modernity at Large: Cultural Dimensions of Globalization*. Minneapolis: University of Minnesota Press.

Berlant, Lauren. 2000. "Intimacy: A Special Issue." Pp. 1–8. in *Intimacy*, ed. Lauren Berlant. Chicago: University of Chicago Press.

Coronil, Fernando, et al. 2001. "Perspectives on Tierney's *Darkness in El Dorado*." *Current Anthropology* 42: 265–276.

Fabian, Johannes. 1983. *Time and the Other: How Anthropology Makes Its Object*. New York: Columbia University Press.

Habermas, Jürgen. 1989. *The Structural Transformation of the Public Sphere: An Inquiry into a Category of Bourgeois Society*. Cambridge: Massachusetts Institute of Technology Press.

Herzfeld, Michael. 1997. *Cultural Intimacy: Social Poetics in the Nation-State*. New York: Routledge.

Kumar, Amitava. 2000. *Passport Photos*. Berkeley: University of California Press.

Mitchell, Timothy. 1991. *Colonizing Egypt*. Berkeley: University of California Press.

Ortner, Sherry. 1995. "Resistance and the Problem of Ethnographic Refusal." *Comparative Studies in Society and History* 2: 173–193.

Peck, Jeffrey. 1996. "From a Literary Critic/Germanist's Point of View: Anthropology." Pp. 13–19 in *Culture/Contexture: Explorations in Anthropology and Literary Studies*, eds. Valentine Daniel and Jeffrey Peck. Berkeley: University of California Press.

Said, Edward. 1978. *Orientalism*. New York: Vintage.

Scheper-Hughes, Nancy. 2000. "Ire in Ireland." *Ethnography* 1: 117–141.

Shryock, Andrew. 1996. "Tribes and the Print Trade: Notes from the Margins of Literate Culture in Jordan." *American Anthropologist* 98: 26–42.

———. 2000a. "Public Culture in Arab Detroit: Creating Arab/American Identities in a Transnational Domain." Pp. 32–60 in *Mass Mediations: New Approaches to Popular Culture in the Middle East and Beyond*, ed. W. Armbrust. Berkeley: University of California Press.

———. 2000b. "Family Resemblances: Kinship and Community in Arab Detroit." Pp. 573–610 in *Arab Detroit: From Margin to Mainstream*, eds. N. Abraham and A. Shryock. Detroit: Wayne State University Press.

Taussig, Michael. 1999. *Defacement: Public Secrecy and the Labor of the Negative*. Palo Alto: Stanford University Press.

Warner, Michael. 2002. "Publics and Counterpublics." *Public Culture* 14: 49–90.
Wilk, Richard. 1995. "Learning to Be Local in Belize: Global Systems of Common Difference." Pp. 110–133 in *Worlds Apart: Modernity through the Prism of the Local*, ed. Daniel Miller. New York: Routledge.
Willis, Paul. 2000. "Manifesto for Ethnography." *Ethnography* 1: 5–17.

PART ONE

Staging and Screening

CHAPTER 2

Striking Samburu and a Mad Cow

ADVENTURES IN ANTHROPOLLYWOOD

Kelly M. Askew

DURING THE ASCENDANCE of the colonial project, British officials decided to construct a railway line from the East African port town of Mombasa westward to Lake Victoria and onward into Uganda. The 1893 declaration of a Protectorate over Uganda, famously described as "the pearl of Africa" by Stanley, all but required a railway if the British were to establish an effective presence there. And an effective presence they very much desired, since Uganda held strategic importance as the gateway to the Nile River Valley. A railway, while extremely costly, would fulfill several key objectives: establish proof of British dominion, deal a decisive blow to the slave trade by dislodging the overland caravans that trafficked in humans, and transport the envisioned mountains of raw cotton Uganda's temperate climate could produce to the coast for shipment to British textile factories. Construction of the Uganda Railway, termed "The Lunatic Line" by the British press, began on May 29, 1896, in a ceremony marked by the 90th Baluchistan Regiment's rendition of "God Save the Queen."[1] Yet all work came to a crashing halt two years later when two man-eating lions developed an insatiable appetite for the (mostly imported Indian) laborers. Big-game hunters and contingents of the British colonial army were all employed in efforts to kill the lions, but before success was achieved, they would kill an estimated 135 people and demonstrate the fallibility of the British Empire.

I wish to thank my colleagues in the Department of Anthropology at the University of Michigan and fellow panelists in the "Knowledge and Practice" session at the 2003 American Anthropological Association annual meetings who offered cogent comments and criticisms to earlier drafts of this essay. Special thanks go to Andrew Shryock who helped me clarify my thinking, offered wonderful editorial suggestions, and provided unceasing encouragement.

Almost exactly one hundred years later, construction began again on the Uganda Railway, this time an imitation built not on the rich clay soils and savanna plains of Kenya but amidst the rolling hills of South Africa's northern Transvaal. This was the central feature of a Hollywood reenactment of the story that has acquired mythic status among hunting enthusiasts and among East Africans who believe the lions were in fact powerful chiefs in lion form dealing a necessary blow to the arrogance of Western imperialism. Some eighty million dollars were spent in the making of *The Ghost and the Darkness* (Paramount Pictures 1996)[2] on, among other things, an international cast and crew, the importation and transplantation of waist-high savanna grass and countless thorn bushes, helicopter delivery of one lone acacia tree (required component of any film set in East Africa), acquisition of a period antique train, and construction of a realistic train depot, bridge, and working railway line. Additional expenses accrued to the recruitment of thirty Samburu warriors from Kenya to act as Maasai warriors (their related, but nonetheless distinct, neighbors) and—sharing the title roles—six talented lions from California, Canada, and France.

Originally hired as the film's Ethnic Music Researcher, then Swahili Dialogue Coach, then Samburu Extras Assistant Coordinator, I participated in the making of this undeniably formulaic Hollywood film. I was party to the delicate cross-cultural negotiations that linked nineteenth-century Kenya, twentieth-century Hollywood, twentieth-century Kenya, and twentieth-century postapartheid South Africa. As Barry Dornfeld (1998:13) notes, anthropological attention to processes of media production has lagged significantly behind that of media reception. Recent progress has been made in ethnographic studies on television production (Dávila 1998; Dornfeld 1998; Michaels 1994; Naficy 1993), journalism (Boyer 2001; Hannerz 2003; Pedelty 1995), music production (Keil and Feld 1994; Manuel 1993; Meintjes 1990, 2003), and advertising (Dávila 2001; Moeran 1996), but aside from Hortense Powdermaker's (1950) monograph, *Hollywood the Dream Factory*, feature film production has remained largely inaccessible to anthropologists.[3] My sojourn in Hollywood allowed a rare ethnographic glimpse into what many consider to be the heart of the "culture industry" (Horkheimer and Adorno 1972).

Hollywood is a powerful and highly influential industry capable of generating and consuming great wealth, typically at the expense of creativity and of people who participate on wholly disadvantageous terms. In her book, Powdermaker described in meticulous fashion the social structure, driving motivations, beliefs, and psychological tendencies of a wide range of people working in the Hollywood hierarchy of the 1940s. Based on my experience, these have changed little over the years. In this essay, I examine Hollywood film production via *The Ghost and the Darkness*, drawing on my participation

FIGURE 2.1. *Simba wa Tsavo.* Cover to the abridged and revised edition of J. H. Patterson's *The Man-Eaters of Tsavo*, translated into Swahili by S. M. Kombo and C. G. Richards (London: Macmillan, 1962), and used throughout East Africa as a standard secondary school text.

in the production process, interviews with a wide variety of people affiliated with the film, the film itself, and relevant written texts including the script, the book on which it was based, and archival materials. Cultural difference is something *The Ghost and the Darkness* not only mass-produced on a global scale, but also required for its manufacture. The attendant representational politics—both onscreen and off—and "culture wrangling" pursued on multiple levels by a diverse array of "actors" constitute my focus here.

Arrivals—Nineteenth-Century Kenya

> Eventually, towards dusk, we arrived at our destination, Tsavo. I slept that night in a little palm hut, which had been built by some previous traveller and which was fortunately unoccupied for the time being. It was rather broken down and dilapidated, not even possessing a door, and as I lay on my narrow camp bed I could see the stars twinkling through the roof. I little knew then what adventures awaited me in this neighbourhood, and if I had realised that, at that very time, two savage brutes were prowling round, seeking whom they might devour, I hardly think I should have slept so peacefully in my rickety shelter.
>
> —Lt.-Colonel J. H. Patterson, *The Man-Eaters of Tsavo* (1907)

The Uganda Railway required the laying of track from Mombasa across some six hundred miles of extreme terrain (including waterless desert, impenetrable thornbush scrub, and the Mau escarpment at eight thousand feet above sea level) to the shores of Lake Victoria where steamships would complete the route to Uganda (see Figure 2.2). For many Britons, the initial price tag of three million pounds (an insufficient amount, as time would tell) for a railway in a distant, inhospitable, and seemingly God-forsaken land militated against arguments for its construction. Yet to imperialists like Lord Frederick Lugard, Sir Gerald Portal, and Prime Minister Lord Salisbury, dreams of establishing a Cape to Cairo travel route and accessing the vibrant commerce of the lake regions were dependent upon a railway from the coast. In his April 1894 report to Parliament, Portal claimed, "The whole problem of the development of East and Central Africa, the prospect of the creation of a profitable British trade, the suppression of internecine religious wars, the security of European travelers, the control of the lake district and of the upper waters of the Nile and, above all, I may confidently add, the only hope of really and definitely killing the slave-trade within a reasonable time—all resolve themselves into the all-important and overshadowing question of transport and communication" (Hardy 1965:40).[4] Abolitionist arguments and commercial potential notwithstanding, political strategists wanted Uganda as a means of safeguarding the Nile and, by extension, the newly minted Suez Canal that reduced by seven thousand miles (forty days) the voyage between England and its foremost colonial interest: India.[5]

John Henry Patterson, British officer, skilled engineer, big-game hunter, and—later in life—ardent Zionist, arrived in Mombasa harbor on March 1, 1898. With a successful record of building bridges in India, he was hired to construct a permanent bridge for the Uganda Railway across the Tsavo River, some 133 miles inland from the coast. The Hindustani linguistic skills he acquired in India proved to be an additional advantage. The bulk of the workforce at Tsavo consisted of Indian "coolies" serving three-year contracts with the railway.[6] Born in Ireland in 1867 to Protestant parents, Pat-

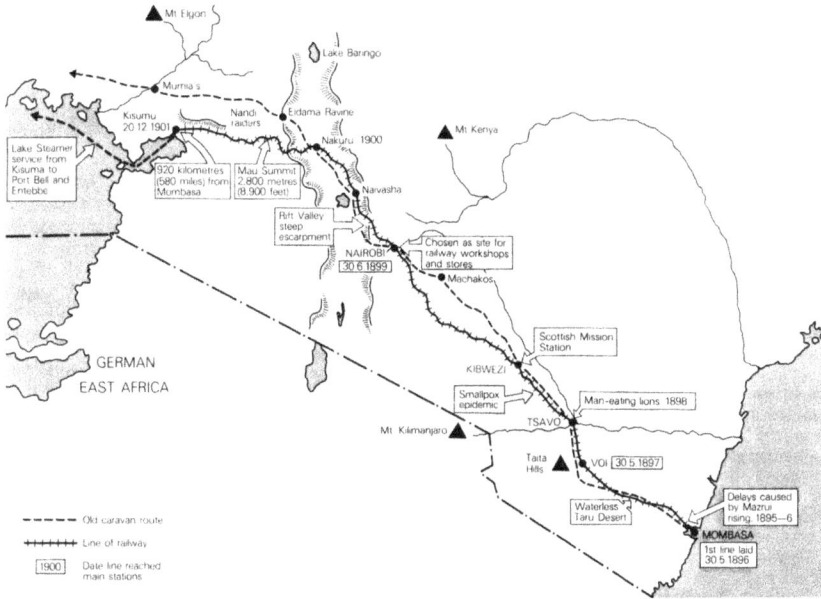

FIGURE 2.2. Map of Uganda Railway. From *A History of East Africa* by E. S. Atieno Odhiambo, T. I. Ouso, and J. F. M. Williams (London: Longman, 1977). With permission of Pearson Education.

terson displayed an early fascination with all matters military, admitting that "as a boy I spent the greater part of my leisure hours poring over the Bible, especially that portion of the Old Testament which chronicles battles, murders, and sudden deaths. . . . I eagerly devoured the records of the glorious deeds of Jewish military captains such as Joshua, Joab, Gideon and Judas Maccabaeus" (Patterson 1916:46, 48). By the time of his death, Patterson would amass several glorious military deeds of his own in the Boer War (1900–1902), for which he was named lieutenant colonel and awarded the Queen's medal, as well as in World War I, when he commanded the first-ever Jewish Battalion. Yet, for all this, it would be his success in tracking and killing the famed "Man-Eaters of Tsavo" that enshrined his name in the annals of history.

. . . our work was soon interrupted in a rude and startling manner. Two most voracious and insatiable man-eating lions appeared upon the scene and for over nine months waged an intermittent warfare against the railway and all those connected with it in the neighbourhood of Tsavo. This culminated in a perfect 'reign of terror' when they actually succeeded in bringing the railway works to a complete standstill.
    At first they were not always successful in their efforts to carry off a victim, but

LIEUT.-COL. J. H. PATTERSON, D.S.O.

FIGURE 2.3. Lt.-Col. John Henry Patterson. Frontispiece to *With the Judaeans in the Palestine Campaign* by J. H. Patterson (London: Hutchinson, 1922). Photo by Vandyk.

as time went on they stopped at nothing, and indeed braved any and every danger in order to obtain their favourite food. Their methods became so uncanny, and their man-stalking so well-timed and so successful, that the workmen firmly believed that they were not real animals at all but devils in lions' shape.

    —Patterson, *The Man-Eaters of Tsavo*

Arrivals—Twentieth-Century South Africa

The movie, the letter explained, is entitled *The Ghost and the Darkness* (henceforth, G&D). Starring Val Kilmer in the role of John Henry Patterson and Michael Douglas as the generic great white hunter, it tells the tale (loosely

FIGURE 2.4.   Michael Douglas and Val Kilmer. Close-up from *The Ghost and the Darkness.* © Paramount Pictures. Courtesy Everett Collection.

based on fact) of the "Man-Eaters of Tsavo," the two lions that inexplicably went on a massive killing spree in Kenya, and the ensuing campaign to stop them.[7] President Theodore Roosevelt, a hunting man himself, called it "the greatest stalk of which we have any record" (Goldman 1996:65). High adventure, exotic setting, blazing hero . . . perfect material for a movie.[8] Included in the letter, which I received in September 1995, was the request that I contact a certain music producer to discuss my potential involvement in researching and providing appropriate East African music for the film.

   I am an anthropologist/ethnomusicologist with extensive research experience in Kenya and Tanzania, specifically on the local and national politics of Swahili musical performance.[9] Originally hired onto the film's Music Department as the "Ethnic Music Researcher," I did a preliminary assessment of the film's music needs as dictated by the script (see Figure 2.5 for a list of the crews/departments involved in *The Ghost and the Darkness*). There were no fewer than seventeen scenes, like the following, that specified people singing, chanting, or humming:

20G   EXT. TSAVO RIVER—BRIDGE SITE 0—DAY   20G

   Masons chip at rocks. We see MAHINA drive them on. There is a sense of
   fatigue. MAHINA, who never tires, begins a chant. And here's the surprise
   —when he speaks, it is always softly, but when he sings, the sound is LOUD.
   HAWTHORNE is watching.

"The Ghost and the Darkness"

CREW LIST

Accounting Department
Animatronics Department
Armoury Department
Art Department
Assistant Directors Department
Camera Department
Casting Department
Catering Department
Construction Department
Editorial Department
Fabricating Department
Greens Department
Grip Department
Kenya Unit
Lighting Department
Locations Department
Makeup & Hair Department
Medical Department
Music Department
Paint Department
Production Department
Publicity Stills Department
Second Unit
Set Decoration & Props Department
Sound Department
Special Effects Department
Stunt Department
Train Department
Transport Department
Video Department
Visual Effects Department
Wardrobe Department
Wranglers

FIGURE 2.5. *The Ghost and the Darkness* crew list.

A couple of other workers pick up the chant. It's pretty. Now a couple more. Prettier still.[10]

With three Kenyans living in Los Angeles at the time,[11] I sang and recorded a number of songs from Kenya and Tanzania (many drawn from my field experiences) that were subsequently reproduced in CD format for the film's director, Stephen Hopkins, to review. In November 1995, producers at Paramount Studios gave me six days' notice that I was being sent to South Africa to facilitate the recording of these songs in Johannesburg by studio musicians. Although set in Kenya, the film was shot in South Africa for numerous economic and political reasons, not the least of which were generous tax concessions and a great welcome from the South African Film Commission (versus bureaucratic difficulties and political obstacles in Kenya; see Kariuki 1995; Screen 2000).[12] In search of a more "authentic African sound," the producers opted to record the songs in South Africa despite the reality that, whether we worked with studio musicians in Los Angeles or Johannesburg, Swahili was not a language the musicians would know.[13]

During the first of three months I would spend in South Africa, my time was split between recording studios in Johannesburg and the film set, located a four-hour drive away in the Songimvelo Game Reserve, near the Afrikaner resort town of Badplaas (lit., "place of baths") in the North Eastern Transvaal. On set, I coached the actors in Swahili lip-synching skills so they could look like *they* (rather than the professionals in Johannesburg) were doing the singing. (All these scenes were cut from the final product; either I was not terribly successful as a coach, or the director feared his film was turning into a musical rather than the action thriller it was intended to be.) When the co-producer discovered my fluency in Swahili, I was hired in a second capacity as the "Swahili Dialogue Coach." This entailed a careful reading of the script for all dialogue flagged as "in native tongue," or, worse, "They JABBER in SWAHILI" (Goldman 1995:63, emphasis in original) and accordingly translate it into Swahili. My job included coaching the actors in the lines I had prepared for them, and being available on set for those moments of inspiration when, for instance, the director would ask, "Kelly, to set the stage for the tensions that exist among the workers, I want these two men to be involved in an argument as Val [Kilmer] walks past. What might they yell at each other in Swahili?"

Finally, I was hired in a third capacity as the "Assistant Coordinator" for thirty Samburu *moran* (bachelor-warriors; see Spencer 1965; Spear and Waller 1993; Holtzman 2001, 2002) flown in from northern Kenya to act in the film. The script called for "FIFTY MAASAI WARRIORS . . . big men, powerful, [who] carry spears and knives and drums and clearly take shit from nobody" (Goldman 1995:63). Samburu are Maa-speaking pastoralists who consider themselves distinct from Maasai but are nevertheless frequently categorized as Maasai by non-Maa-speakers. Because ties already existed with a Samburu self-help association that had been involved in a previous Hollywood production, *The Air Up There*,[14] G&D producers opted to hire Samburu—a known entity—rather than seek out Maasai to play the part. It was only marginally an inaccurate choice. In the 1890s, when the film was set, the Samburu had not yet split off from other Maa-speakers to form a separate subgroup. Serving as the "Samburu Extras Assistant Coordinator" meant negotiating between the production and the Samburu, on set and off, in such matters as communicating the director's requests during filming, co-ordinating daily menus, and organizing shopping expeditions and other pastimes for the many days when they were not needed on set.[15]

Prelude to Scene 98. March 1898. Construction of the Uganda Railway has reached the Tsavo River. A bridge needs to be built across the river and a bright young engineer named John Patterson in the person of Val Kilmer arrives to do just that. He faces a tense situation stemming from the manifold social, ethnic, and religious divisions in the work force: Indian Muslims, Indian Hindus, Sikhs, Arabs, coastal Swahili, and African groups local to the area, including Giriama, Kamba, Kikuyu, and Taita. The very day of Patterson's arrival, a man-eater attacks, seriously wounding one worker. It is discovered that there is not one but *two* man-eaters, who breed terror in the camp as the number of casualties mounts higher each day. As attempts to kill the lions prove unsuccessful, a famous big-game hunter named Remington (Michael Douglas) is called upon. His lion-hunting arsenal includes thirty Maasai warriors—Maasai being famous for their prowess in hunting lions. . . .

On December 14, 1995, I was sent to Jan Smuts International Airport[16] to welcome the thirty Samburu moran hired to play the roles of Remington's Maasai accomplices and their two escorts: Mike McLean, the Samburu Extras Coordinator (I was to be his assistant), and "Ezra," a former councilman from the Samburu District of Kenya.[17] This was not a new experience for Ezra, who had managed the Samburu extras involved in *The Air Up There*. Fluent in the English language and Western manners, Ezra's self-described role was to ensure that the moran "not bring shame on the country of Kenya." Mike, meanwhile, boasted an extensive background in filmmaking, yet this was his first time to Africa. He had been hired on the basis of his reputation in some circles as Hollywood's "indigenous peoples expert," having worked with indigenous people in films shot in Australia and the Solomon Islands. (One might, quite rightly, question the lumping of all "indigenous peoples" together, such that experience working with one group is assumed to be preparation for any other group, but this does not appear to be a concern in the feature film world.) We formed a complementary trio up until the week before the Samburu returned to Kenya. Quite often, the moran would be divided into two groups on set: Ezra would translate for one, and I the other. When Mike and Ezra had to attend to issues such as contracts and payments, I remained with the moran to translate and troubleshoot.

The Samburu were scheduled to appear on camera in Scene 98 within their first twenty-four hours in South Africa. Their own arrival scene, however, was beset with problems. Although they and all their accompanying gear (spears, headdresses, shields) made it safely to Johannesburg, the bus hired to take us to the film set broke down at the airport. During the four-and-a-half hours it took to have a mechanic examine the bus, only to pronounce it unfit for travel and have another bus ordered in its stead, sixty-six Wimpy burgers and thirty-three orders of french fries and sodas were consumed. We arrived at our lodgings late that night, where we were told to be ready for an early afternoon call on set the next day for costuming and makeup.

Ultimately, the delays that are an all-too-common part of the movie-making process forestalled their nineteenth-century arrival in Tsavo, giving the Samburu extras a little more time to combat twentieth-century jetlag and culture shock. Of the thirty, six moran had been involved in *The Air Up There*, so for the majority, much of what they were experiencing was very new. The decision to postpone Scene 98 until the following day was made after we had already traveled forty-five minutes from our accommodations to the set. Having arrived en masse, three moran were selected to try on costumes for the three scenes in which the Samburu would appear: (1) their arrival with Remington [Scene 98], (2) a prehunt ritual/celebration [Scene 106], and (3) the hunt [Scene 108]. Called by the costume team "Arrival Man," "Party Man," and "Hunting Man," respectively, the costumed moran were paraded privately before the director and producers for their approval, evoking discomfiting images of colonizers inspecting their African subjects. The inspection took place at a remove from the area where filming was occurring that day, which at first struck me as odd. However, it became increasingly clear from the discussion that followed, and from the care taken to seclude the Samburu, that the scheduling of the filming of their on-set arrival so soon after their off-set arrival was not coincidental. It was part of a strategy to take full advantage of their newness and exoticism to elicit more "authentic" reactions from the other actors and extras. The camera set-up the next morning, when we filmed Scene 98, confirmed this. The director ordered that cameras and lights be set up for the Samburu POV (point of view). With great anticipation and excitement, the moran had been preparing since before dawn for their debut before the cameras. Yet the cameras were directed not at them but on everyone else in the scene: on Kilmer's Patterson, Douglas's Remington, and the hundreds of extras playing railway laborers. In exploiting and capturing the full impact of twentieth-century

Samburu arrivals, the director effectively enhanced the scripted nineteenth-century Maasai arrivals. He committed to film unaffected expressions of shock and surprise provoked by exotic Others.

On December 12, 1995, two days before I received the Samburu entourage at the airport, I was summoned to a meeting with Michael Douglas at his rented house near the set. The meeting involved some initial Swahili coaching for Scene 98, as well as a discussion of his artistic vision for the Remington/Maasai arrival scene. Whereas the script left much room for interpretation, stating only that "we see FIFTY MASAI WARRIORS moving out of the bush" (Goldman 1995:63), Michael Douglas wanted to insert a call-and-response sequence, wherein he would call out something to the hidden warriors who would then doubly shock the audience with their sudden appearance and an audible response "something like a battle cry." So he asked me to propose a phrase in Swahili for him to call out and something for the warriors to call back in response. I asked for time to consult with the Samburu once they arrived in the country. The invention of tradition does not come easy to an anthropologist.

During our long bus ride from the airport to the Transvaal, I raised this issue with Ezra and Mike. In trying to explain the call-and-response request from Michael Douglas, I drew on a familiar analogy, namely the political call-and-response mantra of the then-current Moi government in Kenya. A fundamental component of any contemporary Kenyan political event is the rallying cry "*Harambee!!*" by a politician and the immediate audience response of "*Nyayo!!*" *Harambee*, a call to work together and a term for community self-help programs, was the political slogan of Kenya's first president Jomo Kenyatta. Daniel arap Moi, who succeeded Kenyatta in 1978 and ruled Kenya with a dictatorial hand for the next twenty-five years, chose *nyayo* (literally, "footsteps") as his slogan, originally to impress upon citizens his desire to follow the economic and political path set by Kenyatta.[18] Being a former politician himself, Ezra readily understood the analogy and promptly denied that there was anything like it in Samburu cultural practice. So creative minds went to work for the sake of Hollywood, and, in the end, Ezra assigned Michael Douglas the call "*Warani!!*" ("Warriors!!"—a Swahili-ized plural form of moran[19]), and told the moran to respond with the guttural coughing sound a Samburu person often makes when startled. The moran agreed that it was a realistic response and, although I had some misgivings about it, I deferred to their cultural authority and the cough was cast.

When we filmed this scene, the first take happened as planned, with Michael Douglas calling out "Warani!" to an apparently empty savannah. The moran, dressed in waist wraps and beaded adornment and bearing shields and spears, were crouched down fully hidden in the imported and painstakingly replanted savanna grass. They arose on cue, running forward to stand together grouped some thirty feet in front of Michael Douglas, who awaited them with his right hand held out palm forward, in a stereotypic cowboy-meets-Indian posture. Once stationary, the Samburu all—in unison—coughed. After the sound died away, the director called, "Cut!" and everyone relaxed. We then waited (as is the norm after every take) for the director to decide whether to reshoot or move to another scene. Michael Douglas and director Stephen Hopkins gathered with producers around the TV monitor and replayed the scene several times, holding a quiet discussion and looking less than satisfied. Finally, Hopkins approached me and asked if it would be possible for the Samburu to extend the cough, that is, to continue producing the sound until he yelled "Cut!" Bemused, I translated the request to the moran who good-naturedly agreed. They assumed their original positions crouched down in the grass and, upon hearing "Warani!!," bounded forward into position where they coughed and whooped and barked for some five minutes. To me, it seemed an eternity. Finally, the director yelled, "Cut!" The immediate smiles on the faces of the director and producers conveyed their satisfaction. THIS was the suitably primitive battle cry they sought. No retake was necessary.

Suffice it to say that Samburu do not engage in communal coughing as a form of greeting. Lacking a "battle cry," they very nearly disappointed expectations until a creative, if inauthentic, solution was found. Some weeks into the shoot, the moran were treated to a private screening of the "rushes" (film takes) in which they appeared. When Scene 98 lit up the screen, with the camera panning slowly from one whooping face to another, the moran burst out in uproarious laughter. They begged for it to be shown again and again, laughing all the harder with every showing. It was so ridiculous that it was funny. But as a memorable image, one that confirms widely held notions of Africans as occupying a lower, more bestial social order, the scene would convey a more serious message to Western audiences. This incident supports Fatimah Rony's contention that "representation of the 'ethnographic' in spectacular commercial cinema takes the form of *teratology*— the study of monstrosity" (1996:160). As men who sound like animals, the Samburu fit a standard definition of the monster as a "composite, incongruous beast" (ibid.). The "Ethnographic" is monstrous, Rony argues,

because he or she is human and yet radically different. Early examples of the monstrosity of the Ethnographic include Regnault's association of race and cranial deformation; Spencer's description of 'naked, howling savages'; the Johnsons' coding of Western Pacific peoples as lascivious cannibals; the obsessive filming of trance (a ubiquitous subject in ethnographic cinema); and the plethora of ways in which indigenous peoples were, through the use of cinematic spectacle, made into Savages (1996:161).

The idea that such a visual moment was needed to establish the relationship between Remington and his Maasai hunters may have made easy sense to the film crew, but it disturbed me. It corresponded to powerful images of self and Other, to images of the white man who has the ability to "command" the natives in their own language. I was keenly aware of the scene's mythical effects, as well as its outright silliness—a double sensation that perhaps explains why I could not laugh at the rushes as freely as the Samburu did.

Blood Brotherhood and a Mad Cow

Theseus, who cleared the roads of beasts and robbers; Hercules, the lion killer; St. George, the dragon-slayer, and all the rest of their class owed to this their everlasting fame. From the story of the Tsavo River we can appreciate their services to man even at this distance of time. When the jungle twinkled with hundreds of lamps, as the shout went on from camp to camp that the first lion was dead, as the hurrying crowds fell prostrate in the midnight forest, laying their heads on his feet, and the Africans danced savage and ceremonial dances of thanksgiving, Colonel Patterson must have realised, in no common way, what it was to have been a hero and deliverer in the days when man was not yet undisputed lord of the creation, and might pass at any moment under the savage dominion of the beasts.
—The Spectator, March 3, 1900

Prelude to Scene 106A. It is evening and Remington, Patterson, the medical officer Dr. Hawthorne, and Samuel (stereotypic sage African elder who advises Patterson) sit cleaning their rifles in preparation for the morning's hunt. The Maasai are gathered together around a fire a small distance away. They start singing a "war chant" and invite Remington to join in.

106A   EXT. REMINGTON AND THE MASAI—NIGHT   106A

The war chant is louder. REMINGTON, drinking, is the center of it all—the loudest chanter.

REMINGTON and the MASAI perform a cow bleeding/blood drinking ritual.

THE MASAI, and they're starting to go a little bit nuts now, the noise building, their bodies movies [sic] in the firelight.[20]

Scene 106A was a dilemma-ridden scene from several perspectives. I was deeply conflicted about the "cow bleeding/blood drinking ritual," as were the producers, albeit for strikingly different reasons. Only director Hopkins appeared not to suffer any concerns going into it, yet it was he who perhaps suffered most in the end. I do believe that, contrary to Rony's disparaging take on commercial film renderings of ethnographic Others, Hopkins wanted to present as accurate and "authentic" a view of Maa-speaking pastoralists as possible. On set, he periodically sought out Mike, Ezra, and me to discuss

Samburu cultural practices, Samburu techniques of lion hunting, and the differences between Samburu and Maasai so he could prepare himself and his crew for filming the Samburu in action. In personal conversations off set, he told me of his travels through Kenya, which included a visit to Maasai areas, and how eager he was to observe, in the filming of Scene 106A, how they bled a cow and drank its blood. He offered his assistance and carte blanche approval for procuring any blacksmithing tools the Samburu might need to manufacture the specialized arrow they use in bleeding a cow. He made it clear that he did not want anything to prevent the scene from being shot in a manner true to Samburu cultural practice.

Imagine, then, his disappointment when, in contrast to the scripted "cow bleeding/blood drinking ritual," the moran explained that neither they nor Maasai perform such a ritual the night before a hunt. Instead, they emphatically affirmed, they get a good night's sleep. It is only in the morning, right before the hunt, that they might adorn their bodies with painted designs, elaborate ostrich feather or lion mane headdresses, and ankle bells.[21] This gave Stephen Hopkins pause, but given that the script and production schedule both called for a prehunt night scene, and given the many artistic and logistical variables that must be weighed in creating a production schedule, he opted to override the Samburu comments and his own personal concern for accuracy and keep it a night scene.

Hopkins then asked what the Samburu or Maasai would actually do when preparing for a lion hunt. Ezra described how moran anoint each other's bodies with red ochre and lime dust, and wear special headdresses and leg-bells, all for an effect designed to frighten and disorient lions. Hopkins asked if the moran would drink fresh blood as part of the preparations. Ezra hesitated, then stated that it *could* happen. It was a far-from-assertive response, motivated, I suspect, by a desire to please and be accommodating. Yet it sufficed to convince the director. The "cow bleeding/blood drinking ritual" was in.

My misgivings over this scene stemmed from my concern with the representation of Maasai as "blood-thirsty," another facet of monstrosity, and the moral implications of this image joining the mostly negative images of Africans (in general) and pastoralists (in particular) already circulating in the global economy of images. While the consumption of raw blood does indeed occur among Maasai and Samburu, it happens only in very select circumstances. Today's Maasai typically reserve the consumption of blood for boys undergoing initiation and new mothers who, it is felt, need additional blood to compensate for that lost during childbirth.[22] In contemporary Samburu communities, moran, junior elders, and boys consume raw blood when an animal is slaughtered, but usually the blood is mixed with milk and fat.[23] In the scripted scene, however, there is nothing to indicate that the blood is mixed with any other substance.

Given the fragmentary nature of knowledge about such practices among
the film's intended audiences, this scene would, in all likelihood, reify and
reinforce existing stereotypes. Rather than humanizing Maasai, it would associate them yet again with enduring images of barbarity. I expressed these
concerns to one of the producers and was told not to worry. The producer
confided that they had no intention of including this scene (despite the director's expectations) because of the potential for trouble with animal rights
activists. Yet I learned from members of the Special Effects crew that they
were ordered, perhaps as a back-up plan, to prepare a contraption to fit
around the cow's neck that would squirt out fake blood. Going into the
shooting of this scene, then, competing and contradictory ideas existed as to
how, if at all, it would be shot.

Luckily, from my perspective, the hapless cow chosen for the scene proved
to be less than cooperative. As soon as it was brought out on set, it sparked
a vociferous discussion among the moran. When the director asked what
they were talking about, I translated: "That's one sick cow! We wouldn't
drink *her* blood. Definitely sick! Look at her swollen udder." Upon hearing
this, the tired and exasperated director (it was around 2 AM at this point)
yelled out to no one in particular, "You bring me a sick cow?! Can't we get
another cow in here?!" A representative of the Animal Wranglers (the unit
responsible for animals used in the film shoot) informed him that the only
other available cows were quite a distance away, and that it would take over
two hours to bring in a substitute. So Hopkins decided to proceed with the
sick cow. She quietly endured the first several takes, just standing in the background while the cameras focused on Douglas/Remington's interactions
with the dancing and singing moran. Then came time for the bleeding
scene. The director asked if the moran were ready and if they had their special arrow. Before anyone could answer, along came the Special Effects crew
with their contraption, to the director's obvious and very public surprise.
Not only *his* surprise. While a tense conversation ensued between director
and producers, the Special Effects team worked to position the contraption
around the cow's neck. She, however, decided that she did *not* want to wear
it and struggled against crew and contraption both, finally throwing herself
down in protest on the ground. Everyone withdrew hurriedly to avoid her
wildly kicking legs and thrashing head. For Hopkins, this was the final straw.
Clearly very angry (and with good reason, for his authority on set had been
seriously undermined by the producers' covert action), he announced that the
scene was scrapped. Silently cheering the cow on, I breathed a sigh of relief.

Unfortunately, the mad cow's victory was short-lived. The sequence made
it back into the film, complete with fake blood spurting from a more com-
pliant cow. Given the lack of transition between a close-up on the spurting
blood and a shot of Douglas/Remington triumphantly holding high, then

drinking from, a cup, we are led to believe that he drinks blood straight from the cow. (The sound editors' insertion of a bovine groan of pain adds to the overall effect.) Interestingly, no moran are seen drinking blood, or anything at all. Audience attention is drawn less to Maasai practices of consuming blood than to the scene's twin themes: (1) Remington's cross-cultural skills and (2) male bonding. The sequence ends with a fade-out of Remington dancing and singing with the moran, reaffirming a more politically correct message of universal brotherhood.

Labor Unrest in Tsavo

The whole of the works were put a stop to because a party of man-eating lions appeared in the locality and conceived a most unfortunate taste for our workmen. At last the labourers entirely declined to go on unless they were guarded by iron entrenchments. Of course it is difficult to work a railway under these conditions, and until we found an enthusiastic sportsman to get rid of these lions our enterprise was seriously hindered.
    —British Prime Minister Lord Salisbury in an address to the House of Lords

On December 1, 1898, after nine months of continued human loss to the ravenous man-eaters, hundreds of panic-stricken Indian "coolies" refused to continue work. "We came from India," they told Patterson, "on an agreement to work for the government, not to supply food for either lions or 'devils'" (Patterson 1907/1927:78). By their sheer numbers, they forced an oncoming train to stop, swarmed onto its cars, and fled Tsavo. The few who remained (about half of whom were too ill to desert) spent their days constructing suspended beds in trees and iron "lion-proof" huts. It was during this time that a long-awaited contingent of thirty British troops finally arrived, yet finding very few people to defend, they promptly left (Hardy 1965:206). For over three weeks, construction of the railway bridge at Tsavo ceased altogether. Work would resume only after Patterson succeeded in killing the two man-eaters.

In the 1996 Tsavo of the Transvaal, a cow was not the only one so dissatisfied with her working conditions as to go on strike. The final days of Samburu involvement with *The Ghost and the Darkness* witnessed a conflict between the production and the Samburu regarding their payment. While the moran were busy on set, their "representative" Ezra had convinced the production's accountant that it would be a grave mistake to pay the moran their salaries and per diem allowances in South Africa for, being irresponsible youths, they would likely waste it all on frivolous purchases. He wanted to ensure that their families benefited from this rare, lucrative opportunity; he thought the wiser course would be to give them their per diems in South Africa and dispense their salaries (by far the greater amount of money) in

Kenya. But being nomadic pastoralists, Ezra further argued, they did not have bank accounts, so the best solution would be to wire all the money into his personal bank account for him to distribute to the moran upon their return. Not surprisingly, he neglected to inform anyone of this arrangement until it was too late and the money had already been transferred. Upon discovering this fact, the moran immediately went on strike, so to speak. Although all their scenes had already been shot, they steadfastly refused to board the bus hired to take them to Johannesburg without receiving either their money or an escort from the production staff who would accompany them to Kenya to ensure that all their money would be paid in full. Failing this, they threatened to occupy their cabins and live off sales of their beadwork until their demands were met.[24]

The fact that the production accountants bought Ezra's story remains the most disturbing aspect of this tale. It would have been inconceivable to treat any other unit of the production in the same way, blindly entrusting one member with all the others' salaries. But in life as in film, the moran were viewed as a collective, so it made sense, according to that logic, to pay them as a collective. In the end, their determined refusal to leave impressed the producers, who later agreed to send Mike and me to Kenya to ensure that everyone received his full wages.

Of Mass Media and Masquerades

At this time the camps were again scattered and spread out for a distance of two or three miles on either side of Tsavo, for I had various works in progress up and down the line. After the return of the lions I sat up in a tree every night for over a week, near some likely *boma*, but all was in vain. Either the man-eaters saw me and went elsewhere, or else I was unlucky, for while I sat watching over one camp the brutes would attack another a quarter of a mile away, and I would have the mortification of hearing the agonised cries of the unfortunate victim as he was being carried off.
    —Patterson, *The Man-Eaters of Tsavo*

In an observation that I would argue is as relevant today as it was during the 1940s, Powdermaker claims that "audiences tend to accept as true that part of a movie story which is beyond their experience" (1950:13). Foreshadowing future developments in film theory, she further argued that movies "have a surface realism which tends to disguise fantasy and make it seem true. . . . If the setting is a New York street, the tendency today is to film an actual New York street. There is, of course, no necessary correlation between surface reality and inner truth of meaning. But if one is true, the other is more likely to be accepted" (ibid., 14). Indeed, a key concern in film theory has been to expose the techniques of realism and the effects of "cinematic apparatus" (Baudry 1986a, 1986b; also Traube 1992) that conceal what

Laura Mulvey (1975/1986) famously called the "look of the camera" and the "look of the audience." Once these are effaced, viewers can be pulled into the narrative and made vulnerable to its ideological effects.

Although *The Ghost and the Darkness* revolves around historical events, considerable liberties were taken to assimilate these events to Hollywood standards of plot development, thus turning "history" into "surface history." A romantic subplot (thought necessary to appeal to female viewers) was created by inserting a fictional wife for Patterson (and a pregnant one, no less).[25] The formulaic "wise African elder"—a leitmotif in African films—appears in the person of Samuel, who serves as Patterson's advisor and source of local knowledge. (In his writings, Patterson gives no indication of having taken advice from anyone.) The Remington (Michael Douglas) character is yet another creation, a composite "great white hunter" representing all those who came to Tsavo in answer to the following ad (Hardy 1965:151):

REWARD

The Managers of the Uganda Railway, having been incommoded by the Depredations of Man-Eating Lions, will pay or otherwise discharge the sum of TWO HUNDRED RUPEES for the skin of any Lion shown to the satisfaction of the Managers to have been destroyed within one mile on either side of the Railway line and to a distance of five miles East and West of the River Tsavo. Such skin and entirely reasonable proof of Vicinity to be delivered at Tsavo Station within 12 Hours of the demise of the animal.

— G. Whitehouse, Chief Engineer
Kilindini, July 1898

These are but a few examples of how the concern for "authenticity" and historical accuracy so frequently invoked by the G&D director, producers, costumers, and other sections of the crew were combined with genre requirements to produce "surface realism." As commercial enterprises geared toward financial profit, Hollywood films typically fall back on established conventions. "A feature of all mass production," states Powdermaker, "is the uniformity of the manufactured product. Hollywood has tried to achieve this by seeking formulas that it hopes will work for all movies and insure their success" (1950:40). Pierre Bourdieu makes a similar argument in his essay, "The Market of Symbolic Goods" (1971/1993). Bourdieu identifies two modes of cultural production: (1) the *field of restricted production*, wherein cultural producers produce goods for other cultural producers (such as high art and academia), and (2) the *field of large-scale production*, wherein cultural goods are produced for nonproducers, namely "the public at large." Whereas the former disavows economic profit and restricts consumption of its products to producer-consumers endowed with specific cultural competencies (acquired through education, specialized training, and exposure to "refined" tastes and styles), the latter is economically driven and "submits to the laws of competition for the conquest of the largest possible market" (1993:115). In efforts to attract the most consumers, Hollywood, perhaps the emblematic case of large-scale production, predictably resorts to "tried and proven techniques" that displace unconventional talent and imagination. In the world of cinema, one can apply Bourdieu's model by contrasting the restricted field of art house and experimental films to Hollywood mass market films, "the one a field that is its own market, allied with an educational system which legitimizes it; the other a field of production organized as a function of external demand, normally seen as socially and culturally inferior" (ibid., 130).[26]

Formulaic depictions of Africans abound in countless media products, and increasingly they take the form of Maasai, who, in large-scale cultural production, have become iconic Africans. One finds Maasai advertising Nike-brand running shoes, inspiring Ralph Lauren's fashion designs,[27] positioned in intentionally stark contrast to *Sports Illustrated* bathing suit models (Figure 2.6),[28] endorsing Japanese blood purification tonics and Land Rover vehicles, all the while "aestheticized and reinvented as proud nonconformists: the last living sign of a 'primordial' Africa" (Kasfir 1999:69; what Rony terms the "taxidermic" impulse in ethnographic spectacle, 1996:101ff, 195–6).[29] Just as Native Americans were reduced in Hollywood Westerns to the single image of Plains Indians (Leuthold 1995), so too is Africa's immense diversity being summed up synecdochically in the Maasai. When presented in feature films, Maasai characters rarely constitute anything more than props, exotic background scenery, or expendable dramatic devices.[30] They typically appear in groups, almost never developing individual personalities that might humanize them and make them appear less foreign and unapproachable. This was born out in G&D, where the Samburu extras were only filmed in groups, continually reshuffled by production assistants, with the camera moving quickly from one face to the next, rarely settling on one for any length of time to avoid rendering that person recognizable. In their analysis of *National Geographic* magazine photographs, Catherine Lutz and Jane Collins found a similar pattern: "People coded black or bronze were more likely to be photographed in large groups than those coded white. . . . They were more often portrayed as part of a mass, perhaps thereby suggesting to readers that they had relatively undifferentiated feelings, hopes, or needs" (1993:163).

The Samburu were, in effect, part of a larger investment in surface realism that shaped G&D in all its phases, from preproduction, to filming, to postproduction. The selection of South Africa for the film shoot required substantial investment in the Greens Department (the unit responsible for landscape), to make the Transvaal appear as a believable Tsavo. Tens of thousands of dollars were spent in hand-planting ten acres of tall savanna grass and additional acreage of thornbush scrub. After trucking in and transplanting

FIGURE 2.6. Model with Maasai in background from 1998 issue of *Sports Illustrated*. Photo by Walter Chin, *Sports Illustrated* 88, no. 7 (February 20, 1998), p. 74.

six eight-ton truckloads of thornbushes every day for six weeks, the local variety was deemed not thorny enough (compared to the Tsavo variety), so the Greens crew painstakingly glued on additional rubber thorns. An acacia tree had to be procured for the scenes in which Patterson spends the night in a tree hoping to nab the man-eaters. Acacia trees are few and far between in the Transvaal. One was finally found and delivered via helicopter together with an avocado tree purchased from Afrikaner retiree Marie Coetsee (Snyman 1996:16–17). The film purchased her tree for 1000 South African rand (275 U.S. dollars at that time), but then paid $36,000 to helicopter it and the acacia to the set! Countless truckloads of rich red clay soil were brought in to cover up the sandy gray soil of Songimvelo.[31] When a nine-year drought broke just as filming got fully under way, the red clay soil turned into red clay muck that filled everyone's boots and turned the film set into a mud wrestler's paradise. The rain fell so heavily that by the end of the shoot, the set was accessible only by raft. (It was quite appropriate that for holiday gifts, the production gave every member of the cast and crew heavy-duty rain slickers bearing lion insignias.) Towering anthills were constructed out of fiberglass, animatronic lions produced for close-up shots, two bridges built across the Nkomazi River to represent the Tsavo Bridge at different stages of construction, and an actual railway line was laid to support an antique steam engine borrowed from a railway museum. And playing the lead roles of "Ghost" and "Darkness" (names by which the Tsavo man-eaters are re-membered for their respective light and dark coloring) were not African li-ons, but rather lions imported from France, Canada, and the United States.

Similar discontinuities surrounded the use of language and music in the film. Since filming began a few weeks before I arrived in South Africa, any scene containing Swahili dialogue filmed during that time was shot instead in a mixture of Zulu and Xhosa. The final film thus contains Zulu, Xhosa, the Samburu dialect of Maa (songs sung by the moran in Scene 106A), and Swahili. My efforts, moreover, to create Swahili dialogue that matched the script went unnoticed since virtually none of it was translated via subtitles. It remained anOther language, incomprehensible to the majority of audi-ence members.[32] Back in Los Angeles during postproduction, I oversaw ADR (Automatic Dialogue Replacement) sessions for the scenes requiring background Swahili dialogue. The first day we recorded, six Africans were hired as vocal actors, only three of whom spoke Swahili. (Fortunately, I managed to convince the ADR supervisor that hiring only the Swahili speakers the next day would speed things up considerably.) Parallels arose on the music side of things, such as when I was assigned the task of making over one thousand Venda, Swazi, and Zulu extras look like they were singing in Swahili, and, as already mentioned, when I taught the (mostly Zulu and Xhosa) Johannesburg studio musicians to sing in Swahili. Not only did these musicians offer an "authentically African" sound, it was a tried-and-true commercially successful sound given the global popularity of Paul Simon's *Graceland* album, which some of them had collaborated on.[33] In all these cases, liberties were taken with "accuracy," yet justified on the basis of not being too far off the mark.

While few would argue that Hollywood is bound to the same standards of truth-telling as, say, documentary film, what is curious about all the above is the stridency with which Hollywood producers espouse authenticity and accuracy as desired goals. Cinematic story telling is believed to be an art, and art sometimes requires that "truth" be compromised.[34] Hollywood films lib-erally employ "movie magic" to smooth over historical, cultural, political, musical, linguistic, and other inaccuracies. Despite their ability to "touch

up" what seems inauthentic, and thus dispense with accuracy in the most literal sense, Hollywood filmmakers continue to fetishize the idea of accuracy.
As one of the promotional slogans of G&D put it, summing up the irony of
surface realism: "Only the most incredible parts of the story are true." Realism is ingrained in Hollywood's narrative style, as convention and technique, and this is why the stereotypes Hollywood disseminates continue to
have a tremendous effect on how international audiences see themselves,
Others, and the world.

The tensions that arise between artistic and economic goals in large-scale
cultural production are probably inevitable (see Powdermaker 1950:25–29;
Bourdieu 1993:115–30). Barry Dornfeld discusses these conflicts in his analysis of *Childhood*, a PBS documentary series, in which the cinematic priorities of producers sometimes ran afoul of what academic advisors to the series
deemed necessary content (Dornfeld 1998:73–76). G&D perfectly exemplified this tension as well. Nicknamed "Claws" or "Paws" by the crew, G&D
was identified by its screenwriter, William Goldman, as "a cross between
Jaws and *Lawrence of Arabia*" (Goldman 1996:66). It could potentially appeal
to two different kinds of audience: action adventure thrill-seekers and film-
goers interested in history and cross-cultural experiences. With the promise
of bigger profits from the former, the film eventually took on more of an
action flavor, rendering "historical and cultural accuracy" less important. In
fact, the producers hotly debated the merits of bringing Samburu all the way
from Kenya. They decided at one point to forego the considerable costs this
would entail [35] and hire Zulu extras to play the Maasai instead (no doubt, because Zulu fit into similar "warlike" stereotypes). It was only through the intervention of director Stephen Hopkins that the Samburu won the role. [36] In
all these negotiations, the power of "surface realism," as a production value
and modus operandi, influenced decisions and helped me whenever I lobbied for greater "accuracy" or "cultural sensitivity."

Like other fields of cultural production, the motion picture industry is an
intersection of complex, variable interests. It cannot be reduced to a monolithic style or intent. Likewise, audiences for Hollywood films are not uniformly skeptical, critical, or likely to believe what they see on the screen.
That being said, we should not dismiss the social consequences of the cultural (mis)representations Hollywood filmmakers produce on a massive scale.
As noted earlier, restricted fields of cultural production, such as art films, require relatively high levels of cultural competence from consumers, whereas
large-scale Hollywood productions require much less. This does not prevent
Hollywood from serving as an authoritative source of knowledge for some
publics or as a popular guide to sentiment. The fragmentary, highly com-
pressed images of other cultures Hollywood produces substitute all too easily for more complex representations, which can take many years to produce
and are hard to conventionalize. Large-scale production demands that com-

plexity be simplified, and social psychologists capture its reductive logic well when they define stereotypes as cognitive strategies employed to streamline an excess or a scarcity of information (Fiske and Neuberg 1990; Hewstone and Stroebe 2001; Leyens et al. 1994).

An extensive literature exists detailing the media strategies that mark and magnify cultural, racial, ethnic, and gender differences (Hall 1981, 1989, 1997; Berg 2002; Davis 1996; Faris 1996; Kratz 2002; Lester 1996; Lutz and Collins 1993; Mengara 2001; Reader 1981; Rony, 1996).[37] Drawing attention to these strategies and their power is a necessary intervention, one that could parallel the strides made by feminist film critics in combating the prevalence of patriarchal representations of women (Doane et al. 1984; Kaplan 2000; Traube 1992). Ella Shohat and Robert Stam, for instance, argue that increased attention to media stereotypes can identify (1) widespread patterns of prejudice, (2) the psychological impact on those stereotyped, and (3) the social functions of stereotypes (Shohat and Stam 1994:198–204).[38] Portrayals of Africans as Maasai, of Maasai as warriors, and of Maasai warriors as drinkers of raw blood are not, in and of themselves, false or negative. Certainly, some Africans are Maasai, some Maasai are warriors, and Maasai warriors sometimes drink raw blood. Problems arise when, through repeated media representation of a highly delimited set of images circulating globally, these portrayals constitute most of what Western audiences know about Africa.

That Hollywood produces stereotypes is, of course, a well-known and widely criticized fact, yet the extent to which this critical knowledge is itself part of the stereotyping process is not generally understood. Inequalities of power lend far more political, symbolic, and economic weight to what European and American publics think of Samburu than what Samburu think of Americans and Europeans. When attempts are made to counter (in film) stereotypical depictions of Samburu/Maasai, the alternative images are inevitably selected and framed in reaction to dominant, Western ideologies, such as those distinguishing "savagery" from "civilization," and this strategic move strengthens the evaluative position of globally dominant publics. My desire to eliminate the "cow bleeding/blood drinking ritual" scene from G&D was a tacit recognition of this asymmetry, since it was based entirely on my own sensitivity to the opinions and imagined reactions of Western audiences.

The Samburu extras, however, did not share my concerns. They felt no embarrassment, no "rueful self-recognition" (Herzfeld 1997:6) that would indicate an awareness of how their appearance in the film might be interpreted negatively by others. They knew they were being represented in odd ways, but their obvious enjoyment of the rushes suggests that they found their screen image humorous, not disconcerting or offensive. As Samburu develop a greater familiarity with "metropolitan" sensibilities, which they undoubtedly will over time, their knowledge of how they are presented in feature films will more likely be accompanied by hurt and indignation. The outraged response of Africans living in Paris to the initial screening of Jean Rouch's *Les Maîtres fous*, with its depiction of possessed Songhay migrants in Ghana eating dog flesh (Stoller 1992; Loizos 1993), is worth recalling here, as is Talal Asad's (1986) insistence that cultural translation never occurs on equal terms.

Culture Wrangling and Cultural Intimacy

The literary or artistic field is a field of forces, but it is also a field of struggles.
—Pierre Bourdieu, *The Field of Cultural Production* (1993)

In presenting Samburu concerns to the film company while relaying the filmmakers' requests on set and off to the Samburu, I trod an infamous path. An anthropologist was involved in early preparations for German director Werner Herzog's *Fitzcarraldo* (1982), a movie set in late-nineteenth-century Peru that depicts the career of rubber entrepreneur Carlos Fermín Fitzcarrald. Fitzcarrald's pursuit of rubber in an inaccessible area of the Amazon (the only area not already claimed by other rubber barons) led him to drag two steamships over a mountain at the cost of countless Indian lives. His success in finding a navigable river pass (that bears his name today) enabled the arrival of thousands of rubber tappers who killed any Indians who resisted or refused to work. Many more Indians were sold into slavery to Bolivian and Brazilian landowners. For Herzog's film, the anthropologist prepared a contract with the Aguaruna community of Peru in whose territory Herzog wanted to film, but they refused to sign in memory of the suffering Fitzcarrald had inflicted on Amazonian peoples. When Herzog decided to go ahead and film anyway, the Aguaruna burned down the set and all but chased Herzog from Peru. The film was stalled for over a year until new elections brought a more favorable climate. Herzog tried again in a different area with a different Indian community—the Muchinguenga—and won their acceptance by promising them land titles. It took four years before Herzog finally succeeded in completing the film, and he left in his wake "ethnic conflict, food shortages, sickness—to the community of only 60 people," several deaths by food poisoning and drowning, and no land titles.[39]

Anthropologists, by virtue of our participatory methods and long-term involvements, cultivate intensely personal relationships with the people we study. If successful, ethnography begets what Michael Herzfeld calls *cultural intimacy*, namely, "recognition of those aspects of a cultural identity that are considered a source of external embarrassment but that nevertheless provide insiders with their assurance of common sociality" (1997:3). Although

Herzfeld developed this concept to describe self-recognition among members of a national community, I believe it explains much that is distinctive about ethnographic encounters. The privileged forms of knowledge born of these encounters bring with them the joys of being accepted as an insider (of sorts) and the concomitant challenge of wielding this knowledge in a culturally responsible manner. As Andrew Shryock points out in the introduction to this volume, ethnographers are forever navigating between public and private concerns, between public and private forms of representation, and we need to face the fact that public applications of our knowledge make many of us "applied anthropologists," whether or not we elect to be designated as such. We should also accept the fact that public applications of our knowledge will produce situations (like the ones I faced on the set of G&D) in which the "embarrassments" we feel will prove that we are not really insiders at all, but intermediaries who try to manage or create sensitivities that do not yet exist in the various cultural locations we transect.

Hollywood feature films are a form of representation oriented not only to localized publics but to publics the world over. Should anthropologists involve themselves in these undertakings, given the entrenchment of formulaic conventions and the drive toward profit that motivates so many Hollywood productions? Should anthropologists play the role of manager, defender, and activist on behalf of persons and groups who appear in mass-mediated cultural representations? I expect some would say no. Instead, anthropologists should facilitate the bearing of this burden by members of the communities in question, helping them develop and pursue their own strategies of self-presentation. The successes of some anthropologists who engage in media-based cultural activism (Ginsburg 1994, 1995, 1997; Michaels 1994; Prins 2002; Turner 1991, 1992, 1995; Worth and Adair 1972/1997) show clearly that this is a viable alternative. Yet it is probably not wise to assume that "members of a community" will do media work well simply by virtue of "membership" (Ruby 2000:218), or that they will be less likely to cater to political interests, that they will not engage in stereotyping, or that they will treat members of their own group with respect. The transformation in consciousness, described by Terence Turner, that allowed Kayapo to view visual media "not merely [as] *means* of representing culture, actions, or events and the objectification of their meanings in social consciousness, but themselves the *ends* of social action and objectification in consciousness," (1991:307) is not always present. Moreover, it is possible to conceptualize access to mass mediation (visual and otherwise) as an "end" of a different kind.

Postcards abound in Kenyan shops picturing Maasai in traditional clothing wielding video cameras (playing on a perceived incongruity between tradition and modernity), but the overwhelming majority of Samburu who worked on G&D expressed little or no interest in media production as identity politics. The only position on the topic I ever heard voiced by Kipsang, Lologol, Naukat, Leparpoorit or any of the other moran was that film production—as an activity initiated by others for others—constituted a means of personal and familial economic advancement.[40] In cases like these, or until these young men or other Samburu take an interest in media production as a kind of representational politics (as Navajo, Aboriginal Australians, Kayapo, and other communities have done), does it not behoove anthropological interlocutors to play an active part in managing the fields of cultural production in which mass-mediated images of difference are made?

As a person who identified affectively with both the Samburu I met on G&D and other members of the production team, I was embarrassed by the insensitivity of Hollywood filmmakers (who belong, in many ways, to my own cultural world) and by their willingness to circulate images equated with savagery and monstrosity. Inhabiting multiple, shifting spheres of cultural intimacy is a common predicament for anthropologists—indeed, one could argue that ethnographic insight is not possible without it. Anthropologists who apply their insights to the creation (or merely the analysis) of mass-mediated forms of popular culture must face the added challenge of straddling multiple fields of cultural production: some "restricted," others "large-scale." The conflicting standards of these fields are very hard to finesse—which is why so many of my colleagues have concluded that "Hollywood is no place for an anthropologist"—yet as mass media become more ubiquitous, and cultures are increasingly "mediatized," our attempts to avoid interstitial positionings will fail.

And this is why I consider Hollywood as good a place as any for anthropological intervention. Global flows of media products are crashing along at breakneck speed. People learn about other cultures more commonly through film and other mass media vehicles than—we must admit—through anthropological monographs. This fact alone should be reason enough to do whatever can be done to assist in the production of cultural representations that are more highly nuanced and less reductive. As Roy Rappaport has argued in a not unrelated context, "We have at least as much to gain from engagement as we have to give" (Rappaport 1993:296). Hollywood producers will continue to make films based on tried-and-true formulas as long as they lack alternatives, but they are not uniformly committed to the traditional way of doing things. Director Stephen Hopkins chose not to portray moran drinking blood and rejected the proposal that Zulu be cast as Maasai. He fought for cultural accuracy and, while he did not always achieve it, his belief that it is important did influence a number of his decisions and made him open to critique and suggestion. The producers, while arguably not as committed to accuracy as Hopkins, nevertheless conceded to his demand for Samburu extras, committed the necessary resources, and sent Mike and me to Kenya with the moran to set right an accountancy wrong.

With this hindsight, I therefore suggest *culture wrangling* as a useful way of conceptualizing what highly public uses of anthropological knowledge entail. In the production memo confirming my employment as the Samburu Extras Assistant Coordinator, I was given a "position as assistant during these early days of Samburu wrangling."[41] Dictionary definitions of "wrangling" encompass, on the one hand, dispute, quarreling, winning through argument, and, on the other hand, herding (of cows and other livestock), with its connotations of channeling, navigating, and directing. Any anthropologist, any person, who has lived between and across cultural boundaries —and has helped others move through these spaces—will be familiar with the tensions, continual reassessment, endless self-doubt, and constant need for tact and diplomacy that come with "wrangling." The more frequently invoked concepts of "cross-cultural understanding," "cultural relativism," "cultural translation," and, yes, even "cultural intimacy," fail to convey the difficulties intrinsic to the social (and emotional) equations they seek to explain. I would go so far as to argue that culture wrangling characterizes even the most private of anthropological encounters, since every piece of ethnographic knowledge we collect has to be categorized as something to be guarded or something potentially to be revealed in our analyses. Issues of concealment, censorship, and partial, full, and no disclosure are magnified when our audiences include the moviegoer, the museum visitor, the radio listener, or other imagined observers.

So what were the greater challenges I faced during my sojourn in Anthropollywood? Given that it was my first experience on a major film, I was positioned quite low in the production's pyramidal structure, despite my role as a knowledge specialist, and this certainly was a handicap. Yet experience on one high-profile film, I have found, has opened the door to other opportunities for film work, and while each additional experience has produced its own vexations, I find myself better able to maneuver; as with any new field experience, prolonged involvement increases one's facility and cultural fluency. I remain all the more convinced that room exists not only for expanded ethnographic analyses of film and other media production, but for anthropologists to lobby for increased access to the lucrative employment opportunities that multinational media industries can offer to the human communities they depict. I see no reason why we cannot attack cinematic stereotypes at the symbolic/representational level even as we help people find jobs, acquire marketable skills, and build community institutions at the economic/practical level.

Of course, the politics of symbols and payrolls are not the only (or even the most pressing) difficulties that confront the wrangler. The realities we faced in postapartheid South Africa, where the label "African" has a unique, tortured history, shaped daily life for the moran in ways none of us foresaw. These realities presented themselves whenever I accompanied the moran on shopping expeditions during their days off. Although dressed in Western-style clothing, like everyone we encountered (see Figure 2.7), the moran nevertheless attracted overt stares and covert gossip. Their lanky build, pierced ears, bead bracelets, and ever-present *lringu* (wooden clubs) gave away their non–South African origins and invited questions from gregarious onlookers about life "there in Africa"—as though South Africa were not part of the same continent. Over time, another problem arose in the steadily increasing numbers of South African women who flocked to the area of our cabins. They were great admirers of the moran and caused Mike and me no small amount of concern, given the high rate of HIV infection in South Africa (whereas HIV was not yet a danger in Samburu areas). There were yet more problems with people—on set and off—treating the moran like inanimate objects by posing for pictures with them without their permission. Our complaints on this matter led to the release of a production-wide memo reminding everyone that the Samburu were guests of the production and deserved the highest respect.[42]

Ezra's duplicity posed another unanticipated challenge, but the fact that we negotiated a solution ensuring salaries in full for all the moran made me glad in the end that I had stayed and not quit (as I was many times tempted to do). In all honesty, however, perhaps my greatest challenge on *The Ghost and the Darkness* was breaking the bad news to my Samburu friends that the glory of killing the lions would be reserved, in this case, for Michael Douglas and Val Kilmer, and, worse yet, that they would be portrayed walking away from the hunt early and empty-handed. *That*, and trying to explain that the million-dollar trained lions on set were *not* to be killed, proved the true test of my skills as a culture wrangler. It made me recognize (and rue) the many ways in which my odd line of work was connected to the colonial world the film sought to depict and managed, on screen and off, to reproduce.

Coda

What it will cost no words can express;
  What is its object no brain can suppose;
Where it will start from no one can guess;
  Where it is going to nobody knows.
What is the use of it none can conjecture;
  What it will carry there's none can define;
And in spite of George Curzon's superior lecture,[43]
  It clearly is naught by a lunatic line.[44]

FIGURE 2.7. Samburu extras from *The Ghost and the Darkness* during the Christmas holiday break, Kromdraai, South Africa, 1995. Photo by author.

In *The Man-Eaters of Tsavo*, John Patterson reveals clearly his passion for the hunt and his exacting attitudes toward work (which made him decidedly unpopular among those who worked for him). What also emerges, however, is an anthropological curiosity that led him to devote two chapters of the book to ethnographic descriptions of Swahili, Taita, Kamba, Maasai, Okiek ("N'Derobbo"), Kikuyu, and Kavirondo peoples he met during his time in Kenya. Descriptions of Patterson from other sources indicate that he was never without a notebook, in which he recorded grievances and fines against those workers whom he considered lazy or inept (Hardy 1965; Miller 1971). In all likelihood, these notebooks also served as repository of his ethnographic observations.

Patterson exhibited as well a penchant for cross-cultural comparison. In describing an encounter he had with Taita women, who displayed a great admiration for the embroidered garment of his Indian servant, he noted, "[T]his took their fancy immensely; they examined every line most carefully and went into ecstasies over it—just as their European sisters would have done over the latest Parisian creation" (Patterson 1907/1927:49). On another occasion, when searching for a water supply for his workers, Patterson came across a Maasai man who claimed knowledge of a nearby pond. Patterson "asked if the place was far away, and got the reply in Swahili: *'M'bali kidogo'* ('A little distance'). Now, I had had experience of *M'bali kidogo* before; it is like the Irishman's 'mile and a bit'" (Patterson 1907/1927:226). Another Maasai man once asked him "if my country was nearer to God than his. I am afraid I was unable conscientiously to answer him in the affirmative" (Patterson 1907/1927:262). His fervent commitment in later years to the establishment of a Jewish army and Jewish state indicated a willingness to think and act outside the social boundaries of his cultural and religious upbringing, the consequences of which seem to have been ostracism from the British establishment that had once proclaimed him a hero.[45]

Viewing his life as a whole, one can argue that Patterson, too, was a culture producer and culture wrangler. He coordinated and managed enterprises involving British and Indians in India, Indians and Africans in Africa, British in South Africa, and Jews in Gallipoli, Egypt, and Palestine. In contributing his labor and skill to the railway project, in helping to expand and defend the British Empire, and in writing several books about his experiences afterward, he helped script the physical and representational narrative of British colonial domination with all its attendant struggles, conflicts, and contradictions. While he did not always endear himself to those with whom he worked (in fact, attempts were made on his life during his time in Tsavo by more than man-eaters), he nevertheless appears to have demonstrated a significant and rather uncommon degree of respect for other cultures. As is the case with many an anthropologist, the cost of this heavy investment in other ways of living, thinking, and meaning was personal estrangement. Patterson traveled the globe and was fêted by world leaders from Queen Victoria to Theodore Roosevelt to Mary Lee, daughter of General Robert E. Lee. Yet with his unconventional position in favor of the establishment of an Israeli state, his open criticism of British policy in Palestine, and his ties to noted Zionists (especially David Ben Gurion, first prime minister of Israel, and Vladimir Jabotinsky, reputed founder of the underground Irgun Zvai Leumi army, both of whom served under Patterson in World War I), Patterson fell from official favor. He eventually moved to America, where he remained active in the Zionist cause right up to his death in June 1947. And where did he settle? Where else but Los Angeles, the home of Hollywood, that would give him in return the gift of immortality.

Notes

1. London *Times*, Tuesday, June 30, 1896, p.5, col. 2.
2. A Constellation Films production, executive producers Michael Douglas and Steven Reuther, written by William Goldman, produced by Gale Ann Hurd, Paul Radin, and A. Kitman Ho, directed by Stephen Hopkins, music by Jerry Goldsmith, distributed by Paramount Pictures Corporation. Release date: October 11, 1996.
3. Elizabeth Traube, however, has written an incisive analysis of feature film texts that relates 1980s Hollywood films to the political context of their production: *Dreaming Identities: Class, Gender, and Generation in 1980s Hollywood Movies* (1992).
4. See also the report on the Uganda Railway in the London *Times*, Monday, August 16, 1897, p.6, cols. 1–3.
5. Miller 1971:242–3.
6. Between 1896–1903, a total of 31,983 Indian laborers were brought in for this purpose, of which 6,454 were invalided back to India and 2,493 died. See Hardy 1965:315; Miller 1971:391n; Tignor 1976:96.
7. For recent efforts to unravel the mystery surrounding the Tsavo man-eaters, see Peterhans et al. 1998, and Caputo 2002.
8. In fact, *The Ghost and the Darkness* was at least the second film made of this story. The first, *Bwana Devil* (1952), also happened to be the first fully 3-D movie.
9. I have been working in East Africa since 1987 (see Askew 2002).
10. William Goldman, *The Ghost and the Darkness*, 7th draft, rev. October 31, 1995, scene 20G, p. 24.
11. Musicologist Jean Kidula, linguist Mwaka Angaluki, and visiting Swahili poet Ahmed Sheikh Nabhany.
12. Filming ran from November 1995 through March 1996.
13. Properly speaking, the name of the Swahili language is "Kiswahili," but for ease of comprehension, I will use the more common "Swahili" to refer to the language as well as a culture area.
14. A Hollywood Pictures production starring Kevin Bacon; executive producers Lance Hool and Scot Kroopf, written by Max Apple, produced by Robert W.

Cort, Ted Field, and Rosalie Swedlin, directed by Paul Michael Glaser, distributed by Buena Vista Pictures. Release date: January 7, 1994. The plot centers on a basketball recruiter (Bacon) who goes to Africa in search of talent and discovers it in a Samburu community. It also was filmed in South Africa.

15. The nine days that the Samburu were needed on set were spread out over a six-week period.

16. The airport has since been renamed Johannesburg International Airport.

17. I use a pseudonym to protect his identity.

18. As Angelique Haugerud points out, however, Moi redefined his usage of *nyayo* several times since its introduction: "the meaning of the *nyayo* slogan gradually shifted from "I (President Moi) will follow Kenyatta's footsteps" to "Follow my footsteps." Later it changed again, as Moi asserted that it referred to the footsteps of Kenyans' ancestors, saying *nyayo* springs from a "universal African spirit—the spirit of the forefathers'" (1995:82).

19. In Samburu linguistic practice, by contrast, the plural form of *moran* is *elmoran*. My thanks to Jon Holtzman, an anthropologist with extensive research in Samburu communities, for enlightening me on this and on other Samburu practices. Additional assistance from Bilinda Straight, another anthropologist working in Samburu communities, is gratefully acknowledged.

20. Goldman, *The Ghost and the Darkness*, scene 106A, p. 70.

21. According to Jon Holtzman, one contrast between contemporary Maasai and Samburu is that Maasai have more ritualized practices surrounding the hunting of lions than Samburu do (personal communication, September 26, 2002). As mentioned previously, however, the Samburu would not have had very different practices from Maasai at the time the events in this film were taking place. For a description of a Maasai lion hunt, see Queeny 1954. I thank Dorothy Hodgson for this reference.

22. Dorothy Hodgson, personal communication, October 17, 2002.

23. Jon Holtzman, personal communication, September 26, 2002.

24. According to some of the moran, it was widely believed that Ezra had received more than his fair share of Samburu salaries on *The Air Up There*.

25. While I cannot with certainty say that he never married, he makes no mention of a wife in any of his writings, and his works are all autobiographical in nature (aside from *Man-Eaters*, these include *In the Grip of the Nyika*, *With the Zionists in Gallipoli*, and *With the Judeans in the Palestine Campaign*; also Jabotinsky et al. *The Battle for Jerusalem*). Moreover, one of my meetings at Paramount studios included a lawyer assigned to the film who, in tracking down copyright information on Patterson, revealed that Patterson had died alone and dependent on the charity of a Los Angeles family who had taken him in during his later years.

26. For more on how experimental films derive their position from opposition to Hollywood, see Mendik and Schneider 2002.

27. "Taking Stereotyping to a New Level in Fashion," *New York Times*, Tuesday, June 3, 1997, A21.

28. *Sports Illustrated* 88, no. 7 (February 20, 1998), 66–74.

29. See also Bruner and Kirshenblatt-Gimblett 1994; Bruner 2001; Galaty 2002; Hodgson 1999, 2001; Kratz and Gordon 2002; and Straight 2002.

30. Some examples are *North* (1994), *The Air Up There* (1994), *White Mischief* (1988), and *Out of Africa* (1986).

31. The actual amounts in South African rand (the rate of exchange was $1 = R3.6) were as follows: R34,000 for thorn trees; R27,000 for replanting them; R50,000 for red soil; R9,000 for grass; R3,500 for the avocado tree (price of acacia tree unknown); R130,000 to deliver the trees by helicopter.

32. Had I known this ahead of time, I might have been inclined to compose some subversive dialogue for the private entertainment of Swahili speakers!

33. A similar conflation occurred in Disney's animated feature film *The Lion King*, which, although clearly set in East Africa (with views of Mt. Kilimanjaro, the Serengeti, and wildebeest migrations), included identifiably South African musical vocals and melodic styles.

34. See Bourdieu's essay "Manet and the Institutionalization of Anomie" in *The Field of Cultural Production*.

35. These costs included airfares, salaries, per diems, housing, and food for the thirty moran plus their official chaperone and two coordinators.

36. He offered to subsidize some of the costs involved in bringing the Samburu to South Africa.

37. For an overview of this literature, see Askew and Wilk 2002.

38. See also Lutz and Collins 1993; Callimanopulos 1983.

39. *Cultural Survival Quarterly* 7, no. 2 (1983), 27. See also the Les Blank film *Burden of Dreams* (1982).

40. Although Samburu have yet to exploit visual media for the purposes of identity politics, they are not identity ingenues. As Sidney Kasfir (1999) has discussed, Samburu moran quite effectively cater to tourists on the beaches in and around Mombasa by exploiting Samburu/Maasai social and physical distinctiveness.

41. Memo dated December 19, 1995, from Mike McLean to Grant Hill.

42. Memo dated December 16, 1995, from coproducer Grant Hill to all cast and crew.

43. British Under-Secretary of State for Foreign Affairs (1895–1898), a vocal proponent of the Uganda railway.

44. Published in *Truth*, a private newspaper established by anti-imperialist critic Henry Labouchere (Miller 1971:286).

45. His death in June 1947 received no mention in the London *Times*, and only minimal coverage in the *New York Times* (June 20, 1947) and *Time* magazine (June 30, 1947).

References Cited

Asad, Talal. 1986. "The Concept of Cultural Translation in British Social Anthropology." Pp. 141–64 in *Writing Culture: The Poetics and Politics of Ethnography*, ed. James Clifford and George E. Marcus. Berkeley: University of California Press.

Askew, Kelly. 2002. *Performing the Nation: Swahili Music and Cultural Politics in Tanzania*. Chicago: University of Chicago Press.

Askew, Kelly, and Richard R. Wilk, eds. 2002. *The Anthropology of Media: A Reader*. Malden, Mass.: Blackwell Publishers.

Baudry, Jean-Louise. 1986a. "Ideological Effects of the Basic Cinematographic Apparatus." In *Narrative, Apparatus, Ideology*, ed. Philip Rosen. New York: Columbia University Press.

———. 1986b. "The Apparatus: Metapsychological Approaches to the Impression of Reality in Cinema." In *Narrative, Apparatus, Ideology*, ed. Philip Rosen. New York: Columbia University Press.

Berg, Charles Ramírez. 2002. *Latino Images in Film: Stereotypes, Subversion and Resistance*. Austin: University of Texas Press.

Bourdieu, Pierre. 1971/1993. "The Market of Symbolic Goods." Pp.112–41 in *The Field of Cultural Production*. New York: Columbia University Press.

———. 1993. *The Field of Cultural Production*. New York: Columbia University Press.

Boyer, Dominic. 2001. "On the Sedimentation and Accreditation of Social Knowledges of Difference: Mass Media, Journalism, and the Reproduction of East/West Alterities in Unified Germany." *Cultural Anthropology* 15 (4): 459–91.

Bruner, Edward M. 2001. "The Maasai and the Lion King: Authenticity, Nationalism, and Globalization in African Tourism." *American Ethnologist* 28 (4): 881–908.

Bruner, Edward M., and Barbara Kirshenblatt-Gimblett. 1994. "Maasai on the Lawn: Tourist Realism in East Africa." *Cultural Anthropology* 9 (2): 435–70.

Callimanopulos, Dominique. 1983. "Film and the Third World." *Cultural Survival Quarterly* 7 (2): 24–27.

Caputo, Philip. 2002. *Ghosts of Tsavo: Stalking the Mystery Lions of East Africa*. Washington, D.C.: Adventure Press.

Dávila, Arlene. 1998. "*El Kiosko Budweiser*: The Making of a 'National' Television Show in Puerto Rico." *American Ethnologist* 25 (3): 452–70.

———. 2001. *Latinos, Inc. The Marketing and Making of a People*. Berkeley: University of California Press.

Davis, Peter. 1996. *In Darkest Hollywood: Exploring the Jungles of Cinema's South Africa*. Athens, Ohio: Ravan Press and Ohio University Press.

Doane, Mary Ann, Patricia Mellencamp, and Linda Williams, eds. 1984. *Re-Vision: Essays in Feminist Film Criticism*. Frederick, Md.: University Publications of America.

Dornfeld, Barry. 1998. *Producing Public Television, Producing Public Culture*. Princeton, N.J.: Princeton University Press.

Faris, James C. 1996. *Navajo and Photography: A Critical History of the Representation of an American People*. Albuquerque: University of New Mexico Press.

Fiske, Susan T., and Steven L. Neuberg. 1990. "A Continuum of Impression Formation, from Category-based to Individuating Processes: Influences of Information and Motivation on Attention and Interpretation." In *Advances in Experimental Social Psychology* 23, ed. Mark P. Zanna. San Diego: Academic Press.

Galaty, John G. 2002. "How Visual Figures Speak: Narrative Inventions of 'The Pastoralist' in East Africa." *Visual Anthropology* 15: 347–67.

Ginsburg, Faye. 1994. "Embedded Aesthetics: Creating a Discursive Space for Indigenous Media." *Cultural Anthropology* 9: 365–82.

———. 1995. "Mediating Culture: Indigenous Media, Ethnographic Film, and the Production of Identity." Pp. 256–91 in *Fields of Vision: Essays in Film Studies, Vi-

sual Anthropology, and Photography, eds. Leslie Devereaux and Roger Hillman. Berkeley: University of California Press.

———. 1997. "'From Little Things, Big Things Grow': Indigenous Media and Cultural Activism." Pp.118–44 in *Between Resistance and Revolution: Cultural Politics and Social Protest*, ed. Richard G. Fox and Orin Starn. New Brunswick, N.J.: Rutgers University Press.

Goldman, William. 1995. *The Ghost and the Darkness*. 7th draft, rev. 31 October.

———. 1996. "Tracking 'the Ghost and the Darkness.'" *Premiere* 10 (3): 65–68.

Hall, Stuart. 1981. "The Whites of Their Eyes: Racist Ideologies and the Media." Pp.128–38 in *Silver Linings: Some Strategies for the Eighties*, ed. George Bridges and Rosalind Brunt. London: Lawrence and Wishart.

———. 1989. "Cultural Identity and Cinematic Representation," *Framework*, No. 38.

Hall, Stuart, ed. 1997. *Representation: Cultural Representations and Signifying Practice*. London: Sage Publications.

Hannerz, Ulf. 2003. *Foreign News: Exploring the World of Foreign Correspondents*. Chicago: University of Chicago Press.

Hardy, Ronald. 1965. *The Iron Snake*. London: Collins.

Haugerud, Angelique. 1995. *The Culture of Politics in Modern Kenya*. Cambridge: Cambridge University Press.

Herzfeld, Michael. 1997. *Cultural Intimacy: Social Poetics in the Nation-State*. New York: Routledge.

Hewstone, Miles, and Wolfgang Stroebe. 2001. *Introduction to Social Psychology*, 3d ed. Oxford: Blackwell.

Hodgson, Dorothy L. 1999. "'Once Intrepid Warriors': Modernity and the Production of Maasai Masculinities." *Ethnology* 38 (2): 121–50.

———. 2001. *Once Intrepid Warriors: Gender, Ethnicity, and the Cultural Politics of Maasai Development*. Bloomington: Indiana University Press.

Holtzman, Jon. 2001. "The Food of Elders, the 'Ration' of Women: Brewing, Gender, and Domestic Processes among the Samburu of Northern Kenya." *American Anthropologist* 103 (4): 1041–58.

———. 2002. "Politics and Gastopolitics: Gender and the Power of Food in Two African Pastoralist Societies." *Journal of the Royal Anthropological Institute* 8 (2): 259–78.

Horkheimer, Max, and Theodor Adorno. 1972. *Dialectic of Enlightenment*, trans. John Cumming. New York: Herder and Herder.

Jabotinsky, Vladimir, John Henry Patterson, Josiah Wedgewood, and Pierre van Paassen. 1941. *The Battle for Jerusalem*. New York: The American Friends of a Jewish Palestine.

Kaplan, E. Anne, ed. 2000. *Feminism and Film*. Oxford: Oxford University Press.

Kariuki, John. 1995. "Missed Chance! Why Film about Kenya Was Made in South Africa!" *Sunday Standard* (Nairobi, Kenya), 31 December.

Kasfir, Sidney Littlefield. 1999. "Samburu Souvenirs: Representations of a Land in Amber." Pp.67–83 in *Unpacking Culture: Art and Commodity in Colonial and Postcolonial Worlds*, eds. Ruth B. Phillips and Christopher Steiner. Berkeley: University of California Press.

Keil, Charles, and Steven Feld. 1994. *Music Grooves: Essays and Dialogues*. Chicago: University of Chicago Press.

Kratz, Corinne A. 2002. *The Ones That Are Wanted: Communication and the Politics of Representation in a Photographic Exhibit*. Berkeley: University of California Press.

Kratz, Corinne A., and Robert J. Gordon. 2002. "Persistent Popular Images of Pastoralists," *Visual Anthropology* 15: 247–65.

Lester, Paul Martin, ed. 1996. *Images That Injure: Pictorial Stereotypes in the Media*. Westport, Conn.: Praeger.

Leuthold, Steven M. 1995. "Native American Responses to the Western." *American Indian Culture and Research Journal* 19 (1): 153–89.

Leyens, Jacques-Philippe, Vincent Yzerbyt, and Georges Schadron. 1994. *Stereotypes and Social Cognition*. London: Sage.

Loizos, Peter. 1993. *Innovation in Ethnographic Film: From Innocence to Self-Consciousness, 1955–1985*. Chicago: University of Chicago Press.

Lutz, Catherine A., and Jane L. Collins. 1993. *Reading National Geographic*. Chicago: University of Chicago Press.

Manuel, Peter. 1993. *Cassette Culture: Popular Music and Technology in North India*. Chicago: University of Chicago Press.

Meintjes, Louise. 1990. "Paul Simon's *Graceland*, South Africa, and the Mediation of Musical Meaning." *Ethnomusicology* 34 (1): 37–73.

———. 2003. *Sound of Africa! Making Music Zulu in a South African Studio*. Durham, N.C.: Duke University Press.

Mendik, Xavier, and Steven Jay Schneider. *Underground USA: Filmmaking Beyond the Hollywood Canon*. London: Wallflower Press, 2002.

Mengara, Daniel M., ed. 2001. *Images of Africa: Stereotypes and Realities*. Trenton, N.J.: Africa World Press.

Michaels, Eric. 1994. *Bad Aboriginal Art: Tradition, Media, and Technological Horizons*. Minneapolis: University of Minnesota Press.

Miller, Charles. 1971. *The Lunatic Express: An Entertainment in Imperialism*. New York: Macmillan.

Moeran, Brian. 1996. *A Japanese Advertising Agency: An Anthropology of Media and Markets*. Honolulu: University of Hawaii Press.

Mulvey, Laura. 1975/1986. "Visual pleasure and narrative cinema." In *Narrative, Apparatus, Ideology*, ed. Philip Rosen. New York: Columbia University Press.

Naficy, Hamid. 1993. *The Making of Exile Cultures: Iranian Television in Los Angeles*. Minneapolis: University of Minnesota Press.

Patterson, John Henry. 1907/1927. *The Man-Eaters of Tsavo and Other East African Adventures*. New York: Macmillan.

———. 1909. *In the Grip of the Nyika: Further Adventures in British East Africa*. London: Macmillan.

———. 1916. *With the Zionists in Gallipoli*. New York: George H. Doran Company.

———. 1922. *With the Judeans in the Palestine Campaign*. London: Hutchinson & Co.

Pedelty, Mark. 1995. *War Stories: The Culture of Foreign Correspondents*. New York: Routledge.

Peterhans, Julian C. Kerbis, et al. 1998. "Journal: Man-Eaters of Tsavo." *Natural History* 107 (9): 12–14.

Powdermaker, Hortense. 1950. *Hollywood the Dream Factory*. Boston: Little, Brown and Company.

Prins, Harald E. L. 2002. "Visual Media and the Primitivist Perplex: Colonial Fantasies, Indigenous Imagination, and Advocacy in North America." In *Media Worlds: Anthropology on New Terrain*, eds. Faye D. Ginsburg, Lila Abu-Lughod, and Brian Larkin. Berkeley: University of California Press.

Queeny, Edgar Monsanto. 1954. "Spearing the Lions with Africa's Masai." *National Geographic Magazine* 106 (4): 486–517.

Rappaport, Roy. 1993. "Distinguished Lecture in General Anthropology: The Anthropology of Trouble." *American Anthropologist* 95 (2): 295–303.

Reader, Keith. 1981. *Cultures on Celluloid*. London: Quartet Books.

Rony, Fatimah Tobing. 1996. *The Third Eye: Race, Cinema, and Ethnographic Spectacle*. Durham, N.C.: Duke University Press.

Ruby, Jay. 2000. *Picturing Culture: Explorations of Film and Anthropology*. Chicago: University of Chicago Press.

Screen Africa. 2000. "Six Good Reasons to Film in South Africa." *Africa News Online, Arts and Entertainment*, February 21, 2000. Available at http://www.africanews.org/culture/stories/20000221/20000221_feat1.html.

Shohat, Ella, and Robert Stam. 1994. *Unthinking Eurocentrism: Multiculturalism and the Media*. London: Routledge.

Snyman, Dana. 1996. "Electronic Lions and Stick-On Thorns," *You Magazine* (South Africa), 11 January, pp.16–17.

Spear, Thomas, and Richard Waller, eds. 1993. *Being Maasai: Ethnicity and Identity in East Africa*. London: James Currey.

Spencer, Paul. 1965. *The Samburu*. London: Routledge and Kegan Paul.

Stoller, Paul. 1992. *The Cinematic Griot: The Ethnography of Jean Rouch*. Chicago: University of Chicago Press.

Straight, Bilinda. 2002. "From Samburu Heirloom to New Age Artifact: The Cross-Cultural Consumption of Mporo Marriage Beads." *American Anthropologist* 104 (1): 7–21.

Tignor, Robert L. 1976. *The Colonial Transformation of Kenya: The Kamba, Kikuyu, and Maasai from 1900–1939*. Princeton, N.J.: Princeton University Press.

Traube, Elizabeth G. 1992. *Dreaming Identities: Class, Gender, and Generation in 1980s Hollywood Movies*. Boulder, Colo.: Westview Press.

Turner, Terence. 1991. "Representing, Resisting, Rethinking: Historical Transformations of Kayapo Culture and Anthropological Consciousness." Pp.285–313 in *Colonial Situations: Essays on the Contextualization of Ethnographic Knowledge*, ed. George W. Stocking Jr. *History of Anthropology*. Vol. 7. Madison, Wis.: University of Wisconsin Press.

———. 1992. "Defiant Images: The Kayapo Appropriation of Video," *Anthropology Today* 9: 5–16.

———. 1995. "Objectification, Collaboration, and Mediation in Contemporary Ethnographic and Indigenous Media," *Visual Anthropology Review* 11 (2): 102–6.

Worth, Sol, and John Adair. 1972/1997. *Through Navajo Eyes: An Exploration in Film Communication and Anthropology*. Albuquerque: University of New Mexico Press.

CHAPTER 3

Egyptian Cinema On Stage and Off

Walter Armbrust

Introduction: Putting Egyptian Films in Their Place

Opinions on Egyptian films are often guided more by the head than the heart. Regardless of class, level of education, and even national origin, fans of Egyptian cinema implicitly compare Egyptian films negatively with their Western counterparts. This is an ethnographic problem. In formal terms comparison is meaningless due to the vastly different circumstances of film production in Egypt (and in Europe for that matter) as opposed to Hollywood. But in cultural terms, if an invidious distinction is nonetheless implicit in all objectifications of "Egyptian cinema," then it becomes desirable to avoid objectifying contexts if one is interested in learning how Egyptian films are woven into everyday life. The presence of a foreigner such as myself, however, inevitably creates precisely the context of objectification I wish to avoid. In a nutshell, it is difficult for me to talk about Egyptian films with those who enjoy them without inadvertently putting the cinema "on stage."

I encountered a familiar instance of this problem recently at a dinner in Oxford. The dinner was hosted by a group of visiting Palestinian and Arab-Israeli academics. All had grown up watching Egyptian films and were as familiar with the stars and famous films as most Egyptians. Some of those in attendance knew I was interested in Egyptian cinema because they had attended a lecture I gave the year before on representations of Americans and Jews in Egyptian films. Indeed, it appeared that one reason I was invited to dinner was to meet a colleague who was planning a research project on Palestinian cinema. However, the guest of honor was a London-based Arab League official of Palestinian origin. He knew about my research interests only because I had told him myself. He eagerly introduced this conversational thread:

I saw an excellent Egyptian film recently on satellite television. I can't remember the title, but it was an old one from the 1950s—the black and white ones are always the best. This one starred 'Umar al-Sharif, Su'ad Husni, Hind Rustam, and Yusuf Wahbi. Wahbi plays a rich businessman. In real life he was a serious theatre man, a student of George Abyad, but in this film he does a comic role, which was unusual for him. Su'ad Husni plays his daughter—and in the film she's a bit of a party girl. Wahbi wants to marry her off to his brother's son, but his wife is trying to match the girl with *her* brother's son, and her brother's son is as frivolous as the daughter. So Wahbi hatches a plot to make it look like *his* brother's son is having an affair with a beautiful actress. The actress is the Hind Rustam role. When the news about the alleged affair gets back to the daughter, she becomes much more interested in her father's brother's son than she had been. But then the actress, whom the characters in the film didn't really know, actually comes into their lives.

As the synopsis lengthened I thought I might have guessed the title: "This is *Rumors of Love*, isn't it?" I said. "Yes!" he said enthusiastically. "That's it. That's definitely the film. It was really excellent, nothing like the awful films they make these days."

   At face value this seemed like an excellent entree for an ethnography of popular Egyptian media. With no prompting, my cosmopolitan Palestinian informant had volunteered extensive commentary about a mainstream commercial Egyptian film. A plot revolving around parents trying to marry their daughter to rival cousins should be an anthropologist's dream. Cousin marriage, preferably to the father's brother's son or daughter, is the hoariest issue in Middle Eastern ethnography. So much the better if it comes dressed up in fancy villas and fast cars. Furthermore, listening to a London-based Palestinian comment on an Egyptian film added a dash of transnational spice, as did the invocation of 'Umar al-Sharif—the same "Omar Sharif" who became well known to American audiences. *Rumors of Love* was al-Sharif's nineteenth Egyptian film, made in 1960. He made three more Egyptian features, then left for Hollywood in 1962 to make *Lawrence of Arabia*, followed by a string of Hollywood and French films, a few of which were quite respectable, and international prominence as a bridge columnist. Al-Sharif's transnational "oriental" persona even has a presence in a lengthy anthropological analysis of *Lawrence of Arabia* (Caton 1999). What an ethnographic smorgasbord! It was, but not quite in the way it might first have seemed.

   Rumors of Love was a lucky guess. I had not seen it. I had, however, glimpsed the opening credits of the film once on television in Cairo. The first minutes of the film were memorable—the credits superimposed on images of upper-class people engrossed in gossipy-looking telephone conversations. So I remembered the title and that al-Sharif and Su'ad Husni appeared in it. The vivacious Husni, who later became known as "Cinderella of the Egyptian screen," began her career in 1959. Al-Sharif left for Hollywood soon after. They could not have overlapped in Egyptian cinema for long, so *Rumors of Love* seemed a likely candidate for the narrative my informant was describing. When I checked al-Sharif's and Husni's filmographies later, I found that it was the only film the two appeared in together.

Despite the promising enthusiasm of my informant and my lucky guess of the film's title, I expected that the conversation would not really be about popular Egyptian cinema. It was unusual for a film like *Rumors of Love* to be avidly discussed in this sort of setting, if not completely beyond the pale. As a Palestinian, my interlocutor had less cultural investment in Egyptian cinema than a well-educated and cosmopolitan Egyptian might. It was not *his* nation being represented by these films after all, though the pan-Arab distribution of Egyptian films makes them to some extent a common cinematic patrimony of the Arabic-speaking world. In the end our conversation about *Rumors of Love* was significant for its capacity to establish a common idiom, giving me an opening to demonstrate, in less than five minutes, that I was not an Egyptian film neophyte. But now that my cards were on the table, it was his turn to place himself.

I was not the least bit surprised when the Arab League official quickly steered the conversation toward Youssef Chahine, Egypt's most cosmopolitan director, whose films are regularly screened in European and American film festivals, and who is the recipient of a lifetime achievement award from the Cannes Film Festival. I am not a fan. I quickly opined that Chahine, a filmmaker since the late 1940s and still an active director in the twenty-first century, made his best film, *Cairo Station*, in 1958. I added that, while I find interesting moments in many of Chahine's films (more than one can say about many directors), I find virtually all of them to be impaired by a cloying pretentiousness. The problem is worse in his more recent films. The Arab League official and several others at the dinner agreed that recent Chahine films—from roughly the 1979 film *Alexandria . . . Why?* on—have been unforgivably self-obsessed. We were left with a comfortable middle ground consisting of Chahine's earlier work, which we all admired to some degree. We had found each other.

One of our group mentioned that an English-language book had been published recently on Chahine. I supplied the name of the author: Ibrahim Fawal. Fawal was a Palestinian American student who came to Oxford after retirement to write a dissertation on Chahine. He finished his dissertation— very quickly published by the British Film Institute on the occasion of a Youssef Chahine retrospective—shortly before I arrived at Oxford. Though Fawal is not Egyptian, the opening page of his book states that "mirroring Egypt's personality on the screen has been Youssef Chahine's lifetime obsession" (2001:1). A few lines later Egypt comes in for some withering criticism: "Throughout his long career, Chahine has doggedly pursued a complex cinema of ideas in a country prone to sentiment and escapism rather than sophistication and serious art" (2001:1). One wonders how a cinematic oeuvre devoted to mirroring a nation of sentimental escapists avoids cinematic escapism, but Fawal's real point is that Chahine is a misunderstood artist. This may well be true, but what is most interesting about Fawal's book is less its capacity to mirror "Egypt's personality" than its ability to mirror the conversation I was having with my dinner hosts about Youssef Chahine. The "Chahine Conversation" is a predictable phenomenon that has less to do with the films themselves than with strategies to achieve social distinction. I had been forced into the same conversation a few months earlier when former United Nations Secretary-General, Boutros Ghali, came for lunch at St. Antony's, my Oxford college. I had no intention of trying to discuss films with Dr. Ghali but was forced to do so when the head of my college outed me as an Egyptian film specialist. Boutros Ghali's response to my reluctant query about his opinion on Egyptian cinema was predictable: "I only like films of Youssef Chahine. The rest are unwatchable. My wife loves old Egyptian films and watches them on television all the time. But I find them intolerable."

No doubt Dr. Ghali was giving a sincere opinion. Nonetheless, it should be noted that Youssef Chahine is the quintessential safe dinner topic, particularly when the dinner guests are a mixed lot that includes foreigners. This is paradoxical given that Chahine's academic reputation as an important director is founded on his *transgressiveness*. His films, particularly his post–*Alexandria, Why?* films, humanize homosexuals, Jews, and Europeans, all either absent or crudely caricatured in most other Egyptian films. None of these films were financed by profits from the Egyptian film market; he increasingly works through European capital, a fact that raises hackles in his own country. Yet Chahine's cinematic transgressiveness is never discussed in detail in such places as the dining room of St. Antony's College, or the living room of Palestinian academics entertaining non-Arab guests. I have never heard the plot of a Chahine film described in as much detail or with as much obvious pleasure as that of *Rumors of Love*; never heard Chahine praised for boldly depicting French and British colonialists as "real people," too—who would have imagined it?[1]

I have on many occasions heard Chahine's name invoked as a sign of sophistication, rather like American academics disclaiming, often implausibly, any interest in television. Every modern society has equivalents of the Chahine Conversation, in which icons of sophistication are used performatively. It is not just a matter of dropping Chahine's name at strategic moments, as if the true sophisticate is the person who really "owns" Chahine's art and reveals his or her ownership at precisely the right time. Nor is it simply a matter of revealing one's "true" preferences. Indeed, if one assumes that sophisticates enjoy Chahine films, while others prefer popular films, the Palestinian intellectual's enthusiastic description of *Rumors of Love* makes no sense, and neither do the responses of many other people in many different circumstances.

A common criticism of anthropological approaches to mass-mediated popular culture is that they tend to be "thin." One way that ethnographies of mass media can address such concerns is by rooting mass-mediated phenomena in "social, cultural, and political dynamics of particular communities" (Abu-Lughod 1999:111). At the same time, part of the difficulty in understanding mass media ethnographically is to avoid the temptation of implicitly matching subgroups with genres: elite films should mirror the sensibilities of elites, and popular films reflect those of the masses. One must also avoid the opposite tendency. To note that the "middle-class," or "nationalist," or "elite" sensibilities exhibited in media texts align poorly with the empirical realities of actual lives is merely to state the obvious. The diffused nature of mass media makes an easy correspondence of content and audience much harder to establish than it seems to be in more conventional ethnographic settings.

Obviously the real issue is not the desirability of situating media in the social dynamics of communities. This is a given. But how does one contextualize such dynamics when the communities in question are conversant with complex discursive practices that alter the ethnographic object of analysis the instant one attempts to examine it? Matching, or mismatching, texts to communities—even communities of textual producers—does not necessarily provide sufficient analytical purchase on the sort of exchange described earlier. Mass-mediated texts are historically structured; they are imbricated in a complex public culture that is not reducible to communities. The point is not merely to repeat the old analytical blunderbuss of "the global" constructing "the local." It is rather that the phenomena to which the phrase "Egyptian cinema" refers have an identifiable history which lies not outside the boundaries of the various communities concerned with Egyptian cinema, but outside the boundaries of what anthropologists are normally inclined to include in an ethnography.

Consequently, this essay seeks to expand the boundaries of the ethnographic imaginary. What follows is mainly an analysis of the historiography and genre divisions of Egyptian cinema. These are not "nonethnographic" matters, as many anthropologists imagine them to be on the grounds that they lie somewhere outside the limits of the verbalized discourse on the cinema that counts as conventional ethnographic evidence. Indeed, my essay examines precisely what makes ethnography "thick" when the communities in question include vast numbers of people who are literate and not socially marginalized. This historiography is implicated in the performative aspects of film discourse for such people; therefore, to analyze cinema (or any other form of mass media in Egypt) without taking it into account is to risk writing a sound-bite ethnography—one that imparts a superficial ethno-graphic feel without addressing important aspects of social context. Dis-courses on historiography and genre are as much a part of the social, cul-tural, and political dynamics of statements made about the films of Youssef Chahine—and about such films as *Rumors of Love*—as are the details of what neighborhoods or regions people reside in, or how they earn their living.

The reason I wrote this essay in the first instance was to try to make sense of my own experiences in organizing and commenting on film festivals staged for international audiences.[2] I have never found such events to be satisfying. In the United States, Egyptian films are seen as a projection of Egyptian cul-ture. Having worked on several Egyptian film festivals, I knew that all films are problematic when presented in a context not structured by the private pleasure of watching films. Egyptian participation in film festivals provokes accusations of misrepresentation by Egyptians, almost without exception. Festivals can spotlight ambiguities between the private pleasure that audi-ences take in popular genres and the duties of public representation that compel praise of films with which many spectators feel little emotional res-onance. Formal discourse on Egyptian films emphasizes realist films;[3] pri-vate pleasure emphasizes musicals that appear at first glance to be the most "Westernized" films in the Egyptian cinema. The latter are often dismissed as trivial. But if the goal of a film festival is to facilitate intercultural com-munication, they should be highly prized.[4]

   Part of the difficulty in staging such films for audiences unfamiliar with them is that viewers lack the intertextual resources required to establish the sort of social relationships that facilitated my exchange with the Palestinian Arab League official. When intertextual resources are shared, even to a lim-ited degree, the nature of communication changes. It does not matter if the Palestinian intellectual and I agree about the films of Youssef Chahine. The important point is that we could locate each other in a cultural field. Two important elements of this field are how films are remembered historically, and how they are ranked hierarchically. No two people ever understand a film in exactly the same way, but the capacity for sharing a film's cultural field can, to some extent, be conveyed.

Genre

Genre and periodization are often structured through nationalist narratives that privilege realism. Benedict Anderson argues famously that realist narra-tives suit nationalism particularly well because realism, in the literary form of the novel, puts diverse elements of a national community in temporal syn-chronicity (Anderson 1991). Most commercial films are structurally influenced by the novel, hence the point Anderson makes about the novel's temporal and spatial dimensions—the simultaneity of events and characters that so neatly mirrors the "imagined community"—should, purely in terms of form, also apply to films that are not often thought of as important to nationalism: musicals, comedies, and dance films, for example.[5] However, one obvious way that many musicals differ from films that lend themselves easily to nationalist discourse is their lack of "seriousness of purpose." Unserious films do not adapt well to political goals. But in informal settings exactly the *opposite* is true—music, at least in Egypt, is probably the *most* potent force for evoking shared national sentiment. The music in question is mostly commercial.[6] Commercial musical films, often packaged with comedy and dance, are crucial to the development of musical culture in Egypt. It is therefore common for an individual to be passionate about the capacity of music to evoke a highly valued in-group identity (often extolled in the Arabic-language press) and yet be alarmed at the idea of including musicals in an international film festival.

Many "nationalist films" are not simply those built around nationalist themes, but rather films that fit within a nationalist narrative of cinematic development. For example, *The Sin* (al-Haram), a film made in 1965, is highly regarded as an example of the best kind of evolution of the Egyptian cinema. Made during a decade in which Egyptian cinema was nationalized, *The Sin* tells the story of a peasant girl who is raped by a son of the old, prerevolutionary elite. Adapted from a novel by prominent writer Yusuf Idris, and filmed on location in the Egyptian countryside, *The Sin* addresses politics by making prerevolutionary Egyptian society into a villain. While the film offers no explicit narrative of nationalist struggle, it does construct images of folk authenticity, which are commonly instrumentalized by nationalist ideologues (Bendix 1997) and in this case pointedly juxtaposed to "inauthentic" Westernized elites.

A recent book gives a splendid example of how formal contexts elevate realism, thereby obscuring broader dynamics of how cinema functions in society. In 1996, Egypt marked the one hundredth year of world cinema by issuing a volume entitled *Egypt: 100 Years of Cinema* (Bahgat 1996) to commemorate the best of Egyptian cinema. Published by the government-funded Cairo Film Festival Press, *100 Years of Cinema* featured the results of a referendum by one hundred filmmakers and film critics on the best one hundred Egyptian films of all time.[7] By my count, of the top one hundred Egyptian films, there were forty-three realist films, nineteen melodramas, fourteen political films, eleven musicals, nine mythological or historical films, four art films, and three comedies. In my categorization I was generous with the musicals. For example, I counted the 1972 film *Pay Attention to Zuzu* as a musical. The film does have music, though it might be more reasonable to categorize it as a dance film on the grounds that the music is always subordinated to dance; indeed, the dance component of the film was the reason for its great commercial success. I emphasize that this was the *only* film out of the top one hundred that could plausibly be called a dance film. It is, however, a particular kind of dance film, focusing on a college student, Zuzu, who studies by day and dances at weddings by night. Though the wedding performances are a family trade, honor demands that she hide her profession from fellow students. Zuzu's identity is eventually revealed by a jealous rival, and she is publicly ridiculed by a quasi-fundamentalist fellow student. Zuzu realizes that she cannot be a modern college student while working in such a backward profession. Her response to the dilemma is to renounce dancing.

Pay Attention to Zuzu neatly illustrates how genre hierarchies are made. The plot revolves around the necessity of keeping "Oriental" dance, a widely shared element of local culture, off stage. Oriental dance is, moreover, a practice many find quite enjoyable and believe to be strongly marked by a specifically Egyptian "feel."[8] The fate of Su'ad Husni, the actress who played Zuzu in the film, adds to the film's complex legacy. Husni died tragically in 2001, probably by suicide, while in London for medical treatment. She was an accomplished actress from an artistic family, and *Zuzu* was her signature film. Indeed, it is sometimes still hailed as the most commercially successful Egyptian film ever made (Adli 1996:267). Husni's death caused an outpouring of tender memorialization.[9] Known as the "Cinderella of the Arab screen," she was a beloved figure by all accounts. However, two years earlier when I helped organize a U.S. tour of Egyptian musicals, the reactions of Egyptian officials to our requests to include *Zuzu* in the program ranged from unhelpful bemusement to polite refusal. We wanted the film on the grounds that its songs are still well known and loved, that it was an extremely popular film, and that it was illustrative of musicals at a certain point in the history of the cinema. But we had to do without *Zuzu*, even though it had been ranked number seventy-nine in the poll. Neither government nor private-sector officials had the slightest interest in making a copy available.

However, the officials' refusal to help us obtain a print of *Zuzu* for our program was a blessing in disguise. *Zuzu* would have been fearsomely difficult to contextualize for American audiences. Most would have loved it for what they would view as its delightful kitschiness.[10] The film is also of intense interest to a large and active community of American Oriental dance enthusiasts who, despite their general attitude of (not necessarily well-informed) goodwill, are usually kept very much at arm's length by academics, Arab Americans, and Arab expatriates in the United States. But aside from the uneasy encounter of American belly dancers and Arabs in America, the film would have been difficult to explain because it featured complex social and political dynamics. The lyrics to the songs were written by Salah Jahin, a major colloquial poet prominent in the Nasser era. The events of the film take place on a college campus that was, at the time, aflame with unrest. Those events were alluded to in the film, rather obliquely it is true, but more directly than in subsequent films, which tended to make increasingly Islamist-oriented student politics invisible. *Zuzu*'s bubbly style belies the fact that it depicts (in a stylized manner) a clash between Leftist students and Islamists who were being nurtured by the Sadat regime in a desperate effort to build a counterweight against opposition to new American-oriented policies it wanted to implement. This understated perceptiveness makes the relatively high regard for the film in the *Hundred Years* poll comprehensible. But at the end of the day *Zuzu* was still a dance film, and hence not to be exhibited for foreigners.[11]

The presence of nineteen melodramas out of the top one hundred films might come as a surprise. It could have been more. I counted the 1954 film *They Made Me a Criminal* as a musical because it contains three songs by Hoda Sultan, a significant musical and dramatic figure of the 1950s (Armbrust 2002).[12] But *They Made Me a Criminal* has an impeccably melodramatic lineage. It is an Egyptian version of the American film *Angels with Dirty Faces* —a tale of two young men, one of whom grows up to be a priest (in the Egyptian film an Imam), and the other a criminal.

Melodrama figured heavily in the referendum because it, like realism, serves the agenda of nationalists. Though critically discounted due to its straightforward appeal to emotion, depiction of polarized forces, and neat resolution of conflicts, melodrama functions through moral clarity. It is, for all these reasons, highly conducive to didacticism, and therefore useful to an elite that sees itself as a social vanguard. This may be the reason for melodrama's place in a poll that was, after all, a quasi-official statement. It does not mean that Egyptian critics accept melodrama in the abstract, nor does it mean that audiences liked the films for the same reasons that the critics and filmmakers who voted in the referendum liked them. The heightened emotions of melodrama are pleasurable, but the referendum was not about the celebration of private pleasures.

Realist films outnumbered melodramas by (in my count) forty-three to nineteen. But the dominance of realism in the poll was actually greater than forty-three out of one hundred films would suggest. At the pinnacle of the referendum, eight out of the top ten films could plausibly be called realist works.[13] Three of these eight were based on novels, and two others were made from screenplays written by Nobel Prize Laureate Naguib Mahfouz during the 1950s, when his work had a well-publicized realist orientation.[14]

Of the two nonrealist films among the top ten, one was "mythological." This was a 1969 art film called *The Mummy*, directed by Shadi Abd al-Salam.[15] Based on history, the film tells the story of a tomb of pharaonic mummies discovered in the 1880s in upper Egypt, first by illiterate villagers who profited from the find by selling artifacts to European antiquities collectors, and then by an Egyptian Egyptologist, who endeavoured to preserve the find, catalogue it for science, and, more important, facilitate a rational scientific exploration of Egyptian identity. Despite its historical theme, Shadi Abd al-Salam's *Mummy* is no realist film. It features a slow, undifferentiated pace, geometrically choreographed movement of people through surreal pharaonic ruins, sparse dialogue in literary Arabic, and a cast that featured only one star (Nadiya Lutfi) in a brief nonspeaking part. *The Mummy* is more a beautiful painting than a realistic vision of Upper Egypt. It is a mythic narrative.[16]

One other film in the top ten, *The Flirtation of Girls* at number nine, appears anomalous. *The Flirtation of Girls* was an all-star revue made in 1949, showcasing five megastars of the 1930s and 1940s. Nationalism figures strongly in how the film is remembered because its stars became canonical figures.[17] It can be admired more safely in formal contexts than most musicals; consequently, *The Flirtation of Girls* is the exception that proves the rule. Given the overtly nationalist framing of the poll, it can only have been ranked so highly because the five stars in the film are overwhelmingly evocative of public national identity, thereby allowing the film to transcend the generally off-stage position reserved for musicals in polite discourse.

The Flirtation of Girls was the only musical in the top ten. By my perhaps overgenerous count there were eleven musicals in the top one hundred. After *The Flirtation of Girls* almost all of the other ten musicals were ranked toward the bottom of the list. The didactic *They Made Me a Criminal*, perhaps more melodrama than musical, is number twenty-six. After that the next musical is *A Bullet in the Heart*, at number sixty-five. Yet even the inclusion of musical films in the lower reaches of the referendum required a rationale other than quality. An article interpreting the results of the referendum suggested that certain films were included only because "they reflect a purely nostalgic value" (Yusuf 1996:29). The section of the article that made this designation for musicals was labeled "Folklore of the Cinema." Ten of the eleven films I counted as musicals were included.[18] Only *They Made Me a Criminal* escaped the accusation that it was on the list as a sentimental favorite and not for its artistic merit. Most of the musicals—including even the highly ranked *Flirtation of Girls*—were damned in the interpretive article by faint praise. As the author put it, "This is a nostalgia that does not obey critical analysis in the strict sense, but it should not be discounted, because this aspect of consciousness makes the cinema a type of contemporary 'folklore,' and is an important feature of cinematic taste." Important, but acknowledged in public only grudgingly.

Periodization: The Dialectic of History and Genre

In the hierarchy of genre that shapes public memory of Egyptian cinema, realism and nationalist agendas sweep music, dance, and comedy off stage.[19] Memory is shaped by historical forces and as an act of interpretation in retrospective rescripting. By the standards of the genre hierarchies that organize Egyptian cinema, the story of Egyptian cinema is one of the creation of a "national style" rooted in realism. It is also a story constructed around a motif of rise and decline.

The formative years of Egyptian cinema are from the early 1930s until the later years of World War II. All histories agree that the most important development of this period was the creation of a comprehensive film studio on Egyptian soil, owned by Egyptians, and eventually, staffed by Egyptians. This was Studio Misr, "The Studio of Egypt," created by industrialist Tal'at Harb. Harb's enterprises flourished during the interwar period, from roughly 1920, when he founded the Bank of Egypt, to 1939, when he was forced by political rivals to resign as head of the bank. He initiated other large-scale industrial enterprises ranging from cotton ginning to producing concrete, shipping and aviation, plus, of course, the film studio (Davis 1983; Hasan 1986). Tal'at Harb is remembered for having developed the Egyptian economy in the teeth of foreign occupation. His companies, including the film studio, were seen as de facto national institutions. A statue of Tal'at Harb stands prominently in downtown Cairo in a square named for Tal'at Harb, which is on Tal'at Harb Street.

Studio Misr was meant to have created a solid foundation for the Egyptian film industry. The reason for this is obvious: Studio Misr aspired to put the means of production in Egyptian hands. The early years are therefore depicted as a kind of mini–golden age of Egyptian cinema. When the studio began making feature films in 1935, many of the productions directly reflected the values of the studio. The most famous of these films was *Determination*, made in 1939.[20]

Determination tells the story of a young capitalist who wants to make his mark as an independent businessman in the import-export business. In other words, he aspires to be Tal'at Harb, the captain of Egyptian industry. The film is not remembered for glorifying the figure of the studio owner, but as the founding text of Egyptian cinematic realism. Consequently, in the referendum on the best Egyptian films of all time *Determination* was the top film. Like *The Flirtation of Girls*, the high ranking of *Determination* was explained in the interpretive article as owing to nostalgia, but in this case, a proudly proclaimed and explicitly nationalistic nostalgia:

It was as if the Egyptian intellectuals and film specialists who participated in the recent referendum felt deep in their collective consciousness that the culture of this nation . . . extends much deeper than is apparent at the current moment in which Egyptian culture . . . is in crisis. Perhaps *Determination* is not the absolute best in intellectual and artistic terms, but its capturing the highest rank in the referendum reflects a sincere desire to search for the powerful roots that can make the great tree grow and bloom (Yusuf 1996:18).

Studio Misr was initially more a prestige project than a moneymaker. Unfortunately Tal'at Harb could ill afford such a luxury when his fortunes took a turn for the worse at the end of the 1930s. Studio Misr tried to defray the cost of its investment in filmmaking infrastructure by renting its facilities to other filmmakers, and even to the British during World War II. As the most comprehensive filmmaking facility in the Arab world, Studio Misr monopolized the crucial processes of developing and printing film. Before Studio Misr, Egyptian filmmakers had to go to Europe to develop, print, and edit their films. Once the new Egyptian studio made its facilities available for rent, dependence on European technical expertise lessened. However, Studio Misr also reveals much about of the chronic problems the Egyptian film industry has faced throughout its history.

The fundamental problem from which all the others derived is that the Egyptian film industry was, from the beginning, undercapitalized. This did not necessarily mean that films were unprofitable. It did mean that the profits always tended to be fragmented, and this ultimately proved disastrous. An often-repeated apocryphal story has it that at a certain period (roughly the late 1940s or early 1950s) the Egyptian cinema was the second most profitable industry in the country, after cotton. In reality, economic studies indicate that the industry was chronically cash poor and, almost from its beginning, sought government intervention to regulate markets, protect local product from foreign competition, and subsidize production (Flibbert 2001; Hasanayn 1995). Furthermore, Egypt has always been underserved in terms of its exhibition capacity.[21] It comes as no surprise that this is true in comparison to the United States, which has long been the best-screened nation in the world. But given Egypt's well-known dominance of Arabic-language film production, it is surprising that over time Egypt fares poorly even in comparison to "less developed" countries.[22] The screen density of Egypt, however, exceeded that of the rest of the Arab world. As a result, not only was the domestic film market relatively anemic, but exports to other Arab countries had only limited potential for covering the costs of a film. Nonetheless, as the costs of making films rose, exporting to other Arabic-speaking markets became a vital part of the business. The lack of exhibition capacity was indicative of a general problem in industrial organization.

Though the Egyptian film industry is often called "Hollywood on the Nile," it was never organized along the lines of Hollywood, as a vertically integrated monopoly. Instead, Studio Misr, the business best positioned to build a local cinema monopoly, cut back on production in the 1940s and rented itself to other filmmakers.[23] Labor, specifically of the star actors, constituted a far higher percentage of the total costs of producing Egyptian films than was the case for Hollywood films because studios never put actors under fixed, long-term contracts. Indeed, by the mid-1940s demand for Egyptian films was high and the quantity of films leaped. Yet the people jumping into the breach to fill this demand were a mélange of investors, including actors, rather than vertically integrated studios. It is alleged that the money being invested in films by this time was actually coming from war profiteers (Aliksan 1981:24; al-Sharqawi 1970:103–105). Thus at a time of expansion in the film market, the major studio of the day was competing with minor entrepreneurs on an oddly equal footing. This would not have happened if the established studios had built a monopoly capable of snuffing out competition, instead of being satisfied with relatively static rent seeking. Studio Misr in particular, with control of developing and printing facilities, seems to have fed the competition by making its facilities available to the highest bidder. It was very common to see films financed by a haphazard, ever-shifting pool of investors, shot at the smaller studios, but developed and printed by Studio Misr.[24] The owners of Studio Misr made profit without risk, but they also contributed to a fragmentation of profits by accommodating new competitors rather than expanding their own business.

One famous Studio Misr production from World War II, called *Black Market* (1946), articulated the studio's predicament. *Black Market* is often credited as a crucial step toward creating a realist film tradition after *Determination* (Abu Shadi 1996:114). Made seven years after *Determination*, the film is number thirty-four in the one hundred best films poll. Its subject is war profiteering. World War II is depicted as a great hardship for Egypt, but, as is often the case, wartime also brought opportunities for some. The British needed labor, and thousands of men came to Cairo from the countryside to work for good wages, even as others were suffering from economic dislocations. The migration of men to the cities, and their relative prosperity, created an opportunity for Egyptian filmmakers. Competition was muted because of the relative absence of foreign (particularly European) films. Film production leaped from around a dozen films per year in 1942 to fifty-three per year in 1946. Production stayed at roughly that level until the mid-1990s.

In 1946, *Black Market* depicted war profiteers as tasteless and evil parasites. Ironically, money from war profiteering and smuggling is alleged to have been a crucial source of capital fueling the expansion of the film industry. Furthermore, the scorn heaped on war profiteers in *Black Market* resembles the way film production from the mid-to-late 1940s is frequently described: tasteless, exploitative, cheap, and utterly unprincipled. Late 1940s cinema is sometimes described as "the cinema of war profiteers." It appears that Studio Misr saw the writing on the wall, realizing that its chance to dominate the film industry was slipping away as new competitors captured much of the market. Just as these infuriatingly vulgar, cheap, and tasteless films were entering the theaters, Studio Misr produced *Black Market*, which angrily condemned vulgar, cheap, and tasteless war profiteers. These were the same characters who, it seems, were laundering their ill-gotten gains by investing in film production, which was now a direct competitor to Studio Misr's own products. Five new studios were built during the 1940s, but Studio Misr's strategy for staying in business was to continue renting out the parts of the filmmaking process it still monopolized, particularly developing and printing film.

Numbers tell the story. In 1939, when *Determination* was made, Studio Misr produced four films. Total production for that year was only fifteen films, hence Studio Misr directly produced 26 percent of the market. In 1946, when *Black Market* was released, Studio Misr's production was only three films, but the total number of films made that year was fifty-two. Thus from 1939 to 1946, Studio Misr's share of the market dropped from 26 percent to about 6 percent. The market wanted more Egyptian films—total production more than tripled. New producers would not have entered the business if they did not believe there was potential to make a profit. It is often said that Egyptian film production was crippled by the inability of Egyptian producers to get screen time for their product—foreign films dominated screens, leaving no room for local products.[25] Though it is true that by the 1990s Hollywood decisively dominated Egyptian film markets, in the mid-1940s, when Egyptian cinema underwent its great expansion, it is more likely that the problem was not the dominance of foreign films but the inability of Egyptian filmmakers to supply enough production to satisfy local demand. If Studio Misr had been able to operate in the 1940s like a Hollywood studio, it would have expanded production, built theaters, and created its own distribution network.[26]

From the late 1950s through the 1960s a more monopolistic market was established, but by way of nationalizing the film industry rather than through less intrusive methods of structuring the market, such as imposing tariffs, instituting a cultural policy favoring filmmakers, or regulating the importation of foreign competition. Most crucially, starting in 1960, the state undermined its own film industry by building a television infrastructure without ever enabling the owners of film archives to rent their product to television stations at fair market value.[27]

At the time of its ascendance, Studio Misr operated in a highly competitive market in which all major facets of the trade were unsynchronized (Flibbert 2001:110). The studio might have lived up to its later reputation as a solid foundation for Egyptian film production if it had created a monopoly.

Instead, Studio Misr kept production flat, rented out its facilities to its competitors, and left the crucial foreign distribution system in the hands of businessmen who made no films but always ended up with a crucial share of the profits. Film production was oriented more toward the efforts of individuals who rented filmmaking facilities than it was toward studio production.

The 1930s and 1940s were important because it was at this time that the basic economic patterns of Egyptian film production were set. Except for the 1960s, when the cinema was nationalized, variations on these economic patterns persist. Film production in Egypt resembles what would be termed "independent" production in the United States, but with the cumbersome caveat that in Egypt most of the budget goes to the star actors. Filmmaking in Egypt is like making a film on *Blair Witch Project* resources, but being required to cast Mel Gibson and Julia Roberts in the leading roles.

Film Festival Redux

What I have just described differs from the conventional narrative of Egyptian film history, the outlines of which are an element of widely shared public culture. Studio Misr lived within and typified the shaky market structure of Egyptian cinema, but this aspect of its history is rarely emphasized. Instead, Studio Misr is inevitably described as an engine of the early Egyptian film industry. Madkour Thabet, former director of the High Institute for the Cinema, was typical in stating flatly that

Studio Misr and its school became a solid foundation for the cinema industry in Egypt. It had been planned with this intention in mind as expressed by Talaat Harb, in his speech at the inauguration ceremony on 12 October 1935. He said it was one of the industrial economic projects of Bank Misr aiming at making available all the requirements of making films to all workers in this field. . . . The success of the part played by Studio Misr was an incentive for other studios to be established" (Thabet 1998:17).

An article in *100 Years of Cinema* discusses the importance of Studio Misr in nearly identical terms. Its title, "Studio Misr: School of the Egyptian Cinema" (Ibrahim 1996), highlights the way the institution is remembered. Ibrahim states that the "company believed Studio Misr should serve the Egyptian cinema, and not just its own films. The studio therefore opened its doors to various other companies that wanted to make Egyptian films" (ibid.:159).

If it is true that Studio Misr was created with altruistic goals—that it generously opened its doors to its competitors—then in economic terms it would be more reasonable to argue that Studio Misr did *not* contribute to a sound basis for an Egyptian film industry. Creating a monopoly capable of effectively pressuring the government to protect and promote the film industry, as did the American film industry (Putnam 1997), would have been far more beneficial to Egyptian filmmaking in the long run. The problems the industry faced were only partially to do with equipment and materials; flaws in the business structure were much more serious. Yet arguments for the importance of Studio Misr tend to conflate the infrastructural contribution of the business with a mystique predicated more on the quality of its films than on economics. Again, the article in *100 Years of Cinema* is instructive. According to Ibrahim, "the opening of Studio Misr was considered the beginning of a new and important stage in the history of Egyptian cinema. All of the company's films were high-quality productions intellectually, artistically, and in terms of craft. None of its films could be considered silly or vulgar" (1996: 162). But "silly" and "vulgar" were precisely the terms used to describe many of the films produced by Studio Misr's competitors in the mid-to-late 1940s, when the Egyptian film industry underwent its most significant expansion. Many of those films were, in fact, obviously made by filmmaking neophytes. But when film critics of a later age disparage this kind of production in aesthetic or even quasi-moral terms, they miss the point of what was happening.

The beloved *Flirtation of Girls* was in fact one of these cheap productions of the late 1940s. In terms of plot and structure it bears all the marks of the "silly" or "vulgar" films disparaged in *100 Years of Cinema*. But the reason for the film's lasting success is not just the presence of stars who later became recognized as national icons. *The Flirtation of Girls* is genuinely a great musical, and an excellent comedy. Furthermore, it was not made in a vacuum. Two other examples of films from this supposedly decadent period of Egyptian cinema are *The Beau's Hanky* and *Dark and Beautiful*, from 1949 and 1950 respectively. Both should be strong candidates for a film festival focusing on Egyptian musicals.[28] They feature early examples of the film work of the dancers Tahiya Karioka (in *The Beau's Hanky*) and Samiya Gamal (in *Dark and Beautiful*). Karioka and Gamal are household names in Egypt.

As dancers, Gamal and Karioka are very much part of the "off stage" element of Egyptian cinema. Everybody who watches Egyptian films knows and loves them, but short of a heroic effort by a determined film festival organizer, one rarely sees them in international film festivals. Samiya Gamal appears only once in the referendum on the best one hundred films of all time. In a 1950s film called *The Beast* she plays the girlfriend of the villain, a criminal who terrorizes the Upper Egyptian countryside. Although Gamal's dancing in *The Beast* was superb, many of her other films showcase her talents more directly. In all likelihood *The Beast* is not included in the referendum as a nod to Samiya Gamal's talent, but as an outstanding example of director Salah Abu Sayf's early work. Abu Sayf, it almost goes without saying, is famous as a link on the great chain of nationalist realism. He was the assistant director of *Determination*, and a close friend and artistic associate of Naguib Mahfouz.

Tahiya Karioka also appears only once in the referendum, in *Pay Attention to Zuzu*, the antidance parable mentioned earlier. This was made in 1972 long after Karioka's 1930s-to-1950s heyday. Again, it is a safe bet that Karioka's lone film in the referendum had little to do with what attracted her fans, namely her dancing. She was, in any case, too old to dance in this film. Nonetheless, Karioka was a major figure of twentieth-century Egyptian culture. When she died recently, even the eminently cosmopolitan Edward Said saw fit to publish a respectful obituary (1999). In the same vein as the interpretive article in *100 Years of Cinema*, which explained away the embarrassing presence of a handful of musicals, Said discounted Karioka's films. As previously mentioned, the *100 Years of Cinema* article justified the inclusion of "weak genre" films on the basis of nostalgia. Likewise Said, in his obituary for Karioka, asserted that her films were vastly inferior to her live performance. This may be true, but it completely ignores the fact that people wrote obituaries for Karioka precisely *because* of her film career. No dancer famous only on the cabaret stage has ever received an obituary in all the major newspapers.

As films, Gamal's *The Beau's Hanky* and Karioka's *Dark and Beautiful* are delightful. The dialogue slips in and out of rhymed prose. The music seems continuous, giving a feeling more of comic opera than of narrative film. Both films found ways to overcome low budgets and production values. They look like quick episodic adaptations of stage routines, but all the same they are marvelous, energetic films bursting with creativity. They're not cheap, vulgar, and exploitative, as the champions of Studio Misr claim. This is not strictly my own interpretation. These two films are remembered fondly by Egyptian audiences and are still marketed to them in the video and satellite television media.

Fast Forward to the Present

Usually the history of Egyptian cinema is a narrative of the rise and fall of a realist aesthetic. The "rise" sets the conditions under which realism, the most favored genre for nationalist presentation of the cinema, can flourish. In this sense the initial rise of the Egyptian cinema set the stage for the preeminence of Studio Misr in the 1930s. Studio Misr produced all kinds of films, but in public contexts, the studio's crowning achievement was realism.[29]

The basic narrative is as follows: the cinema is founded in the early 1930s by ambitious entrepreneurs, but these pioneers work strictly as individuals and fail to establish an industry controlled by Egyptians. Studio Misr steps in during the mid-1930s to create a filmmaking infrastructure, and for a brief time a golden age prevails because Studio Misr has both the resources and the aesthetic vision to produce a cinema the nation can be proud of. Then from the mid-to-late 1940s Studio Misr falls victim to hard times caused by the Second World War, even as its competitors flourish. The ability of studios other than Studio Misr to thrive during the war is attributed to the willingness of brash newcomers to pander to vulgar desires of the audiences. Belly dancers and singers occupy the place once held by more elevated Studio Misr productions (Salih 1986). By the end of the 1940s the Egyptian cinema has gone through its first rise and fall cycle.

What happens next? Briefly, in the 1950s—really beginning in 1952, when the Free Officers come to power and Egypt finally frees itself from colonialism—the cinema again gathers steam, mainly (in the Rise and Fall narrative) in the quality of films being produced. The entire industry achieves a fairly high standard of production values—often just a notch or two below mainstream Hollywood films in terms of craft. Since about fifty films a year are being produced in the 1950s, the variety and sophistication of films gradually increases. The public narrative of Egyptian cinema portrays certain directors active during the 1950s as having planted the seeds for the more fully developed realism of later periods, particularly the nationalized cinema of the 1960s. Indeed, most of the directors who made highly acclaimed films during the 1960s learned filmmaking during the commercial cinema of the late 1940s and 1950s. It is merely assumed that the work of these directors could never come to complete fruition in the context of a commercial cinema, and this assumption serves as the cultural and aesthetic basis for the next stage in Egyptian film history, which was nationalization of the cinema.[30]

The period from 1963 to 1971 witnessed the second rise of Egyptian cinema. Although there is fierce disagreement about the legacy of 1960s public sector cinema, it would not be wrong to say that a majority (a complicated majority with a variety of motivations) considers the 1960s to be the pinnacle of Egyptian cinema.[31] Roughly a quarter of the one hundred best films are from this era. By the early 1970s direct government funding of films ended, though the state maintained control of the means of production, as it still does. Economically, this mixed system yielded poor results, and by the 1990s film production dropped precipitously. Currently, a significant proportion of films are made as coproductions, bypassing the weak Egyptian market. Youssef Chahine, whatever his virtues as a filmmaker, pioneered this mode of European-funded production in Egypt. But the Egyptian state has not disappeared from the business of filmmaking. It built a lavish new Media Production City near Cairo which, in concert with state investment in satellite broadcasting and a cautious liberalization of local broadcasting regulations, is a sign of the priority given to maintaining Egypt's high profile in Arabic-language media production. Filmmaking is part of these initiatives, but there is little evidence that the outcome of the Media Production City will be a revived cinema. Few would characterize the present as the beginning of an Egyptian filmmaking renaissance. Most consider it a period of decline.

Conclusion

Imagine an ethnography of Egyptian cinema spectatorship that seeks to refrain from engagement with the periodization and genre issues discussed earlier. It is easy for most anthropologists to do so. There are many conventional reasons for ignoring such matters. Most obviously, periodization and genre look too much like straight history or film studies issues. While they might be useful for general background, they surely do not get at the micro-relations immanent in personal interaction, do they?

So why not leave history to the historians, and film studies to the film scholars, and concentrate instead on placing the immediate experience of film in a "thickly described" social context? But what social context? The reason we should not cede these matters to the historians is that the issues addressed here must be *part of* a thick ethnographic description. This should be unsurprising, as mass media, if they do nothing else, extend the boundaries of access to discourses and, in doing so, potentially reshape the ways in which discourses are perpetuated or changed. Nonetheless, ethnographers find it difficult to focus on the scale of the discourses that are the subject of this essay. It is as if we see the world through either a microscope or a powerful telescope, but have no device capable of focusing on the medium distance.[32] The ethnographic microscope puts the reader into socially inflected localizing conversations, which should illuminate media texts from the perspective of both the lifeworlds of "consumers" and those of media producers (Abu-Lughod 1999:113). Our global telescopes, meanwhile, bring remote social facts—everything from imported television programs to an iniquitous world economic system—into crystal clear focus in ethnographies of local practice. For some ethnographic contexts microscopes and telescopes may be adequate tools. But not, I think, for the context of educated Egyptians who feel they have made a social investment in modern life. In this case the naked eye might be better for discerning a cultural scale that anthropologists often miss.

The group in question here—"educated Egyptians" or even "educated Arabic-speakers"—is amorphous, numbering in the millions, and divided by multiple social and economic fissures. This hardly makes them unimportant. On the contrary, literate "middle-class" Egyptians (in orientation if not in terms of material well-being) are politically and culturally powerful and are well aware that they have shared histories and identities. The social machinery for constructing a sense of common identity for such people is complex, but not mysterious: it has been produced historically through media, national institutions, and common experiences of events and processes, all of which are reflected and shaped by the cinema and other forms of mass communication. This does not by any stretch of the imagination mean that we should be satisfied with writing homogenizing ethnographies of "national culture." It does mean that to understand how media affects peoples' lives we must grasp the ways that people relate disconnected cultural dimensions, a process that is less one of homogenization than one of "indexing" objects, practices, and texts by reference to an implicit hierarchy of connected and therefore coherent meanings (Peterson 2003:267). Cultural fields such as the Egyptian cinema are particularly important to this process because they occupy an accessible, intermediate position between the nearest and the most distant cultural phenomena.

The institution of the film festival provides a good framework for thinking about how this indexical process works. As interpreters of cultural difference, film festivals are made to bridge near and far perspectives. Furthermore, the film festival is more than a metaphorical image for my own analysis: it is implicit generically in discourse on Egyptian cinema. The film festival was certainly an unspoken presence when I delivered the first draft of this essay to a mostly Egyptian and highly privileged audience at the Egyptian Embassy in Washington, D.C. On that occasion I kept a compilation of video clips from the films I was talking about running silently in the background. One response from an Egyptian member of the audience was, "Why don't you show more film clips from old movies and talk about them? Those are the films we love." My film clips had been predominantly of dance films from the 1940s and 1950s. Indeed, at almost every Egyptian film festival at which I have spoken in the United States somebody in the audience has asked, "Why are the old films so much better than the ones they're making now?" Sometimes the questioners mean old films such as *Determination* or *The Sin*, but they often elaborate on what they mean by "old films" in a way that makes clear that such films are inseparable from the formally disapproved genres adapted from Hollywood: musicals, dance films, melodrama, and popular comedies. It is understandable that most of these films should be excluded from a "best of" list on the basis of many criteria commonly used by filmmakers; but when an inescapable criterion for "best of" is the capacity to express national or cultural identity, then excluding the films that are not just the most popular, but also the most meaningful and, "off stage," the most cared for, becomes problematic. And the gap between "best of" and "best representative of national culture" becomes an overwhelming (though rarely discussed) factor in the actual staging of Egyptian films for non-Egyptian audiences—an enterprise that explicitly seeks to interpret cultural difference.

The rhetoric of art appreciation so often used to categorize Egyptian films is often taken literally by cultural interpreters such as film festival organizers. It should not be taken literally by anthropologists, because the result is paralysis with respect to the films produced mainly in Egypt for Egyptian and Arabic-speaking audiences and an inevitable gravitation toward works that are directed by Arabic-speaking filmmakers yet produced by European funding agencies: in other words, the Youssef Chahine model. For film festival organizers this is done ostensibly on grounds of quality; it is also a practical necessity of selecting films on a limited budget. The selection of coproductions is also buttressed, however, by systematic denial of alternatives by both Egyptian and Western participants in the events. The alternatives are much more interesting to anthropologists.

Anthropologists should not make the same mistake as film festival organizers. I began this essay by describing how the subject of Egyptian films arose between a group of Palestinian and Arab-Israeli scholars and myself. The object of the conversation was simply to talk about films. Egyptian cinema was a cultural field that we shared to some extent, even though none of us was Egyptian. Having recognized each other on this common cultural field, the films not suitable for display (such as *Rumors of Love*) were discretely moved off stage, and the more suitable films (by Youssef Chahine) were brought into view. The trajectory of such a conversation is hardly predetermined. Indeed, similar discourse can just as easily lead to misrecognition. Literate urban Egyptians, for example, are well aware of Chahine as a public intellectual whose name is bruited about in the press with regularity. Like Boutros Ghali, they are often of the opinion that Chahine is Egypt's ambassador to the world, a fine director who rises above the commercial muck that passes for Egyptian cinema, and therefore just the person a foreigner like you should know about. On other occasions, however, in conversations with less obviously privileged Egyptians, it is Chahine's famed transgressiveness—rarely mentioned by the social class that "owns" him—that is most evident.

I experienced a striking instance of how films can index social relations one summer in the late 1990s. I was in Cairo, staying with a friend who was working on a Ph.D. at Cairo University. He was a new father, and in order to give his wife a few moments of peace, he had taken the baby out to a café, where we met a friend of his. We were three men, a baby, and a *shisha* (water pipe), which was being passed among us (not, of course, to the baby). My friend's friend taught computer courses at an adult education program attached to Cairo University. The man was by no means destitute, but teaching wages in Egypt are notoriously low, and in income he was roughly

lower-middle class (but only by taking into account his potential for teaching private lessons; his night-school job offered no more than a poverty-level
wage). My friend told the computer technician of my interest in films. His
reaction was a vehement rant:

Everyone in the artistic milieu is utterly corrupt. Youssef Chahine is the worst. His
films are made for foreigners, and all the foreigners want is to make Egypt look like
a bunch of fags [*khawalat*—a reference to the homoeroticism in some of Chahine's
films]. All these show-business people are the same. Even Nur al-Sharif [an upper-
middle-brow actor generally known for having some artistic ambition]. They're all
whores, men and women alike, and they're all going to be punished by God. Why,
there's a film starring 'Aqila Ratib. She plays an actress, and her daughter is one too
—she's played by Shadia. But the mother tries to keep her daughter out of the profession because it's immoral. But then a great writer thinks she's perfect for the starring role in his next play.

His synopsis was long and ended in ever fiercer denunciations of the acting and filmmaking professions. What does an anthropologist do with such
a conversation? It was in no way a "natural" occurrence of discourse, for the
obvious reason that my friend had motivated it by telling his friend that
I was interested in Egyptian films. But perhaps there is no such thing as a
"naturally occurring" discourse. Did it help establish a social context for our
fleeting relationship? I think it did. But the important thing is that it did so
more reliably—more "thickly" one might say—if one could relate it to the
larger cultural field of Egyptian cinema revealed by discourses on film history. These are constructed in the implicit assumption that the object of criticism is in some sense "on stage." There was no doubt that at least some of
this man's indignation derived from precisely the on stage quality of cinema
discourse. I was, after all, a foreign interpreter of his culture. His overt moralizing gave a hint of Islamist ideology, which would not have been out of
place for his socioeconomic status and profession. But there was also ample
reason not simply to plug him into the Islamist slot. His extensive, detailed
film synopsis marked him as a fan, even if he was an Islamist, and even if he
did tie his description of a film plot back into the language of moral denun-
ciation. His invocation of Aqila Ratib and Shadia—starlets of the 1940s and
1950s—linked him to a common language of nostalgia for the "old" films
as surely as his moral outrage tied him to the language of Islamist politics.
These are precisely the sorts of things that can be mapped onto the politics
of genre hierarchies. I am confident that he would have had a wonderful
time talking to the Palestinian Arab League official about *Rumors of Love*.

    An ethnography of a mass medium cannot simply match films to classes
of spectators, or indeed, to classes of producers. If one did this the computer
technician in Cairo would be slotted into a moralizing "film-hater" category; one might have glossed over his suspiciously detailed knowledge, only

possible through hours of immersion in the films he professed to despise. And absent a means to steer the conversation toward cinematic icons of social distinction, the Palestinian intellectual in Oxford might have looked like "just" a popular film fan. But there are webs of meaning and discourses that connect the two men. These are constructed by means that are often not counted as ethnographic evidence—in this case, discourses on the periodization and genre hierarchies of Egyptian cinema. Generally speaking, these issues are emblematic of a large range of cultural practices that can be obscured by a "bifocal" gaze that takes into account only "local" and "global" processes. It is a difficult scale of discourse to see, given the methodological proclivities of anthropology, but one that nonetheless rewards attention.

Notes

1. But see Fawal (2001) and Massad (1999) for academic appraisals of the transgressive themes in Chahine's work.

2. The primary organizer of these events was Livia Alexander, then a student, now a professional film festival organizer (see http://www.arteeast.org/). I selected films, wrote publicity material, and spoke to audiences. The sponsoring agency was the American Research Center in Egypt in partnership with a number of cultural venues, including the Lincoln Center in New York, the International House of Philadelphia, the Washington Film Festival, the Boston Museum of Fine Arts, and the Art Institute of Chicago.

3. There are many ways to achieve an effect of realism in films. In Egypt, realist cinema usually focuses on lower class or rural characters (but pointedly in contrast to other classes or social groups) and is structured through a dominant narrator's perspective. See Shafik (1998) for an excellent analysis of the many complications in producing effects of realism in Arab cinema.

4. What are the goals of a film festival? In metropolitan contexts featuring non-metropolitan works, Karen Schwartzman describes the film festival as a juggling act motivated by "the desire to solve the problem of foreignness by overcoming difference or to communicate foreignness by revealing difference" (Schwartzman 1995: 90). Her formula transposes easily to the goals of anthropology. However, filmmakers themselves often object strenuously to the de facto employment of their work as ethnographic material. Undoubtedly the ethnographizing of films happens most predictably to Third World directors, regardless of their backgrounds or of the quality of their work.

5. These three genres often overlap; to talk about one in the Egyptian cinema is to talk about all three. Obviously this point cannot be generalized. It certainly would not hold for Indian films, and possibly not for Hollywood films.

6. By contrast, some music was explicitly nationalist and state sanctioned, particularly in the 1960s, when Egypt nationalized its cinema. See Shay (2002) for more on nationalist agendas for producing populist art.

7. The premise and methodology of the poll was identical to that of the decennial *Sight and Sound* poll of the best ten films of all time.

8. The most eloquent formulation of the notion that only someone from the East can appreciate the subtleties of the art—its "feel"—can be found in a remarkably essentialist obituary for the Egyptian dancer Tahiya Karioka (Said 1999).

9. The news of Husni's death came on 23 June 2001 ("Rahil Hazin l-Sindirilla al-Sinima al-'Arabiyya ba'da Mu'ana Tawila ma' al-Marad fi al-'Azima al-Britaniyya," *Al-Ahram*, p. 1). The *Hundred Years* volume listed Fatin Hamama as the top female star ('Adli 1996:259–260). Su'ad Husni was second in terms of the number of her films that appeared on the "best one hundred" list (nine), and was considered the top female star of the 1970s ('Adli 1996, 267). But the article in the volume on the 1970s (al-Nahhas 1996) focused almost exclusively on political films criticizing the Nasser era, and mentioned *Zuzu* only briefly as a "social film" (ibid., 191).

10. After Su'ad Husni died the Anglophone Egyptian press did make efforts to contextualize her for its readership, a substantial portion of which is non-Egyptian. *Al-Ahram Weekly* ran three articles on Husni, by director Muhammad Khan, and journalists Mona Anis and Safynaz Kazem (Khan 2001; Kazem 2001; Anis 2001). All made reference to *Zuzu* in interesting ways. Kazem expressed admiration for Husni, but went out of her way to point out that she did not like *Zuzu*. Khan expressed admiration for her talent as a singer and dancer, and mentioned the recurrence of songs from *Zuzu* in Husni's self-presentation (such as on her telephone answering machine and in a gathering in France where she treated friends to a song from the film). Anis invoked Walter Benjamin to muse about the difficulties Husni had in dealing with the commoditization of a star's personal life, which was most intense in the context of *Zuzu*. All three profiles of Husni were affectionate, but Khan's was alone in not expressing some form of disapproval for *Zuzu*.

11. After Husni's death *Zuzu* was exhibited to at least one foreign audience, in Paris, at the Institut du Monde Arabe 6th Annual Arab Film Festival (June 29–July 7, 2002), in a retrospective of Husni's work. The film itself received a more sympathetic presentation in French than it had in English (Salmawy 2001a). However, in the overall program *Zuzu*'s position was analogous to its position in the "100 Best Films" poll—it was the only one of its kind. Furthermore, the same journalist who wrote sympathetically of *Zuzu* in the French version of *al-Ahram* barely mentioned the film in his report on the festival in the Arabic *al-Ahram* (Salmawy 2001b).

12. Abu Shadi, however, categorizes *They Made Me a Criminal* as a work of realism on the grounds that Naguib Mahfouz wrote the screenplay, and that it "shows how an ordinary person can become a criminal" (1996, 115–116). The protagonist, however, is not what most Egyptians would recognize as "an ordinary person," but an orphan (and hence, in local terms, already bereft of the family authority that should guide him away from a life of crime). Furthermore, the film's depiction of nightclubs, singing, and dance are pure mainstream 1950s Egyptian cinema.

13. The realist films were: *Determination* (number 1); *The Land* (2); *Cairo Station* (4); *The Sin* (5); *A Woman's Youth* (6); *A Beginning and an End* (7); *The Bus Driver* (8); and *The Tough Guy* (10). The two exceptions were *The Mummy* (number 3), a work of mythical representation, and *The Flirtation of Girls* (9), a musical comedy.

14. These were *A Woman's Youth* (number 6) and *The Tough Guy* (number 10). Although after the 1950s much of Mahfouz's writing was of a more allegorical nature, his nonrealist works were not the basis of films. Of the full one hundred best

films, Mahfouz is credited with having written the screenplay or story of twelve (al-'Ashari 1996:220).

15. Abd al-Salam died young, leaving *The Mummy* as his only full-length feature film. In 1969, when it was made, *The Mummy* was ignored in Egypt. It created a sensation in foreign film festivals, and was finally released in Egypt in 1975, but to absolutely no popular acclaim. Later intellectuals came to admire the film greatly, and considerable academic literature in Arabic and English has been devoted to it (including a special issue on *The Mummy* of the literary periodical *Al-Qahira* no. 159, February 1996; and in English a special issue of the periodical *Discourse* [1999. v. 21 (1)] subtitled "Middle Eastern Films Before Thy Gaze Returns to Thee," which includes a translation of *The Mummy*'s script; see also Colla 2000).

16. Colla (2000) discusses the nationalist context of both the film and the events on which it was based. He suggests that while nationalism must be an element of any reading of the film, the form and significance of nationalism shifts over time.

17. Three of the five stars were Nagib al-Rihani, Layla Murad, and Anwar Wagdi, all of whom were huge stars of the early years of Egyptian cinema. *The Flirtation of Girls* also included cameo appearances by Yusuf Wahbi and Muhammad Abd al-Wahhab. Wahbi, the "theater man" mentioned by the Palestinian intellectual in his description of *Rumors of Love*, was a forceful leading man and a founding figure of the Egyptian theater and cinema. Abd al-Wahhab was one of the greatest figures of twentieth-century Arabic music. For more on *The Flirtation of Girls* see Armbrust (2000).

18. They are: *Dinanir, A Bullet in the Heart, Love and Revenge, The Flirtation of Girls, Our Sweet Days, Wife Number 13, Sins, Father Is Up the Tree, Pay Attention to Zuzu,* and *Soft Hands.*

19. A nationalist memory of American or British cinema would do exactly the same thing. However, the actual *public memory* of American and British film is not overtly shaped by nationalist agendas. In fact, musicals fared slightly worse in the *Sight and Sound* top ten films poll than in the Egyptian poll, with only *Singing in the Rain* at number ten. However, the other top ten films in the *Sight and Sound Poll* were diverse in terms of genre, and not notably slanted toward realist films. Nor is there anything comparable in the United States and Europe to the disjunction in Egyptian and Arab discourse between strongly expressed nostalgia for "old films" (particularly musicals and comedies) in informal settings, and systematic exclusion or marginalization of such films in formal settings.

20. For more on *Determination*, see Armbrust (1996), in which it is referred to as *Resolution.*

21. One way of estimating the capacity of a film market is by "screen density" (the number of movie screens per one million of population). Putnam notes that in the 1990s screen density in the United States was the highest in the world, at one hundred screens per one million people (Putnam 1997:320). For France it was eighty, for Britain thirty-four (ibid., 320). According to Hasanayn (1995:246) Egypt had 162 theaters in 1992, very few of them multiplexes (meaning the number of screens did not differ greatly from the number of theaters). If one assumes 170 screens, the screen density for Egypt, with a population of fifty-nine million, would be 2.74 screens per million people. Most theaters are concentrated in Cairo and Alexandria.

22. Egypt reached its peak number of theaters in the 1950s, at 450 (Hasanayn 1995:246). Its screen density at that time, with a population of twenty-three million, was 19.6 screens per million. In the 1950s, India, with a population of 395 million, had a screen density of 8.1 (based on 3,200 theaters, few if any being multiplexes [Barnouw and Krishnaswamy 1963:142]). While screen density in Egypt declined from 19.6 in the 1950s to 2.74 in the 1990s, in India screen density rose from 8.1 in the 1950s to 12 in the 1990s (based on a population of one billion and an estimate of twelve thousand theaters.

23. Flibbert notes that the Misr Company for the Theater and Cinema (the parent company of Studio Misr) did attempt to create a monopoly in postwar years through mergers and acquisition of producers and exhibitors, but to no avail (2001:153). The reasons for the failure are not mentioned, but Flibbert suggests that there was little coordination between producers and insufficient governmental regulation of the competition.

24. Al-Sharqawi lists 120 production companies active between 1945 and 1952, up from twenty-four in the previous period (1970:101–105).

25. This is a point made by Vitalis (2000), to which much of my discussion of film economics is indebted.

26. Flibbert finds that Egyptian cinema was in fact best off economically when the local market tilted toward monopoly. But monopoly was not associated with the initial rise of Studio Misr (when its most highly praised films were produced). The wartime expansion took place when foreign competition was relatively absent and production was still "disorganized" and "almost speculative" (Flibbert 2001:111). Production might have collapsed soon after the war if the Egyptian government had not provided some protection for local producers (ibid., 112).

27. By 1969 Egypt was estimated to have half a million television sets in operation, and the state subsidized the installation of television sets in rural areas (Boyd 1982:48–49). The rental of films to content-hungry television stations allowed Hollywood to profit from the new medium of television (Putnam 1997:235–240). In Egypt television, though just as hungry for content, was state-owned and therefore not likely to pay high rents for films that were, in any case, more often owned by distributors than producers. The effect on the film industry was catastrophic.

28. We attempted to get these films for our 1999 ARCE Egyptian film festival, which showcased musicals. But as nominees for an American film festival these films were nonstarters. The only mainstream musicals we were able to get other than *Ghazal al-Banat* were second-rate films provided by the widow of the films' star. No assistance, institutional or commercial, was forthcoming from the Egyptian side for acquiring these films.

29. Six Studio Misr productions appear in the *100 Years of Cinema* referendum on the best one hundred Egyptian films poll: *Determination* (1); *Lashin* (22); *Black Market* (34); *Salama Is Well* (76); *Si 'Umar* (81); and *Love and Revenge* (91). *Determination* and *Black Market* are considered early landmark's of cinematic realism. *Salama* and *Si 'Umar* are comedies, the former, like *Determination*, extolling a Tal'at Harb-like business empire. *Love and Revenge* is a melodrama.

30. The economic rationale for state promotion of the film industry was com-

pelling. Nationalization was part of a larger turn to socialism by the Egyptian state in the early 1960s.

31. The economic impact of the public sector is an even more contentious issue. See "Al-Nass al-Kamil" (1993) for estimates of the losses incurred by the public sector cinema. The significance and accuracy of these figures are disputed by partisans of public sector cinema.

32. This phenomenon, described elsewhere as "bifocality" (Peterson 2003:264–265), is as relevant to informants' views of the world as it is to analytical strategies.

References Cited

Abu-Lughod, Lila. 1999. "The Interpretation of Culture(s) after Television." Pp. 110–135 in *The Fate of Culture: Geertz and Beyond*, ed. Sherry Ortner. Berkeley: University of California Press.

Abu Shadi, Ali. 1996. "Genres in Egyptian Cinema." Pp. 84–129 in *Screens of Life: Critical Film Writing from the Arab World*, ed. Alia Arasoughly. Quebec: World Heritage Press.

'Adli, Nadir. 1996. "Ahamm al-Nujum fi tarikh al-Sinima al-Misriyya." Pp. 254–267 in *Mi'at Sannah Sinima*, eds. Ahmad Ra'fat Bahgat. Cairo: Matbu'at Mahragan al-Qahirah al-Sinima'i.

Aliksan, Jan. 1981. *Al-Sinima fi al-Watan al-'Arabi*. Kuwait: al-Majlis al-Watani lil-Thaqafa wa al-Funun wa al-Adab.

Anderson, Benedict. 1991. *Imagined Communities: Reflections on the Origins and Spread of Nationalism*. London: Verso.

Anis, Mona. 2001. "Before the Public Gaze." *Al-Ahram Weekly Online* 540 (28 June–4 July 2001). Available at http://weekly.ahram.org.eg/2001/540/cu5.htm, accessed April 18, 2004.

Armbrust, Walter. 1996. *Mass Culture and Modernism in Egypt*. Cambridge: Cambridge University Press.

———. 2000. "The Golden Age before the Golden Age: Egyptian Cinema before the 1960s." Pp. 292–327 in *Mass Mediations: New Approaches to Popular Culture in the Middle East and Beyond*, ed. Walter Armbrust. Berkeley, Calif.: University of California Press.

———. 2002. "Manly Men on the National Stage (and the Women Who Make Them Stars)." In *Histories of the Modern Middle East: New Directions*, eds. Israel Gershoni, Hakan Erdem, and Ursula Woköck. Boulder, Colo.: Lynne Rienner.

'Ashari, Fathi al-. 1996. "Al-Qissa wa al-Hiwar: fi Afdal Mi'at Film Misri." Pp. 218–224 in *Mi'at Sannah Sinima*, eds. Ahmad Ra'fat Bahgat. Cairo: Matbu'at Mahragan al-Qahirah al-Sinima'i.

Bahgat, Ahmad Ra'fat, ed. 1996. *Mi'at Sannah Sinima*. Cairo: Matbu'at Mahragan al-Qahirah al-Sinima'i.

Barnouw, Erik and S. Krishnaswamy. 1963. *Indian Cinema*. New York: Columbia University Press.

Bendix, Regina. 1997. *In Search of Authenticity: The Formation of Folklore Studies*. Madison: University of Wisconsin Press.

96   Walter Armbrust

Boyd, Douglas. 1982. *Broadcasting in the Arab World: A Survey of Radio and Television in the Middle East*. Philadelphia: Temple University Press.

Caton, Steven. 1999. *Lawrence of Arabia: A Film's Anthropology*. Berkeley: University of California.

Colla, Elliott. 2000. "Shadi Abd al-Salam's *al-Mumiya*: Ambivalence and the Egyptian Nation-State." Pp. 109–143 in *Beyond Colonialism and Nationalism in the Maghreb*, ed. Ali Ahmida. New York: Palgrave.

Davis, Eric. 1983. *Challenging Colonialism: Bank Misr and Egyptian Industrialization, 1920–1941*. Princeton, N.J.: Princeton University Press.

Fawal, Ibrahim. 2001. *Youssef Chahine*. London: BFI.

Flibbert, Andrew. 2001. "Commerce in Culture: Institutions, Markets, and Competition in the World Film Trade (Egypt, Mexico)." Ph.D. dissertation, Columbia University.

Hasan, Ilhami. 1986. *Muhammad Tal'at Harb: Ra'id Sina'at al-Sinima al-Misriyya*. Cairo: al-Hay'a al-Misriyya al-'Amma lil-Kitab.

Hasanayn, Nasir Galal. 1995. *Al-Ab'ad al-Iqtisadiyya li-Azmat Sina'at al-Sinima al-Misriyya*. Cairo: al-Hay'a al-Misriyya al-'Amma lil-Kitab.

Ibrahim, Munir Muhammad. 1996. "Studyu Misr: Madrasat al-Sinima al-Misriyya." Pp. 158–166 in *Mi'at Sannah Sinima*, eds. Ahmad Ra'fat Bahgat. Cairo: Matbu'at Mahragan al-Qahirah al-Sinima'i.

Kazem, Safynaz. 2001. "Sister to the Moon." *Al-Ahram Weekly Online* 540 (28 June–4 July 2001). Available at http://weekly.ahram.org.eg/2001/540/cu4.htm, accessed April 12, 2004.

Khan, Mohamed. 2001. "In the Present Tense." *Al-Ahram Weekly Online* 540 (28 June–4 July 2001). Available at http://weekly.ahram.org.eg/2001/540/cu2.htm, accessed April 12, 2004.

Massad, Joseph. 1999. "Art and Politics in the Cinema of Youssef Chahine." *Journal of Palestine Studies* 28 (winter): 77.

Nahhas, Hashim al-. 1996. "Malamih Asasiyya fi Sinima al-Saba'inat al-Misriyya." Pp. 189–193 in *Mi'at Sannah Sinima*, eds. Ahmad Ra'fat Bahgat. Cairo: Matbu'at Mahragan al-Qahirah al-Sinima'i.

"Al-Nass al-Kamil li-Taqrir al-Niyaba al-'Amma bi-Hifz al-Tahqiq fi Qadiyat Khasa'ir al-Qita' al-'Amm." 1993. *al-Sinima wa al-Tarikh* 7: 77–91.

Peterson, Mark. 2003. *Anthropology and Mass Communication: Media and Myth in the New Millennium*. Oxford: Berghan Books.

Putnam, David. 1997. *The Undeclared War: The Struggle for Control of the World's Film Industry*. London: Harper Collins.

Said, Edward. 1999. "Farewell to Tahia." *Al-Ahram Weekly Online* 450 (7–13 October). Available at http://weekly.ahram.org.eg/1999/450/cu4.htm, accessed April 12, 2004.

Salih, Taufiq. 1986. "Al-Waqi'iyya . . . 'Sinima al-Shabab' wa Mashakil al-Qita' al-'Amm: Hiwar ma' Taufiq Salih" (conducted by Sa'id Murad). In *Maqalat fi al-Sinima al-'Arabiyya*, by Sa'id Murad. Beirut: Dar al-Fikr al-Jadid.

Sallitt, Dan. 2002. "Sight Unchanged: How Did the Film Canon Get So Stodgy?" *Slate* (August 20). Available at http://slate.msn.com/?id=2069759, accessed September 24, 2002.

Salmawy, Mohamed. 2001a. "Soad Hosni et la fin d'une époque." *Al-Ahram Hebdo* 356 (Mercredi 4 Juillet).

Salmawy, Mohamed. 2001b. "Daura Dhahabiyya li-Mahrajan al-Sinima." *Al-Ahram*, July 8, p. 13.

Schwartzman, Karen. 1995. "National Cinema in Translation: The Politics of Film Exhibition Culture." *Wide Angle* 16, no. 3: 66–99.

Shafik, Viola. 1998. *Arab Cinema: History and Cultural Identity*. Cairo: The American University in Cairo Press.

al-Sharqawi, Galal. 1970. *Risala fi Tarikh al-Sinima al-'Arabiyya*. Cairo: al-Sharika al-Misriyya lil-Taba'a wa al-Nashr.

Shay, Anthony. 2002. *Choreographic Politics: State Folk Dance Companies, Representation and Power*. Middletown, Conn.: Wesleyan University Press.

"Sight and Sound Critics Top Ten Poll 2002." 2002. *Sight and Sound* (September). Available at http://www.bfi.org.uk/sightandsound/topten/index.html, accessed September 24, 2002.

Thabet, Madkour. 1998. *Egyptian Film Industry*. Cairo: Ministry of Culture.

Vitalis, Robert. 2000. "American Ambassador in Technicolor and Cinemascope: Hollywood and Revolution on the Nile." Pp. 269–291 in *Mass Mediations: New Approaches to Popular Culture in the Middle East and Beyond*, ed. Walter Armbrust. Berkeley: University of California Press.

Yusuf, Ahmad. 1996. "Istifta' haula 'Ishq al-Sinima wa al-Watan." Pp. 15–38 in *Mi'at Sannah Sinima*, eds. Ahmad Ra'fat Bahgat. Cairo: Matbu'at Mahragan al-Qahirah al-Sinima'i.

Additional Readings

Bindari, Mona, Ya'qub Wahba, and Mahmud Qasim, eds. 1994. *Mausu'at al-Aflam al-'Arabiyya*. Cairo: Bayt al-Ma'rifah.

Bradshaw, Peter. 2002. "Movie Is in a League of Its Own, But Not on My List." *Guardian* (August 9). Available at http://www.guardian.co.uk/Archive/Article/ 0,4273,4479519,00.html, accessed September 24, 2002.

Dougherty, Roberta. 2002. "The Egyptian Musical Film: Diagesis Derailed?" Paper presented at the conference of the Middle East Studies Association, Washington, D.C.

Farid, Samir. 1986. "Surat al-Insan al-Misri 'ala al-Shasha bayn al-Aflam al-Istahlakiyya wa al-Aflam al-Fanniyya." Pp. 205–214 in *Al-Insan al-Misri 'ala al-Shasha*, ed. Hashim al-Nahhas. Cairo: al-Hay'a al-Misriyya al-'Amma l-il-Kitab.

James, Nick. 2002. "Nul Britania." *Sight and Sound* (September). Available at http:// www.bfi.org.uk/sightandsound/2002_09/feature01_nulbritannia.html, accessed September 20, 2002.

Jameson, Fredrick. 1986. "Third-World Literature in the Era of Multinational Capitalism." *Social Text* 15: 65–88.

Sadoul, Georges. 1966. *The Cinema in the Arab Countries*. Beirut: Interarab Centre of Cinema and Television.

Sakr, Naomi. 2001. *Satellite Realms: Transnational Television, Globalization and the Middle East*. London: I. B. Tauris.

Solomons, Jason. 2002. "There's More to Film than Citizen Kane." *Observer* (August 11). Available at http://www.guardian.co.uk/Archive/Article/0,4273,4479519,00.html, accessed September 24, 2002.

Select Filmography:

Alexandria, Why? (*Iskindiriya, leh?*). Chahine, Youssef. 1979. Cairo and Algiers: Misr International and Algerian Television.

The Beast (*al-Wahsh*). Abu-Sayf, Salah. 1954. Cairo: Aflam al-Hilal.

The Beau's Hanky (*Mandil al-hiluw*). Kamil, 'Abbas. 1949. Cairo: Nahhas, Film.

Black Market (*al-Suq al-suda'*). Tilmisani, Kamil al. 1945. Cairo: Studyu Misr.

A Bullet in the Heart (*Rasasa fi al-qalb*). 1944. Karim, Muhammad. Cairo: Aflam Muhammad 'Abd al-Wahhab.

Cairo Station (*Bab al-hadid*). 1958. Chahine, Youssef. Cairo: Jibra'il Talhami.

Dark and Beautiful (*Asmar wa gamil*). Kamil, 'Abbas. 1950. Cairo: Shuruq Film.

Determination (*Al-'Azima*). Salim, Kamal. 1939. Cairo: Studio Misr.

The Flirtation of Girls (*Ghazal al-banat*). Wagdi, Anwar. 1949. Cairo: Sharikat al-Aflam al-Muttahida (Anwar Wagdi wa Sharikahu).

The Mummy (*al-Mumia'*). 'Abd al-Salam, Shadi. 1969 (1975 in Cairo). Cairo: Hay'at al-Sinima.

Pay Attention to Zuzu (*Khalli balak min Zuzu*). Imam, Hasan al. 1972. Cairo: Takfur Antonian.

Rumors of Love (*Isha'at hubb*). 1960. 'Abd al-Wahhab, Fatin. Cairo: Jamal al-Laythi.

The Sin (*al-Haram*). Barakat, Henri. 1965. Cairo: al-Sharikah al-'Ammah lil-Intaj al-Sinima'i (Filmintaj).

They Made Me a Criminal (*Ga'aluni mugriman*). Salim, 'Atif. 1954. Cairo: Farid Shawqi.

Widad (*Widad*). Kramp, Fritz and Jamal Madkur. 1935. Cairo: Studio Misr.

PART TWO

Exhibitionism

CHAPTER 4

Wedded to the Republic

PUBLIC INTELLECTUALS AND
INTIMACY-ORIENTED PUBLICS IN TURKEY

Esra Özyürek

LIKE MANY VISITORS to "Family Albums of the Republic," an exhibit held at the Imperial Mint Building in the courtyard of Topkapı Palace, I was curious to see the official wedding ceremonies conducted as part of the display. During my third visit to the exhibit, a smiling, enthusiastic guard informed me at the gate, "Today at four o'clock we have a wedding. Be sure to be there." It was already close to four, so I rushed to the wedding room, which was decorated with life-size black and white wedding pictures of Turkish citizens from different periods and diverse ethnic and class backgrounds. The room was already filled with stylishly coiffed guests in three-piece suits and fine dresses. Journalists were also on hand, as were a small number of exhibit visitors, and guards who were peeking in. Soon, the bride and groom arrived in a car adorned with flowers and ribbons. The bride, in her early twenties, had her dyed-blonde hair put up and wore heavy makeup and a low-cut, sleeveless white wedding gown. A red ribbon belt signaled her reproductive powers, and several gold coins attached to her dress were wedding gifts from the guests. The groom, who appeared to be about ten years older than the bride, wore a dark suit and a colorful tie. They looked just like any other middle-class, urban, secular couple. What distinguished them were the not-so-small pictures of Mustafa Kemal Atatürk pinned to their chests.

I am thankful to Andrew Shryock for his encouragement and criticism on many versions of this paper. The research for this article was conducted as part of a larger ethnographic project on the privatization of state ideology in Turkey (Özyürek 2001a), and some results of this work have already appeared in Özyürek (2001b). I collected the material about the exhibits presented here by attending both of the exhibits every day during the month of October 1998, observing visitors, and interviewing exhibit organizers, visitors, and guides.

FIGURE 4.1. A wedding ceremony at the "Family Albums of the Republic" exhibit. Photo by author.

The couple's Atatürk pictures delighted Ayfer Atay, the secularist mayor of Beşiktaş, who was to preside over the ceremony.[1] After the mayor put on the red coat symbolizing his office, he began the civil ceremony with a speech emphasizing the importance of the ritual:

This is the seventy-fifth anniversary of the Republic. It is an especially important anniversary because of the attacks against the Republic. Along with the precautions taken against these attacks, the government wanted to have celebrations with great popular participation. Accordingly, the History Foundation organized the "Family Albums of the Republic" exhibit. Today, we are adding a new family album to it. One of the most important gifts of the Republic is the civil wedding ceremony. Due to the anniversary of the Republic, these friends we have here will marry in a civil marriage. Instead of an Islamic marriage, which prioritizes man over woman and allows him to divorce his wife by saying "be divorced" (boş ol) three times, we will have a civil ceremony, which is based on equality and gives security to women. Thank you for allowing me to perform this historic wedding.

Atay's speech, which stressed the political nature of the wedding, received loud applause from the guests. Later he performed the brief official ceremony by asking the bride and groom whether they wanted to marry each other of their own free will. He then turned to the audience and made the customary wish: "May all the single people gathered here today also marry soon" (*Darısı bekarların başına*).

In many ways, the wedding ceremony I describe was typical. Its location in a museum was unique, however, as was the fact that this display of "equality" and "free will" took place as part of "Family Albums of the Republic," an exhibit organized by the Economic and Social History Foundation (History Foundation), a nongovernmental organization. The larger exhibit, which commemorated the seventy-fifth anniversary of the Republic in 1998, showed scenes of domestic intimacy drawn from three generations of Turkish family life. At the same time, the Yapı Kredi Bank organized an exhibit entitled "To Create a Citizen," which focused on the private lives of Turks during the 1930s. Private sector investment in Republic Day celebrations is a recent trend in Turkey, and it is explicitly dedicated to a public redefinition of the ideal model of Turkish national intimacy. The new model is designed to suggest that, from the earliest days of the Republic, Turkish citizens have *voluntarily* embraced secularism and modernity, much as the bride and groom whose wedding I observed were embracing each other freely.[2]

This new model departs markedly from an older symbolism of paternalistic, state-centered intimacy, which is epitomized by the veneration of Atatürk, founding father of the country. Modernity and secularism, in this more established view, are gifts given by Atatürk to his children, who should be thankful and cherish these gifts because the father figure, who knew their true value, instructed them to do so. Atatürk was conspicuously absent from the exhibits I examine in this essay, but the visitors (as well as the couples who were married in the "Family Albums" display) routinely invoked paternalistic notions of intimacy—which stress obedience and respect, not choice and desire—to express their relationship to Turkish modernity and the state. The new public interest in the private lives of Turkish citizens, I will argue, is one arena of cultural production in which Turks are struggling to reconceptualize the emotional content of citizenship and decide what form of government is most appropriate for Turkey as it relocates itself in the changing power dynamics of the post–Cold War era.

This essay will show how public intellectuals in Turkey have tried to cultivate a voluntaristic sense of national identification by resorting to—but also opposing—the idea of a state-sponsored, mass-mediated public. My approach diverges from others in this volume because it does not concentrate on the uneasy location of the ethnographer between the contradictory demands of "cultural intimacy" and mass mediation. Rather it takes one step back and looks at how the conflicted relationship between these analytical fields emerges in the first place. Public officials, in Turkey and elsewhere, frequently take the lead in crafting the collective intimacy motifs that turn government jurisdictions into "homelands," and they can do so because meta-phors of domesticity effectively define and naturalize broader power relations within the nation-state (Yanagisako and Delaney 1995). Likewise, profes-sionals who have access to public media, such as intellectuals (Verdery 1991), journalists (Boyer 2001), TV producers (Abu-Lughod 2002), and advertising agents (Mazzarella 2003), play a privileged role in defining metaphors of col-lective familiarity. Of course, public intellectuals and state officials rarely create these frames of self-recognition from scratch; instead, they "selec-tively formalize intuitive and informal schemes of differentiation . . . and then publicize the results . . . as accredited knowledge of social self and other" (Boyer 2001:461). By focusing on two exhibits that sought to rede-fine a nationally shared domestic intimacy in Turkey, I aim to highlight the fact that a sense of collective familiarity is not always already there before it is adapted for public display. Intimacies are often actively shaped and trans-formed by local agents with the power to represent and, in turn, are ac-cepted, negotiated, or simply refused by local publics. Furthermore, a shared sense of familiarity usually relies on (and flourishes in relation to) publicity, instead of taking shape in private domains that somehow exist apart from a mass-mediated public culture.

Agents of Public and Cultural Intimacy

Although they analyze expressions of intimacy at different points in time (the eighteenth and twentieth centuries) and in different places (Western Eu-rope and the eastern Mediterranean), both Jürgen Habermas (1989) and Mi-chael Herzfeld (1997) point to the unexpectedly broad political implications of a culturally shared intimacy.[3] According to Habermas, the intimate emo-tional structures of the bourgeois family played a decisive role in the forma-tion of a "rational-critical public sphere" in early modern Europe. By the eighteenth century, Habermas argues, the conjugal patriarchal unit had be-come the dominant household form in Europe. Ownership of domestic property and a claim to familial intimacy made the bourgeois man feel like an independent human being who could participate in the public arena as an equal, regardless of his social status.[4] Such feelings, appropriate to the pri-vate man, did not develop just because domestic units became smaller in size and more autonomous. Rather, it was the specific condition of experienc-ing emergent forms of conjugal intimacy as qualities oriented toward an ex-ternal audience that made men feel part of a new public. In Habermas's words, the "sphere of the public arose in the broader strata of the bourgeoi-sie as an expansion and at the same time completion of the intimate sphere of the family" (1989:50).

Unlike Habermas, who discusses the political consequences of a publicly open communication of intimate feelings, Herzfeld writes about the discreet expression of a shared sense of national belonging that reveals itself through "rueful self-recognition" and "inward acknowledgement" of cultural traits that cause embarrassment when outsiders observe them (Herzfeld 1997:6). The sensibility Herzfeld describes could have come into being only in the nineteenth century, since its possibility depends on a nationally accessible public sphere. Despite their differences in focus, however, I would suggest that Herzfeld's concept of "cultural intimacy" is similar to Habermas's bourgeois intimacy at several levels. First, both scholars emphasize how intimacy is a socially constructed emotion (whether publicly or discreetly) quite similar to what Raymond Williams calls a "structure of feeling" (Williams 1977). More important, both scholars recognize the socially and politically transformative capacities of intimate expression. Just like the bourgeois intimacy that shaped the public sphere in Europe, cultural intimacy pervades national identities, giving rise to feelings of "common sociality" and "familiarity with the bases of power" (1977:3).

Habermas and Herzfeld also share a tendency to turn a blind eye toward the possibility that publicly recognized intimacies might be intentionally fabricated. The two scholars assume that public expressions of intimacy are an unintended outgrowth (an "expansion" or "completion") of the informal interactive styles that predominate among family members and fellow nationals. They assume that once publicly expressed (or publicly hidden, in Herzfeld's discussion), these culturally based intimacies alter political formations or hold them in place. What is missing from their analysis is a recognition of situations, common now throughout the world, in which publicly shared conceptions of intimacy do not correspond neatly to sentiments or social practices that precede acts of public display. Lauren Berlant alludes to this kind of relationship between intimacy and publicity when she claims that "the inwardness of the intimate is met by a correspondence of publicness" (Berlant 2000:1). I would take her point a step further and argue that, in some cases, the inwardness of intimacy is actually constituted, and thus preceded, by publicness.

Nilüfer Göle has argued that the Turkish public sphere does not fit the Habermasian model of an organically formed arena that expands out of and completes a particular form of domestic culture. Rather, it "provides a stage for the didactic performance of the modern subject in which the nonverbal, corporeal, and implicit aspects of social imaginaries are consciously and explicitly worked out" (2002:177). I agree with Göle's assertion that the public sphere in Turkey is more didactic and performative than rational-critical and discursive. The museum exhibits I discuss in this essay were designed to be instructive, to teach visitors a new model of citizenship. They were not meant to inspire a rational-critical discourse on state-citizen relations in Turkey. Moreover, the exhibit work itself suggests that didactic performances of this sort, precisely because they are public, must involve carefully planned displays of intimacy and emotional identification. It is no coincidence, then, that these exhibitions made family life their principal focus.

Metaphors of Familial Intimacy in Nationalism and Neo-Liberalism

The effectiveness of kinship metaphors in defining state-citizen relations is well known. Throughout the nineteenth and twentieth centuries, nationalist ideologues typically conceptualized the relationship between the nation and the land, the nation and the state, and the state and its citizens as a family relationship (Skurski 1994; McClintock 1997; Shryock and Howell 2001). Nationhood is often based on the idea of fraternity among male citizens (Mosse 1985; Pateman 1988; Hunt 1992), which is established through imagining the homeland as a woman who needs to be loved and protected by her men (Najmabadi 1997). Such ideas legitimize the power of the nation-state over its population and turn the nation into a sphere in which men and women "naturally" play out their gender roles (Williams 1995; Nagel 1998). Turkish nationalism is no exception to this rule. Carol Delaney (1995) argues that the foundation of Turkey was based on the metaphor of the rebirth of the nation through the union of the motherland (Anadolu) and the father leader (Atatürk). The single-party regime of the early Turkish Republic used the family metaphor in order to define ideal citizens as children of the state who were eternally indebted to the parent (Şerifsoy 2000).

New conceptualizations of nation and state typically go hand in hand with efforts to reorganize family and gender relations (Jayawardena 1986; Phillips 1988; Abu-Lughod 1998). As Suzanne Brenner states, regarding the policies of the New Order regime in Indonesia, "the family often takes the foreground as the site on which the seeds of a 'modern,' 'orderly,' and 'developed' nation can be planted" (1998:228). In the Turkish case, officials of the new nation-state worked hard to break up extended family ties that challenged the authority of the state (Kandiyoti 1991). In her analysis of the relationship between gender and nationalism in Turkey, anthropologist Nükhet Sirman argues that, whereas "men needed to be *pasha*s of the large households in order to have power in the old order; in the new order all husbands would be pashas. The classless society ideal would be realized in the fraternal community based on the assumption that men [who all own a family] would be equal" (2002:238). When the Turkish Republic was founded in 1923, the first policies of the new regime involved regulating family and gender relations. Turkish officials adopted the Swiss Civil Code, which replaced Islamic marriage with civil marriage, abolished polygamy, and gave women the right to initiate divorce and to keep children after divorce.[5] They also actively encouraged women to take part in public life through education, working outside the home, or simply by unveiling (Göle 1996). In this way, the state became involved in the regulation of one of the most intimate spheres of life, formerly handled by religious communities or by male heads of households.

In the early-twenty-first century, as centralized states are losing ground in their control over the redistribution of power and wealth (Omae 1995; Sassen 1996; Steinmetz 1999), the intimate metaphor of the family is gaining new currency in international and Turkish political discourse. Neo-liberal politicians and experts, who promote replacing both state and society with the market, pay central attention to family matters. In this millennial moment, the conjugal family represents the epitome of the private sphere, where individuals voluntarily enter into truly binding relationships without the involvement of the state. In the United States, for example, "family" has been a central concept for national policies and citizenship debates since Reagan's presidency. Lauren Berlant argues that "the intimate public sphere of the U.S. present tense renders citizenship as a condition of social membership produced by personal acts and values originating in or directed toward the family sphere" (1997:5). Accordingly, politics is conceptualized as something that does not take place in relation to a shared public and does not recognize a shared public good.

In countries like Turkey, which have a strong state tradition, the concept of a shared public sphere is still central to politics. Yet the global ideology of neo-liberalism and the local controversy between Islamism and secularism in Turkey make familial intimacy the center of politics in a peculiar way. Since the 1990s, increasing numbers of Islamists, Kurdish nationalists, and liberal intellectuals have argued that the oppressive reforms of the Turkish state are creating a secular public sphere that is not effectively integrated with the intimate zones of domestic life, ethnic identity, or religious belief. Secularist Turkish intellectuals now face the challenge of promoting the Turkish state and modernity as one that fits the new symbolism of neo-liberal market ideology.

The museum exhibits I analyzed on family, marriage, and the private life of Turkish citizens emphasized both the voluntary and contractual nature of European bourgeois concepts of conjugal intimacy, highlighting their separation from the state. Organizers utilized displays of a modern and secular domestic life to symbolize the free and willing relationship citizens have fostered with the state and its modernization project since the early years of the Republic. The wedding ceremonies featured in the "Family Albums" exhibit underlined the voluntary nature of the marriage contract and the mutual desire of bride and groom. In the civil ceremony, which Turkish authorities adapted from Western counterparts, one of the few questions wedding officials are required to ask is whether both partners decided to marry of their own free will. In the Turkish case, a civil ceremony involves an additional level of choice. Although it is illegal to be married only through Islamic rites, it is still a widely practiced alternative. Thus, when Turkish couples choose to make their contract through civil marriage, they also agree to have the most intimate aspects of their lives shaped by the laws of a conspicuously Westernizing state.

A Civilian Celebration of the Turkish Republic

As Mayor Atay noted in his speech to the wedding assembly, the seventy-fifth anniversary of the Turkish Republic was commemorated in an exceptional political context. During the fervently celebrated Republic Day of 1998, politicians and politically active citizens debated and discussed the past, present, and future of their country. Although not traditionally a significant number, the seventy-fifth anniversary became the most widely and enthusiastically commemorated one in the history of the Turkish Republic. The form and content of the celebrations can be read as an instrumental attempt to rethink the role of the Turkish state at a time when its founding principles and legitimacy were being challenged by local opposition leaders as well as international funding agencies. Although their demands on the Turkish state differ, all oppositional groups criticize it for being oppressive and limiting political, social, and economic freedoms. Each of these challenges materialized due to major political events that unfolded just before the celebrations.

First, the Islamic Welfare Party, which held the prime ministry in the governing coalition in 1996 and put forward Islamic demands, was banned by the secular military. Renamed the Virtue Party, the same group continued to challenge secularist groups by declaring that the Turkish state was undemocratic. Second, shortly after the anniversary celebrations, Abdullah Öcalan, leader of the armed separatist group the Kurdish Workers Party (PKK), was arrested in Italy following a fourteen-year guerilla war. This further roused nationalist feelings and hatred toward the Kurdish uprising among many Turkish citizens. Finally, Turkey was moving closer to being a candidate member of the European Union, but was also being continuously criticized by the EU, the World Bank, and the International Monetary Fund for limiting political and economic freedoms.

Turkish politicians who came to power after the Islamist government was overturned and the Welfare Party was banned, in addition to citizens who supported this intervention, used the seventy-fifth anniversary as a means to state their opposition to recent assaults on Republican principles. For the first time in Republican history, private organizations and foundations outside the immediate authority of the state organized a major part of the Republic Day celebrations. At a time when the government was not legitimated by votes, Republic Day celebrations became a tool to demonstrate public support for the 1997 military intervention and the government it established.

The Economic and Social History Foundation, founded in 1991 by two hundred academics and intellectuals in order to "develop and spread historical consciousness in Turkey," took a leading role in organizing and implementing the seventy-fifth anniversary as a "civilian" celebration, as opposed to an "official" one. Although during its early years the History Foundation repeatedly emphasized its independence from the state and placed itself in opposition to the Turkish History Institute, which was founded in 1935 to write the official history of the new nation, in 1998 they received major funding from the government to organize the celebrations. When the Islamist government was in power, the chair of the foundation, İlhan Tekeli,[6] told me that he and his friends "thought about what to do to stand up against the Islamists." The idea they came up with was to organize a Republic Day celebration that would emphasize the founding principles of the Turkish Republic and the underappreciated popular support for it.

İlhan Tekeli appealed to President Süleyman Demirel and suggested that the social situation in Turkey required a change in the nature of celebrations: "Recent threats against the Turkish Republic in terms of its unity and modernization added significance to the celebration of the Republic . . . . Developing innovative celebrations is an urgent necessity in Turkey in order to meet these desires and to provide celebrations that fulfill their social functions" (Tekeli 1998:21). Tekeli was suggesting that participatory celebrations would be a powerful statement against the Kurdish uprisings and Islamic politics, which threaten Turkey's founding official ideologies of national homogeneity and secularism. The new celebration, Tekeli proposed, would be likened to a festival and be organized around three concepts: mass participation, spontaneity, and enthusiasm.[7] Through such a conceptual reorganization, the celebration would allow citizens to express freely their support for the Turkish state. More important, by framing their voice as enthusiastic and spontaneous, it would give supporters of the Turkish state legitimacy against oppositional groups. Pro-government citizens would appear as individual customers choosing to support the official ideology based on their own free will rather than as people forced to take part in a state-planned celebration.[8] One way to spread this perspective was to rewrite the history of the Turkish Republic as one that fits a neo-liberal symbolism that fetishizes the market and contractual relationships in the private sphere.

Family Albums of the Republic and Multicultural Citizenship

One of the major activities of the History Foundation during the seventy-fifth anniversary was organizing an exhibit called "Three Generations of the Republic," which demonstrated the holistic changes that have taken place in the private lives of citizens since the foundation of the Republic. Such a strategy diverged from earlier depictions of Republican history that concentrated on the public achievements of the modernizing state, including developments in education, economy, the legal system, and international relations. The most popular section of the exhibit, entitled "Family Albums of the Republic," concentrated on family life and a display of "family albums" constructed by the organizers using pictures collected from seventeen real families. Each album was accompanied by personalized stories of the changes three generations of family members had experienced since the founding of the Republic.

Family pictures and family albums are popular media used around the world to produce domestic intimacy and display it to others. Families actively manipulate the way they appear in these pictures and select only particular images to be included in albums. As Susan Sontag put it eloquently, "each family constructs a portrait chronicle of itself—a portable kit of images that bear witness to its connectedness" (1977:8). Most often, family pictures and albums represent the family as if it were part of a unit larger than itself. At the same time, they exclude many personal relationships from the record. Given all the emotional and arduous work that goes into defining who are the significant members of "a family," it is interesting to explore how exhibit organizers narrated and represented the "families of the Republic."

Even though Republican modernity aimed to suppress different ethnic identities, the exhibit organizers showcased the diversity of Turkish citizens. Each of the seventeen families displayed in the exhibit represents a different ethnic, religious, or class background in Turkish society. The exhibit included Jewish, Greek, Armenian, Kurdish, Alevi (Alawite), Bektashi, Circassian, and Sunni Turkish families. The organizers also characterized class diversity, displaying two poor working-class families side by side with one of the richest families of Turkey: the Eczacıbaşıs. They also complemented families from metropolitan Istanbul with those from Anatolian cities and villages. In this respect, the exhibit made a statement about the multicultural nature of the Turkish Republic and the intimate connections of such diverse citizens to each other as if they were a family.

This novel "mosaic" approach to the Turkish nation/family was shaped by, and is a reaction to, Islamist, Kurdish, and liberal critiques of the homogenization policies of the Turkish state. According to the 1924 Treaty of Lausanne, only Christians and Jews were considered "minorities." The Turkish state resisted accepting any other groups, such as Kurds, as minorities, or as non-Turk for that matter. Despite this official position, in the 1990s a group of Islamist and liberal intellectuals engaged in a vibrant discussion of multiculturalism in Turkey. The most important factors that led to the development of this discussion were the increasing demands of Kurds and of religious people to be recognized by the state as distinct groups with cultural rights. A group of Islamic intellectuals led by Ali Bulaç (1992, 1993) suggested that Islamic law is multicultural because it allows different groups to have their own laws and regulations.[9] Supporters of this argument, including the now-banned Welfare Party, emphasized that the Ottomans had allowed different religious groups to have their own laws and courts and were tolerant of religious differences. Particularly evident in their party propaganda for the 1994 elections, the Welfare Party leaders repeatedly emphasized that their social model for Turkish society allows for multicultural practices rather than suppressing cultural differences as the current Turkish government does.

In reaction to such critiques, "Family Albums of the Republic" depicted the family of the Turkish Republic as one in which diverse cultures coexist and intimately relate to each other. The exhibit suggested that, if different groups have assimilated over time, they have done so by choice. Between the lines, the "Family Albums" exhibit also recognized the hardships religious minorities such as Greeks, Jews, and Armenians have faced. Such incidences of ethnic discrimination were (and still are) hidden from public scrutiny in more conventional expressions of Republican modernity. For instance, the exhibit made reference to the infamous September 1955 anti-Greek riots in Istanbul, the 1942 "Wealth Tax" for non-Muslims (which caused thousands of citizens to end up in work camps), and even the 1915 massacre of Armenians. Yet the main text accompanying the exhibit emphasized similarities and commonalities among Turkish citizens. The text reads:

Different regions, different classes, different occupations, different beliefs, different languages. . . . Despite the differences similar joys, similar sorrows. Babies, whether they are baptized or circumcised, bring happiness. Wedding pictures are full of hope. Brides and grooms smile at the cameras. In pictures students wear black uniforms and white collars or private school uniforms. Facial lines are formed as a result of the weight of the years, and those who are lost. . . . Joys and sorrow, which would not change much, even if we chose different families.

The exhibit organizer, Oya Baydar, told me that one of the main goals of the exhibit was to show how a diverse range of citizens throughout the country participated in Turkish modernization. Likewise, the co-organizer, Feride Çiçek, explained how curators chose to display pictures that were "typical" and would help visitors remember parallel transformations that had occurred in their own families. The official wedding ceremonies that accompanied the exhibit emphasized the continuous, contractual, and commonplace nature of Republican modernity.

Similarly, exhibit panels showed families becoming homogenous, secular, and westernized. For example, over three generations the women of the Edhemağalar family unveil and even start wearing bathing suits; the Alevi

Tanrıverdi family lose their positions of religious leadership in their community; the Türkoman Hacimirzaoğlu family cease being nomads and settle down in a village. As the first generation builds a mosque, the following generations build a school; the second- and third-generation members of the Kurdish Kalkan family no longer engage in polygamy and wife beating; the extended Bektashi family of the Ulusoys divides into nuclear families.

As the family stories on display emphasized certain kinds of transformations, they silenced others that point to the failure of Republican ideals. Although over the last two decades more families have become religious and started to live according to Islamic principles, no second- or third-generation woman in the exhibit was veiled. This was in contrast to the exhibit's tendency to accept the ethnic differences of family members. According to organizers, the ideal family of the Turkish Republic is one in which members chose to assimilate and follow the modernist teachings of the Republic despite their differences. In other words, the exhibit celebrated a domestic intimacy that voluntarily internalizes the effects of Turkish state policy regarding homogenization, secularization, and a specific version of modernization.

To Create a Citizen

A private bank, Yapı Kredi, organized "To Create a Citizen: Introduction to Warfare for Creating a Modern Civilization," the second major exhibit commemorating the seventy-fifth anniversary of the Republic.[10] Despite its militaristic title, reminiscent of the language of the initial years of the Republic, this exhibit also concentrated on mundane transformations in the daily lives of citizens in the 1930s. More important, it emphasized how people readily internalized modernist transformations even in the most intimate aspects of their lives.

Located on İstiklal Caddesi, the busiest avenue of Taksim in Istanbul, the exhibit was easily noticed despite the competing advertisements and signs on the hectic pedestrian-only boulevard. The nationalist songs and marches from the 1930s that radiated from the exhibit made it the center of attention. Passersby on the street could not help but see the external part of the exhibit, which consisted of six bright red walls covered with black and white pictures of ordinary citizens from the 1930s and 1940s. Each wall symbolized one of the six principles of Kemalist ideology. The walls were built in the shape of the six arrows of Atatürk's Republican People's Party. Their bright red color was reminiscent of both the Turkish flag and the official emblem of the RPP.

In the corridors formed between the six walls, four of the six Kemalist principles were emphasized: nationalism, populism, statism, and republicanism. The pictures on the walls showed changes in public life that resulted

FIGURE 4.2. "To Create a Citizen" exhibit (exterior). Photo by author.

from the application of these principles by the single-party regime. For example, in the corridor representing statism, there were pictures of workers in state-owned factories; the corridor devoted to populism displayed pictures of peasant children in Republican schools; pictures of Turkish politicians and political meetings were displayed in the corridor of republicanism; and pictures of small producers who were supported by heavy taxes on imported goods appeared in the nationalism corridor. Along with pictures there were quotes of the two presidents of the period, Mustafa Kemal Atatürk and İsmet İnönü, as well as some popular songs and sayings. Both the idea of setting up exhibits on the street and the graphic designs used were suggestive of the propaganda methods favored by the single-party regime. Because there was no guiding text that situated the exhibit in the framework of 1998, viewers could feel they had (re)entered the world of the single-party regime. Life-size images of citizens from the 1930s merged with pedestrians walking beside them in the street.

The corridors between the arrow walls led visitors to the second part of the exhibit, located inside the building. Unlike the first part of the exhibit, which concentrated on public transformations, the second part was about changes in the private sphere. It displayed pictures of women, children, and youth, each a social category the single-party regime placed great emphasis on transforming and making part of public life. The location of the second part of the exhibit and the material displayed there referred to a separation of public and private spheres, yet at the same time demonstrated the continuity between them. The internal space of the exhibit represented the two remaining Kemalist principles: laicism and revolutionarism.

The last two principles of the Kemalist regime were represented by transformed images of formerly private persons, depicting women in European clothes in nightclubs, girl scouts in orderly lines, and young men and women doing gymnastic demonstrations in stadiums. In addition to pictures, there were also personal items of Mustafa Kemal Atatürk, İsmet İnönü, and Vehbi Koç, a Turkish Muslim businessman who became rich during the early years of the Republic. Their tuxedos, rather than Atatürk and İnönü's military uniforms, were on display. These three men probably wore these costumes during the balls organized in the 1930s and 1940s in order to westernize Turkish people. Along with the display of women's ballroom dancing clothes, this section featured a privately enjoyed (yet publicly oriented) European bourgeois lifestyle during the single-party era.

The new private sphere of the young Republic was best characterized in this exhibit by a "modern" living room from the 1930s, which contained European furniture such as armchairs, a coffee table, and a radio. Along with pictures of women dressed in European clothes, this room symbolized how public efforts to create modern bourgeois citizens were integrated into the

FIGURE 4.3. "To Create a Citizen" exhibit (interior). Photo by author.

private lives of the people, transforming their lifestyles and habits.[11] The small size of the room and the presence of only two armchairs suggested that some early Republican Turks were already living in nuclear monogamous families, which Habermas saw as the basis of the European public sphere.[12] The furniture also implied that the new Republican Turkish family that lived in this room sat on armchairs instead of cushions; ate on the table rather than the floor; and listened to the radio to feel that they were part of the new "imagined community" (Anderson 1991) of the Turkish nation instead of reading the Qur'an and thus being part of the Muslim world. The exhibit declared that ordinary people long ago transformed their habits and lifestyles according to European standards in the domesticity of their homes, outside the direct authority of the state.

The architecture of a museum space and the way it is organized for visitors to walk through is at least as important as the material exhibited (Benett 1995). The architectural design of "To Create a Citizen" was especially important in the absence of guiding texts that could tell the visitor what or how to think. The act of entering the exhibit from the public sphere of the street and progressing toward a representation of a domestic living room was possibly the only thread the visitor could follow as a link to the different parts of the exhibit.

Visitors to the exhibit came from İstiklal Avenue, along which hundreds of thousands of people pass every day. İstiklal Avenue was built in the nine-

teenth century as one of the first westernizing efforts. As such, it houses all
the institutions commonly associated with the European bourgeois public
sphere, from cafés and salons to theaters. Based on the model of a wide Parisian boulevard, it cuts across districts and connects them (Çelik 1986). This
new boulevard is obviously different from the cul-de-sacs of Istanbul, where
people who are not part of the local neighborhood are not expected to wander freely (Eickelman 1974; Abu Lughod 1987). Target visitors for the exhibit were passersby who already were part of the nonhierarchical public
space of the avenue. When they encountered the exhibit, they started walking through one of the corridors created by the six two-meter-high red walls.

Although creating a sense of freedom similar to the avenue, all corridors
in the exhibit led visitors toward a particular point. They merged at the entrance to the second part of the exhibit, which depicted how earlier citizens
of the Republic transformed their private lives freely. Moreover, according to organizers, the corridors directed visitors from the east toward the
west, iconically representing the way Kemalist principles directed Turks
from their Eastern roots toward Western civilization as they transformed
even the most intimate spheres of their lives. These architectural details were
carefully planned. According to Ahmet Özgüner, one of the exhibit organizers, "The structure has its own language. People can enter from any point
and wander around. They can reconstruct the Republican ideology in the way
they perceive it. After wandering freely they merge in one point."[13] Since
the exhibit represented the Kemalist single-party era, the unforced guidance
built into its architecture could be interpreted as a statement against contemporary critics of the early Republican regime, who define it as authoritarian and the Turkish citizens as victims of state oppression. The exhibit architecture suggested that Turkish people acted with a sense of freedom as
they incorporated Kemalist principles in their daily lives and became citizens
through this process. Though not forced to do so, early Turkish citizens still
chose to move in the direction the Republican regime showed them.

A guided sense of freedom is at the same time iconic of the way Yapı
Kredi Bank exhibit organizers saw their role in relation to Republican ideology. This became clear to me during my interview with Münevver Eminoğlu, coordinator of the Yapı Kredi exhibit space. When I asked her why
a private bank like Yapı Kredi went to the trouble of organizing an exhibit
for the seventy-fifth anniversary, she said there was nothing special about it
because the bank always tries to create exhibits that are in line with public
discussions. For example, shortly after "To Create a Citizen," the bank
sponsored a display of arts and crafts celebrating the seven hundredth anniversary of the founding of the Ottoman Empire. In response to a question
about the absence of any explanatory or guiding texts in the exhibit, however, Eminoğlu stated the role of her institution more explicitly: "We want

everyone to read the exhibit in the way they want to. We want them to understand what they can. We are not the state. We are not going to say things by hitting them over the head."

For Eminoğlu, it would be inappropriate for a private bank to assume the manner of the state and say things forcefully. Rather, Yapı Kredi should create choices and discreetly guide customer-citizens toward the product it promotes. In other words, even when engaged in political affairs, the bank should act in accordance with market principles. As Yapı Kredi chooses freely to support the secular principles of the Republic, it takes on the qualities of the ideal citizen, as did early Republican citizens, who voluntarily followed the official ideology and embraced common interests determined by the state. According to this model, the bank, the early Republican citizen, and the contemporary exhibit visitor freely and willingly submit to the state's broader project and equate their private interests with those of the state.

The Public Audience of Republican Intimacy

In redefining Turkish intimacy, Republic Day exhibits addressed a Turkish-speaking audience.[14] Yet the organizers of the Yapı Kredi Bank exhibit also took into account the imaginary gaze of a foreign—yet familiarized—Europe. Much like the cultural intimacy Herzfeld describes, the Turkish privacy on display in "To Create a Citizen" was explicitly constructed to avoid embarrassment, as if imaginary European Union officials would be scrutinizing the exhibit to determine whether Turks are truly modern and European. In this case, however, it was not the general public but the exhibit organizers who defined the "embarrassing" aspects of the Turkish identity as paternalistic submission to Atatürk as well as the militaristic and hence anti-European nature of Turkish modernity. In my interview with Zafer Toprak,[15] main curator of the Yapı Kredi Bank exhibit and original organizer of "Family Albums of the Republic," he pointed out that his goal in putting up these exhibits was to prepare the Turkish public to be part of the European Union.[16] Two years after the exhibit was set up, he defined the main emphasis of the exhibit as the universal (read European) rather than the Turkish character of Kemalist reforms. One of the effective tools he utilized was to choose pictures that did not give clues about their Middle Eastern context:

We chose pictures of people who do not carry any national characteristics. You can show these pictures to people in any country and no one could be able to tell that people in the pictures are Turks. We were not in search of the Turkish identity.

At a time when Turkey's full integration into the European Union was being earnestly discussed, de-emphasizing the nationalist character of the Turkish Republic's foundational principles was a noteworthy political statement. It asserts both to Turks and to the imaginary European viewer that Turkey has been part of Europe since its foundation as a modern state. Another strategy Toprak followed in order to establish a historical connection between Turkey and Europe was to highlight aspects of the early Republican regime that mimicked Europe, rather than demonstrating how the same regime also defined itself through the wars it fought with Western powers:

In these exhibits we started with the national struggle and ended with the Republic. We chose a very peaceful discourse and emphasized commonalities [with Europe]. We could have celebrated the national values as well. . . . For example, when I chose pictures of İsmet İnönü and Celal Bayar, I only used their pictures with Western clothes instead of uniforms. I wanted to show that now Turkish society is ready to be part of the European Union.

According to Toprak, a nonmilitaristic representation of the Turkish Republic, in which Turkish citizens have transformed all aspects of their lives, would move contemporary Turks beyond their nationalist feelings and toward integration with Europe. Furthermore, realizing this deep congruity between Turkey and Europe, the European officials would admit Turkey into the Union. The militaristic and patriarchal feelings associated with the early Republican era no longer match the contemporary ideals of European modernism, which, as Toprak understands it, promotes voluntarism and free will in state-citizen relations.

Toprak stated that one of the most important functions of the exhibit was to help Turks evaluate the early Republican period as a completed stage in history that allows them now to move into the next stage. Namely, it aims to equip citizens to move beyond the nation-state into a global era as part of the European Union:

We need to evaluate our past. The European Union is beyond the nation-state stage. We do not need to go out to the streets and yell "fully independent Turkey." We need to provide an easy transition [to the European Union]. That is our duty.

Toprak's emphasis on the European Union at first sight appears different from Tekeli's stress on public support for the Turkish Republic's secularist and unitarian principles. In fact, the views of the two organizers are parallel in the sense that they both call attention to how citizens willingly accept the modernist principles of the Republic apart from state pressure. Both organizers concentrate on transformations in the lives of ordinary citizens and make a statement about the deep effects of Turkish modernization on private lives. Exhibits prepared by both organizers presented ideal citizens as those who willingly abandoned non-Kemalist practices in order to make themselves part of the larger project of national progress. Turkish citizens appear as both privately and publicly committed to Turkish modernity, just like the officially wedded spouses in a love marriage.

Not Love but Arranged Marriage to Turkish Modernity

Despite the organizers' intentions, however, my interviews with exhibit visitors and the notes they wrote in exhibit guest books make clear that most visitors did not interpret the Republican intimacy on display as a symbol of voluntary and loving engagement with Turkish modernity. Instead of seeing the exhibits as places where private individuals could come together to witness transformations that occurred in the lives of older fellow citizens, visitors perceived the exhibits as contact zones between themselves as citizens and a powerful state that had shaped them. Although in neither exhibit was there a picture of the founding father of the Turkish state, visitors found ways to venerate Atatürk and even tried to communicate with him. The exhibits reminded them not of a voluntary love affair between equals, but of their obligation to the founding father who arranged a fitting marriage for them. This sentiment was especially clear in the exhibit notebooks of "To Create a Citizen."

Yapı Kredi always provides visitor books at its exhibits, but never had they been so popular. During "To Create a Citizen," thousands of visitors filled 1,600 pages in eight books. On many pages there were multiple messages, and most notes were written collectively by groups of students, families, brothers and sisters, or couples. Remarkably, almost all the notes were written to Atatürk. The majority consisted of short formulaic messages referring to the Turkish state as Atatürk's trust (*emanet*) and describing the right way of acting as the path provided by him: "My Father (*Atam*), I am responsible for your trust" or "We are on your path, my Father." Contrary to the exhibit's statement about how Turkish citizens found their own path toward Turkish modernization, Republican visitors claimed that they were merely walking in the path Atatürk had shown them.

Many visitors used the notebooks to express their love and commitment to the leader, rather than the modernization project itself:

If you lived, I would spend my whole life by kissing your hands.
[name]

We never did or will forget you. You are an immortal treasure. If we live independently and freely today, we owe it to you. I am sure that you see us and realize the condition of the country. I will always love you.
Respectfully
[name]

Most exalted of the exalted, Atam,
As youth we promise to protect what you have left us. We will live only for you. We will receive strength when we look at your pictures and we will keep walking faster and stronger.

I love you.
We did not forget the reason of our existence [i.e., Atatürk].
Bakırköy Lycee
[name]

In the same notebooks many visitors promised Atatürk that they would fulfill *his* goals by being good citizens, protecting the Republic, and teaching new generations Republican ideology:

Atam, I promise that I will protect this republic, which you founded by putting your life in danger. I also promise that I will raise new Republican generations. Sleep comfortably.
[name]

Great Leader (*Ulu Önder*) Atatürk;[17]
I fought and fought all over Anatolia, hungry, thirsty, in cold or hot, in order to protect the republic to which you entrusted us and to raise new generations who believe in the homeland, the flag, and you. I did great amounts of work for your children, because I am a teacher of your children. You told me that "the new generations will be your work of art." Following this principle I dedicated my life to them. I have been working and working for thirty years. I will work more. May your soul be pleased (*ruhun şad olsun*).
May the seventy-fifth anniversary of the Republic be celebrated by the whole nation.
Atam, the Republic is entrusted to us. Sleep well. With my endless love.
We are with your principles.
[name]

Although many visitors told Atatürk they were following his path, some confessed that they or their fellow citizens could not and asked for forgiveness.

My Exalted Ancestor (*Yüce Atam*);
As I write these words to you my head is bowed [with embarrassment] because we could not take responsibility for (*sahip çıkamadık*) the Republic you left us. You did everything in order to elevate the Turkish youth. Your aim was to have the Turkish youth carry the Turkish nation to a better place. I hope you will forgive me for this: but maybe you were wrong for the first time in trusting in the Turkish youth. Probably you do not hear or see your followers, but I am sure you feel them at a far away place.
My Father, do not forget that, even if it is not everyone, the Turkish children who love their country are always on your path. We are the guardians of this nation.
[name]

Dear Atatürk,
As of 1998 we accomplished a lot in the path you set towards reaching contemporary civilization. But there are people who try to divide the nation by acting as if

they are Atatürkist or Republican. As a real Atatürkist I really regret this situation. We love you and miss you.

[name]

Of the visitors and guides at "Family Albums of the Republic" I was able to interview, none saw voluntarism or individual choice as a fundamental aspect of the Republican regime. Most often the exhibits made them nostalgic for Atatürk's presidency, when the Turkish Republic rigidly forced its principles on people. My friend Hatice was among the devoted Republicans who spared at least half her day to visit the exhibit.[18] Hatice and I met at the entrance of "Family Albums of the Republic" on a Sunday afternoon. She told me that she "felt awful" after visiting the exhibit. I was eager to learn what stirred such strong emotions. She started talking without waiting for our tea to be served: "When you look at those old pictures, you see that people were more decent, their faces were glowing (*yüzleri aydınlıktı*), they had a sense of responsibility. We do not have that any more."

For Hatice, as it was for many other visitors, the exhibit represented the "golden era" of the early Republic. She believed that in the early days, when citizens could not choose their government, people were filled with Republican enlightenment and felt responsible for the nation rather than themselves. Unlike exhibit organizers who emphasized free-willed engagement with the state, for Hatice the best part of the Republican project was its success in achieving total submission. "In the old days," she said, "even the stupid ones followed orders [of the state]. They wanted to do what they were supposed to be doing. But now it is not like that. People have no belief, no hope, no aim. No one believes in either the nation or order."

As a devoted Republican, Hatice believes that the end of the single-party regime and transition to democracy was the starting point of selfishness in Turkey. "Things started to change in the 1950s. In the exhibit they tell about the transition to the multiparty system, but they do not tell about the compromises (*verilen tavizler, yavşaklıklar*)." Her argument is similar to that of many Republicans who claim that the transition to democracy, which brought the rule of the people rather than the state, inhibited the Turkish nation from reaching the highest Republican goals. This position presupposes that an authoritarian, elitist state is better prepared than a democratic one to bring its citizens to the level of Western civilization.

Many visitors to the exhibit, as well as the guides, shared Hatice's impression that the Republican project deteriorated after the 1950 elections. When I followed people visiting the exhibit, I was surprised to see how many visitors interpreted the display as a representation of a past utopia. Comments about how people were happy in the old days, looked clean, and had enlightened faces, came up repeatedly. A middle-aged male visitor shouted,

"The disaster (*rezalet*) started here!" when he saw a famous political campaign ad used by the Democrat Party during the 1950 elections. In his mind,
the first free elections diminished the authority of the state, and populist
politicians prioritized the immediate interests of their voters rather than the
public good. The same visitor became nostalgic when he and his wife looked
at the old stadium demonstrations: "Look at these pictures! People have a
smile on their faces. There are no strange, nonsensical (*abuk sabuk*) people
around. If you were to take this picture now, it would be full of men with
beards or long hair. This picture is taken without their noticing it, and
everyone looks happy."

Beards and long hair on men are symbols of opposition in Turkey. The
latter is commonly associated with either Islamic mystics or, more likely,
"rockers," rebellious youth, whereas "beards" is code for religious conser-
vatives. Uncontrolled hair for both men and women means not being controlled by an authority figure, such as a father, husband, or the state (Delaney 1994).[19] Thus, the visitor's comment about hair is very telling. What
he meant is that people were obedient to the paternalistic state in the past,
and this made them happy. Today, by comparison, individuals are free to develop oppositional political ideologies of their own, and this clearly upset the
exhibit visitor. Such freedom, he no doubt believed, leads to chaos and un-
happiness by breaking up the homogeneity of the nation and diluting the
complete obedience of citizens to the Turkish (father) state.

Guiding the Youth, Guarding the Republic

My last source of information about the interpretation of the exhibits comes
from the guides for "Three Generations of the Republic." They were enthusiastic, college-aged men and women, whose duties were to give information to visitors, make sure the multimedia functions of the exhibit ran
smoothly, and lead groups of students through the exhibit. During my interviews with nine guides, I discovered that these young men and women,
drawn from a pool of middle-class, urban, secular university students, were
very proud of their jobs. When Özlem, a second-year student of chemistry
at Istanbul University, said, "I really like what I am doing. I would do it even
if they did not pay me," other guides nodded enthusiastically.

The guides were given no specific training. At first, they simply toured
the exhibit on their own and told visitors whatever they considered important. In that sense, their views did not necessarily reflect the exhibit organizers' intentions, but were very much their own. Although hired primarily
to watch over groups of student visitors, the guides took their responsibilities seriously and saw it as an important Republican duty to create good citizens who appreciate the Republican project. Serving as guides transformed

them from university students who work for pocket money to good citizens devoted to a public cause. Most important, the guides internalized the didactic function of the public intellectual in Turkey and embraced the mission of educating young visitors about the virtues of the republic.

During one of their breaks, I asked a group of guides what kinds of things they told students. Özlem replied first: "I want all the children to be Republicans. I pay the most emphasis to elementary school children, because they are young, and I can mold them." At this point, Selda added, "I personally really enjoy giving consciousness to students because they are very ignorant. I think 80 percent of the exhibit should be geared towards children. I want them to know that Suna Kan [a famous violinist] is also a woman of the Republic." Taner joined in, saying, "I try to teach them that they should know the value of the Republic regime that we have, so they can protect it when they grow up." To these college students, being an exhibit guide was a political mission. They were teaching Republican values. By introducing youngsters to classical music performers and other modern products of the Republican regime, they hoped to turn students into devoted Republican citizens rather than critics.

Some guides were very direct in teaching students how they should protect the Republic. For example, when I followed Özlem, who was guiding a group of middle school students in front of a panel about national celebrations, she gave them advice: "In the old days people commemorated the national days with much enthusiasm. Today, we should do the same as well." At other times the guides were subtle about giving their messages. They worked hard to fulfill their mission of inculcating Republican ideology and came up with creative ways to have their teachings better heard by students. Özgür, who at the time was a third-year engineering student at Yıldız Technical University, told me about the methods he used to influence students.

The couple of hours they spend in the exhibit may change these students. So I do my best to influence them. I talk about Atatürk like a human being. I tell about his human side, his loneliness. I call him "that guy" (*o herif*) for example. Then they really listen to me and understand that this exhibit is something different from their history books. And my messages hit the target.

Özgür's approach was indeed innovative. Having recently been a high school student himself, he was aware that students were tired of studying the virtues of the republic over and over again. To hold the attention of students who are adept at closing their ears to propaganda, Özgür related his message in ways that echo those favored by the Yapı Kredi Bank and the History Foundation. This newly intimate style, whether it is conveyed in a casual way of talking about Atatürk or in the carefully considered text and physical layouts of museum exhibitions, has slanted the Republican message toward more voluntaristic models of citizenship. For Özgür, however, and perhaps for most of his student listeners, another set of messages still came through, and it would seem that these messages were more easily felt and understood.

Conclusion

The way the "Family Albums of the Republic" and "To Create a Citizen" exhibits frame the Republican past and its domestic intimacy is closely re-lated to both the particular historical process in which citizenship developed in Turkey and contemporary debates about this issue. Since its beginning in the nineteenth century, Turkish modernization has developed as a top-down project in which a modernizing elite defines the collective interests of Turkish citizens (Mardin 1962; Bozdoğan and Kasaba 1997; Keyman 1997). Hence, Turkish citizenship has corresponded more to a "classical" model than a "liberal" one, according to a popular way of categorization, wherein citizens are defined through their duties toward the state rather than their rights (Kadıoğlu 1998). The modernist Turkish state frequently interfered in, manipulated, and defined the boundaries of domestic lives and made sure that citizens engaged in the necessary practices of modernity in private so they could, as an aggregate of individuals, constitute a modern and secular public sphere. Changing marriage rules, taking control of religious practices, and engaging in clothing reform are some of the ways in which this inter-vention took place. Thus, both exhibits, which focus on the personal lives of new Turkish citizens, reflect the Republican state's longstanding pre-occupation with intimacy as a tool for creating a modern, secular public in Turkey.

The new, voluntaristic models of national identification I discuss in this essay, however, must also be understood as reactions to contemporary Is-lamist, Kurdish, and liberal critiques of the Turkish state, all of which define the state's modernization policies as externally imposed and, therefore, op-pressive and inauthentic. Private exhibit organizers, who display a secular, modern Turkish domesticity to the public, claim that Turkish citizens have voluntarily and intimately internalized Republican principles, even in areas of private life that are outside state authority. Because organizers are non-governmental, their involvement in Republic Day celebrations also serves as proof of deliberate, unprompted support for the modernist principles of the Turkish state.

In this essay I have tried to show that ideas about family relationships are deeply intermeshed with Turkish perceptions of the public sphere. Early Republican government officials and contemporary public intellectuals are united in seeing private lives as appropriate sites for shaping public behavior and creating ideal citizens. Unlike early Republican officials, however, who saw the family as a sphere of direct control and manipulation, contemporary Republican intellectuals depict the family as a site of voluntary, affective identification. To counter increasing criticism of Turkish modernization as a project externally imposed by the state, public intellectuals who are anti-Islamist and pro–European Union are fashioning a history of the Turkish Republic that is Habermasian in its assumption that an "authentically" modern public sphere must be related to an "authentically" intimate private sphere. Yet in contrast to Habermas's concept of *other-oriented intimacy*, in which the subjective experiences of the new bourgeois family flowed naturally into the rational-critical public sphere, which "expanded" and "completed" them, the contemporary Turkish government and its allies fabricate *intimacy-oriented publics*. They take an active, calculated role in displaying images of secular and modern family life as proof of the willing, collectively shared, and intimately internalized relationship of Turkish citizens to Turkish modernity. By redefining the appropriate models of national intimacy, exhibit organizers also assert a close historical connection to the West and hope to include Turkey in a post–Cold War European cultural and political intimacy.

Most visitors to Republican exhibits were receptive to the multivalent symbols of family and intimacy as interpretive tools they could use to appreciate their own history and connection to the state. However, they tended to understand the relationship between Turkish modernity and familial intimacy not in the neo-liberal framework of voluntarism, but in the étatist-nationalist model of paternalism and obligation. In both exhibits the images of early Turkish citizens reminded visitors of the founding father who modernized the nation. They repeatedly referred to their desire and need to follow Atatürk's path in order to be modern. They also voiced nostalgia for the days when the founding father was alive and the paternalistic state made the best decisions for its citizens. If organizers hoped to depict the relationship between the modernizing Turkish state and its citizens as a love marriage wherein partners freely choose each other, for Republican visitors the intimacy on display brought to mind a protective parent-child relationship. The couple who married as part of "Family Albums of the Republic," with Atatürk pictures on their chest, transformed a personal relationship into a performative symbol of their commitment to the secular, modernist principles of the Turkish Republic. As Republicans are challenged by oppositional groups in Turkey, they act out their belief that ideal citizens of Turkey should be wedded to the Republic because this union was arranged by the founding father who knew what was best for his citizen children.

During my interviews with exhibit organizers, I noticed that they were unaware of the contradiction between their aims and visitors' interpretations. Instead, the organizers embraced the traditional role of the cultural elite in Turkey by introducing the newest European conceptions of modernity into Turkish political life. In the models of national intimacy they newly endorsed, the authoritarian aspects of Turkish political identity are coded as embarrassing in relation to neo-liberal ideology and the political culture of the European Union. Earlier codes had merely required that nonmodern aspects of life, such as the veiling of women, be hidden from view or confined to the private sphere, and these moves were understood as obligatory acts of submission to the state. The new conventions, by contrast, aim to conceal the paternalistic inclinations of the Turkish state (and its supporters) by delegating much of the state's representational agenda to NGOs and commercial interests, such as private banks, which speak a market-oriented language of autonomy and choice. These organizations can now teach ordinary Turkish citizens to embrace the modernist state freely and establish nonhierarchical relationships with it.

These lessons in modernity, oddly enough, are taught in ways that ignore their most obvious implications. A citizen free to embrace Republican principles is also free to reject them, as many Turks are doing. If this rejection is seen as illegitimate, or unacceptable, then the authenticity of "intimacy-oriented publics" can once again be cast in doubt by critics of Republicanism. Whether these critics are domestic or foreign, their relationship to the Turkish state is hardly nonhierarchical. In this sense, recent efforts to translate the neo-liberal ethic of government into local public culture seem to be reproducing the authoritarian, elitist tradition of modernism in Turkey. The gap between what Republic Day exhibits were meant to achieve and what they actually accomplished widens as (or precisely because) new models of Turkish national intimacy trigger a deeply felt paternalism that, among Turks of diverse backgrounds, is now associated with an obsolete political style and, no less consistently, with commitment to Republican ideals.

Notes

1. Beşiktaş is one of the oldest, most central, and overpopulated parts of Istanbul. Two million middle- and upper-middle-class inhabitants live in this residential and business district.

2. Throughout its seventy-five year history, the Turkish state has taken the leading role in narrating and celebrating the Republic. For a history of the celebrations, see Öztürkmen 2001.

3. For a critical discussion of the link Habermas establishes between intimacy and publicity and the contemporary implications of this relationship for the "heteronormative order" of the contemporary United States, see Berlant (1997) and Berlant and Warner (2000).

4. By the seventeenth century, many European scholars, including John Locke,

saw the family as the ideal contractual relationship outside state authority. Margaret Somers (1999) discusses how Locke's ideas have influenced contemporary forms of antistatism in Anglo-American political culture.

5. Republican reformers chose the Swiss Civil Code because at the time it was the most recently revised one (Berkes 1964/1988).

6. İlhan Tekeli is a Professor of Urban Planning at the Middle East Technical University in Ankara.

7. In the 1970s, 1980s, and early 1990s Republic Day celebrations were limited to poorly attended military and student parades in stadiums or town centers and badly acted and outmoded nationalist skits in schools.

8. Yael Navaro-Yashin mentions other attempts in the 1990s, when the Turkish press and municipalities presented themselves as entities "outside the state" and adopted "an appearance of spontaneity" in their open support of the state (2002: 127–154).

9. Ali Bulaç based this argument on an agreement the Prophet Muhammad made with three Jewish tribes in Medina.

10. In Turkey it is common for banks to fund cultural events such as exhibits, concerts, and plays. Yapı Kredi Bank not only funds cultural events, it runs its own publishing house and is very active in displaying exhibits about important historical and contemporary events.

11. In her work on architecture during the early Republican period, Sibel Bozdoğan demonstrates how the modern, cubic architecture and interior design of the 1930s became "visual markers of a thoroughly transformed, Westernized, and secularized lifestyle" (2001: 197).

12. In their extensive study of Istanbul households between 1880 and 1940, Cem Behar and Alain Duben (1991) show how ideals of the European bourgeois family such as conjugal companionship, the nuclear domestic unit, and an emphasis on "quality" upbringing for children had become popular among the upper classes even before the establishment of the Turkish Republic.

13. *Cumhuriyet*, October 31, 1998.

14. Seventy thousand people visited "Three Generations of the Republic" in Istanbul and Ankara. Most visitors to this exhibit were students on school tours. Although there is no socioeconomic data on these visitors, research conducted by the History Foundation on another exhibit about the history of Istanbul displayed at the Mint Building is informative. According to this research, most visitors to the Istanbul exhibit had high levels of education and income and defined themselves as people who have a habit of visiting museums. In other words, they had the living standards and habits Kemalist reforms tried to create. In these exhibits, they had a chance to see and celebrate how their ideology came into being. Most visitors to "To Create a Citizen," by contrast, were curious pedestrians who ran into it. There was greater variety in their backgrounds and approach to Republican ideology.

15. Zafer Toprak is a Professor of History at Boğaziçi University in Istanbul.

16. After long years of negotiation, Turkey became a candidate member of the European Union at the beginning of 2000. However, Turkey was not included in the Union during the major expansion that took place in December 2002.

17. It is customary to capitalize the first letters of phrases that refer to Atatürk. This practice marks his superiority to all other human beings.

18. Hatice, who comes from a farming family in central Anatolia, was in her mid-30s at the time of the interview and worked as a sociologist for a research institute. She has strong Republican values and voted for the nationalist and center-left Democratic Left Party in the 1999 elections, and for the secularist and social democrat Republican People's Party in the municipal elections.

19. It is common for middle- to lower-class men to grow a mustache when they establish their own families and are free of their father's authority. Yet in recent decades it has become fashionable and a sign of "modernity" to have a bare upper lip.

References Cited

Abu Lughod, Janet. 1987. "The Islamic City—Historical Myth, Islamic Essence, and Contemporary Relevance" *International Journal of Middle East Studies* 19: 155–176.

Abu-Lughod, Lila. 1998. *Remaking Women: Feminism and Modernity in the Middle East*. Princeton, N.J.: Princeton University Press.

———. 2002. "Egyptian Melodrama—Technology of the Modern Subject?" Pp. 115–133 in *Media Worlds: Anthropology on New Terrain*, eds. Faye D. Ginsburg, Lila Abu-Lughod, and Brian Larkin. Berkeley, Calif.: University of California Press.

Anderson, Benedict. 1991. *Imagined Communities*. London: Verso.

Behar, Cem, and Alain Duben. 1991. *Istanbul Households: Marriage, Family, and Fertility 1880–1940*. Cambridge: Cambridge University Press.

Benett, Tony. 1995. *The Birth of the Museum: History, Theory, Politics*. London: Routledge.

Berkes, Niyazi. 1964/1988 [1964]. *The Development of Secularism in Turkey*. New York: Routledge.

Berlant, Lauren. 1997. *The Queen of America Goes to Washington City: Essays on Sex and Citizenship*. Durham, N.C.: Duke University Press.

Berlant, Lauren. 2000. *Intimacy*. Chicago: University of Chicago Press.

Berlant, Lauren and Michael Warner. 2000. "Sex in Public." Pp. 311–330 in *Intimacy*, ed. Lauren Berlant. Chicago: University of Chicago Press.

Boyer, Dominic C. 2001. "On the Sedimentation and Accreditation of Social Knowledges of Difference: Mass Media, Journalism, and the Reproduction of East/West Alterities in Unified Germany" *Cultural Anthropology* 15, no. 4: 459–491.

Bozdoğan, Sibel. 2001. *Modernism and Nation Building: Turkish Architectural Culture in the Early Republic*. Seattle: University of Washington Press.

Bozdoğan, Sibel, and Reşat Kasaba, eds. 1997. *Rethinking Modernity and National Identity in Turkey*. Seattle: University of Washington Press.

Brenner, Suzanne April. 1998. *The Domestication of Desire: Women, Wealth, and Modernity in Java*. Princeton, N.J.: Princeton University Press.

Bulaç, Ali. 1992. "Medine Vesikası Hakkında Bazı Bilgiler." *Birikim*. 38/39.

———. 1993. "Medine Vesikası Üzerine Tartışmalar." *Birikim*. 47.

Çelik, Zeynep. 1986. *The Remaking of Istanbul: Portrait of an Ottoman City in the Nineteenth Century*. Seattle: University of Washington Press.

Delaney, Carol. 1994. "Untangling the Meaning of Hair in Turkish Society." *Anthropological Quarterly* 67, no.4.

———. 1995. "Father State, Motherland, and the Birth of Modern Turkey." Pp. 177–200 in *Naturalizing Power: Essays in Feminist Cultural Analysis*, eds. Sylvia Yanagisako and Carol Delaney. New York: Routledge.

Eickelman, Dale. 1974. "Is there an Islamic city? The making of a quarter in a Moroccan Town." *International Journal of Middle East Studies* 5: 274–294.

Göle, Nilüfer. 1996. *The Forbidden Modern: Civilization and Veiling.* Ann Arbor, Mich.: University of Michigan Press.

———. 2002. "Islam in Public: New Visibilities and New Imaginaries." *Public Culture* 14, no. 1: 173–190.

Habermas, Jürgen. 1989. *The Structural Transformation of the Public Sphere: An Inquiry into a Category of Bourgeois Society.* Translated by T. Burger and F. Lawrence. Cambridge, Mass.: MIT Press.

Herzfeld, Michael. 1997. *Cultural Intimacy: Social Poetics in the Nation-State.* New York: Routledge.

Hunt, Lynn. 1992. *The Family Romance of the French Revolution.* Berkeley, Calif.: University of California Press.

Jayawardena, Kumari. 1986. *Feminism and Nationalism in the Third World.* London: Zed Books.

Kadıoğlu, Ayşe. 1998. *Cumhuriyet İdaresi Demokrasi Muhakemesi.* Istanbul: Metis.

Kandiyoti, Deniz. 1991. "End of Empire: Islam, Nationalism, and Women in Turkey." Pp. 22–47 in *Women, Islam and the State*, ed. Deniz Kandiyoti. Philadelphia: Temple University Press.

Keyman, Fuat. 1997. "Kemalizm, Modernite, Gelenek." *Toplum ve Bilim* 72: 84–99.

Mardin, Şerif. 1962. *The Genesis of Young Ottoman Thought. A Study in the Modernization of Turkish Political Ideas.* Princeton, N.J.: Princeton University Press.

Mazzarella, William. 2003. "'Very Bombay': Contending with the Global in an Indian Advertising Agency" *Cultural Anthropology* 18, no. 1: 22–71.

McClintock, Anne. 1997. "No Longer in a Future Heaven: Gender, Race and Nationalism." Pp. 89–112 in *Dangerous Liaisons: Gender, Nation, and Postcolonial Perspectives*, eds. Anne McClintock, Aamir Mufti, and Ella Shohat. Minneapolis: University of Minnesota Press.

Mosse, George. 1985. *Nationalism and Sexuality: Middle-Class Morality and Sexual Norms in Modern Europe.* Madison, Wis.: University of Wisconsin Press.

Nagel, Joane. 1998. "Masculinity and Nationalism: Gender and Sexuality in the Making of Nations" *Ethnic and Racial Studies* 21, no. 2: 242–269.

Najmabadi, Afsaneh. 1997. "The Erotic *Vatan* (Homeland) as Beloved and Mother: To Love, to Possess, and to Protect" *Comparative Studies in Society and History* 39, no. 4: 442–467.

Navaro-Yashin, Yael. 2002. *Faces of the State: Secularism and Public Life in Turkey.* Princeton, N.J.: Princeton University Press.

Omae, Ken'ichi. 1995. *The End of the Nation-State: The Rise of Regional Economies.* New York: Free Press.

Öztürkmen, Arzu. 2001. "Celebrating National Holidays in Turkey: History and Memory." *New Perspectives on Turkey* 25: 47–75.

Özyürek, Esra. 2001a. "Nostalgia for the Modern: Privatization of the State Ideology in Turkey." Ph.D. thesis. The University of Michigan.

———. 2001b. "Cumhuriyet'le Nikahlanmak: 'Üç Kuşak Cumhuriyet' ve 'Bir Yurttaş Yaratmak' Sergileri" Pp. 185–214 in *Hatıladiklarıyla ve Unuttuklarıyla Türkiye'nin Toplumsal Hafızası*, ed. Esra Özyürek. Istanbul: İletişim.

Pateman, Carole. 1988. *The Sexual Contract*. Stanford, Calif.: Stanford University Press.

Phillips, Joan. 1988. *Policing the Family: Social Control in Thatcher's Britain*. London: Junius.

Sassen, Saskia. 1996. *Losing Control? Sovereignity in an Age of Globalization*. New York: Columbia University Press.

Şerifsoy, Selda. 2000. "Aile ve Kemalist Modernizasyon Projesi, 1928–1950." Pp. 155–188 in *Vatan Millet Kadınlar*, ed. Ayşe Gül Altınay. Istanbul: Iletişim Yayınları.

Shryock, Andrew, and Sally Howell. 2001. "'Ever a Guest in Our House': The Emir Abdullah, Shaykh Majid Al-Adwan, and the Practice of Jordanian House Politics, as Remembered by Umm Sultan, the Widow of Majid." *International Journal of Middle East Studies* 33, no. 2: 247–69.

Sirman, Nükhet. 2002. "Kadinlarin Milliyeti." Pp. 226–244 in *Modern Türkiye'de Siyasi Düşünce: Milliyetçilik*, eds. Tanil Bora and Murat Gültegingil. Istanbul: İletişim.

Skurski, Julie. 1994. "The Ambiguities of Authenticity: Dona Barbara and the Construction of National Identity." *Poetics Today* 15: 605–642.

Somers, Margaret R. 1999. "The Privatization of Citizenship: How to Unthink a Knowledge Culture." Pp. 121–161 in *Beyond the Cultural Turn: New Directions in the Study of Society and Culture*, eds. Victoria E. Bonnell and Lynn Hunt. Berkeley, Calif.: University of California Press.

Sontag, Susan. 1977. *On Photography*. New York: Farrar, Straus and Giroux.

Steinmetz, George. 1999. "Introduction: Culture and the State" Pp. 1–49 in *State/Culture: State Formation after the Cultural Turn*, ed. George Steinmetz. Ithaca, N.Y.: Cornell University Press.

Tekeli, İlhan. 1998. *Ankara, Istanbul, İzmir için Cumhuriyet Geçitleri ve Şenlikleri: Kuramsal Hazirlik ve Tasarım Çalışması*. Istanbul: Tarih Vakfı Yayınları.

Verdery, Katherine. 1991. *National Ideology Under Socialism: Identity and Cultural Politics in Ceaçescu's Romania*. Berkeley, Calif.: University of California Press.

Williams, Brackette. 1995. "Classification Systems Revisited: Kinship, Caste, Race and Nationality as the Flow of Blood and the Spread of Rights" Pp. 201–238 in *Naturalizing Power: Essays in Feminist Cultural Analysis*, eds. Sylvia Yanagisako and Carol Delaney. New York: Routledge.

Williams, Raymond. 1977. *Marxism and Literature*. Oxford: Oxford University Press.

Yanagisako, Sylvia, and Carol Delaney. 1995. "Naturalizing Power." Pp. 1–24 in *Naturalizing Power: Essays in Feminist Cultural Analysis*, eds. Sylvia Yanagisako and Carol Delaney. New York: Routledge.

CHAPTER 5

Intimacy and Hegemony in the New Europe

THE POLITICS OF CULTURE
AT SEVILLE'S UNIVERSAL EXPOSITION

Richard Maddox

WE OWE TO MICHAEL HERZFELD (1997) a new way of understanding the "social poetics" of politics and solidarity within nation-states and other kinds of emergent contemporary polities. His discussion of cultural intimacy stresses the stereotypical, somewhat embarrassing forms that informal expressions of common identity often take, and it contrasts these everyday sorts of metaphoric predications (see Fernandez 1986) with the more official, formal, and overwhelmingly positive ideological representations that are normally associated with expressions of nationalism, ethnic or regional distinctiveness, and the like. In southern Spain, for example, when Andalusians say, "We are *medio moro* [half Moorish]," they are usually making a sort of rueful confession of an open secret, which both indicates something that Andalusians feel they have in common with one another and recognizes that this commonality might not be altogether praiseworthy, as in "Yes, it has taken thirty years to fix the highway; well, we are *medio moro.*" Even so, such invocations of intimacy are normally somewhat ambiguous and are easily given more or less positive inflections in accordance with the requirements of the particular situations in which they are voiced. For instance, being "*medio moro*" may summon into presence the glories of medieval Córdoba, or it may serve as a way of contrasting southern charms with the austere and "cold" temperaments of Castilians and other northerners, or it may even express empathy with North African immigrants.

The goal of this essay is to explore the most important ways in which such notions of cultural intimacy were deployed in and around the universal exposition that was held from April to October 1992 in Seville (Expo '92) and to relate these local usages to the broader hegemonic and counterhegemonic strategies and structures that were involved in efforts to create a "new Spain" and a "new Europe" during the exposition. As the essay demonstrates, while the garb and substance of "intimacy" may vary from place to place, the politics, dynamics, significance, and structural and historical roots of intimacy are not always exclusively or even predominantly local.

Expo '92 and Cosmopolitan Liberalism

To understand the politics of cultural intimacy in Seville in 1992, it is first necessary to appreciate what it was that Sevillanos (citizens of Seville) and others had to be intimate about at that particular time. Expo '92 was originally conceived as an event to celebrate the five hundredth anniversary of Columbus's first voyage, and it proved to be spectacular both in scope and scale. Located on La Isla de la Cartuja (a peninsula of previously undeveloped land that lies between two branches of the Guadalquivir River, just to the west of the historic center of Seville), the site of the world's fair contained the pavilions of 112 countries, seventeen autonomous regions of Spain, and twenty-nine multinational corporations and international organizations, as well as a dozen or so large thematic pavilions. Over its six-month course, the Expo was visited by perhaps fourteen million people and by seventy-seven heads of state or government. In short, Expo '92 was a very big deal for a relatively small city whose metropolitan population numbered somewhat less than a million people. Moreover, coinciding with the exposition were hundreds of other conferences, ceremonies, and activities associated with the fifth centenary observations of Columbus's voyage, with Madrid's tenure as the "Cultural Capital" of Europe, and with the Olympic Games of Barcelona. All of these events of 1992 (the so-called miraculous year) were sponsored, largely financed, and ultimately controlled by the Spanish government. Through the events, the government aimed to "re-found the state," to "change the image of Spain," and to demonstrate that the legacy of backwardness from nearly forty years of authoritarian dictatorship under Franco had finally been transcended and that a fully modern country committed to democracy was ready to assume a prominent role in the creation of the European Union and a new Europe "without borders" in the 1990s (DD 23 Aug 1992:12).[1]

To help accomplish these goals, the Expo's designers naturally sought to develop an appropriate vision of culture, society, and history for the event. Acutely aware that previous universal expositions had been criticized as vehicles for the promotion of nationalist pride, imperialist ambitions, and capitalist expansion, they were determined to minimize such criticism. Therefore, from the very beginning, when the official theme of the Expo was announced as "The Age of Discoveries," they warned prospective participants that

an excessively nationalistic attitude, ethnocentric in its aspirations, would be in flagrant contradiction with the philosophy of Expo '92 and the interpretation of its theme which celebrates precisely the universality of man's capacity for discovery—man understood as a species above and beyond his nationalistic and ideological prides and prejudices—with a view to stimulating the elaboration of genuinely universal global bases for peaceful co-existence on the symbolic occasion of both the turn of the century and that of a new millennium (Office of the Commissioner General 1987:42).

So instead of simply indulging in some of the more traditional forms of nationalist self-glorification, the Expo essentially promoted a vision of Spain, Europe, and the world in keeping with the tenets of what may be called "cosmopolitan liberalism." Cosmopolitan liberalism is a term I use to refer to an emergent and somewhat inchoate set of cultural and political strategies that involve a reworking of some of the elements of conventional liberalism in order to legitimate state and corporate power in ways that are better suited to the recent, rapid, and radical transformations not only of Spanish society but of the contemporary European and global political and economic order.

Like other forms of liberalism, cosmopolitan liberalism ultimately derives most of its intellectual authority from its association with two Enlightenment traditions: (1) a universalizing minimalist ethical humanism of individual rights and freedoms and (2) a maximalist philosophical and scientific rationalism that constitutes human beings, history, societies, and cultures as objects of knowledge, judgment, and governance (see Toulmin 1992). Owing, however, to the way in which these Enlightenment traditions have been affected by the pressures and constraints exerted via the transnational processes alluded to earlier, cosmopolitan liberalism is distinguished by several crucial hallmarks.

First, cosmopolitan liberalism has a highly charged, ambivalent, and bipolar view of cultural diversity. On the one hand, it represents cultural diversity as an expression of human freedom and a vital source, spur, and locus of organic creativity and vitality—hence, current preoccupations with tolerance, pluralism, and multiculturalism in liberal societies. On the other hand, it depicts cultural differences and divisions, particularly those related to racism, ethnic nationalism, and religious prejudice, as the root causes of most of the conflict, hatred, and suffering in human history and especially as the source of most of the troubles in the post–Cold War era. As a result, cosmopolitan liberalism defines its overriding political and cultural mission as one of domesticating the world, making difference both safe and productive.

Second, in keeping with this vision, cosmopolitan liberalism places extraordinary emphasis on developing strategies of mediation to foster inter-changes that bring divergent traditions and practices into active relation with one another. In the economic sphere, for instance, the expansion of free trade, the fluid movement of global capital, and the extension of basic processes of commodification that make divergent values partially com-mensurate with one another are celebrated not merely because they prom-ise to increase wealth and gradually improve conditions of life everywhere but also because they create pathways that bring peoples and cultures to-gether and generate new forms of interdependence. More broadly, cosmo-politan liberalism anticipates an emergent global cultural ecumene character-ized by the proliferation of what Richard Wilk (1995) aptly terms "structures of common difference." Each of these structures generates diffuse and com-plex transcultural systems "for communicating difference," structures that focus and permit particular sorts of competition but place formal and prac-tical constraints on conflict. Wilk discusses beauty pageants in Belize and the Caribbean, but what he says of them can be applied to the Expo in Seville, the Olympics in Barcelona, and countless other contemporary cultural phe-nomena. Such structures provide vehicles for the dissemination of cosmo-politan liberalism insofar as they realize its fundamental aims of promoting diversity and particular kinds of freedoms in ways that also strengthen or at least do not seriously threaten the primacy and dynamism of actually exist-ing liberal institutions, values, and worldviews that have primarily been de-fined by "the West."

However, the full cultural force that cosmopolitan liberalism exerts by giving pride of place to what are essentially neofunctionalist strategies for the mediation and domestication of difference can be appreciated best when this form of liberalism is considered from a third, more directly political, perspective. Both liberal internationalism and cosmopolitan liberalism sup-port global cooperation, promote an expanded role for international organi-zations, and pay homage to the almighty, if remote, god of macroeconom-ics. But what is distinctive about cosmopolitan liberalism is the stress that it places on transforming an international regime based on the sovereign power of nation-states. Cosmopolitan liberalism holds that in the interests of free-dom, peace, and progress, critical dimensions of state power should be par-tially or wholly devolved and redistributed not just "upward" to suprastate and transnational bodies (such as the European Union) but also "down-ward" to subnational regional or ethnic and political communities (such as Catalonia or Scotland) and "outward" to public and private entities (such as national and transnational corporations, autonomously chartered agencies, and other nongovernmental organizations). This does not, however, mean that the state itself, much less the forms of coercive, regulatory, and disci-plinary power associated with it, will wither away. On the contrary, intrinsic to the logic of cosmopolitan liberalism is the notion that even as the state divests itself of some of its monopolies, it must also shoulder many of the new burdens involved in the increasingly indispensable, complex, and multidimensional functions of policing and coordinating the dense networks of interrelationships that exist among overlapping but quasi-autonomous entities, interests, processes, peoples, and cultures. This vision of cosmopolitan polities that orchestrate ever-increasing multilayered interdependence and heterogeneity goes well beyond the concepts of mediation as interest balancing or as compensatory equalization by a centralized authority as they have been elaborated in either the laissez-faire version or the welfare state version of classic liberalism. Indeed, in what Manuel Castells (1998: 316) calls "the network society," the idea of "universal bargaining" becomes the dominant logic of every kind of sociopolitical relation (see also Rose 1996).

At the Expo, a vision of the world consistent with the emerging tenets of cosmopolitan liberalism was communicated to visitors in many different ways. For example, the design and contents of the dozen or so thematic pavilions and exhibitions devoted to culture, science, and technology conveyed a vision of history that stressed both human diversity and historical processes of convergence. In this regard, the message was that both the legacies of the past and the many tools that contemporary knowledge and technology have provided will ensure the continuation of progress as each culture and tradition becomes better able to contribute to the solution of universal social, environmental, and human problems. An "interactive" vision of history and progress was also evident in the way Spain represented itself as occupying a liminal, betwixt-and-between, crossroads-of-the-world position. This representation was reinforced through the contents of the Spanish national pavilion, which was divided into two main sections, one of which celebrated regional differences and popular customs and the other of which emphasized the country's contributions to European and world civilization. More generally, throughout the Expo, a near obsession with communications media and a highly self-conscious demonstration of the widest imaginable variety of media technologies and performance genres conveyed a nearly absolute faith in communication as a human good that inevitably breaks down barriers between groups and forges forms of "solidarity through interchange," which will eventually lead to the creation of "one single world common to all its inhabitants" (Office of the Commissioner General 1987:8).

The Expo, Efficacy, and Intimacy

Exactly what sort of impact the Expo organizers supposed that the Expo pavilions and events were going to have on visitors was never completely clarified. One of the explicit aims of the exhibition was to change the image of Spain for foreigners, but it is evident that the organizers also saw the Expo as an opportunity to tutor Spaniards themselves by providing them with a more optimistic and inspirational vision of their country's present and future place in Europe and the world.

In general terms, there is no doubt that the Expo's sponsors desired Spaniards to regard themselves as good Europeans and cosmopolitan citizens of the world—citizens who are tolerant of other cultures, who accept the need for and inevitability of an increasing interaction and interdependence of different peoples in order to facilitate progress and limit conflicts, and who at the same time take pride in their own regional and national traditions and the contributions of these traditions to human happiness. The realization of these positive values and pluralist dispositions virtually seemed to require contemporary people to have at least some conscious sense of self and society as constituted by multiple, overlapping, and ideally complementary cultural identities that are primarily based on membership in different sorts of communities, such as local, ethnic, national, and religious communities.

Beyond this, however, the Expo also consistently represented an essentially two-tiered version of global society. Something akin to an appropriately domesticated, highly mediated, and up-to-date version of Marx's distinction between bourgeoisie and proletarians, the Expo version of global society distinguished between what might be termed "experts and discoverers" and "just plain folks." Throughout the exhibition, the highest virtue and authority were almost universally associated with first-tier members in various realms of endeavor (Columbus, the Buddha, Isaac Newton, a modern medical researcher, a computer programmer, an astronaut, and so forth), who, along with loyal sponsors and assistants, were depicted as actively employing the resources and tools of representation and reason "to solve the problems of humankind" (Office of the Commissioner General 1987:43). The second tier was depicted as tens of thousands of images of smiling faces and ordinary individuals happily going about their daily business. Thus, the imagined social world of the Expo appeared to rest on the foundation of a presumed elementary hierarchy of talent, vision, merit, and achievement that extended across cultural boundaries. In terms of its class dynamics, the Expo can probably best be regarded as a celebration of the leadership of an increasingly cosmopolitan, meritocratic professional-managerial elite of policymakers, scientists, academics, and others who are supposed to be essential for the expansion of knowledge and for the smooth day-to-day functioning and long-term development and integration of both Europe and a new liberal world order (see Hannerz 1990).

Yet the message that organizers wished to convey through the Expo and the message that visitors actually perceived were by no means necessarily the same thing. Indeed, one of the most difficult aspects of understanding the

significance of the Expo and other highly mediated mass events lies in trying to gauge the efficacy and impact of such events on their intended audiences. The problem of efficacy has as a result been approached from a wide
range of theoretical perspectives. On one end of the spectrum, it is possible
to view these events as instantiations of Guy Debord's "society of the spectacle." From this perspective, the Expo can be regarded as one of those
"completely equipped blocks of time" (Debord 1977:152) that advanced
capitalist societies ostensibly market for purposes of entertainment, pleasure,
and edification. Such blocks of time offer people highly contrived and
strictly limited experiences whose purported effect is to further the creation
of a society populated by distracted, bemused, docile, and apolitical masses.
On the other end of the spectrum, analysts of mass events can take heart
from approaches such as those inspired by the work of Michel de Certeau
in *The Practice of Everyday Life* (1984). Though scarcely less critical of advanced
liberal societies and fully aware of all the forces making for conformity and
limiting autonomy, de Certeau suggests that many (if not most) people are
able to adapt what is given to them by their social environments and to put
it to use for their own diverse purposes. Thus, visitors to a mass event such
as the Expo can be expected to make their own itineraries and to interpret
and experience the event in ways that may not correspond to and may even
oppose official expectations and programs. Even many highly structured and
constraining situations leave more space for social and cultural creativity, improvisation, and choice than is usually apparent at first sight, and it is common
for people to exercise their "tactical" capacities. This approach to understanding mass culture is particularly useful for exploring the gaps that usually exist between formal representations and informal popular practices and
understandings. The danger of the approach is that it may overestimate the
reality of or potential for criticism, change, and resistance in everyday forms
of cultural improvisation, rule bending, and spontaneous social innovation.

More broadly, the posing of such starkly contrasting theoretical perspectives indicates the complex dialectic of freedom and nonfreedom that still
exists at the heart of liberal societies and at the same time it invites us to plunge
more deeply into ethnographic explorations of the specific constraints and
pressures and the nature of the practical conditions and contingencies that
influence the responses of different sorts of people to public events. And it
is at this crucial juncture that a better understanding of the politics of cultural intimacy has a great deal to contribute toward understanding the force
and efficacy of events like the Expo. For just as the Expo organizers sought
to instruct and familiarize the Expo visitors with an emergent and still
somewhat inchoate official orthodoxy that served to legitimate processes of
Europeanization, many of the visitors clearly succeeded in partially reincor-
porating these images of the new world order into already existing and

essentially self-validating systems of values and purposes that tended to max-imize their sense of mastery and autonomy over the Expo's social and cul-tural milieu or at least to insulate and protect them from any threats that they perceived this milieu might pose. The visitors sought, in other words, to make what was most strange and new about the Expo more familiar and manageable; and in doing so, they naturally appealed to values of intimacy and invoked broadly shared common understandings that tended to rein-force, rather than to transcend, stereotypical forms of regional, national, class, political, and other forms of identity and association. This happened in an almost endless variety of ways and affected everything from how families planned their visits to the event to how residents of Seville remembered the Expo after months and years had passed.

In the sections that follow, I describe three of the most important forms that the public politics of intimacy took for Sevillanos at the Expo in 1992. A discussion of these forms of intimacy—which I characterize as skeptical, communalist, and exclusionary intimacy—will set the stage for a brief anal-ysis of the historical roots and future prospects for the politics of intimacy in the new Europe.

Skeptical Intimacy and the Politics of State Patronage

From its beginnings, the Expo was defined as a great undertaking of the Spanish state. This undertaking was to be carried out by the national gov-ernment, which had been in the hands of the Socialist party (El Partido So-cialista Obrero Español, or PSOE) since 1983, and many questioned whether the Socialists would use the Expo primarily as a vehicle to further their own interests or as a means to promote the interests of Spain as a whole. Although members of the PSOE were heavily committed to a cosmopolitan, liberal, and Europeanist vision of Spain, they also clearly viewed the Expo through the narrower lens of partisan national, regional, and local politics. From this perspective, the Expo project, whose site was supposed to be converted into a high-tech research and development park in 1993, was part of a strategy to secure the party's crucial southern electoral base against other political forces, including the center-right Partido Popular and a small (but still po-tentially threatening) regionalist political formation known for most of this period as El Partido Andalucista. Thus, the Expo represented the most pub-lic face of a broader effort to reap the political benefits of promoting the overall modernization and development of Andalusia, a region that in the early 1990s ranked third in unemployment among the European Union's 171 regions and ranked 152nd in per capita gross domestic product (*DD* 10 Jul 1992:55).

Harmonizing the divergent interests and aims of those involved in planning the Expo was no easy matter. Indeed, from its inception, the Expo project was fraught with conflict. The Socialists' first serious error was to nominate architect Ricardo Bofill for the crucial office of commissioner general of the Expo. Bofill was well known internationally, and because he was not formally a member of the PSOE, his appointment would preserve the nominal status of the Expo as a "nonpartisan" state project while still permitting the Socialists to take the lion's share of political credit for the event. However, because Bofill is a Catalán, his nomination immediately produced howls of protest from Seville, where the consensus was that there were many Andalusians who would be well qualified to fill the post. Thus, having started out by offending the very region that it was intent on court-ing, the government rushed to make amends by reversing itself and appoint-ing Manuel Olivencia, a law professor at the University of Seville, to the post of Expo commissioner general. This choice was a fateful one. Although the Olivencia appointment was generally popular in Seville, it vastly annoyed many Socialist militants, who regarded the professor as representative of the city's right-wing elite. The militants' unremitting opposition to Olivencia eventually led to the counterbalancing appointment of Jacinto Pellón, an en-gineer and a Socialist supporter with minimal Andalusian connections, to the important position of executive director of the State Society for the Uni-versal Exposition. This placed Pellón in charge of the construction and day-to-day administration of the Expo while leaving Olivencia in charge of the more "cultural" aspects of the Expo, including the design and contents of the theme pavilions and the organization of a program of performances, cer-emonies, and so forth.

Not altogether surprisingly, this arrangement soon degenerated into a struggle for ascendancy within the Expo organization, which became a sort of two-headed monster with each head trying to cannibalize the other. The relatively small commissioner general's office contained a number of local academics and managed to preserve something of the tone and values of a classic Andalusian *tertulia*, a circle of friends and "friends of friends" who are bound to one another by shared outlooks and experiences as well as by com-mon interests and purposes. In contrast, the higher and middle levels of the much larger State Society tended to be staffed by non-Andalusian Socialist technocrats who had or wished to have careers in public administration or in the most advanced and highly corporatized sectors of the economy. Many of these functionaries were relatively young, were highly ambitious, and en-joyed conveying the impression that they were rising managers and experts who brooked no nonsense.

The intensity of the struggle between the partisans of "Don Manuel" and the partisans of "the Engineer" waxed and waned over time, and battles were fought on a number of different fronts. One form the struggle took was a series of disputes over the design and contents of the Expo. The Olivencia group wished to stress a humanistic, highbrow Expo of "ideas," while the Pellón group was skeptical of this approach and was somewhat more concerned with organizing a great spectacle of diversions and entertainments. This disagreement was but one of several variations on the theme of official formality versus populist intimacy that surrounded the event. However, the most serious disputes tended to arise when members of the commissioner general's staff sought to assert their legal preeminence in policymaking and to exercise their responsibilities for auditing accounts and overseeing the activities of the State Society. These efforts were evidently often stiffly resisted by the State Society's directors through the use of classic bureaucratic tactics of delay and obfuscation. As a result, the commissioner general's staff came to believe that their office was the target of a series of hit-and-run raids whose ultimate aim was to turn Olivencia into a mere figurehead by slowly eroding his practical control over one aspect after another of the Expo.

Olivencia's supporters, opposition politicians, and some members of the press responded to the perceived secretiveness of the State Society directors by raising questions concerning how the massive resources under the control of the State Society were being expended. There was certainly some cause for concern about this issue. Beginning in the late 1980s, one rumor after another emerged concerning the methods of Socialist party financing or the personal greed of well-placed party regulars. Indeed, in early 1990, the taint of corruption reached Seville when news broke that Juan Guerra, the brother of Spain's vice president, had grown suddenly rich by setting up an office for influence peddling in the local party headquarters (*EPI* 19 Feb 1990:14). Moreover, it began to become fairly clear that favoritism was present in the contracts awarded by the State Society for work on the Expo. Only about 7 percent (45 of 668) of these contracts involved open competitive bidding, and the remainder either were directly awarded or were granted after a minimal number of private proposals were solicited (*ABC* 19 Apr 1992:55). This practice allowed ample scope for the Socialists and their allies to engage in mutual back-scratching, as can be seen, for example, in the case involving a construction firm called Dragados. Both before and after the Expo, Jacinto Pellón was one of the directors of this firm; and during Pellón's tenure as director of the State Society, Dragados became the largest single beneficiary of Expo largesse, receiving about 17 percent of the money awarded through the State Society and the Ministry of Public Works for the construction of Expo-related projects (*ABC* 3 Apr 1992:56–57; *ABC* 19 Apr 1992:55; *EP* 22 Jul 1990:4).

This type of apparent favoritism was not technically illegal, and despite many charges and countercharges about Socialist party graft and Expo graft, no great financial scandal has ever come to light concerning the Expo itself.

What is crucial to note is that the paucity of reliable information about Expo financing did virtually nothing to discourage the widespread suspicion that there was much amiss inside the Expo. In fact, a few news reports and persistent rumors and gossip were all that were necessary to convince most people that the Expo represented a typical example of "politics as usual." In other words, the politics of intimacy at the Expo began even if it did not end with the notion that for all its high-blown rhetoric and noble aims the event was beset with a set of well-known liabilities that were part and parcel of Andalusian and Spanish political culture and identity.

Cronyism, factionalism, graft, backstabbing, unchecked personal ambitions, greed, envy, secret deals, and unspoken agreements were pretty much assumed to be the order of the day. As one Sevillano said when I asked him how the preparations for the Expo were going, "*Hombre, es nada más que un choque . . . una pelea . . . una cosa política*" ("Man, it's nothing but a collision . . . a fight . . . a political thing"). This basic conviction, in tandem with a lack of much real knowledge, created a space of skeptical doubt that was usually filled with negative stereotypes of what northerners, southerners, academics, politicians, and bureaucrats were supposed to be like. If there was an innocent victim here or there (Olivencia was usually cast in this role), it was nonetheless assumed that most of the officials who occupied the higher echelons of the Expo organization were culpable to some degree for all the internal conflicts and rivalries. Depending on their political loyalties, some people were inclined to view the Expo's problems as a legacy of the authoritarian political culture of patronage and *amiguismo* (the inclination to favor one's self, friends, associates, allies, and party to the detriment of fair practices and the public interest) of the Franco regime, while others argued that the difficulties were mostly attributable to the contemporary dynamics of what was sometimes called "egosocialism," a term used to invoke the arrogance and lack of accountability of many militants of a political party that had been too long in power.

As a result, the tensions surrounding the Expo reinforced two of the most enduring features of Spanish political culture. The first is the conviction that politicians and officials of the state are not so much representatives or mediators who act in the interests of all as they are members of an entrenched, elite "political class" who pursue their own interests with little real regard or respect for the opinions or needs of ordinary citizens. The second is the closely linked notion that ideologies and policies often amount to little more than the vehicles of and camouflage for what are essentially intensely personalized conflicts among power-hungry "big men" and their clients. As the party in charge of the Expo, the PSOE was affected most by these perceptions, but opposition politicians were also seen as stamped from the same basic mold, even if the immediate circumstances cast them into the role of whistle-blowers. This belief reaffirmed long-held perceptions in Seville of a deep chasm between the interests of the state and those of ordinary people who could do little but shrug their shoulders and make the best of the way things worked on the basis of their familiarity with the basic motivations, interests, and values of people in power. This kind of political realism in turn tended to undermine the Expo's promotion of cosmopolitan liberalism, an idea whose legitimacy depended precisely on the credibility of the claims of politicians and other agents of the state to act as rational, pragmatic, and neutral mediators of cultural differences and conflicts of interest.

Communalist Intimacy and Local Politics and Culture

The high general level of skepticism about the Expo project and about who was likely to be profiting from it had a profound impact on democratic politics in Seville. By the spring of 1991, a dispute between Olivencia and Pellón about the pricing of admissions to the Expo, which was, of course, a matter of great interest to local residents, had spilled over into the municipal electoral campaign. Some months earlier, Pellón had challenged Olivencia's authority by independently announcing that a one-day ticket to the Expo would cost about forty dollars and by proposing a restrictive policy concerning season passes. This led Olivencia to threaten to resign, and it simultaneously created a political crisis for the Socialist-controlled government of Seville because it threatened the easy access of Sevillanos to the Expo site. It also played into the hands of Alejandro Rojas Marcos, a leader in the regionalist Partido Andalucista who had earlier led a protest march to retake the "Bastille" of the Expo for the people of Seville and now began accusing Seville's current mayor of kowtowing to the Expo organization and the national government.

In effect, Rojas Marcos launched his own campaign for the mayoralty by demanding that Sevillanos be given special Expo privileges and prices on the grounds that they had already made and would continue to make the greatest sacrifices to ensure that the event was an international success. During the ensuing electoral campaign, Socialist opponents of Rojas Marcos pointed out that there was no legal basis for favoring Sevillanos over others, but this did not deter him. Instead, at every opportunity, Rojas Marcos gave a strongly local and Andalusian inflection to the issues surrounding the Expo, continually stressing the "uniqueness" of Seville. With his Socialist opponent clearly in his sights, he made many proclamations such as the following: "To be a Sevillano is not only to have been born in Seville. To be a Sevillano is a form of being, of feeling, of loving, of living" (*DD* 21 May 1991:21). This appeal to intimate involvement and local control won the hearts and minds of many people in the city and thereby helped Rojas Marcos to be elected in June 1991 as Seville's mayor, a position that had been occupied by the Socialists for nearly a decade. The defeated and somewhat shell-shocked Socialist opponent attributed his loss to Rojas Marcos's success in attracting a backward-looking "folkloric vote," and he later lamented that his "apparent weakness" was that he had adopted "a more civilized and European posture" in an effort to overcome "local atavisms and family demons" (*DD* 26 Apr 1991:3).

The loss of Seville was a stunning defeat for the Socialist party, which now faced the intolerable prospect of having a non-Socialist commissioner general of the Expo and a non-Socialist mayor of Seville greeting the dignitaries and visitors to the exposition in 1992. In short order, therefore, Olivencia was fired and Pellón became for all practical purposes the supreme commander of the Expo. Thus, less than a year before the Expo was to open, Seville was governed by a regionalist who was committed to defending the city's interests and culture vis-à-vis the Expo and the state, while the Expo was ruled by an abrasive and unpopular technocrat.

An uneasy truce between these two natural antagonists prevailed for some months, but scarcely a week after the Expo opened, Pellón proclaimed that "the Expo is not just for Sevillanos" and suspended the sale of Expo season passes. In response, Rojas Marcos and other local politicians represented this decision as "a declaration of war" against the city and pledged to undertake redressive action. The main themes sounded in this storm of words were that the decision and everything related to it were "unjust," "a barbarity," "disrespectful," "shameful," "a mockery," "an abuse of citizens' rights," and "a deception" and that the people of Seville had "suffered" and would continue to suffer from the acts and arrogance of Expo officials (*DD-ex* 23 Jun 1992: 6–8; *DD-ex* 26 Jun 1992:6; *EC-ex* 23 Jun 1992:2–4). From there, matters degenerated to a point where Pellón was publicly booed and ridiculed when he appeared at an opera performance in Seville, and Rojas Marcos later got the same treatment from Socialists when he visited the Expo.

The public brouhaha over the season passes gave melodramatic form to the critical underlying issue of whether the Expo was to be understood and dealt with as an artificial and essentially foreign body temporarily implanted by the state or as a new urban zone that should be fully incorporated into and controlled by the city of Seville for the sake of its residents. This issue was never satisfactorily resolved either legally or politically. However, in spite of the event's official cosmopolitanism, most Sevillanos chose to talk and act in ways that attempted to make the Expo their own. Rather than regarding themselves as simple tourists or service employees of the Expo, they saw themselves as the true hosts of the event and generally aimed to be hospitable by introducing visitors not just to the Expo but also to the pleasures and values of a distinctive local way of life that celebrates intense, tradition-based forms of face-to-face sociability. As Rojas Marcos had stated during his speech on the opening day of the Expo, the crucial role that Sevillanos had to play was to show Seville's visitors how "to live life more intensely" (*ABC* 21 Apr 1992:8).

In other words, Pellón's attempt to bar the gates to the Expo had only encouraged Sevillanos to understand the hitherto somewhat incipient and repressed split between the official liberal values promoted by the Expo and the tradition-based values of the city as a cultural cleavage of monumental proportions. Indeed, as a result of the conflict, it seemed as if Sevillanos renewed their resolve to treat the Expo simply as Seville's newest neighborhood—an island offering an ideal place for walks along the river, conversation, drinking, eating, singing, dancing, and romance, particularly in the evenings after most of the Expo pavilions had closed and admission prices to the site were lowered. Thus, through the more or less spontaneous (but not by any means entirely unconscious or unintended) efforts of Sevillanos, two Expos came to exist. The first, Expo Día, or the "daytime Expo," was the one characterized by hordes of tourists waiting in lines in Seville's sweltering heat to catch a glimpse of the wonders of the world. The second, Expo Noche, or the "nighttime Expo," was dominated by Sevillanos who invaded the island during the hours when admission prices were reduced and sought to charm and seduce (sometimes quite literally) their guests. Expo Noche was characterized not by the formalities and busy pursuits of the day but instead by the pleasures of relaxed and spontaneous social intimacy. The distinctive structures of feeling during Expo Noche resonated with those of the traditional cultural forms of the fiesta and the *paseo* (leisurely walk or stroll), rather than with those of the modern museum or amusement park. And because of this, Expo Noche provided an alternative and distinctively local way of appreciating and experiencing the human intercourse made possible by gathering together the "whole world on an island."

Ultimately, the existence of these two quite different Expos did the event no harm as a tourist attraction. On the contrary, perhaps the most common answer to the endlessly repeated survey question, "What's the best thing about the Expo?" was "Seville." But the Expo clearly failed to transform Sevillanos into the ideal subjects of cosmopolitan liberalism, subjects who fluctuate between one identity and another and are grateful to experts for the direction and benefits they provide. Instead, it led to the reanimation of a rooted, populist, egalitarian alternative that involved more than just the commercial exploitation of local custom and color—an alternative perhaps best characterized as a cosmopolitan localism that was grounded in intimate values of communal hospitality and mutual respect and was as tolerant of the differences among ordinary people as it was skeptical of the policies of encompassing corporate and state institutions directed by elites. Again and again, and in a wide variety of ways, it seemed that Sevillanos had asserted that one cannot really be a full citizen of Spain, Europe, or the world without primary ties and participation in the way of life of a particular place.

Exclusionary Intimacy and the Limits of Cosmopolitan Liberalism

To appreciate something of the range of ways in which notions of cultural intimacy were invoked at the Expo, it is necessary to discuss briefly a darker side of the cultural politics of the event. This dimension of the Expo involved the use of state power and the manipulation of public opinion to police and repress cultural differences and dissent, rather than to tolerate them.

Although most of the time visitors were barely aware of it, the Expo was in some of its aspects less an island open to the world than a fortress, panopticon, and high-security zone of limited access, electronic surveillance, and crowd control—a zone that was closely (though often virtually invisibly) guarded by thousands of agents of state security. The primary justification for the heavy security measures surrounding the Expo was to guard against terrorist attacks, particularly by Euskadi Ta Askatasuna (ETA), the clandestine Basque independence group that has been engaged in a bloody and protracted armed struggle against the Spanish state for decades. Fears of ETA attacks were not unfounded. As late as December 1991, ETA had planted three bombs in Seville. The quite reasonable right of Expo visitors to be protected from violence, however, tended to be conflated both by officials and by many members of the press with the far more problematic notion that visitors' fun at the Expo ought not to be dampened by protesters. Thus, many steps were taken to limit and at times repress even nonviolent dissent.

The core of the resistance to the Expo consisted of domestic environmentalists and pacifists loosely linked to a network of representatives of indigenous peoples from Latin America and activists from elsewhere in Europe. However, a number of autonomous individuals and progressive sectors, including anarchists and Socialist and Communist youth groups, were also involved in actions against the Expo. For instance, El Patio de la Asociación por Derechos Humanos de Andalucía formed a network of groups that included the Critical Architecture Collective, the Ecological Pacifist Confederation of Andalusia, other "greens," and similar groups. In turn, this local coalition had ties to another coalition of indigenous Latin American groups that was called Conic, or the Coordinator of Indigenous Organizations of the Continent, and was planning large demonstrations against the fifth centenary observations in October in Seville, Madrid, Barcelona, and other places. In addition, under the title of "Disenmascaremos '92" ("We Will Unmask '92"), leaders from a number of these groups were organizing a schedule of anti-Expo protests that stretched throughout the summer (*EC* 16 Apr 1992:43). Beyond denouncing the "genocide of 1492," neocolonialism, and racism, the activists hoped to focus public attention on more specific issues, such as Latin American foreign debt, immigration policy in Europe and the Americas, the loss of biodiversity in the Amazon, and the social, economic, and environmental consequences of the advent of the single market in Europe. In sum, the loosely affiliated groups of protesters were quite similar in their aims and composition to the antiglobalization coalitions that emerged later in the 1990s in the United States and Europe, although in 1992 the dissenters at the Expo did not use the term "antiglobalization" to represent what they had in common.

To begin the protests and also to honor the legacy of Bartolomé de las Casas, an event called El Encuentro Internacional de Solidaridad (International Encounter of Solidarity) was to be held in Seville from April 17–23, 1992, to coincide with the opening of the Expo. This event was to include a number of peaceful protests and marches. Indeed, many of the primary organizers of the event were committed pacifists. Nevertheless, authorities in Seville were hostile to these plans and refused to issue permits for the marches and demonstrations. Alfonso Garrido, a delegate of the government of Andalusia, argued that it was "obvious that the rights of the majority of citizens have to be protected" and that the demonstrations would constitute a threat to public order and were clearly unsuitable for El Paseo de Colón, a "touristic zone" near the Expo. In addition, he related the planned actions to disruptions that had occurred the previous October when another, evidently unrelated group had entered the Cathedral of Seville and performed a "pagan exorcism" invoking the Pachamama before the tomb of Columbus. To no avail, representatives of Disenmascaremos '92 protested Garrido's statements and the decision to deny the permits (*EC* 24 Apr 1992:22; *EP* 31 Mar 1992:2).

On the evening of April 19, a serious clash occurred between police and about four hundred youths who had been attending a rock concert in the center of Seville. Whether the youths were simply being rowdy or had a serious purpose is unclear. In any case, the youths had gathered in La Plaza de San Marcos just as worshippers were leaving a service held in the church there. The police evidently received reports that some of the youths had shaved heads and were damaging cars and spray-painting the walls with anti-Expo and other slogans, while other rioters were masked and were "communicating with one another by radio." The reports were sufficiently alarming that authorities instructed a special police antiriot unit to restore order. The unit attacked the crowd with truncheons, riot guns, and rubber bullets. This created utter chaos, as panic-stricken youths and churchgoers alike fled the onslaught and sought refuge in surrounding streets. As a result of this display of overwhelming force, three people suffered serious gunshot wounds, dozens of others were beaten and fled to hospitals, and dozens more were jailed. Three hours passed before calm was completely restored (*ABC* 20 Apr 1992:58).

The next day, a relatively small crowd of Spanish and foreign demonstrators attempted to block the Barqueta bridge to the Expo to show their revulsion for "neocolonialism, slavery, and exploitation," to demand freedom for those detained by police the night before, and to denounce police brutality (*DD* 21 Apr 1992:5). This demonstration was also broken up by police, and a number of people were arrested. In addition, security forces raided a camping site on the outskirts of Seville and arrested (on obscure grounds) another two dozen people who were thought to be planning acts against the Expo. After these arrests were made, a total of about eighty people from Andalusia, the Basque country, Catalonia, Austria, Germany, Sweden, Turkey, and elsewhere were being held by the police on a range of charges (*DD* 22 Apr 1992:8A).

According to official commentary on the events, responsibility for everything that happened could be laid at the feet of Disenmascaremos '92. Indeed, rather than making any effort to distinguish among the various sorts of demonstrators and demonstrations, official spokespersons seemed to be determined to lump them all together and to link them to ETA. For example, much was made of the purported fact that a couple of the people arrested after the rock concert carried a general set of instructions from the anarchist union La Confederación Nacional de Trajabadores (CNT) on what to do if arrested. Moreover, security officials suggested that the protesters had suspicious links to ETA and foreign subversives. One of the Basque groups, Amaikurko Quetzal, whose members had taken part in the demonstrations, supposedly had ties to the ETA front party, Herri Batasuna. However, the evidence for these and similar claims turned out to be rather thin. For instance, in the case of Amaikurko Quetzal, the connection between the group and ETA was that an ETA militant had been captured a few years previously with literature from the group in his possession (*DD* 22 Apr 1992:8A). No matter. The police were convinced (or at least they tried to convince others) that it was more than likely that a broad conspiracy was afoot to disrupt the inauguration ceremonies and, if possible, to shut down the Expo (*DD* 21 Apr 1992:5).

Representatives of Disenmascaremos '92, CNT, and other groups denied these accusations and insinuations. Indeed, they asserted that all of the demonstrations and events that had happened so far had been spontaneous and unplanned and that there was no conspiracy. Moreover, a Disenmascaremos representative noted that the group was firmly opposed to all forms of violence and insisted that his group intended to confine its efforts to "conferences, debates, and peaceful acts" (*DD* 23 Apr 1992:6). Furthermore, the resisters countercharged that the security forces had detained people illegally, had used excessive force in taking demonstrators into custody, and had withheld food from some youths for up to thirty hours while they were in custody (*DD* 20 Apr 1992:5; *DD* 1 May 1992:16).

Respect for the letter of the law, including perhaps basic civil rights, was not, however, at the top of the list of official priorities at the moment. In short order, the courts freed about twenty Spanish youths, sentenced a handful of others to lengthy jail terms, and directed that about fifty foreign detainees be interrogated by the authorities and then expelled from Spain (*EC* 24 Apr 1992:22; *EP* 23 Apr 1992:1). Moreover, the protesters' complaints about official distortions of the facts and violations of civil rights had little effect on what the authorities were saying, on what the press chose to emphasize, or on what the public seemed to accept as true. On the contrary, legitimate forms of protest were effectively tainted by being associated with random "Punk" violence, which was in turn linked to terrorist plots and conspiracies. Editorialists in the local press chimed in by characterizing those under arrest as "outsiders," "barbarians," "savages," and "huns" and by depicting local peaceful resisters as if they were the dupes of foreign agitators and terrorists. Just so no one would harbor doubts about who the true defenders of civilization and natural decency were, one editorialist observed that "the Indian may cultivate his myths, may protest, [and] may do what he wishes" but "he must let others have their fiesta in peace" (*DD* 21 Apr 1992: 5; *DD* 23 Apr 1992:3).

So much for the Expo that promised something for everyone. So much for the free movement of people and ideas in a Europe without borders. So much for cosmopolitan pluralism and openness. Invocations of an intimate community of local citizens and ordinary Expo visitors who shared common values and desires were used to circle the wagons around the Expo and to exclude "undesirable" outsiders, even though quite a large number of these outsiders happened, in fact, to be Andalusians and other Spanish citizens. And so much as well for open resistance to the Expo. The calm of the Expo was never seriously disturbed again. As local activists readily admitted, they were intimidated because the authorities had made it clear that there was quite literally no place for radical dissent at the Expo or in Seville in 1992.

More broadly, however, the politics of intimacy in the skeptical, communalist, and even exclusionary forms it took at the Expo revealed the limits on the efficacy of the event in creating a new image of Spain and of Spanish people either for themselves or for outsiders. At almost every turn, informal shared understandings of people's positions, motives, and interests and stereotypical ideas about regional, class, national, and other forms of identity undercut some of the key hegemonic representations of cosmopolitan liberalism and reconfirmed Sevillanos' understanding of the character of politics in Spain, of the distinctiveness of local culture, and of their own somewhat marginal place in the contemporary world. Thus, even if the Expo largely succeeded in normalizing images of the new Spain and the new Europe by making them more familiar elements in the inventory of contemporary culture than they had been in the past for Andalusians, it clearly failed in converting many people into enthusiastic adherents of the emergent ideology of cosmopolitan liberalism or in dramatically transforming them into the docile and pliable subjects that this way of looking at the world appears to mandate.

Cultural Intimacy and the New Europe

Without question, many aspects of the cultural politics surrounding the Expo were shaped by the particularities of Andalusian and Spanish history and society. Nevertheless, the skeptical, communalist, and exclusionary forms of the politics of intimacy are by no means limited to this milieu.

For example, what I refer to here as the skeptical form of the politics of cultural intimacy is clearly demonstrated in Cris Shore's *Building Europe* (2000), an ethnographic account of the European Commission in Brussels. Indeed, despite the fact that this key bureaucratic organ of the European Union (EU) has an official ideology based on meritocratic values and the standards of "legalistic rationalism," Shore (2000:173) argues that its "debates about nationalism, supranationalism, and the 'European interest' are played out against a background of political patronage and personal networking, self-interest and elite-formation." As a result, the EU hallways in Brussels are full of gossip and rumors of cronyism and corruption, and negative stereotypes of national identities flourish as a powerful counterpoint to the official rhetorics of cosmopolitanism. Thus, to the avowed, if perhaps somewhat hypocritical, dismay of (mostly northern) EU functionaries, it is widely believed that the smooth operation of the European administration is continually being disturbed by officials from (mostly southern) regions where "giving jobs and awarding contracts to family and friends is not perceived as morally wrong or untoward" (Shore 2000:213). Evidence of the resentments, rivalries, and machinations generated by this politics of intimacy erupted into public view when charges of scandal led to the mass resignation of the whole governing council of the European Commission in 1999 (Shore 2000:200–201).

Similarly, the almost daily press coverage of ethnic and regional disputes, concerns about immigration, and the like remind us that the communalist and exclusionary forms of the politics of intimacy also flourish in contemporary Europe. But what are we to make of the widespread occurrence of the politics of intimacy in its various forms?

Those scholars who embrace theories of practice that place primary emphasis on how culturally mediated interests shape the talk and behavior of social actors will be inclined to attribute the widespread occurrence to interrelated and comparable situational pressures and constraints. From this perspective, the similar dynamics of the contemporary politics of intimacy in Seville, Brussels, and elsewhere in Europe can itself be primarily viewed as evidence of the force of processes of European integration and the impact of increasingly homogeneous mass media on the lives of individuals from different countries, classes, and social groups. For this reason, everywhere we look we can expect to find complaints about the power and lack of accountability of state and corporate technocrats, concerns about the vitality of local communities, and anxiety about alien invaders of social space. This way of representing the politics of intimacy as a response to bureaucratization, massification, globalization, and the like is "antiessentialist" in spirit and is compatible with what Hans-Rudolf Wicker has called the "magic terms" of contemporary social analysis: "reflexivity, fluidity, negotiability, situativity, transitivity, hybridity, and process" (Wicker 1997:4). And, as Wicker also argues, this practice-oriented theoretical approach serves at least to some extent to legitimate the contemporary workings of advanced capitalism and global political reorganization by taking as its fundamental assumption or root metaphor that flux, radical transformation, continual change, and the fragility of all identities are the essence of social reality. However, this seems a rather peculiar point at which to conclude a discussion of the politics of cultural intimacy, because the poetics of intimacy (whatever else it may be about) clearly does not place a high value on undermining the stability of informal, everyday sorts of social knowledge. Recognizing that the dynamics of the practical politics of cultural intimacy in contemporary Europe often takes the form of compensatory, counterhegemonic reactions to the dislocations and further concentration of power and authority that are a crucial aspect of processes of macroregional and global integration no doubt explains a great deal. But it should not obscure the persistence of some important historical continuities and structural regularities.

Indeed, the contemporary politics of cultural intimacy reveals the continuing presence of once dominant and now displaced, fragmented, transformed, and subordinated cultures of organic personalism that have given a distinctive form to European societies for centuries. Moreover, the dilemmas arising from the intersection of the politics of intimacy and the projects of cosmopolitan liberalism in Seville, Brussels, and elsewhere suggest that the tensions between two fundamental ways of constituting the self and society—one based on organic personalism and the other based on universalistic individualism—have not ceased to influence contemporary social and political life in the new Europe.

From this perspective, both the reaffirmation of communalist values (including hospitality, friendliness, generosity, openness, and a spontaneous passion for life) and the worries about favoritism, secrecy, cunning, envy, and alien outsiders on the occasion of the Expo are testimony to the continuing force of a personalist worldview that places primary emphasis on extensive and deep knowledge of the motivations and desires of the self and others. Both the positive and the negative dimensions of the contemporary politics of intimacy ultimately derive from traditional cultural formations whose three pillars were orthodox (primarily Catholic) religion, secular ideologies of honor, and spiritual and worldly patronage that corporate bodies and persons of superior virtue and authority were obliged to offer others in accordance with their just desserts. Grounded in notions of spiritual hierarchy and organic unity, the ethos of personalism involved a concentric extensionalist cultural logic whose moral and political burden was to incorporate as wide as possible a circle of others into intimate communities of truth and virtue. The most important metaphoric representations of this way of viewing the world were familistic and tended to revolve around hierarchical or egalitarian representations of the obligations of parents to children and of siblings to one another.[2] It is therefore no mere coincidence that tales of bad patrons, cunning officials, rebellious communities, and exclusionary political strategies abound as much in descriptions and perceptions of the Expo as they do in the Spanish literature of every era, from *El poema del Cid* to *Fuenteovejuna* and beyond.

Nevertheless, according to standard liberal accounts of the history of European modernity, this traditional personalist and corporatist hegemonic formation has been or is being almost wholly superseded by a more or less enlightened egalitarian individualism with its emphasis on basic freedoms and rights, consumerism, the salutary pursuit of self-interest, contractual law, civic voluntarism, and characteristic state and capitalist institutional forms. In this context, cosmopolitan liberalism represents the newest stage in the evolution of modern forms. Just as the defeated Socialist candidate for the mayoralty of Seville in 1991 attempted to relegate his opponents to the dustbin of history by accusing them of appealing to "local atavisms and family demons," modernists tend to regard personalist themes and values as residual legacies that should and soon will be overcome. Yet this view is misleading, because it fails to recognize the historical force of the continual tensions, contradictions, accommodations, and syncretic graftings and regraftings of personalist and individualist forms of representation and practice that still exist in European societies.

Just spending a few attentive hours in almost any European bar or café will confirm that modern individualism is not the only (or necessarily the most popular) tune playing on the cultural jukebox. Although the personalist aspects of cultural intimacy are probably most deeply grounded in the informal, face-to-face relations of family and social life, they also have a larger (if often somewhat obscured and overlooked) public and official presence. Even if we leave aside the continuing influence of traditional institutions, such as the Catholic Church, and limit our consideration to the realm of politics and ideology, it is not difficult to discern the influence of personalist values and appeals on a variety of forms of cultural intimacy. The distinctive political rhetorics of both of the primary transnational ideological blocks of the EU, for example, are redolent with appeals to personalist values of intimacy as well as to the values of modern individualism: Socialists and Social Democrats extol the values of fraternal solidarity and attack privilege, while Christian Democrats and their allies of the center-right continue to maintain some allegiance to neocorporatist models of cooperation and integration that are intended to mitigate class and other tensions. In this way, displaced and transformed versions of organic personalism act as ideological brakes on neoliberal free-market fundamentalism and have thus far helped to preserve the basic structures of the postwar West European welfare state. Moreover, as Michael Herzfeld (1997) has convincingly argued, most contemporary and highly domesticated forms of nationalism appeal to notions of cultural intimacy through their invocations of the nation as a family and their discussions of the European "family of nations."

It is in the double character of the nation-state itself that the grafting of notions of organic personalism and corporatism with egalitarian individualism and instrumental rationalities is most obvious. Even so, one increasingly prominent aspect of the transnational project of making a new Europe and strengthening the sense of a new transnational European identity involves distinguishing European culture from other traditions. In this effort, the United States is often identified as suffering from the effects of excessive competitive individualism, while the Islamic world is represented in terms of excessive communalist traditionalism. This kind of representation places Europe in a mediating position characterized by a balance between intimacy and freedom, common values and pluralism, tradition and modernity.

Paying more attention to the ways in which the personalist dynamics of cultural intimacy interact with the ideologies of modern individualism may help dispel the illusion that the increasing power of technocracy within the EU, along with the so-called democratic deficit that attends it, will herald the end of politics. If we better understand what is at stake in each of the varieties of proliferating liberalism that have emerged since the revolutions of 1989, we may gain a better sense of what forces have the potential for generating new social movements and issues, and we may also gain a better sense of the limits of entrenched institutional power. As the Expo showed, even the expenditure of massive resources to promote the projects of cosmopolitan liberalism may have limited efficacy and produce quite unexpected counterhegemonic political effects. But the task of paying greater heed to the politics of cultural intimacy ought to extend far beyond the realm of mass-media events and orchestrated spectacles. In this respect, it is important to recall that in April 1992, while the Expo opened with a massive celebration of the global influence of European culture and the advent of a Europe without borders, the Bosnian war also erupted. And in 1992, while a Spaniard's claim to be *"medio moro"* could be interpreted as a source of either pride or mild embarrassment, a Bosnian's claim of mixed identity might make him or her a target of ethnic cleansing. Thus, as a guideline for future work, it seems reasonable to suggest that when we have a theoretical approach to European political culture that can offer compelling accounts of events that range from mass-media spectacles to acts of genocide and can help us comprehend how such events are historically, processually, and structurally interrelated, then we will really have made some progress.

Notes

1. All English translations of Spanish sources are my own. In the text, parenthetical references to Spanish newspapers—for example (*DD* 23 Aug 1992:12)—indicate the source, day, month, year, and page number of the material cited. The following abbreviations are used: *ABC* = *ABC*, Seville edition; *DD* = *Diario 16*, Seville edition; *DD-ex* = *Diario 16*, Seville edition, special section on Expo '92; *EC* = *El Correo*; *EC-ex* = *El Correo*, special edition on Expo '92; *EP* = *El País*, Andalusian edition; and *EPI* = *El País*, international edition.

2. The anthropological literature on religion, honor, and patronage in the traditional cultures of Europe and especially in the Mediterranean region is vast. For an extended discussion of the particular approach taken here, see Maddox 1993.

References Cited

Castells, Manuel. 1998. *End of Millennium*. Vol. 3 of *The Information Age*. Oxford: Blackwell.

Certeau, Michel de. 1984. *The Practice of Everyday Life*. Translated by Steven Rendall. Berkeley: University of California Press.

Debord, Guy. 1977. *Society of the Spectacle*. Detroit: Black and Red.

Fernandez, James. 1986. *Persuasions and Performances: The Play of Tropes in Culture*. Bloomington: Indiana University Press.

Hannerz, Ulf. 1990. "Cosmopolitans and Locals in World Culture." Pp. 237–52 in *Global Culture*, ed. Mike Featherstone. London: Sage Publications.

Herzfeld, Michael. 1997. *Cultural Intimacy: Social Poetics and the Nation State*. New York: Routledge.

Maddox, Richard. 1993. *El Castillo: The Politics of Tradition in an Andalusian Town*. Champaign: University of Illinois Press.

Office of the Commissioner General. 1987. *Outline of Contents: Sevilla 1992 Universal Exposition.* Seville: Oficina del Comisario General de España para la Exposición Universal de Sevilla 1992.

Rose, Nikolas. 1996. "Governing Advanced Liberal Democracies." Pp. 37–64 in *Foucault and Political Reason,* eds. Andrew Barry, Thomas Osborne, and Nikolas Rose. Chicago: University of Chicago Press.

Shore, Cris. 2000. *Building Europe: The Cultural Politics of European Integration.* New York: Routledge.

Toulmin, Stephen. 1992. *Cosmopolis: The Hidden Agenda of Modernity.* Chicago: University of Chicago Press.

Wicker, Hans-Rudolf. 1997. "Introduction: Theorizing Ethnicity and Nationalism." Pp. 1–41 in *Rethinking Ethnicity and Nationalism: The Struggle for Meaning and Order in Europe,* ed. Hans-Rudolf Wicker. Oxford: Berg.

Wilk, Richard. 1995. "Learning to Be Local in Belize: Global Systems of Common Difference." Pp. 110–33 in *Worlds Apart: Modernity through the Prism of the Local,* ed. Daniel Miller. New York: Routledge.

PART THREE

Sex, Food, and Spirits

CHAPTER 6

Sexual Secrets

CANDOMBLÉ, BRAZIL, AND THE MULTIPLE
INTIMACIES OF THE AFRICAN DIASPORA

J. Lorand Matory

THROUGHOUT THE late nineteenth and twentieth centuries, scholars and thinkers confronting the challenge of how the Others of the Atlantic nation-state should be included have looked to Candomblé for answers. Since Brazilian Raymundo Nina Rodrigues's studies of this religion (1905/1988, 1905/1945, 1896/1900/1935) inaugurated Afro-Brazilian studies as we know it today, Candomblé has been celebrated not only as a uniquely pure manifestation of African culture in the white-dominated Americas but also as an exemplary case of women's power in a male-dominated world. Amid this adulation stands the apparent irony that some very famous priests have been men and, for many international opinion makers, the scandal that many of them appear to have been "passive homosexuals."

As George Mosse (1985) has pointed out, conformity to certain norms of sexual conduct has long been a key symbol of membership in the European nation-state and acceptance of its broader social expectations.[1] Moreover, homosexuals, Jews, and Gypsies have figured as overlapping and analogous counterimages of such membership and conformity. Sexuality is a particularly rich area in which to discuss the dynamics of imagined communities, for several reasons. First, it is a site of fantasy, daily performance, and dissimulation. While people might appear to be conforming to the norms of one imagined community, their visible actions, as well as their private symbolisms and narratives, might simultaneously embody alternative imaginations of self and community. Second, people's judgments about whom they can divulge these alternatives to are themselves indicative of the forms of hierarchy and community that shape the shared social world. Matters that one

discusses only among insiders and not with members of higher or lower social strata are described by James C. Scott as "hidden transcripts" (1990).

For example, adherents and advocates of Brazilian Candomblé gossip
among themselves about each other's sex lives, but one of my priest friends
in Candomblé has denied the relevance of the matter and urged that it not
be discussed in print.[2] Nigerian Yorùbá people typically do not talk about
sex with people much older or younger than themselves, and, of course, age
is a major idiom of hierarchy in Yorùbáland.[3] One worthy hypothesis is that
West African Yorùbá people's relative silence about sex reveals not its unimportance but its centrality to the social order.[4] The prominence of male homosexuals in Candomblé might generate similar hypotheses. Since the 1930s,
it has been an object of international controversy in which much more than
the priests' sexual conduct is at stake. The respectability of the nation and
the status of women internationally are also in question. As a Brazilian colleague pointed out to me, there might be no more homosexual men in the
Candomblé priesthood than in the Roman Catholic priesthood, the psychiatric profession, or even the general population. I have no way of verify-
ing such claims in a statistically reliable way. Yet numerous nonhomosexual
priests have told me that they or their families struggled against their calling
for fear that, once it became common knowledge that they had been possessed
by Candomblé gods, other people would assume they were homosexual.

In the absence of proof to the contrary, Bahians tend to assume that a male
possession priest is a *bicha* or *adé* (that is, a man who is sexually penetrated).
In fact, many probably are, and many are not. In the allied tradition of
Cuban Santería, or Ocha, most male possession priests I know might be
described as homosexual. They and my priestess friends discuss the matter freely. Moreover, the oft-repeated official prohibition on the entry of
women, homosexuals, and people possessed often by their gods into the
Cuban Ifá divination priesthood entails an implicit recognition that all of
these groups are strongly present—symbolically and demographically—in
the broader Cuban-inspired Ocha tradition. I have not observed anything
describable as homosexuality in the West African Yorùbá possession priesthood, though later in this essay I will detail one striking account thereof reported to me by a highly reliable Yorùbá scholar.

I am the first to publish the argument that indigenously Cuban and Brazilian suppositions about the homosexuality of priests are logically and historically related to the transvestism of their West African counterparts, but
I am not the first to discuss these geographically separate traditions individ-
ually. Nor am I the first author to face stiff opposition to even the most
oblique mention of homosexuality in relation to Candomblé. I feel compelled to speak of this matter both despite and because of the controversy.
On the one hand, the homophobia of nationalists neither needs nor deserves

my silent complicity. On the other, the process by which nationalists and other powerful opinion makers have imposed an official stigma on what appears to be part of a circum-Atlantic cultural tradition deserves explanation in itself. To keep silence on this set of rumors and symbolic continuities is to accept as natural a politically informed choice to regard these continuities as embarrassing. Indeed, there are Cuban and Brazilian priests who find personal affirmation in my analysis, a fact equally worthy of explanation and unworthy of ignoring.

Of course, ritual secrecy undoubtedly defines the boundaries of òrìṣà-worshipping priesthoods, but, like families and other bounded groups, the sacred communities of the black Atlantic keep secrets whose significance to the group is debated. Which leads me to the third reason why sex is a rich site in which to discuss the dynamics of imagined communities. Sex is a classic object of what Herzfeld calls "cultural intimacy"—that is, a sensibility that encourages state elites to propagate official visions of the nation-state that exclude embarrassing aspects of national cultural life, even though these aspects of life are the focus of family feeling within the nation and the very reason for many people's loyalty to the nation-state (Herzfeld 1997: 1–36). Implicit in this model is Herzfeld's concept of "disemia," a term he uses to describe the tension between the state's official (and respectable) representation of the nation and the people's candid recognition of the nation's collective "flaws." According to Herzfeld, this candid recognition enables ordinary people to advance alternative versions of the nation's historical foundations, to legitimize alternative claims on or against the state, and to feel the affection for the nation that is crucial to the nation-state's survival.

What I would add to this picture is an emphasis on the *multipleness* of the communities that can be constructed around similar collective "flaws." Among these communities are religions, sects, regions, nations, transnational communities and movements, and supranational civilizations, such as "Europe," "Latin America," and "the African diaspora." That is, the nation-state is subdivided, cross cut, and encompassed by other imagined communities that are structured by numerous disemias of their own. Moreover, I will argue that the nation-state does not imagine itself, or its "flaws," independently of the subnational, supranational, and transnational communities that coexist with it. Overlapping imagined communities are often constituted by diverse interpretations of overlapping secrets, or "flaws," and elaborate defenses against their telling. Often, the flaws of one imagined community are the virtues of another, and intercommunity debates over whether a specific phenomenon is a flaw or a virtue are regularly a source of ideological and organizational change.

The Brazilian white elite, for instance, long felt embarrassed under the gaze of North America and northwestern Europe, particularly since Frenchman Arthur de Gobineau and other racists diagnosed Brazil's generally dark racial makeup as a permanent obstacle to its national progress. By segregating its diplomatic corps and navy, the Brazilian state consequently endeavored to hide the nation's true complexion from the world. Yet prosperous, literate, and Anglophone Afro-Brazilians who traveled back and forth to West Africa from the late nineteenth to the mid-twentieth century brought to Northeastern Brazil the idea that the Yorùbá were superior to other Africans. Because Northeastern white and mulatto elites could reason that this fact made their region (which had received a disproportionate number of proto-Yorùbá and proto-Jeje captives)[5] superior to the economically dominant Southeast (which had received a disproportionate number of non-Yorùbá Central Africans), Northeastern scholars like Edison Carneiro took up the cause of a Yorùbá-centered discourse of African dignity. Once an affirmation of Northeastern regional worth, Carneiro's Yorùbáphilia has gradually become an important feature of Brazilian cultural nationalism and of its projection abroad. Thus, the disemic tension between the official protection of national secrets and the celebratory popular revelation thereof is embedded in bigger, messier debates, with the result that, in Brazil, the early-twentieth-century state's official concealment of its large black population has given way to a Northeastern-inspired public emphasis on the superiority of certain kinds of African roots.

In this essay, I will illustrate the *diversity* of the imagined communities that have struggled over the meaning of Brazil's national "flaws," showing how a dialogue of overlapping disemias has reshaped Brazilian national consciousness and popular conceptions of Candomblé leadership as well. Specifically, I will document a series of controversies related to sexual secrets, showing how these secrets constitute a wide array of communities that share (and frequently transcend) the geography of Northeastern Brazil.

Cultural Intimacy and the Transnational Feminism of Ruth Landes

This saga of sexuality and secrets begins with Ruth Landes's *City of Women* (1947) and the consequences of its revelation and reinterpretation of Brazilian national secrets. Landes's research was initially embarrassing to Euro-Brazilian nationalists for two reasons. First, in a country ambivalent about its racial and cultural blackness, she studied Candomblé. However, as a Boasian, she studied it not as a racial flaw to be hidden but as proof of the richness of a transnational African legacy and, more important, of the potential for women's equality in her own country, the United States. The final two paragraphs of the book summarize how Landes saw her relationship to the guardians of Brazilian cultural intimacy.

When I left Rio for the United States, Brazilian friends escorted me to the boat, and one of them said, half teasing but with a certain defiant patriotism, "Now you can tell them that no tigers walk in our streets."

I nodded, and added: "I'll tell them also about the women. . . . Will Americans believe that there is a country where women like men, feel secure and at ease with them, and do not fear them?"(1947:248).

In her study of Candomblé in Brazil, a country she knew to be highly sexist, Landes avowed she had found evidence of a "cult matriarchy." In the Brazilian state of Bahia, she reported that women ruled the religious affairs, and therefore the most *important* affairs, of the black people. In her search for a primordial alternative to the lamentable condition of her home audience and herself, she had discovered Bahia, of which she declared, "I know by now that women are the chosen sex [in Bahia]. . . . I take it for granted just as I know in our world that men are the chosen sex" (1947:202). Like Margaret Mead, as some would argue, Landes slighted or distorted a great deal of evidence in her analysis (Freeman 1983; Healey 1998/2000:93). For example, to account for the significant number of men leading Candomblé temples during her visit, she claimed they were violating "African tradition" because of their own psychological problems and the ritual laxity of the women, who, according to Landes, had only recently begun to initiate men.

To prove that the statistical majority of male priests in Candomblé was abnormal and a result of recent corruption, Landes violated Brazilian cultural intimacy yet again by reporting the widespread view that male possession priests were *adés*, or, in Landes's medico-pathological parlance, "passive homosexuals." Further, their entry into the priesthood was to be blamed on a new generation of supposedly lackadaisical, untraditional Candomblé priestesses serving the *caboclo* Indian spirits (Landes 1940). Through her choice to call them "passive homosexuals" and in her exposition, Landes argued that male possession priests belonged not to a religious tradition but to a disease category. This revelation was far more embarrassing to the light-colored Brazilian bourgeoisie than was her foregrounding of black culture. Landes's account of gender roles in the Candomblé priesthood is historically incorrect, though it has come to be regarded as factual by most subsequent students of this religion. Just as importantly, her revelation of a "homosexual" presence in that priesthood provoked a series of defensive responses by the scholarly representatives of other imagined communities who regarded that presence as a collective "flaw."

These responses are brightly illuminated by Herzfeld's concept of "cultural intimacy." Moreover, they help to account for a series of changes in the popular conception of Candomblé, for an emergent hierarchy in the distribution of government and private patronage among temples, and for the trajectory of at least two scholarly careers—those of Ruth Landes and Yorùbá sociologist Oyeronkẹ Oyewumi. Landes's discussion of sexual matters particularly discomfited her Brazilian scholarly colleagues, even those who would have been perfectly happy for her to write about the cultural and demographic importance of Afro-Brazilians. These colleagues were clearly more attuned to international standards of national respectability and more concerned about guarding the cultural intimacy of Brazil than were the priests and subjects of the trans-Atlantic sacred nations. A variant on such cultural intimacy seems to motivate Yorùbá nationalists' response to my own published argument about the gender symbolism of the Brazilian, Cuban, and Nigerian òrìṣà priesthoods. The twist in this case is that the argument of my major Yorùbá nationalist critic, Oyeronkẹ Oyewumi, rests on the assertion that "authentic" Yorùbá culture is superior due to its alleged lack of the flaws she attributes to the West: homosexuality and gender itself. Homophobia is a common adjunct of nationalism; it is no surprise, then, that it has also become an important tropic operation in a range of communities within and beyond the nation-state. Indeed, it is common ground on which Northeastern regionalists, Brazilian nationalists, Yorùbá nationalists, and transnational feminists can struggle over the meaning of the *adé* priest and the importance of keeping him a secret.[6]

Contrary to Landes's assertion, male leadership in Candomblé is an old phenomenon. Throughout the nineteenth century, men outnumbered women in the Bahian Candomblé priesthood. Indeed, the increase in *female* leadership was the more recent phenomenon (Harding 2000:71–74).[7] Butler believes that a tradition of exclusively female temple leadership began with the foundation of Casa Branca, or the Ilê Iyá Nassô temple, in the mid-nineteenth century, relatively late in the documented history of Candomblé religious activity in Brazil (Butler 1998:193–209). Without making claims about the relative numbers of male and female priests, Butler believes that the ideal of female leadership gained prestige due to the concentrated attention to, and protection of, the Casa Branca temple and its offshoots by scholars and other bourgeois elites (Butler, personal communication, 12/3/02). There is evidence, as Butler suggests, that the idea of an exclusively female temple leadership was promoted by influential scholars in the 1930s and 1940s. However, evidence that this idea existed in Candomblé discourse or practice before the mid-twentieth century is unclear.

In the 1930s, male priests still outnumbered female priests (Corrêa 2000: 245; Carneiro 1948/1986:104). Nonetheless, since the publication of Landes's work (1940, 1947), the scholarly literature has come to speak with one voice on the matter: in the Candomblé priesthood, "women are the chosen sex." Landes herself inaugurated the description of Candomblé as a "cult matriarchate" and a "city of women." She introduced into the Brazilian national debate over the legitimacy of Candomblé the medical-pathologizing logic of "homosexuality," which not only cast male priests as diseased but also alienated them from any legitimate *cultural* tradition (see also Bastide 1961:309; Ribeiro 1969:122). Moreover, the Freudian notion that "homosexuals" are men who identify excessively with the mother figure appeared to bolster Landes's argument that women are the paradigmatic leaders of the religion: men who aspired to become leaders had to imitate them.

As Landes herself reported, however, the apparent "abnormality" of many male priests seems not to have troubled other priests or adherents of Candomblé. As priests, these men were "supported and even adored by those normal men of whom they were before the butt and object of derision" (Landes 1947/1994:37; 1940:393). And, in the late 1930s, Landes noted that Edison Carneiro, who served as her principal guide in Bahia, personally admired the beauty and liveliness of male homosexual priests (Landes 1947/1994:37). However, over the course of their friendship, Landes appears to have changed Carneiro's mind, or at least his public posture toward male priests, in a manner contrary to the convictions of most adherents of Candomblé. His subsequent publications appear to reflect embarrassment over Landes's revelation of Bahia's "intimate" cultural secrets. Despite his private comfort with the *adé* priests, Carneiro's later published work dismisses them, and all male priests, as unrepresentative of Candomblé tradition and describes their numerical predominance as recent. He added to his indictment the vocabulary of the Brazilian state's efforts to regulate the practice of the healing arts, calling the male priests not only "effeminates" but also "charlatans" and "sorcerers" (Carneiro 1948/1986:104–106). Nostalgia for an undocumented time when Candomblé was its true, all-female self had been a linchpin of Landes's argument and would become a *deux ex machina* in Carneiro's as well.

Male priests (and the priestesses who had allegedly admitted them to the priesthood) became scapegoats for everything powerful outsiders might find to condemn in the religion. Like Landes, Carneiro argued that almost all male priests were uninitiated frauds, commercializers, tyrannical leaders, poor administrators, and practitioners of evil magic. They were said to gossip like women and to be sexually confused. Not even the most gymnastic, speculative arguments were barred in the effort to dismiss male priests and thereby guarantee the international respectability of a tradition supposedly made authentic by their absence. While male chief priests were accused of not believing in the "evil" magic they used to exploit their clientele, female chief priests were credited with an innocent, if naïve, belief in the innocuous magic they practiced (Carneiro 1948/1986:103–109). Carneiro also suggested that male priests belonged mostly to the "least respectable" and least "orthodox" nations of Candomblé—that is, to the Angola, Congo, and caboclo nations (as opposed to the "orthodox" Nagô and Jeje). In truth, the personnel and ritual content of these nations had long overlapped. Yet Carneiro, moved by the desire to spare his region embarrassment and to save his priestess friends from persecution, invented a tradition and constructed around it boundaries that legitimized the Nagô and Jeje priestesses by vilifying and delegitimizing the male priests.[8]

Edison Carneiro published *Candomblés da Bahia* in 1948, after Landes's two major publications on the subject (1940 and 1947) had already appeared. He was clearly influenced by Landes, but his own work was marked by a more ambiguous style of exposition. On the one hand, he reproduced the opinion that female leadership is the primordial norm of Afro-Bahian religion, thus affirming the respectability of the *real* tradition (that is, the selected subset of past and present Candomblé practice that *he* deemed respectable within the imagined community of his region and nation). On the other hand, his degree of knowledge did not allow him to ignore a vast body of facts that would suggest the contrary. For example, Carneiro credits the nineteenth-century African-born priest Bambuxê (Baṁgboṣe) with initiating Aninha, the future chief priestess of the Opô Afonjá temple. Carneiro also documents the esteemed leadership of the Yorùbá/Nagô babaláwo diviners Martiniano do Bonfim and Felisberto Sowzer, and he mentions numerous eminent male leaders of Jeje and Nagô temples who were alive during his time. Nonetheless, for all the contrary evidence that he himself recorded, Carneiro's synoptic statements about the "tradition" seem designed to satisfy the same partisan notions of respectability Landes invoked. Carneiro wrote:

> Of the 67 temples registered in the Union, 37 were directed by priests and 30 by priestesses. It seems, however, that there were not always priests and priestesses and that, in the past, Candomblé was, distinctly, the domain of women. . . . Only the Congo temples can be seen as an exception. . . . In contrast to the inner strength that emanates naturally from the Nagô and Jeje priestesses, the male priests of the Angola nation, of the Congo nation or the *caboclos* are almost all improvised, self-made, "learning one song here and another song there," as the Nagô and Jeje leaders say (1948/1986:84–86).

A comparison of Carneiro's informal remarks to Landes in 1938–39 with those in his own publication of 1948 suggests that he had not thought of Candomblé's "passives" as much of a secret before 1938. They became a secret only in the wake of published accounts by Ruth Landes, whose revelations triggered a vicious response from Arthur Ramos, a famous Brazilian physician, nationalist, folklorist, sometime state functionary, academic gatekeeper, and culture broker extraordinaire. Faced with a powerful international gaze, Ramos flatly denied Landes's claims about a "cult matriarchate" and a significant homosexual presence in Candomblé. Moreover, he worked hard to foreclose future professional opportunities to Landes after she returned to the United States, enlisting North American anthropologist Melville J. Herskovits in the project of defaming her (Corrêa 2000:242–46).

A close observer of Bahia and a close friend of Landes, Carneiro could not deny the newly embarrassing reality, but he was in a position to marginalize it authoritatively. As he wrote *Candomblés da Bahia* (1948/1986) for publication by the State Museum of Bahia under the collective scrutiny of Arthur Ramos, Ruth Landes, the nationalists, and the international community, Carneiro clearly labored under a kind of self-censorship. His written account deferred self-consciously to nationalist and international notions of respectability. *Candomblés da Bahia*, it seems, was created *para inglês ver*, "for the English to see," a Brazilian expression redolent with the real history of Bahia, in which dissimulation has long been a characteristic response to the foreign gaze (see Fry 1982).

The Penalties of Revelation and the Transformation of Communities

Multilateral debates over which secrets to keep, who can speak them, and in what company, have far-reaching social and material consequences. Indeed, these debates are crucial in shaping scholarly careers and human communities alike. Landes's career, for example, was made and unmade by her revelations. *The City of Women* would eventually bring her fame, but she was unable to hold a job befitting her qualifications after the book's publication. Landes blamed Ramos's anger over her revelation of "homosexuality" for much of her professional undoing (Corrêa 2000:246−48).[9] For three decades after obtaining her Ph.D., Landes was unable to secure a regular academic position (Healey 1998/2000:88).

The controversy Landes provoked seems also to have transformed the material wealth and prestige of Bahia's Candomblé temples, as well as the standards of priestly qualification within each of them, since the mid-twentieth century. The sense, common among Bahia's light-colored elites, that the alleged homosexual presence would diminish their esteem in the eyes of richer regions of Brazil and more "advanced" nations has certainly been one of the motives behind Brazilian scholars' disproportionate attention to—and, later, the Brazilian government's disproportionate financial support and moral endorsement of—female-headed Candomblé temples. Once an embarrassment to the bourgeois nation-state, the Candomblé priestess eventually attained pride of place in Northeastern regionalism and its close ally, Brazilian nationalism. She certainly benefited from her superficial likeness to the Black Mammy (or *Mãe Preta*) who had become an object of nostalgic adulation in Gilberto Freyre's influential narrative of *mestiço* nationalism, *Casa-Grande e Senzala* (*The Masters and the Slaves*, 1933/1986). The Candomblé priestess is represented in numerous journalistic accounts as gentle and generous to her white children, but also stern enough to control her black children (see also Silverstein 1979). These are the terms of her incorporation into the nationalist narrative, and they appear to be an equally significant reason why, since the 1960s, the city government of Salvador, the Bahian state, the Brazilian federal state, businesses, and national media outlets have lent disproportionate moral support and funding to the female-headed temples. This is not to say that more than a few temples have benefited. It is also worth emphasizing that most Afro-Brazilian women have not benefited at all from their inclusion in the Freyrean narration of regional and national history. In 1980, for example, the average white woman earned 69 percent of the average white man's salary. In turn, the average black man (*preto*) earned only 63 percent, the average black woman (*preta*) only 38 percent, and the average mulatto woman (*parda*) earned only 36 percent of the average white man's earnings. Any casual visitor to Brazil notes immediately that black and mulatto women are egregiously overrepresented among domestic servants, accounting for over 80 percent of that employment category in a society only 45 percent black or mulatto (Agentes de Pastoral Negros 1990: 26, based on the 1980 Brazilian Census [IBGE]; Heringer et al. 1989:11). Despite omnipresent public affirmations that Brazil is not racist, 60 percent of black and mulatto men avow on surveys that whites are racist; black and mulatto women are even *more* likely (69 percent) to say so, indicating a widespread dissatisfaction with their social experience and offering little evidence to support Landes's view of gender equality in black Brazil or her sense of a general white male preference for Afro-Brazilian *women* over Afro-Brazilian men (Singer 1995:70; Landes 1953).

In short, my argument is not intended to diminish the important role women have played in the founding and edification of Brazilian Candomblé since the nineteenth century. Rather, it is to reconsider the chronology and conditions of a female triumph that is both recent in genesis and unique in the Yorùbá-Atlantic world. Priestesses have always been important leaders in Candomblé, as in its West African antecedents and its contemporary West African Yorùbá counterparts. To understand the preeminence they enjoy in Candomblé today, however, one must attend not to a substrate of ancient matriarchal traditions, but to a set of fairly recent cultural interventions that, from the 1930s onward, have enabled a few priestesses to acquire a mighty set of advocates in the overlapping communities of Brazilian nationalism and transnational feminism.

How the Priestesses Use Their Opportunity

Women, in their capacity as wives and mothers, have long occupied a paradigmatic role in the symbolism of the possession priesthoods of the Bight of Benin. No doubt they did so in nineteenth-century Bahia as well. However, men in both West Africa and Brazil have, for just as long, convincingly appropriated that symbolism in constructing their own priestly authority, and the nineteenth-century evidence suggests that men have always outnumbered women as the chief priests of Bahian Candomblé. The regionalist, nationalist, and transnational feminist sensibilities that converged in Bahia in the 1930s, however, provided significant new symbolic grounds for the authority of the priestesses—grounds that, with equal novelty, delegitimized male priestly authority. Thus, if female chief priests had not always been preeminent in Candomblé, they certainly came to be so in the wake of Landes's intervention and the gradual embrace of Candomblé within the cultural intimacy of the Brazilian nation-state. Since then, women priests have been far more successful than males at making alliances with light-skinned, prosperous, Western-educated men, many of whom classify themselves as white. Women have somehow managed to attract more touristic, journalistic, and ethnographic attention to their houses as well, even in a society as thoroughly patriarchal as Brazil.

For journalists who know nothing about the ritual protocols that insiders regard as the main key to priestly success, another criterion of success, one more accessible to outsiders, has become the focus of commentary: namely, the priestess' talent for cultivating "friends on all social levels" (*amigos em todas as camadas sociais*). Successful priestesses publicly broadcast their interest in fostering extensive, class-crossing friendship networks. Whatever their personalities, ritual competency, or grievances, dark-black and middle-aged-to-elderly women in Bahian society can wittingly or unwittingly take advantage of a well-established cultural image in Brazil, one that is especially useful in attracting those seeking the literal or metaphorical "snuggly embrace" of the black matriarch.

Since the 1990s, this phenomenon has found its greatest exemplar in *Mãe* Stella, who, like a series of Yorùbá/Nagô priestesses since *Mãe* Aninha—particularly *Mães* Senhora, Olga, and Menininha—has ridden the momentum of her illustrious predecessors and, by the force of her own character, has augmented it. *Mãe* Stella was the first priestess offered the opportunity to explain, in the national press, women's preeminence in her religion. Though *Mãe* Stella belittles none of the men whose initiation, knowledge, and "spiritual disposition" qualify them for the priesthood, she, too, joins Landes in characterizing Candomblé as a "matriarchate," for which she offers the following historical and psychological reasons. First, Candomblé was "brought [to Brazil] by three ladies, *Iyás* Deta, Kala and Nassô, three people from the kingdom of Xângo, who had the courage, even with all the repression, to do their Candomblé." Second, the priestly title "Iyá Nassô" ("Mother Nàsó" in Brazilian Nagô) alludes to the fact that a woman is the palace chief and head of the Ṣàngó priesthood in the Ọ̀yọ́ kingdom (see Johnson 1897/1921:63–4; Babayẹmi 1979:16). Third, since female domestic slaves had free time and both the competency and the option to cook, they were also uniquely able "to continue practicing their original religion." Indeed, something in the experience of enslaved and freed Afro-Brazilians encouraged an extraordinary *elaboration* in the votary cuisine of the gods. Finally, explains Mãe Stella, "I think that a woman always has a special little maternal way of taking care of things. Men too take care, but it is not the same thing." Thus, she reflects on what draws a following to any given priest: "That doesn't mean that the man lacks the capacity to be a priest [*babalorixá*]; it's that the woman is the mother figure, and when people come into a Candomblé temple, they are looking for more of that snuggly embrace [*aconchego*]. Women have the capacity to offer more tenderness. It's just that." [10]

Stella appropriately highlights the importance of the "mother figure," or the psychological *image* of the mother, since the representational tropes attractive to bourgeois noninitiates are often at odds with the personalities and ritual roles of actual priestesses. For example, many of the chief priestesses of Candomblé are not snuggly or affectionate at all, and more than a few are childless by choice. For someone not in search of a conventional "mother" figure, the description of their manner that first comes to mind is "executive." Moreover, while plenty of male and female initiates *can* cook very well, Candomblé-related "domestic services," as Carneiro describes them, are preferentially assigned not to just any woman but to women consecrated to female gods (Leão Teixeira 1987 : 44 – 45; Azevedo Santos 1993 : 52 – 54). In other words, many women are disqualified in principle, and many men are qualified in practice. Such gendered subtleties have been of little interest, however, in the politically purposive analyses of Landes, or the journalists and scholars who have found *City of Women* congenial to the self-image of the *mestiço* nation or to the primitivist search for a real-world matriarchy that appeals to some feminists (see Healey 1998 /2000 on Landes's "primitivism").

Even Herskovits's assessment seems more indebted to the gender tropes of the bourgeois nation-state than to his ethnohistorical knowledge of the African diaspora. He argues that women predominate among Candomblé initiates because their time and earnings are more dispensable to the consanguineal family than are men's. However, this argument is surely more a mid-century white bourgeois projection than a reality of most Afro-Brazilian women's lives. The production of counterfactual images of blacks and Indians in journalism, folklore, and anthropology has been a central element in white creole representations of national community in the New World. And such images—like that of the *Mãe Preta*, or "Black Mammy"—can become the prisons—or the tools of the real people so represented.

Priestesses, Too, Question the "Matriarchate"

Notwithstanding the harmony of black female religious authority with white sentimentality about the Black Mammy and with transnational feminist imagery of "cult matriarchy," leading priestesses' own talk about gender and authority belies—and at times consciously negates—the simplistic characterization of the Candomblé as "matriarchal." For instance, *Mãe* Stella and the mothers of the great "traditional" temples *do* tend to avow publicly that women possess a special acumen for priestly duties. The gender of the sacred agency defining their authority, however, often explicitly contrasts with the priestesses' personal sexual identity. In response to one of the numerous journalists seeking an explanation for the "cult matriarchate," the chief priestess of Bahia's adamantly "African" Opô Afonjá temple made it clear that, for her, for her predecessor *Mãe* Senhora, and in the "African tradition" followed by their lineage generally, the consummately *macho* god Xangô has always been the real "boss" (*chefe*).[11] Also recall the words of the late *Mãe* Nicinha of the Jeje Bogum temple: "In our nation," she told a reporter, "the only person who can occupy this post [chief priest] is a woman who has a male saint [i.e., who is consecrated to and possessed by a male god]."[12] As Leão Teixeira (1987) suggests, the very image of divine authority in Candomblé is masculine. In a further example, the sequence in which the gods are saluted during sacred festivals implies an association between maleness and the rank of seniority among the gods. Older or male gods tend to be saluted earlier in the song sequence, or *xirê*, while younger and female gods tend to be saluted later. The unique ritual prerogatives of men and the restrictions placed on menstruating women and on the daughters of goddesses suggest that priestly ritual competency itself is also coded male (Leão Teixeira 1987:43−4, 48).

Even as journalistic and scholarly discourses around Candomblé bubble over in their praise of female priests, it remains the case that Candomblé ritual *marginalizes* females far more than West African *òrìṣà*-worship does. In Yorùbá *òrìṣà*-worship, women priests *are* prohibited from performing certain types of sacrifice, but, as entities who "mount" and are literally addressed as the "husbands" (*ọkọ*) of their worshippers, *goddesses* possess no less authority, competency, or seniority than male gods (Matory 1994). Likewise, in Yorùbá family life, a woman's long-term male sexual partner and all of his kin, male or female, are called her "husbands" (*ọkọ*), and, to all of them, she is a "wife" (*ìyàwó*). In Yorùbáland, femaleness does not diminish the husbandly authority of a goddess, any more than it diminishes that of a female "husband." Nor, in Yorùbáland, does maleness exclude a man from becoming a *wife* to the gods. What Landes read as the criterion of "femininity" in the service of the Nagô gods (1940:386, 393) seems closely connected to the West African Yorùbá criterion of "wifeliness," which is not restricted to any particular biological sex. Thus, there are some differences between the gender concepts of Candomblé and those of the West African Yorùbá religion. What they have in common, however, is just as significant. They both elude de-

scription as "matriarchal," and neither offers much evidence for homophobic readings of African tradition.

If the black priestesses of Bahia have been transformed from national
"flaws" into evidence of national ideals, and certain priestesses enjoy ample
opportunity to assert themselves in the public sphere, this empowerment can
be understood only in relation to the status of male chief priests, who have
become a dirty secret and are now thrust into the shadows and subject to
new forms of silencing. As the reader will see, the gendered logic specific to
Candomblé and the forms of male privilege that structure Brazilian society
as a whole nonetheless give male priests a leadership advantage in all but the
most highly institutionalized, state-supported, and media-endorsed temples.
Thus, the scholarly literatures of Brazilian nationalism and transnational feminism that employ Candomblé as allegory have a skeleton locked in their
shared closet: the fact that most Bahians think male Candomblé possession
priests, including the heads of temples, are typically *adés*, or as Landes put it,
"passive homosexuals." And, far from considering them abnormal, most
Bahians have long thought that *adés* are normal in this role. Indeed, the idea
of a straight man being possessed or initiated is strange to them.

Mounted Men: The Overlooked West African Precedents of the Adé Priest [13]

Years ago, I publicly proposed an explanation for this locally perceived nor-
mality of "passive homosexuals," or *adés*, as possession priests and therefore
as the heads of temples. The debate it engendered demonstrates that the African diaspora is constituted by secrets and can be reconstituted through
reselections and reinterpretations of secrets that need to be defended. This
debate illustrates rather clearly how diasporas are related to other imagined
communities—to regions, nations, religions, and transnational feminism—
by the manner in which they are connected "intimately" to the same
secrets.

There are no reliable statistics on how many Candomblé priests engage
in passive homosexuality. Nor does my thesis concern their actual numbers.
Rather, I wish to understand why so many members and cognoscenti of
Candomblé assume—with or without statistical accuracy—that male initiates in the possession priesthood are normally *adés* and why many Afro-
Brazilian men who love men feel at home in Candomblé. Today there are
numerous explanations for *adés'* alleged prominence among Candomblé possession priests. Before we can understand them, however, we must identify the set of symbolic contrasts of which the "passive homosexual" in Brazil is part.

English-speaking North Americans tend to distinguish sharply between men who engage in sex with other men ("homosexuals") and those who do not ("heterosexuals"). By contrast, Brazilians are far more likely to distinguish men who penetrate others during sexual intercourse (*homens*, or "[real] men") from those who are penetrated (*bichas*, *viados*, or, in Candomblé language, *adés*) (Fry 1986, 1982). Brazilians share this pattern of classification with many circum-Mediterranean peoples, as well as much of premodern Europe, Native America, and most of the rest of the world (Trexler 1995). A contrast between penetrator and penetrated is not the only classification available in Brazil (see Jackson 2000; Kulick 1998; Parker 1998, 1991; Green 1999). However, this particular idiom of sexuality and power is central to most working-class Bahians' vocabulary and negotiation of respect. Even when the Bahians I know use the term *homossexual*, most are referring only to the party in sexual intercourse who is assumed to be habitually penetrated, or "passive." Of course, the real behavior of both homens and *bichas*, or *adés*, is regularly more varied than what is stereotypically attributed to them, and the normative assumption that the "active" party is dominant both in the sexual act and in the nonsexual dimensions of the relationship is often more fantasy than reality (Kulick 1998). However, local *ideological* assumptions and expectations tend to link habitual male "passivity" with transvestism, feminine gestures and occupations, and with the social subordination of the penetrated party.

Why do many Cubans and Brazilians think there is a connection between the possession priesthood and men who love men? Cuban and Puerto Rican adherents of Ocha have told me of the affinity of the goddesses Ochún and Yemayá with *addodis*, or penetrated men.[14] Cuban and Puerto Rican priests also note what they believe to be distinctive levels of prosperity, mobility, and tastefulness enjoyed by such men, qualities that have enabled them disproportionately to spread the Cuban Ocha religion to new locales. Of the Brazilian case, anthropologist Peter Fry suggests that the shared classification of male "passives" and possession cults as "deviant" makes the priesthood an appropriate niche for homosexuals. Following Victor Turner (1969) and Mary Douglas (1966), Fry argues that the *liminal* status of homosexuals in Brazilian national society links them symbolically, in the Brazilian popular imagination, to professions dealing with "magical power" (Fry 1986:138). Various sources do indeed report that male and female homosexuals are generally thought to make superior mediums and that women, who also predominate among temple clients, often prefer male homosexual to male heterosexual priests (Lima 1983:180–82; Leão Teixeira 1987:49–50).

It must be acknowledged that Fry's analysis is far removed from the psychological framework and pathologizing conclusions of Landes and her successors, Bastide (1961:309) and Ribeiro (1969:109–120). Fry's is a symbolic analysis of local images of "magical power" and the role of *inversion* within them. However, in my opinion, the representation of Afro-Brazilian cultural practice as abnormal or inverted is Eurocentric, projecting European readings of the European *Carnaval* onto Afro-Brazilian culture as a whole. Despite the best intentions, this model prioritizes nationalist logics of respectability and normalcy over the distinctly Afro-Brazilian forms of symbolism, logic, hierarchy, and planning that shape these religions. Afro-Brazilian culture ends up looking like a form of "letting loose," a sort of compartmentalized abandon. Indeed, the Europeanist model of Carnaval as social inversion has limited applicability even to the Brazilian Carnaval.

Lima moves in the direction of acknowledging what is *normal* about homosexuality in Candomblé. He argues that both Afro-Brazilian religions and Spiritism have generally shown themselves more *tolerant* than the Roman Catholic Church (1983:167ff). More to the point, Birman shows that Candomblé provides a rationalization for the feminine personalities and homosexual desires of some men. That is, men whose heads are governed by female divinities are expected to share in the female dispositions and desires of the goddesses (Birman 1985; also Leão Teixeira 1987:48; and Landes 1940:395).[15] Thus, according to Candomblé's indigenous personality theory, the homosexuality of male priests is in their "natures" (*naturezas*), is derived from "nature" (*natureza*), and is authorized by the sacred; hence, their attraction to and acceptance in Candomblé.

Fry observes that *bichas*, or "passives," enjoy an advantageous flexibility in the performance of social roles normally reserved primarily for one sex or the other. That is, they can do the cooking and embroidery necessary for the temple, and yet, in Belém do Pará (where Fry conducted his research), they retain the social advantages of men in transactions with the "world of men," of police, judges, doctors, lawyers, and politicians "whose services they themselves may use or broker to clients for their own advantage" (Fry 1986:147–49). In the Bahian case, however, men's advantages over the great Yorùbá/Nagô mothers in this regard are not so evident. What is more evident, and is observed by Leão Teixeira, is that homosexual men bring to Candomblé three other advantages over women: (1) the higher average earnings of men; (2) their license as men to perform all the ritual duties normally *restricted* to men, such as the sacrifice of four-legged animals, the care of the gods Exú (of sex, mischief, and communication) and Ossaim (of herbal medicine) and of the Eguns, or spirits of the dead; and (3) their immunity to the restrictions placed upon menstruating women, who may not, for example, enter the shrine rooms.[16] A woman consecrated to a male god is eligible to receive a further initiation (*mão de faca*) that entitles her to sacrifice birds, but, while menstruating, such an initiated woman cannot even sacrifice birds (Leão Teixeira 1987:44–5; see Azevedo Santos 1993:52–54 on the servile status of women consecrated to female *orixás*).

My main point is that "cult matriarchy" is not a fact that arises logically out of "tradition." Instead, it is a plausible but *interested* and *contested* construction of tradition. Despite the pronounced homophobia of many Third-World bourgeois nationalists (including a number of prominent Anglophone African elites), one would be hard-pressed to locate the precolonial, "traditional" Yorùbá precedents for the homophobia that Landes, Ribeiro, and Bastide have tried to pass off as psychoanalytic proof of the unsuitability of male priests in the Yorùbá-affiliated Candomblé Nagô. The homophobia that abnormalizes the prominence of "passives" in the Candomblé priesthood has its origins not in aboriginal Africa but in the nationalism and transnational feminism of the mid-twentieth century.

I believe that the proliferation of latter-day explanations of the prominence of "passives" in Brazilian Candomblé and Cuban Ocha priesthoods, and the well-documented history of Candomblé adherents' comfort with *adés* in this role, share a common root. It is evident between the lines of informant testimony in Landes's work in the 1930s, and it is clearly implied by the historical work of James H. Sweet (1996), who argues that transvestites, including homosexual transvestites, were once common in West-Central and southern Africa and that some of these homosexual transvestites were important ritual experts. Such ritual experts, he argued, embodied a set of African "core beliefs" that, as a result of the slave trade, appeared among captives from that region in sixteenth- and seventeenth-century Portugal and Brazil as well. Sweet inverts the Third-World nationalist cliché that homosexuality is a "white man's disease" corrupting the purity of the nation and its "traditional" culture, arguing instead that the *lapse* of homosexuality and transvestism among West-Central African male ritual experts in the postcolonial period resulted from Western missionary and colonial influence.

Though inattentive to these West-Central African traditions, Carneiro argued that male priests (whom he assumed were passive homosexuals) were virtually restricted to the West-Central African-identified Angola and Congo nations (1967:265, 1948/1986:104–106). Male priests, he argued, were "exceptions" deviating from the traditions of the West African–identified Jeje and Nagô nations. The sixteenth- and seventeenth-century records analyzed by Sweet leave unexplained the cultural logic by which West-Central Africans (such as the eponyms of the Congo and Angola nations of Bahia) and their descendants believed ritual expertise to be logically connected to transvestism and homosexual transvestism, or the degree to which they believed the connection to be a strong or necessary one. The historical and ethnographic records of the twentieth century have, however, left evidence of a strong connection precisely in the trans-Atlantic nations of the West African Yorùbá/Nagô/Lucumí and the Jeje, or Ewe/Gen/Aja/Fon-speakers. Moreover, at least in the present day, the shared Yorùbá, Ewe/

Gen/Aja/Fon (E.G.A.F.), and Brazilian Candomblé imagery of marriage to the divinity, who then episodically displaces its bride's personality and consciousness, is foreign to West-Central African religions (Wyatt MacGaffey, personal communication, 1996).

Metaphors of horsemanship, blood kinship, birth, seniority, and marriage shape the sartorial and verbal representation of possession and possession priests among the West African Yorùbá and E.G.A.F.-speakers, and there is every indication that such metaphors were prominent among their eighteenth- and nineteenth-century ancestors. With the financial and political backing of the Ọ̀yọ́ Empire, the Ṣàngó priesthood's manipulation of gender and equestrian symbolism in particular became a critical instrument of political legitimization. Since the collapse of the Empire and the dispersion of its subjects to the New World, these metaphors have undergone multiple reinterpretations suited to the new contexts of their invocation, both in West Africa and at the various sites of New World òrìṣà-worship (Matory 1994). A comparison among contemporary West African, Brazilian, Cuban, and Haitian iconography suggests some common, gendered patterns in the representation of spirit possession among these West African–inspired religions, and Bahian testimony recorded in the 1930s suggests what precedents had to be made secret as feminist scholars, Brazilian nationalists, and, lately, Yorùbá nationalists have each in turn invoked communities through the play of cultural intimacy.

Ọ̀yọ́-Yorùbá worshippers employ and mix multiple metaphors to evoke the nature of people's relationships to the gods. Like Brazilian candomblécistas, West African Yorùbá worshippers of the òrìṣà gods might call any devotee of a god the "child" (ọmọ [Yorùbá]; filho [Portuguese]) of that god. In both traditions, motherhood and fatherhood are used as metaphors of leadership in the worship and activation of the gods. For example, a senior male West African Yorùbá priest of Ṣàngó might be addressed as Bàbá Oníṣàngó ("Father Owner-of-Ṣàngó"); a senior priestess would be addressed as Ìyá Oníṣàngó ("Mother Owner-of-Ṣàngó"). In Brazil, the male head of a Candomblé temple is called a pai-de-santo ("father-of-divinity"), while a chief priestess is called a mãe-de-santo ("mother-of-divinity"). Yet the Yorùbá terms that mark the priest's competency to embody the god and act as his or her worldly delegate rely above all on allied metaphors of marriage and sexuality. According to Edison Carneiro, these metaphors were very much alive in the Brazilian Candomblé of the 1930s, and they were present in local understandings of male and female participation in the priesthood. In the speech of many twenty-first-century Brazilian orixá-worshipers, these metaphors are now dead or dying. Yet the death of a metaphor seldom means that it has lost its effect in communicative and stipulative acts; rather, its effect has become naturalized and implicit. In present-day Brazilian Candomblé, metaphors of marriage and sexuality stand powerfully alongside metaphors of parenthood and birth in the often-contested representation and reproduction of the priesthood.

Most Ọ̀yọ́-Yorùbá possession priests in West Africa are women. Male possession priests, on the other hand, cross-dress. But their cross-dressing requires a culture-specific reading. They dress not as "women" but as "wives" or "brides" (*ìyàwó*), a term that otherwise refers only to women married to worldly men. Novices to the priesthood—male or female—are designated metaphorically as *ìyàwó*, meaning "brides" or "wives." Indeed, Ọ̀yọ́-Yorùbá people not only formed a plurality of the African captives taken to Bahia in the nineteenth century but also furnished the founding priests and priestesses of Bahia's most influential temples. The degree to which Bahians understand the cognate term *iaô* to mean "wife" or "bride" has declined since the 1930s, but the implications of its Yorùbá meaning upon the logic of priestly recruitment have echoed into the twenty-first century. The overlapping implications of West African Ewe-Gen-Aja-Fon vocabulary of spirit possession have faded a bit more since the eighteenth-century era, when these captives predominated in the slave trade to Bahia. In that West African cultural zone, too, most possession priests are women, but there are also numerous men. As in Yorùbáland, male and female possession priests in the E.G.A.F.-speaking region are generically called "wives" (*sì*) of their divinities. However, chief priests in the E.G.A.F. region are called "mothers" (*nọ*) of the god, regardless of their sex.

For months after the initiation, male and female Ọ̀yọ́-Yorùbá novices wear women's clothes: *ìró* (wrap skirts), *bùbá* (blouses), and *ọ̀já* (baby-carrying slings); specifically on ceremonial occasions, they also wear *tìróò* (antimony eyeliner), *làálì* (henna for the hands and feet), delicate bracelets, earrings, and so forth. As mature priests, or *ẹlẹ́gùn*, women and men braid their hair, and follow the latest styles in women's coiffures, but, on ceremonial occasions, they *also* continue to don *tiro* eyeliner, henna, and delicate jewelry. Many uninitiated Yorùbá *women* do these things but, as far as I know, male possession priests are the only men who do so. In the Ọ̀yọ́-Yorùbá town where I conducted my principal West African field research, both the stripweaving of cloth and barkeeping are considered female professions. So, almost predictably, the only male strip-weaver and the only male barkeeper in the town are Ṣàngó possession priests.

Yet the most pervasive and dramatic gendered symbol in the representation of the priests' symbolic role in relation to the gods—from initiation onward—is the complex web of metaphors implicit in the verb *gùn*—meaning "to mount" or "to climb." Indeed, the term for "possession priest" (*ẹlẹ́gùn*) means "the mounted one." The term refers to what a *rider does to a horse* (hence, by analogy, possession priests are sometimes called "horses of the gods" [ẹṣin òrìṣà]). The term gùn also refers to what an animal or a brutal man does sexually to his female partner (and possession by Ṣàngó is often spoken of as a brutal act).[17] The term gùn also refers to what a god—especially Ṣàngó—does to his possession priests. And Ṣàngó's is the most influential possession priesthood not only on the Bight of Benin but, to an even greater extent, among the òrìṣà-worshippers of Brazil, Cuba, Trinidad, and the United States. However we translate the verb gùn into English, the term montar in Caribbean Spanish and Brazilian Portuguese, and the Haitian Kweyòl term monte (all cognates of the English verb "to mount"), encode the same three referents: horseback riding, sexual penetration, and spirit possession.

Duly warned by my colleague Wande Abimbọla, I acknowledge that the English gloss "to climb" better captures the fact that many òrìṣà (though not Ṣàngó) are regarded as rising from the ground rather than descending from above. But this gloss fails to encode the equestrian and sexual implications that are implicit in the terms esin ("horse"), ìyàwó ("bride" or "wife"), and gùn. In fact, the main virtue of the gloss "to climb" is precisely that it sublimates the equestrian and sexual implications of the folk terminology that might appear to stigmatize the religion in the eyes of mightier religions and nations. Hence, it is not my aim (nor is it within my competency) to contradict Abimbọla, who is a widely traveled babaláwo diviner, spokesperson of the priesthood at its Ife heartland, and university professor. Rather, it is to illustrate both the historical roots of a range of such reinterpretations of òrìṣà religions and the forms of cultural intimacy that appear to shape them.

Let me illustrate, then, how Afro-Latins—such as the priests and cognoscenti of the Bahian Candomblé—still construed these West African Yorùbá metaphors in the 1930s, at the time of Landes's research in Bahia. These are Carneiro's words, quoted in Ruth Landes's City of Women:

Sometimes they call a priestess the wife of a god, and sometimes she is his horse. The god gives advice and places demands, but often he just mounts and plays.

So you can see why the priestesses develop great influence among the people. They are the pathway to the gods. But no upright man will allow himself to be ridden by a god, unless he does not care about losing his manhood. . . .

Now here's the loophole. Some men do let themselves be ridden, and they become priests with the women; but they are known to be homosexuals. In the temple they put on skirts and mannerisms of the women. . . . Sometimes they are much better-looking than the women (Landes 1947:37, emphasis added).

This parlance is largely consistent with the West African, Ọ̀yọ́-Yorùbá symbolism of spirit possession I observed among Nigerian Ṣàngó priests of both sexes in the 1980s, but for one detail: the prohibition on the participation of "real men" in the Brazilian Candomblé possession priesthood. Sex was not an infrequent topic of conversation among male friends of my age group in Ìgbòho, and the Ṣàngó priests of both sexes in the town were vocal, and ribald in their humor, about the matter. Yet I never became aware of any commonly used vocabulary in Ọ̀yọ́-Yorùbá language to distinguish "upright men" from a category of men who are "homosexual" or somehow like women.[18] I have never heard any West African òrìṣà priest speak of himself or his fellow priests as anything like a "homosexual" or as engaging in same-sex intercourse. I argue simply that the Afro-Brazilians have *reinterpreted* West African metaphors of spirit possession in the light of Brazilian gender categories. For many Brazilians in the 1930s and now, submission to a god's agency has seemed analogous to sexual "passivity." In other words, a physically mountable man seems highly qualified, in a symbolic sense, to be mounted spiritually, and a spiritually mountable man is strongly suspected of sexual mountability, or "passivity." The metaphor-ridden "loophole" by which Carneiro and his priestly friends understood men to have recently entered the Yorùbá/Quêto/Nagô possession priesthood in the 1930s was virtually identical—in both its terms and its emphasis—to the dominant logic of the Ọ̀yọ́-Yorùbá Ṣàngó priesthood that I observed in the 1980s and others had observed in similar terms since as long as that West African priesthood had been studied (Matory 1994:171).[19] Therefore, my argument has long been that the prominence of adés in the Candomblé priesthood is a reinterpretation of the sacred male transvestism of Ọ̀yọ́-Yorùbá priests.

Were it not for the increasingly vocal homophobia of Anglophone African bourgeoisies and the hot-button nature of sex as an object of cultural intimacy among nationalists, my argument would be not only better substantiated but also little more controversial than Herskovits's view that "shouting" in black North American churches is a "reinterpretation" of African spirit possession (Herskovits 1941/1958:211–16). It would be little more controversial than explaining how the ìdòbálẹ̀ and the ìyíkàà salutes in Cuba and Brazil reinterpret similar gestures in West Africa.[20] I have never said or believed that the West African transvestite priests were or are in any sense homosexual (Matory 1994:208, 1991:22, 520–21, 538). While many have embraced the argument as logical and empirically sound, others have found it easy to misinterpret, either as proof that homosexuality is as widespread and natural in Africa as it is in the West (Murray 1998:100; personal communication, 1996) or as a defamation of authentic, "traditional" Yorùbá culture (Oyewumi 1997:117).

At the time of my research in Ìgbòho, I had never heard of a named or symbolically marked category of men who are penetrated *sexually* by other men, but, in sum, I could see that those who are regularly penetrated *spiritually* by the gods have a great deal in common (sartorially, professionally, and symbolically) with the Brazilian *bicha* or *adé* category. Imagine my sur-

prise when I made the acquaintance of a highly respected Yorùbá art historian from Ọ̀yọ́, whose extended family included many Ṣàngó priests in the
town. During his time among oricha-worshippers in the United States, this
scholar also became aware of the importance of men who love men in the
priesthood. Without having read my work, he had concluded that male-
male sexual conduct among New-World priests was a *continuation* rather
than a reinterpretation of West African religious traditions. He told me that,
on two occasions between 1968 and 1973, he witnessed possessed male
Ṣàngó priests anally penetrating unpossessed male priests in an Ọ̀yọ́ shrine.
He does not know, however, if this practice was widespread or whether it
represented a tradition or norm. Nor do I. As yet, I would extend my case
no further based on this unique testimony, which the original observer (with
a sense of cultural intimacy) has shared with me privately but has himself
hesitated to publish.

The Controversy

Dozens of Yorùbá scholars have written with sharpness and clarity about
gender and gender relations in Yorùbá religion and culture generally (for example, R. Abíọdun 1989; Awẹ 1977; Fadipẹ 1939/1970; Okediji and Okediji
1966; Ogundipẹ-Leslie 1985). However, those discussions have acquired
new dimensions and new content as the numbers of Yorùbá scholars in the
diaspora have increased, as have the occasions for their interaction with New
World priests of the Cuban *orichas*, Brazilian orixás, and African American
orishas. In this context, my argument has recently sparked controversy in a
new diasporic community, that of Yorùbá scholars and African American
priestesses of Yorùbá religion in the United States.

   One Yorùbá scholar in the United States, sociologist Oyeronke. Oyewumi, read my argument and then, in print, accused me of describing the
West African possession priests as "drag queens" practicing symbolic if not
actual homosexuality (Oyewumi 1997:117). I regard this summary as a deliberate misrepresentation of my words and of my argument, but what is more
important is (1) the deep feeling of offense it clearly expresses and (2) the author's rhetorical effort to classify "homosexuals" as Other to a new diaspora
nationalism. This caricature of my work was but one link in Oyewumi's argument: that there is no gender in authentic Yorùbá culture. Like Freyre,
Oyewumi attempts to turn the tables on North American and Western European cultural and racial chauvinism. She does so, however, not through
vivid storytelling but through caricatures of the absolute difference between
"the West" and "the Yorùbá conception." In "the West," argues Oyewumi,
everything about a person's social status is determined by his or her visible
biology (in which Oyewumi includes a person's genotype); that is, by a per-

son's race and sex. Oyewumi then defines "gender" as the allegedly "Western" notion that every aspect of an anatomical female's life is determined by her anatomy, that no cross-cutting identity or category of social belonging (such as kinship, age, or marital status) shapes any anatomical female's social role or status, that every anatomical female is always socially inferior to every anatomical male, that an anatomical female may perform no roles that anatomical males also perform, that the gender categories are determined entirely by the referent's visible or chromosomal biology, and (despite her citation of several scholarly works that discuss third genders or relational gender) that the analytic term "gender" always imposes a binary or dichotomy upon its referents (Oyewumi 1997:ix–xxi, 1–17; see also Amadiume 1987 and Matory 1994 and 1991 for nondichotomous treatments of gender relations in southern Nigerian cultures).

On the basis of this unusual definition of "gender" and a somewhat unempirical assessment of "Western" social life, Oyewumi asserts that "gender" prevails in the West, but not in Yorùbá society, where, she asserts, people's anatomical sex "did not privilege them to any social positions and similarly did not jeopardize their access" (ibid.:78). Only one's age relative to other people, and the family to which one belongs, the author continues, determine anything about one's social status and relationships in authentically Yorùbá society. In evidence, the author cites the extensive gender coding of pronouns, names, kinship terms, and occupational terms in English, as well as numerous Yorùbá pronouns, kinship terms, and occupational terms that, in her opinion, do not encode gender—such as *òun* ("s/he"), *ọmọ* ("child"), *ẹ̀gbọ́n* ("senior sibling or cousin"), *ọba* ("monarch"), *Bàbá Ẹléran* ("butcher [lit., "Senior-Male Owner-of-Meat"]), and *Ìyá Aláṣọ* ("clothier [lit., "Senior-Female Owner-of-Cloth"]).

Oyewumi spends much of her argument explaining away or concealing the gender coding that actually does appear in much Yorùbá terminology and social practice. For example, there are clearly words in Yorùbá for "male" (*akọ*), "female" (*abo*), "man" (*ọkùnrin*), and "woman" (*obìnrin*). The terms of address and reference for parents, senior relatives, senior strangers, and people of almost every occupation indicate the referent's gender—as in *Bàbá Ayọ̀* (the teknonymic "Father of Ayọ̀"), *Bàbá Ẹléran* ("butcher"), and *Ìyáa mi* ("Mommy"). Most professions in Yorùbáland have (and have long had) vastly more of one sex than another practicing them, and virtually all social clubs (*ẹgbẹ́*) are segregated according to sex. Certain Yorùbá religious and political titles are strongly gender-marked, despite their infrequent adoption by a person of the other sex, such as *babaláwo* (a type of divination priest [lit., "senior male-who-owns-the-mystery"]), *baálẹ̀* (nonroyal quarter or town chief [lit., "father of the land"]), *ìyálé* (eldest wife of the house [lit., "mother of the house"]), and *baálé* (head of residential compound [lit., "father of the house"]). It should be noted that these last two terms are *etymo-logically* distinguished *only* by the gender of the referent. Yet in real social life the persons described as "fathers of the house" rank far higher in the house than do the people called "mothers of the house." On the other hand, one of the most important chieftaincies of the nineteenth century was that of the Ìyálóde (the Chief of the Market [lit., "Mother-Who-Owns-the-Outside"]), and, as far as I know, this title has never been held by a man. Moreover, the fact that there are a few female *baálẹ̀*, or "village chiefs," near Oyewumi's hometown should not allow us to overlook the male gendering of power that the term implies, especially if Oyewumi intends to be true to her hypothesis that vocabulary reveals the culture-specific ideology underlying statistics of otherwise unclear implications. In this case, contrary to her general argument, Oyewumi chooses to privilege the statistic of the exception over the linguistically implicit ideology of male dominance (1997:41, 49, 75, 77).

This is a society in which men and women have long worn markedly different styles of clothing, a wife is regularly expected to supply her husband with cooked food (and not vice versa), almost all professional cooks (except in European-style establishments) are women, and the social norms of legitimate reproduction differentially affect the experience of anatomical males and females throughout the life cycle, in ways ranging from infant clitoridectomy to earlier marriage for women than for men, bridewealth, polygyny, the unthinkability of polyandry, viri-patrilocal postmarital residence, the levirate, and the normatively different roles of mothers and fathers in childcare. Oyewumi even makes the credible claim that motherhood is the most honored of Yorùbá institutions, but, given her peculiar definition of "gender," she takes this observation to illustrate the absence of gender in Yorùbá society (ibid.:75). The author claims that polygyny is frequently initiated by the existing wife, that male interests are not supreme in polygynous marriages, that married women's sexual dalliances are tacitly accepted, and that husbands have no rights over the wife's labor. These indications of wifely "agency," alongside Oyewumi's argument that polygyny entails male self-discipline and deprivation, are taken to prove that polygyny is "ungendered" (Oyewumi 1997:61–2). Most of Oyewumi's claims are inconsistent with my observations in Ọ̀yọ́ North, Ìbàdàn, and Lagos during the 1980s and 1990s, and with other scholars' observations during the past two centuries. Even if they were true, however, the claim that they prove an absence of gender in Yorùbá culture follows more from Oyewumi's idiosyncratic definition of gender than from a careful assessment of the empirical data on Yorùbá marriage. They also reflect little knowledge of what has been described as gendered in Western marriage and social life.

The levirate is no longer commonly practiced in Yorùbáland, but the archival records of the Customary Courts during the early colonial period demonstrate, contrary to Oyewumi's claim, that it was often practiced without the widow's consent. Court records from the early twentieth century indicate that adultery was often severely punished, and women were sometimes forced, on threat of violence, to remain in marriages that they wished to leave (Matory 1994:28–44). Oyewumi fails to produce any documentation of her claims that Yorùbá marriage does not and did not, throughout its documented history, entail systematically different social experiences for the male and female partners. The statistical and ideological norm that a wife moves to her husband's natal household and enters as a subordinate to every person previously born to or married into that household is a structural disadvantage that affects most women in this society *because* they are women. These facts are not easily dismissed.

Oyewumi focuses great attention upon linguistic evidence because any claim that present-day Yorùbá culture fails to distinguish men from women or that it offers them equal access and privileges to important social options, is manifestly false. Hence, Oyewumi claims that her analysis reconstructs the *real* Yorùbá culture, which preceded colonization and/or the slave trade, a period to which we have hardly any documentary access. The earliest document the author consults is dated 1829, long after the slave trade had begun to affect the Ọ̀yọ́-Yorùbá, and elides all historical periods that preceded the slave trade and colonization into a single "authentic" prototype, which she believes remains evident and alive only in those aspects of present-day Yorùbá parlance that do not mark gender. When evidently old gender-marked aspects of Yorùbá language are addressed at all, they are excused by various means. For example, *bàbá* ("father" or "senior man") and *ìyá* ("mother" or "senior woman") are said to indicate not only sex but *also* adulthood; therefore they are not gendered, argues Oyewumi. Does it follow, then, that the terms "father" and "mother" in English are not gendered? Oyewumi argues that the term for "bride" or "wife" (*ìyàwó*) is ungendered because it refers to both the female brides of worldly husbands and possession priests regardless of sex. Does the fact that the church is called the "bride of Christ" in English then imply that the English term is also ungendered? Moreover, in English, as in Yorùbá, one could recite an endless list of gender-free references to people without ever proving that the language or the culture is gender-free. Could one ever infer from the gender-neutral English terms "parent," "cousin," "sibling," "child," "president," "prime minister," and "governor" that Anglo-Saxon or Western language and culture are in their essence or once were free of gender and gender hierarchy? I think not. But this is the logic of Oyewumi's linguistic argument that Yorùbá culture, in its deep past and in its present essence, is completely without gender. In this argument, there is a measure of both ethnological naivete and intellectual dishonesty.

Indeed, Oyewumi's argument neatly parallels Gilberto Freyre's claim that Brazil is a "racial democracy" (opposite in character to the United States and the rest of the Euro-Atlantic world) and that analyses of race and racism in Brazil result from the imposition of an imperialist North American logic (Freyre 1933/1986). Both Oyewumi's argument and Freyre's dramatically remind us of the cross-cultural variation in the interpretation of human phenotypes (a point that may have been surprising to the Brazilian general public in the 1930s but is hardly news to the scholars who studied gender in the 1990s). However, the work of Oyewumi and Freyre also alerts us to a genre of nationalistic allegory that is common in a transnational world, where scholars and other workers in the diaspora articulate some of the most emotionally powerful and politically persuasive images in the national imaginaries of the homeland. The Brazilian Freyre also formulated his influential sociomoral allegory during and following his sojourn in the United States. Both arguments rely on the construction of an idyllic past beyond immediate scrutiny. They equally invoke a sense of national honor around the decision to conceal contrary facts that every insider knows.

No careful and knowledgeable student of Brazil could, in my opinion, claim that racism works the same way in Brazil as it does in the United States, but "racism" is a useful analytic category by which to analyze, and rethink, the ways in which discrimination based upon presumed or visible ancestry works in each of the two countries. Likewise, Oyewumi's redefinition of "gender" does little to clarify or improve upon existing discussions under that rubric, many of which subtly analyze the empirical turf Oyewumi considers: the diversity of female roles and powers in Yorùbá society, the ways in which they overlap with men's powers, and the way these differ from the arrangements of roles and powers in other societies. Oyewumi's redefinition of gender does little more than flatten both "the Yorùbá conception" and "the West" into opposite stereotypes. The text itself vilifies not only "the West" but also those eminent Yorùbá scholars whose interpretations differ from Oyewumi's, dismissing theirs as foreign to "the Yorùbá conception" (1997:68). Thus, a pattern of arbitrary essentialization of Yorùbá culture extends not only to her analysis of ethnographically observed, oral historical, and archival materials but also to her critiques of the work of fellow scholars.

A (Culturally) Intimate Gathering of Priests and Scholars

Since Gilberto Freyre organized the First Afro-Brazilian Congress in 1934, dozens of such conferences have brought together priests and scholars intent on rethinking and reorganizing òrìṣà religion. Several conferences have had momentous effects. For example, the 1937 Congress organized by Edison

Carneiro in Bahia culminated in the organization of the Union of Afro-Brazilian Sects, the first organization to unite the Bahian temples and their supporters against police repression. In 1983, Wande Abimbọla and Marta Moreno Vega organized at the University of Ife, Nigeria, the first World Conference of Orisha Tradition and Culture. For the first time a conference brought together scholars and priests of *òrìṣà* religion from Brazil, Cuba, Puerto Rico, Trinidad, the United States, and Nigeria. A dozen such conferences have followed, albeit under an increasingly factionalized leadership. It is against this backdrop that events at a 1999 conference at Florida International University acquire their significance. Titled "*Òrìṣà* Devotion as a World Religion: The Globalization of Yorùbá Religious Culture," this conference brought together dozens of U.S.-based Nigerian, Cuban, Puerto Rican, and native North American scholars with priests of equally diverse national origins.

Whatever its scholarly inadequacies, Oyewumi's argument received a standing ovation from a number of New World *òrìṣà* priestesses in attendance at the F.I.U. conference. One of the priestesses told me that she liked Oyewumi's presentation because of Oyewumi's assertiveness, because she delivered it *ex tempore*, and because she seemed to know what she was talking about. In an apparent effort to support Oyewumi's argument, several senior Yorùbá scholars in attendance offered further examples of Yorùbá gender configurations that might surprise most Americans, such as the Yorùbá practice of calling one's patrilateral relatives *bàbá* (normally meaning "father" or "senior man") and matrilateral relatives *ìyá* (normally meaning "mother" or "senior woman") in certain contexts. One Yorùbá philosophy professor shared with me his strong agreement with Oyewumi but seemed to feel less enthusiastic when I asked him to consider the implications of viri-patrilocal postmarital residence, whereby a woman is normally expected to spend most of her life in a household where she automatically becomes the junior to everyone else in the house. There, she will always owe deference and a measure of servility to those male and female in-laws born before her marriage into the house and to the earlier-married wives, and her rights to land and chieftaincy titles will always be secondary to those of anyone born in the house. When space and resources are limited in her natal home, her claims even there will be subordinate to those of her male agnates, and the rights of her descendants will be subordinate to those of male agnates' descendants. These structural disadvantages affect females systematically, above and beyond the structural experiences shared by persons of the same age, persons of the same kin group, persons of the same profession, and persons with the same amount of money or number of well-placed social contacts.

Others among the senior Yorùbá scholars in attendance restricted their comments to private conversations. One told me that Oyewumi's argument was not significant enough to challenge, though this same scholar apparently advocated for the book to receive the Herskovits Prize of the African Studies Association. Another believed that the culturally appropriate mode of criticism had already been undertaken—that is, some Yorùbá scholars refused to endorse it when asked privately by official agencies. Two scholars told me that public criticism of a junior scholar by senior scholars would have been regarded in Yorùbá culture as bullying (àgbàyà). Yet a female Yorùbá feminist scholar who organized a roundtable at the 2002 African Studies Association meetings in order to contest Oyewumi's conclusions believed that the male Yorùbá scholars in question were trying to silence criticism of Oyewumi's argument because her book reflects positively on them, as it exonerates Yorùbá men of sexism. Thus, in multiple ways, my argument that Yorùbá gender relations and religious symbolism contained precedents for the prominence of adés in the Candomblé priesthood clearly became an object of embarrassment to this diasporic vision of the Yorùbá past and to the communities that defend its selective presentation in public.

Moreover, without consulting any Africanists, much less Yorùbánists, the Sex and Gender Section of the American Sociological Association awarded Oyewumi's *Invention of Women* its 1998 Distinguished Book Award ([selection committee member], personal communication, 2001). The structural nostalgia that has united the Sex and Gender Section of the A.S.A. in common cause with Yorùbá long-distance nationalism is new in some details but is logically similar to the reasoning that united Brazilian nationalism with Landes's transnational feminism. Two years after the F.I.U. Conference, a New World priestess told me she had forgotten the contents of Oyewumi's presentation. What she remembered more was that, despite claiming to represent a traditional African culture, Oyewumi herself did not wear African clothes. This priestess' notion of authenticity and its proper spokespersons remained different from Oyewumi's. Nonetheless, the issue of gender in Yorùbá religion and culture generally is likely to arise at many future conferences of this sort. The debates that ensue will penetrate the community of worshippers and inspire the creation of new traditions and new cultural intimacies.

Conclusion

My point is that diasporas, like nation-states, propagate secrets and defend their own intimate zones. Diasporas often share the *materia prima* of secrets with other, overlapping communities, including regions, nations, civilizations, and transnational social movements. Moreover, these communities regularly contest and reinterpret each other's secrets. In doing so, they inspire the social transformation of the communities that defend those secrets. Implicit is the understanding that the cultural phenomena that nationalists and advocates of reformist movements would hide because they are supposed to be anomalous (and therefore unreal) regularly follow a complex semiotic and social logic of their own, a logic that is subject to politically conditioned historical change, just like any other dimension of culture. The meaning of ritual metaphors is not fixed; the implications of any given metaphor are selectively "highlighted" or "hidden" depending on the personal or political project at hand. Across history, across different nation-states, different regions and different priesthoods, and within the same local priesthood, diverse interests might favor equally diverse readings of the same metaphor. However, like all semantic articulations, ritual metaphors retain traces of their past uses and the aims of past users: any current invocation owes part of its convincingness, its appropriateness, and its meaning to the *history* of its usage.

It is perhaps now easier to understand why—and on whose terms—sentimental and feminist-inspired favoritism toward black women became such an important force in the history of Candomblé. However, such favoritism does not explain why Afro-Brazilians would be likely to believe in female priests in the first place, and the popularity of reputedly "passive homosexual" priests *entirely* escapes explanation in terms of Euro-Brazilian attitudes *or* sponsorship. From the nineteenth century onward, the preponderance of bourgeois European and Euro-American opinion has labeled these men as a pathological type. In fact, the presence of women *and* male "passives" side-by-side in the Candomblé leadership hints at the far older, West African ideological precedents of the gender arrangements in Candomblé possession religion.

Several female-headed Candomblé temples are now officially registered and preserved as monuments of the Brazilian National Patrimony.[21] The great Jeje and Nagô mothers have been able to secure such a position for their temples by dint of their personal ingenuity, their knowledge of state politics, and their deft management of the Brazilian nationalist imaginary. Yet it has taken no less genius—and no less prestigious a trans-Atlantic precedent—for the *fathers* of various Candomblé nations to secure an honored place in the Afro-Brazilian patrimony. It is *they* who have relentlessly faced down the resistance of a powerful, homophobic class of Brazilian nationalists and international opinion makers.

Notes

1. See also Parker, Russo, Sommer and Yaeger (1992).

2. The priest said sex has nothing to do with his religion, a statement that could be construed in multiple ways. Clearly, sacred duties require various periods of sex-

ual abstinence, and many a god requires his or her devotees to abstain and to sleep separately from their spouses on the day of the week devoted to that god. While the conduct of sacred affairs excludes sexuality, this very prohibition manifests the widespread analogy between sacred affairs and the sexual conduct they exclude.

3. Exceptionally, Ṣàngó priests in Ìgbòho often speak openly about sex across age groups.

4. The discretion with which Yorùbá people discuss "witchcraft" (aje) and female barrenness further supports the hypothesis that concerted silence about a phenomenon need not suggest its unimportance.

5. See Matory (1999a) on the trans-Atlantic and recent genesis of the "Yorùbá" ethnic category and Matory (1999b) on the similar genesis of the "Jeje" ethnic category, as well as the colonial-era political struggles and literary movements by which groups so named acquired unparalleled prestige among African-inspired ethnic groups in the Americas.

6. I describe Landes as a transnational feminist not because her scholarly contribution is reducible by any means to a feminist project, though her effort to present Brazil as a living counterexample to Western gender inequality and racism was clearly a major part of her intent in writing The City of Women. It is also true that much that Landes misrepresented in Candomblé is designed to support international resistance to sexism and racism (Healey 1998/2000). Equally important, however, is the fact that her writings have been embraced as truthful and her person adopted as a hero of cosmopolitan feminism by numerous feminist scholars and many members of the general public, including Simone de Beauvoir, Sally Cole, Kim D. Butler, and Rachel E. Harding (see Matory, forthcoming).

7. In the nineteenth-century record, there is evidence of a significant number of male priests even in the leadership of the Jeje and the Nagô (or Yorùbá) nations (Harding 2000:71−4, 77, 103; Carneiro 1948/1986:57, 104−109; Butler 1998:193, 195; Wimberly 1998:82−5).

8. See also Wikan (1977) on the Omani construction of the male homosexual xanith as the antitype of the good woman and as symbolic evidence of women's propriety generally.

9. Indeed, Landes's 1940 article "A Cult Matriarchate and Male Homosexuality" not only asserts the numerical importance of "passive homosexuals" in Candomblé but also identifies a dozen such men by name and describes them in the most demeaning terms possible. However, Ramos's offense did not seem to derive from her violation of these men's privacy and good name.

10. Mãe Stella's testimony is taken from Hamilton Vieira, "A história do Axé Opô Afonjá na homenagem a Mãe Stella," AT, 14 Sept 1989, 2° Caderno, p.3 (Pasta 324, AT archives); "Mãe Stella: 'Se nós não preservamos a natureza viva, termina tudo,'" AT, 30 April 1995, 2° Caderno, p.1, Recorte de Jornais, Bahiatursa office, Salvador; "Sete décadas da estrela do Afonjá," TB, 27 April 1995, Recorte de Jornais, Bahiatursa office, Salvador.

11. See Hamilton Vieira, "A história do Axé Opô Afonjá na homenagem a Mãe Stella," A Tarde, 14 Sept. 1989, 2° Caderno (Pasta 324, AT archives); "Mãe Stella: 'Se nós não preservamos a natureza viva, termina tudo,'" A Tarde, 30 April 1995, 2° Caderno, p.1, Recorte de Jornais, Bahiatursa office, Salvador.

12. "'Cirrum' começou no Bogum e 'Gamo' é a nova yalorixá," *A Tarde*, 30 Dec. 1975, p.3

13. I have presented the main body of this argument in *Sex and the Empire That Is No More* (Matory 1994) and "Homens montados: homossexualidade e simbolismo da possessão nas religiões afro-brasileiras" (Matory 1988).

14. A category of men known as *maricas* or *addodis* has for decades been identified as common in the Yorùbá-affiliated denomination of Afro-Cuban religion called *Regla de Ocha* or Lucumí. They are said to be protected by the goddesses Yemayá and Ochún, who love them dearly. See Lydia Cabrera (1954/1983:56) and Rómulo Lachatañeré (1939/1992:223–224). The earlier of these written accounts dates from the same period as Landes's observations about homosexuals in the Brazilian Candomblé.

15. A number of sex-*changing*, or ambisexual, divinities (like Logunedé and Oxumarê) are said to inspire and legitimize the same-sex desires of their male worshippers. Birman also observes the cultural controversy over whether men start out homosexual, even if their natal relationship to a given divinity made them so, or are turned into homosexuals during the initiation process. Though Birman attributes the former view to priests and the latter to outsiders, some priests have told me that an unscrupulous priest could indeed change the sexual preference of initiands by placing a certain leaf under their sleeping mats in the initiation room.

16. As Andrews shows, men of any given social race earn more on average than the women of that category (1992:252). It has also been observed that, in contexts where light-skinned gay men successfully conceal their sexuality, they possess considerable economic and political advantages over women as a group and blacks as a group (*Veja*, 12 May 1993, pp.52–59). For an explanation of the term "social race," which I use in the absence of an alternative generic term for Brazilian color and status categories, see Wagley 1952/1963:14 and Degler 1971:105.

17. In a probative contrast, the term *mágùn* (lit. "don't mount") refers to a "medicine," or magical application, that kills the paramour of a married woman at the moment he attempts to penetrate her.

18. In contemporary Yorùbá, there is a rarely used term for "butt fuckers" (*adófùrò*; literally, "one-who-fucks-the-anus"). However, I have yet to meet any native Yorùbá-speakers who can confidently specify any category of persons to which it refers. My wife had long thought it meant "vagina fucker" but still could not say whom the term is used to describe. Thus, besides being of rare and obscure usage, the term fails to unite *penetrated* persons within any verbal category. Nor, in any obvious way, does it imply that the penetrated party is male.

19. This priestly cross-dressing has been documented at least since 1910, and there is no reason to believe that it was new at that time.

20. That is, among the West African Yorùbá, *men* prostrate themselves flat on the ground, while the *ìyíkàà* (lying first on one side and then on the other) is the more appropriate gesture for *women* in sacred contexts. In Cuban Ocha and Brazilian Candomblé, by contrast, it is the gender of one's divinity, or "saint," that determines the appropriate style of self-prostration. A person governed by a male saint salutes elders and altars with the *ìdòbálè*, whereas a person governed by a female saint performs the *ìyíkàà*.

21. See "Terreiro Casa Branca, uma decisão histórica da Sphan," ESP, 1 June 1984 (Pasta 22.844, ESP archives); Aureliano Biancarelli, "Estado tomba terreiro de candomblé de SP," FSP, 3 May 1990 (Pasta 22.844, ESP archives); "Bogum quer tombamento para preservar o seu bissecular Terreiro," AT, 24 July 1986, Caderno 2°.

References Cited

Abiọdun, Rowland. 1989. "Women in Yorùbá Religious Images." *African Languages and Cultures* 2, no. 1: 1–18.

Agentes de Pastoral Negros. 1990. *Mulher Negra: Resistência e Soberania de uma Raça*. Petrópolis: Vozes and Quilombo Central—Agentes de Pastoral Negros.

Amadiume, Ifi. 1987. *Male Daughters, Female Husbands: Gender and Sex in an African Society*. London: Zed Books.

Andrews, George Reid. 1992. "Racial Inequality in Brazil and the United States: A Statistical Comparison." *Journal of Social History* 26: 229–263.

Awẹ, Bọlanlẹ. 1997. "The Iyalode in the Traditional Yorùbá Political System." Pp. 144–160 in *Sexual Stratification*, ed. Alice Schlegel. New York: Columbia University Press.

Azevedo Santos, Maria Stella de. 1993. *Meu Tempo É Agora*. São Paulo: Editora Oduduwa.

Babayẹmi, S. O. 1979. "The Rise and Fall of Ọ̀yọ́, c.1760–1905." Ph.D. dissertation, Centre of West African Studies, University of Birmingham, England.

Bastide, Roger. 1961. *O Candomblé da Bahia*. São Paulo: Editora Nacional.

Birman, Patricia. 1985. "Identidade social e homossexualismo no Candomblé." *Religião e Sociedade* 12, no. 1: 2–21.

Butler, Kim D. 1998. *Freedoms Given, Freedoms Won: Afro-Brazilians in Post-Abolition São Paulo and Salvador*. New Brunswick, N.J.: Rutgers University Press.

Cabrera, Lydia. 1954/1983. *El Monte*, 5th ed. Miami: Colección del Chicherekú.

Carneiro, Edison. 1967. *Antologia do Negro Brasileiro*. Editora Technoprint S.A./Ediouro Grupo Coquetel.

———. 1948/1986. *Os Candomblés da Bahia*, 7th ed. Rio de Janeiro: Civilização Brasileira.

Corrêa, Mariza. 2000. "O Mistério dos Orixás e das Bonecas: Raça e Gênero na Antropologia Brasileira." *Etnográfica* 4, no. 2: 233–265.

Degler, Carl N. 1971. *Neither Black Nor White: Slavery and Race Relations in Brazil and the United States*. Madison: University of Wisconsin Press.

Douglas, Mary. 1966. *Purity and Danger: An Analysis of Concepts of Pollution and Taboo*. London: Routledge and Kegan Paul.

Fadipẹ, N. A. 1939/1970. *The Sociology of the Yorùbá*. Ibàdàn, Nigeria: Ibàdàn University Press.

Freeman, Derek. 1983. *Margaret Mead and Samoa: The making and unmaking of an anthropological myth*. Cambridge, Mass.: Harvard University Press.

Freyre, Gilberto. 1933/1986. *The Masters and the Slaves*. Translated by Samuel Putnam. Berkeley: University of California Press.

Fry, Peter. 1982. *Para Inglês Ver*. Rio de Janeiro: Zahar.

———. 1986. "Male Homosexuality and Spirit Possession in Brazil." *Journal of Homosexuality* 11, no. 3–4: 137–153.

Green, James N. 1999. *Beyond Carnival: Male Homosexuality in Twentieth-Century Brazil*. Chicago: University of Chicago Press.

Harding, Rachel E. 2000. *A Refuge in Thunder: Candomblé and Alternative Spaces of Blackness*. Bloomington, Ind.: University of Indiana Press.

Healey, Mark Alan. 1998/2000. "'The Sweet Matriarchy of Bahia': Ruth Landes's Ethnography of Race and Gender." *Disposition XXIII* 50: 87–116.

Heringer, Rosana, Wania Sant'Anna, Sebastião de Oliveira, and Sérgio Martins, coordinators. 1989. *Negros no Brasil: Dados da Realidade*. Petrópolis: Vozes and Instituto Brasileiro de Análisis Sociais e Econômicas (IBASE).

Herskovits, Melville J. 1941/1958. *The Myth of the Negro Past*. Boston: Beacon.

Herzfeld, Michael. 1997. *Cultural Intimacy: The Social Poetics of the Nation-State*. New York: Routledge.

Jackson, Peter A. 2000. "Reading Rio from Bangkok: An Asianist perspective on Brazil's male homosexual cultures." *American Ethnologist* 27, no. 4: 950–960.

Johnson, Rev. Samuel. 1897/1921. *The History of the Yorùbás: From the Earliest Times to the Beginning of the British Protectorate*. Lagos: C.S.S. Bookshops.

Kulick, Don. 1998. *Travestí: Sex, Gender and Culture among Brazilian Transgendered Prostitutes*. Chicago: University of Chicago Press.

Lachatañeré, Rómulo. 1939/1992. *El Sistema Religioso de los Afrocubanos*. Havana: Editorial de Ciencias Sociales.

Landes, Ruth. 1940. A Cult Matriarchate and Male Homosexuality. *Journal of Abnormal and Social Psychology* 35, no. 3: 386–397.

———. 1947. *The City of Women*. New York: Macmillan.

———. 1953. "Negro Slavery and Female Status." *Mémoires de l'Institut Français d'Afrique Noire* 27: 265–268.

———. 1947/1994. *The City of Women*. Albuquerque: University of New Mexico Press.

Leão Teixeira, Maria Lina. 1987. "Lorogun—Identidades sexuais e poder no candomblé." Pp. 33–52 in *Candomblé: Desvendando Identidades*, ed. Carlos Eugênio Marcondes de Moura. São Paulo: EMW Editores.

Lima, Délcio Monteiro de. 1983. *Os Homoeróticos*. Rio de Janeiro: F. Alves.

Matory, J. Lorand. 1988. Homens montados: homossexualidade e simbolismo da possessão nas religiões afro-brasileiras. Pp. 215–231 in *Escravidão e Invenção da Liberdade*, ed. João José Reis. São Paulo: Brasiliense.

———. 1991. "Sex and the Empire That Is No More: A Ritual History of Women's Power among the Ọ̀yọ́-Yorùbá." Ph.D. dissertation, Department of Anthropology, University of Chicago.

———. 1994. *Sex and the Empire That Is No More: Gender and the Politics of Metaphor in Oyó Yorùbá Religion*. Minneapolis: University of Minnesota.

———. 1999a. "The English Professors of Brazil: On the Diasporic Roots of the Yorùbá Nation." *Comparative Studies in Society and History* 41, no. 1: 72–103.

———. 1999b. "Jeje: Repensando Nações e Transnacionalismo." *Mana* 5, no. 1: 57–80

———. Forthcoming. *Black Atlantic Religion: Tradition, Transnationalism, and Matriarchy in the Afro-Brazilian Candomblé*. Princeton, N.J.: Princeton University Press.

Mosse, George. 1985. *Nationalism and Sexuality*. Madison, Wis.: University of Wisconsin Press.

Murray, Stephen O. 1998. "Overview." Pp. 91–109 in *Boy-Wives and Female Husbands: Studies of African Homosexualities*, eds. Stephen O. Murray and Will Roscoe. New York: St. Martins Press.

Ogundipẹ-Leslie, 'Molara. 1985. "Women in Nigeria." Pp. 119–131 in *Women in Nigeria Today*. eds. S. Bappa, J. Ibrahim, A. Imam, F. Kamara, H. Mahdi, M. Modibbo, A. Mohammed, H. Mohammed, A. Mustapha, N. Perchonock, and R. Pittin. London: Zed Books.

Okediji, O. O., and F. O. Okediji. 1966. "Marital Stability and Social Structure in an African City." *The Nigerian Journal of Economic and Social Studies* 8, no. 1: 151–163.

Oyewumi, Oyeronkẹ. 1997. *The Invention of Women: Making an African Sense of Western Gender Discourses*. Minneapolis: University of Minnesota Press.

Parker, Andrew, Mary Russo, Doris Sommer, and Patricia Yaeger. 1992. *Nationalisms and Sexualities*. New York: Routledge.

Parker, Richard G. 1991. *Bodies, Pleasures, and Passions: Sexual Culture in Contemporary Brazil*. Boston: Beacon Press.

———. 1998. *Beneath the Equator: Cultures of Desire, Male Homosexuality, and Emerging Gay Communities in Brazil*. New York: Routledge.

Ribeiro, René. 1969. "Personality and the Psychosexual Adjustment of Afro-Brazilian-Cult Members." *Journal de la Société des Américanistes* 58: 109–120.

Rodrigues, Raymundo Nina. 1896/1900/1935. *O Animismo Fetichista dos Negros Bahianos*. Rio de Janeiro: Civilização Brasileira S.A.

———. 1905/1945. *Os Africanos no Brasil*, 3rd ed. São Paulo: Companhia Editora Nacional.

———. 1905/1988. *Os Africanos no Brasil*, 7th ed. Brasília: Editora Universidade de Brasília.

Scott, James C. 1990. *Weapons of the Weak: Everyday Forms of Peasant Resistance*. New Haven, Conn.: Yale University Press.

Silverstein, Leni M. 1979. "Mãe de Todo Mundo: Modos de Sobrevivência nas Comunidades de Candomblé da Bahia." *Religião e Sociedade* 4: 143–169.

Singer, Paul. 1995. "Radiografia da 'Democracia Racial' Brasileira." Pp. 69–81 in *Racismo Cordial*, eds. Cleusa Turra and Gustavo Venturi. São Paulo: Àtica.

Sweet, James H. 1996. "Male Homosexuality and Spiritism in the African Diaspora: The Legacies of a Link." *Journal of the History of Sexuality* 7, no. 21: 184–202.

Trexler, Richard C. 1995. *Sex and Conquest: Gendered Violence, Political Order, and the European Conquest of the Americas*. Ithaca, N.Y.: Cornell University Press

Turner, Victor. 1969. *The Ritual Process: Structure and Anti-Structure*. Chicago: Aldine.

Wagley, Charles. 1952/1963. Introduction. Pp. 7–15 in *Race and Class in Rural Brazil*, ed. Charles Wagley. New York: UNESCO/International Documents Service, Columbia University Press.

Wikan, Unni. 1977. "'Man Becomes Woman': Transsexualism in Oman as a Key to Gender Roles." *Man* 12: 304–319.

Wimberly, Fayette. 1998. "The Expansion of Afro-Bahian Religious Practices in Nineteenth-Century Cachoeira." Pp. 74–89 in *Afro-Brazilian Culture and Politics: Bahia, 1790s to 1990s*, ed. Hendrik Kraay. Armonk: M. E. Sharpe.

CHAPTER 7

"X Marks the Future of Brazil"

PROTESTANT ETHICS AND BEDEVILING MIXTURES
IN A BRAZILIAN CULTURAL HERITAGE CENTER

John F. Collins

One day I will return, Bahia,
with more time,
to your brown Brazilian breast
To your Churches . . .
And to the tables of your *baiana* market women splashed with an "x"
(and that "x" marks the future of Brazil),
to your houses and colonial mansions smelling
of incense, food, and cocoa
— Gilberto Freyre, "Bahia," 1926/1996

ONCE, LATE AT NIGHT in London, I listened to a Brazilian friend discuss his national culture with a group of cosmopolitan travelers. Many of these professionals had visited his home state of Bahia, a region typically portrayed as Brazil's blackest and most traditional "heart." Significantly, before leaving his home in Salvador, Bahia's capital, my friend had led a community movement that opposed the conversion of his neighborhood, Salvador's Pelourinho Historical Center, into a pastel-hued mnemonic device designed to showcase the Bahian state's version of national pasts. Yet some time after mar-

I thank Nubia Rodrigues, Ordep Serra, Jocélio Teles, Daryle Williams, Andrew Shryock, Michael Herzfeld, and the anonymous reviewers for Stanford University Press for their comments on drafts of this chapter. I alone am responsible for misreadings or misunderstandings of our debates. I am also grateful to the IIE Fulbright Program, Wenner-Gren Foundation for Anthropological Research, the Brazilian PIBIC Program, and the U.S. National Science Foundation for supporting the fieldwork on which this chapter is based. Most of all I am indebted to the members of the Bem Aventurados and S.O.S. Children of the Historical Center, whose insightful analyses of their state government may in fact make possible a new Brazil.

riage to a German woman attracted especially to his aura of African "roots," he found himself alongside me, in the company of a group of European and South Asian scientists keenly interested in Brazilian culture as packaged by his state government. These people in turn found themselves befuddled by my dreadlocked friend's insistence that he did not practice the Afro-Brazilian divination and possession-based religion known as Candomblé.

"Why don't you believe in Candomblé?" they queried, recalling fascinating ceremonies experienced during vacations that led them deep into Salvador's working-class neighborhoods. Facing them, their Bahian interlocutor looked at me for a moment, angry and embarrassed that Candomblé should stand as his audience's referent for his home and Afro-Brazilianness. He then pressed both fists against his chest before crossing and uncrossing his arms while snapping his fingers in a stereotyped imitation of a Candomblé practitioner's invocation of West African *axé*, or spirit. My friend then proclaimed, "I'm proud of my African roots and I don't want to dilute them with the worship of saints and false prophets. Candomblé is based on cultural syncretism, something that effaces my African ancestors so that my country's politicians can profit from my culture!"

My friend told the group that, as a black Brazilian, instead of worshipping at Candomblé temples, he reads the Bible and follows the word of Jah Rastafar-I to keep in touch with his homeland, Africa. Not wanting to anger this man, with whom I felt an especially close kinship since I had recognized his embodied ironization of Candomblé's importance to foreign perceptions of Bahia, I resisted the urge that night to point out that the Jehovah's Witnesses' Watchtower Society had translated and printed his Bible and that I had often heard him beat out alluring Candomblé rhythms on his *atabaque* drums. When I asked later in private how it was that Africa could be reached through the Bible, he sputtered, fumed, and argued that the word of the Christian God presented a road that avoided the transcultural infections of the Brazilian nation while demonstrating the "true truth" (*a verdadeira verdade*), of his people's origins.

Some months later, the Balé Folclórico da Bahia, (Bahian Folkloric Ballet), a dance troupe whose principle performance space lies in the Pelourinho neighborhood that my friend had struggled to wrest from the grip of his state's culture managers, presented four sold-out performances in the North American college town of Ann Arbor, Michigan. Beforehand, thanks to the efforts of the University of Michigan's Center for Latin American and Caribbean Studies, one of the Ballet's directors led a workshop on Bahian arts and culture. There he explained that he draws much of the group's choreography from Candomblé. He also made clear to the rapt audience that Candomblé is absolutely essential to Bahian identity and that almost everyone in Salvador is an adherent, so much so that on Fridays, a day dedicated to Oxalá, a spirit or *orixá* who favors the color white, "the whole city dresses in white."

Perhaps because of experiences in London, or in Salvador, or because I had recently read a Bahian newspaper's account of a Pentecostal who swam through a polluted pond in order to attack, with a hammer, enormous state-funded sculptures of Candomblé deities in Bahia's capital city of Salvador (Sansi 2001), I turned to the Brazilian seated next to me and whispered, "That is, unless you're a Protestant!" We exchanged conspiratorial glances and giggled, for just a moment. I thought then of my fieldwork in Salvador, and the Pentecostal "believers" (*crentes*) who would wake me on Sunday mornings with their door-to-door proselytizing. And I felt a certain attachment to the Brazilian expatriots in the audience in Michigan. It was as if, by dint of long-term residence in Bahia and my perhaps inappropriate comment on the speaker's claim, I had attained anthropological nirvana and joined a circle of national insiders able to make out Candomblé's importance, and Pentecostalism's uncomfortable challenges, to the most basic aspects of Brazilian identities. Such moments of recognition, and their relationship to the representations of Brazilianness currently being put together in the Pelourinho Historical Center, do much to reveal the contours of what I will argue in the following pages is a contemporary shift in the racialized bases of national belonging in Brazil.

Many of the new Protestant denominations so evident today in Brazil, commonly glossed as "Evangelicals" and often described in scholarly literatures as "neo-Pentecostals" to differentiate them from earlier North American missions, insistently attack both Roman Catholicism and Candomblé. In sermons, television and radio broadcasts, in mass rallies in soccer stadiums, and in everyday interactions, a burgeoning number of Pentecostals who stress the gifts of the Holy Spirit made manifest in healing powers and the ability to speak in tongues lambast Candomblé as the devil's religion, as a faith without clear distinctions between good and evil, and as a cult based on multiple deities and idolatry. Given Candomblé's extraordinary importance to Brazilian nationalism, significant sectors of Salvador's populace, and contemporary antiracist struggles, these Pentecostal attacks are both politically sensitive and important to understanding debates over the relationships between domestic habits, religious practices, and state-sanctioned forms of Brazilian public culture.

Social scientists with whom I broach the topic of Pentecostal assaults on Candomblé frequently shudder, expressing dismay and relegating to silence the crude mystifications and ignorance that they assume guide Pentecostal criticisms of this most Brazilian of religions.[1] For most Bahian intellectuals, as well as for the majority of North American Brazilianists and the community organizers and progressive politicians involved in Salvador's antiracist and popular struggles, Pentecostal groups are a source of enormous unease, if not outright embarrassment and anger (Burdick 1998).[2] In the following pages I would like to take a different tack. Rather than denounce Bahia's Pentecostals as opportunists seeking to carve out a diacritical niche in a crowded religious marketplace, as guilty of racism, or as the unwitting victims of imported ideologies and millennial capitalism's distortions of politics and social life, I will explore another possibility. It appears that among certain Pentecostals who have begun to take leadership roles in Salvador's Pelourinho Historical Center, criticisms of Candomblé present a problematic, albeit prescient, indictment of the extent to which their state has sought to draw close to Candomblé in an attempt to occlude its own racist practices. In such a light, Pentecostal practices, overwhelmingly portrayed as embarrassing or even racist counterparts to sanctioned forms of Afro-Brazilian religiosity, help support new forms of Afro-Brazilian politics that challenge dominant narratives of Brazilianness.

Given the extent to which Pelourinho Pentecostals disparage models of twentieth-century Brazilian cultural citizenship constructed around Roman Catholicism, Candomblé, and a powerful ideology of cultural and racial fusion, Pentecostal criticisms of Candomblé seem to be much more than attacks on a *religion*. They are instead one part of a growing popular refusal in Bahia of the accounts of hybridity that have been presented throughout the twentieth century as the foundation of the Brazilian nation.

Before examining contemporary Pentecostal critiques, I offer a short background to the importance of ideologies of mixture in Brazilian life. In doing so I introduce the importance of cuisine in debates about national culture, and I attempt to underscore the novelty of Protestant interventions, the difficulty of analyzing them, and the extent to which attacks on Candomblé strike at the heart of the mediation of public and private so important to the twentieth-century elaboration of a nationalist ideology known as "racial democracy." Following this background, I look closely at the arguments and practices of a particular Rastafarian-influenced Pentecostal community in Salvador's Pelourinho Historical Center, a UNESCO World Heritage Site subject to a massive state-directed gentrification effort during the 1990s. I hope to bring Protestant critique and Candomblé's power into a shared analytical frame and, by doing so, to illuminate historical shifts in the structures of intimacy that are productive of both state and citizen in modern Brazil.

Afro-Brazilian Religiosity, the Modern Nation, and Pentecostal Embarrassments

Perhaps more than any other nation, Brazil is associated at home and abroad with cultural mixture, racial fluidity, and tropical sensuality. Such twentieth-century valorizations of hybridity arose in part as a reaction to late-nine-teenth- and early-twentieth-century European theories of racial degeneracy that predicted the nation's future. These supposedly scientific theories of na-tional progress, or lack thereof, relegated Brazil to underdevelopment as a result of its "infection" by African and Native American blood and custom (Stepan 1991). As a result, by the 1920s a mounting Brazilian valorization of mixture, crystallized most influentially in the work of sociologist Gilberto Freyre whose 1927 poem "Bahia" serves as this chapter's epigram, gave weight to a powerful discourse of tropical Lusophone exceptionalism now known as "racial democracy."

Racial democracy is generally understood as an ideology of racial and cul-tural mixture that gives positive value to the purportedly regenerative fu-sion of Portuguese, African, and Native Brazilian habits and blood. Through this valorization of mixtures that supposedly took place in the relations be-tween masters and slaves in the domestic spaces of the colonial sugar planta-tion in states like Bahia, Brazilians have in effect rehabilitated their national culture and bloodlines for the benefit of foreign eyes. A mixed-race status previously coded as degenerate here becomes a source of pride and strength in the face of foreign racism. Such accounts provide an important context for understanding both the reconstruction of Salvador's Pelourinho Histor-ical Center and Pentecostal critiques of Bahian Candomblé at the end of the twentieth century.

The Pelourinho was declared a national monument and a UNESCO World Heritage Site in the 1980s, but it was only in 1992 that the Bahian state began the major renovation that has transformed the former red light district into a stunningly beautiful heritage zone designed to represent state-sanctioned images of Brazilianness. The neighborhood's importance in the management of national culture, however, extends much further in time. For example, in January of 1927, three years before the rise of Getúlio Vargas' authoritarian regime that would establish Brazil's most important public cul-tural institutions, a young Bahian poet, Godofredo Filho, guided a visiting writer and soon-to-be official in Brazil's IPHAN cultural heritage bureau-cracy through the twisting alleys of Salvador's Pelourinho neighborhood.[3] This man, Manuel Bandeira, a founding figure in the modernist movement that promoted an autonomous Brazilian identity through the celebration of cultural expressions that cannibalized and subverted European cultural forms, wished to experience tropical Bahia's most authentic traditions and charms. His quest led him to the Pelourinho's baroque architecture, abandoned by Salvador's upper classes at the end of the nineteenth century and occupied and subdivided throughout the twentieth century by working families and women of ill repute.

Bandeira later claimed to have adored his tour of Salvador's colonial treasures. In a letter to his mentor, the novelist and poet Mário de Andrade (who would draft the legislation that created the IPHAN cultural heritage bureaucracy in 1937), Bandeira concluded that the "Pelourinho square is the urban space that a Brazilian can show to a Frenchman without worrying about being cuckolded by the Champs Elysée or the Avenue of the Opera." After staking this masculine and vociferously Brazilian claim to autochthonous modernity based on the Pelourinho's architecture, but not necessarily its people, Bandeira continued,

I'm in love with Bahia! It's a stupendous place! THE BRAZILIAN CITY. Hundreds, hundreds, hundreds of huge colonial mansions with four stories and a cellar. If I could, I'd take one back for you and one for me. Mansions with strong and serious signorial lines, with polished rock doorways and family crests, doors of deep hardwoods and baroque peacock's tails—all inhabited by little black ladies, prostitutes and people so poor, so poor, the poorest of them all! You look down through the cracks into a cellar where you would imagine that only rats could live and you see a little altar, lit by a flickering oil lamp.[4]

In a demonstration of the importance of Bahian cuisine to official representations of the nation, at lunchtime Godofredo Filho (who later headed IPHAN's Bahian office) and his guest, Bandeira (who helped establish IPHAN and spent much of his working life singling out Brazilian wonders for inclusion in the register of national historic places) stopped by "Black Eva's" homestyle cooking shack.[5] There, on rough wooden benches and among working-class Afro-Bahians, the future culture managers tested the region's signature African-influenced *moqueca*, a delicacy Bandeira later described as "the most stupendous mixture of palm oil and hot peppers."[6] Even as Bandeira worried about (and seemed to derive a certain titillation from) the degenerate status of the Pelourinho's population of "little black ladies, prostitutes and people so poor, so poor, the poorest of them all," he singled out their food and their altars as examples of the possible redemption of a Brazilian people and a national culture. The multiple meanings of, and paths to, community redemption in twentieth-century Bahia are critical to interpreting today's Pentecostal assaults on Candomblé.

As I will explore later in this essay, Pentecostal challenges to Bahian cuisine and religious practice are enormously threatening to the established bases of Brazilian nationhood. Pentecostalism involves the transformation of private habits and moral frameworks, precisely the stuff of Gilberto Freyre's myth of national emergence through sexual and domestic relations, of Bandeira's enchantment with the Pelourinho and its people, and of the Bahian government's efforts to reconstruct the Pelourinho in the 1990s. Before outlining how the neighborhood's refurbishing depends on the moral retraining of its populace's most private habits, I would like to underscore the extent to which cuisine and religion call forth an imagined private sphere that is purported to stand as the historical source of the Brazilian nation. The extraordinarily influential Freyre, a student of Franz Boas at Columbia, described downtown Salvador in the following manner in his 1926/1996 poem, "Bahia"[7]:

> All of Bahia is one fat maternal city
> As if out of her taut wombs
> From which have arisen so many of Brazil's cities
> still others would emerge
> Into the oily air
> The smell of food
> The smell of incense
> The smell of mulatas
> And the hot breath of sacristies and kitchens

These lines introduce themes central to Freyre's 1933 sociological treatise and foundational nationalist text, *The Masters and the Slaves*. In the author's poetry and prose, childrearing practices, religious beliefs, cooking, and interracial sex appear as vectors for producing as well as making manifest the nation's embodied essences, or what the author calls the "smells" of life in a Brazil becoming modern through the celebration of mixture and tropical fluidity.[8] Freyre's version of what passes as interracial harmony depends on female nursemaids, cooks, domestic servants, and slaves who serve as surrogate mothers and lovers to the white or almost white men who will run Brazil, a process described in "Bahia" as "Mulatas with angelic hands / Making little boys grow bigger / Creating great Sirs almost equal / To those of the Empire." Put another way, in constructing a public Brazil, Freyre conjured up a domestic sphere in which nursemaids' care and the sex between master and slave were mystified as national origins. Not surprisingly, most academics and the Brazilian black movement vehemently contest Freyre's vision today. Yet a valorization of mixture through the imagination of the domestic scene remains influential in many Brazilians' conceptualizations of themselves and their nation.[9]

As suggested in Bandeira's juxtapositions of private religiosity and Bahian cuisine, the state-sanctioned aspects of the history of Candomblé, like that of food, involve the selective appropriation of African traits and the valorization of private mixtures in the service of the nation. With some notable exceptions, until the second half of the twentieth century Candomblé was treated often as an illegal, threatening, and even embarrassing complex of primitive beliefs. Since then, Candomblé has been transformed in the eyes of important sectors of the state, elites, and Brazilians of all colors into a paradigmatically Brazilian cultural form (Birman and Lehmann 1999). The re-

ligion is influential in social scientific and touristic representations of Brazilianness and, especially, Bahian regional identity today.

I cannot do justice here to the many influences, contradictions, and nuances in the approximation of Candomblé, the nation, and an ideology of
hybridity that gained momentum during Getúlio Vargas' 1937–1945 Estado
Novo regime and became especially prominent during Brazil's 1964–1985
military dictatorship (Matory 2001; Teles dos Santos 2000).[10] Nonetheless, a
1998 exchange between a journalist and Bahia's political patriarch, Antônio
Carlos Magalhães, makes clear the importance to political life and regional
identity today of certain types of representations of Candomblé.

> REPORTER: What is Bahianness?
> A.C.M.: It's a spiritual state produced in relationship to this land through which
> one experiences all of Bahia's special characteristics, attributes like religious
> syncretism and cordiality that no other land possesses. The Bahian people are
> the most cordial of any in Brazil. In Bahia there is no racism, no prejudice.
> REPORTER: How can there not be any?
> A.C.M.: No, there isn't any.
> REPORTER: You are a Catholic and you go to Candomblé?
> A.C.M.: I go to Candomblé, but I believe in Dom Eugenio [Bahia's Catholic Bishop
> at the time]. *Anyone who doesn't really know Candomblé cannot govern Bahia.* I
> don't go to Candomblé because of my beliefs, I go on the basis of Bahianness.
> (emphasis my own)[11]

Candomblé's history reflects the process whereby cultural traits considered embarrassing at one historical juncture later come to be valued as expressing Brazil's most essential character, that of creative hybridity. Although
influential intellectuals and practitioners have presented Candomblé since
the late nineteenth century as unceasingly African, in Salvador today the state
government, important media conglomerates, and large segments of the public—like my friend who decried the religion as "syncretic"—understand
this African-derived religion as metonymic of a larger national emphasis on
regenerative mixture. Thus, a religion that was once officially outlawed and
representative of an African population considered degenerate is now presented as essentially Brazilian. In a parallel reversal, Protestantism, a religious
tradition that was once linked to the northern rigor that relegated Brazil
to secondary or tertiary status in the community of nations, is now increasingly associated with attempts at community development, self-help, and
economic improvement among the most impoverished of Brazilians (Chesnut 1997). It is the growth of Protestantism in Bahia, and not just the prevalence of Candomblé there, that figures today as one of Brazil's best-kept
"national secrets."

Given Candomblé's shifting relationship to national embarrassment and
pride, it is significant that in both the anecdotes with which I began this es-

say ironic references to different forms of Afro-Brazilian religiosity—in one case Candomblé, in the other Pentecostalism—provide insiders and ethnographers (quasi-insiders), with a privileged idiom for experiencing feelings of social solidarity coded as Brazilianness. This camaraderie arises not as a result of pride in artistic expressions sanctioned as secure exemplars of national culture, but around the playful recognition that an often obscured but nonetheless well-known and problematic aspect of national life—namely, the reality of a *still unruly* Pentecostalism—has just been brought to light.

Michael Herzfeld has described rueful recognitions of a community's shared blemishes as examples of "cultural intimacy," or a "fellowship of the flawed" (Herzfeld 1997:28) in which frank acknowledgment of habits coded as unseemly may encourage feelings of collective belonging. The changing relationship between the Brazilian nation-state and Candomblé suggests something of the extent to which cultural intimacy is historical and requires historicization. In Bahia, what was once shameful is now celebrated. And precisely at the late-twentieth-century moment when Candomblé appears as resolutely Brazilian, a significant number of Salvador's Afro-Brazilian citizens have begun to follow new forms of Protestantism that state officials, social scientists, culture managers, and sectors of the Bahian citizenry are likely to find offensive and even highly embarrassing. How (and to what extent) people derive a shared identity in relation to such troubling shifts is an open question that warrants ethnographic investigation, something I do not pursue here. Instead, I build on insights gleaned from what Herzfeld calls cultural intimacy in order to raise new questions about national identity and Pentecostalism in Brazil.

At the close of the twentieth century, established notions of Brazilianness leave little room for Bible-thumping, textually obsessed Pentecostal moralists who deny the importance of cultural mixture and sensual miscegenation to official definitions of nationhood. Although Bahia's Pentecostals have not usually targeted something called "the nation" in their attacks on mixture, they actively contest the celebration of Candomblé's orixás and the sexualized mulatta, distinct figures that are nonetheless omnipresent in Brazilian nationalist imagery. Pentecostals often argue that one's race should not be a marker of one's social status and that sexual and affective relations should be based on inner virtues. And they strive at times to valorize black women, and women in general, in the face of a culture that fetishizes brownness as the epitome of feminine beauty (Burdick 1998, 2001). In a related vein, Pentecostals argue that dishes made of the African ingredients characteristic of Bahian cuisine, including coconut milk and *dendê* palm oil, are dangerously mixed. I have often heard them argue that these foods can be traced back to the influence of Candomblé, and hence the devil, and will cause spiritual and physical harm to people who ingest them. In order to contextualize these debates about race, nation, and religion waged around everyday habits, I present a snapshot of Salvador's Pelourinho Historical Center from the perspective of the new millennium.

Restoring the Cradle of Brazil

One of Brazil's most remarkable populist politicians, Antônio Carlos Magalhães, began a massive urban reform and cultural heritage program in the state of Bahia in the early 1990s. Magalhães, a vengeful, masterful manipulator of patronage and state bureaucracy, is often called "ACM," "Tony Malignant," and the "Strong Arm of Bahia." He has been mayor of Salvador twice and filled in as an unelected representative to the lower house of congress during the 1964–1985 military dictatorship. He was national minister of communications in the 1980s, a post that earned his family the Bahian franchise for Rede Globo, one of the worlds' largest television networks. Magalhães has served as governor three times, and he picked his successor to the governor's mansion in 1994, 1998, and 2002. He is the *de facto* owner of Bahia's second-largest newspaper, the *Correio da Bahia*, and much of Salvador's prime real estate.

Critical to the power and future designs of Magalhães and his political coalition is the culture industry, especially as it relates to the images of sensuous, brown, and "traditional" Brazil purportedly exemplified by Candomblé, Bahian cuisine, and the restored spaces of the Pelourinho. This potent relationship is common to heritage centers around the world, since "cuisine, like gentrification, is built on appropriation . . . of segmented vernacular traditions . . . local ingredients and preparations . . . incorporated into new 'classical' cuisine at the center" (Zukin 1991:212). Tellingly, the Pelourinho is often called "the cradle of Brazil" or "Brazil's brown mother" (Gaudenzi 1999). A center of Afro-Brazilian cultural production and political organization, the neighborhood is today in the final stages of a restoration project that has consumed almost US$100 million in state funds since 1992.

The domestic lives of the inhabitants of the Pelourinho have, since the early 1970s, undergone careful measurement and evaluation by the Bahian Institute of Artistic and Cultural Patrimony, (IPAC), the state institution founded in 1967 to prepare the neighborhood for its inclusion in the UNESCO list of world heritage sites. Individuals who successfully conform to government expectations concerning the mostly private qualities necessary to serve as the Bahian version of what UNESCO calls "Living Human Treasures," or "persons who embody . . . the skills and techniques necessary for the production of . . . the cultural life of a people and the continued existence of their material cultural heritage," have been allowed to remain in the restored heritage center.[12] Those deemed problematic or representative of traits unsuitable for consumption by a middle-class and foreign public have received indemnifications averaging US$2000 and been exiled to Salvador's mainly peripheral working-class neighborhoods where, in the eyes of the state, they belong.

The Pelourinho's inhabitants face a state determined to generate political legitimacy and foreign exchange by transforming a former pillory into the nation's consummate space for street life, spectacle, and expressive culture, for architecture presented as an authentic symbol of Brazilian culture, and for the interracial and interclass sexual relations often posed as the glue that binds Latin American national identities (Skurski 1996; Sommer 1991). Nonetheless, as a result of its enormous intervention in residents' private lives, the Bahian state today faces a group of Afro-Bahians made familiar with its modes of governance by more than thirty years of negotiating their quotidian ways of walking, sleeping, dancing, worshipping, fighting, and even making love, and thus their permanence in the neighborhood.

More than just the refurbishing of Latin America's most stunning collection of baroque mansions in an effort to garner tourist dollars, the Pelourinho's gentrification is a eugenicist project, an attempt at improving a population that might serve as symbolic ancestors representative of the nation's African roots. Here historical reconstruction stands not simply as a way of commodifying culture, or even of constructing a people, but of struggling to produce a population whose everyday habits appear to be isomorphic with particular aspects of an imagined Brazil.

Needless to say, there are important divergences between the conceptions of self and community enunciated by Pelourinho inhabitants and the representations marketed by their state. But residents are not some authentically resistant population or a heroic community that rejects the hegemony of the nation-state and thus struggles to close such a gap. Rather, the manipulation of residents' practices helps produce new conceptualizations of collective belonging and protest that both support and undercut Brazil's most salient idioms for national identification. Among these seem to be novel forms of Pentecostal belief and practice. In other words, the Pelourinho, as a self-conscious and tightly ordered representation of what Brazil *should* be, stands as a privileged zone for examining what happens when aspects of what Brazil *should not* be somehow come to public attention.

Sickening Mixtures: Pelourinho Protestantism and Nationalist Cuisine

Anthropologists have long emphasized the importance of foodstuffs in systems of reciprocity and understandings of pollution and social identities (Douglas 1966; Leach 1972; Rappaport 1967). Adults who grew up in the

Pelourinho report that, from at least the 1960s until the 1980s, Pelourinho children, like their peers throughout Salvador, commonly spent September eating copiously at sumptuous meals known as *carurus*. A caruru is named after its main course, a chopped okra, onion, palm oil, and crushed peanut and cashew stew served in honor of the Roman Catholic saints Cosmas and Damian. In Bahia these saints are associated in Candomblé with the Ibêji, the Yorùbá divinity understood to watch over children, especially twins (Verger 1998:569–571). On September 27, and throughout most of the month leading up to this date, Bahia's Roman Catholics and Candomblé believers commonly honor Cosmas and Damian with a late September "children's caruru" or "Saint Cosmas' caruru" that they claim should be eaten by at least seven children (Tavares 1961:149). Many Bahians believe that through the distribution of caruru to children they protect themselves from envy, disease, and sterility while removing obstacles that might impede their attainment of personal and professional goals.

On Cosmas' and Damian's day in 1999 I visited the Rocinha, a section of the Pelourinho populated entirely by working-class Afro-Brazilians. The neighborhood's children raced about, covered in sticky caruru and holding presents offered by those who had prepared the meal served in the historical center's restored streets. Yet this caruru was special. Due to residents' intransigence and competing ownership claims by wealthy Bahians and the state and federal governments, the Rocinha in 1999 was one of the last areas of the Pelourinho where IPAC had not yet divided residents into those fit to remain and those to be removed. Most important, unlike similar meals throughout the 1970s and 1980s, the 1999 caruru was not distributed by the Pelourinho's powerful Afro-Bahian entrepreneurs.

Instead of the respected neighborhood women who owned bars, small stores, food stands, restaurants, and brothels before the Pelourinho's restoration, the 1999 sponsors were mainly IPAC employees and middle-aged bourgeois women from outside the neighborhood, known as "madames" by residents who had often worked as domestic servants in such people's homes. The identities of the purveyors of the caruru, who traveled to the historical center to distribute food as a part of a tradition of paying "promises" that they understood to reinforce regional Bahian identities, seem to have played an important part in neighborhood residents' denunciations of caruru, mixture, and their state in a language of Pentecostal censure. In their condemnation of both IPAC and Candomblé, residents frequently asserted that the food distributed belonged to the devil. This is a way of explaining the world that is quite salient in Pentecostal discourse in Brazil. For example, as a young boy made his way along the muddy path that gives access to the area's homes, his mother began swatting at him with a broom, shouting, "Where the hell have you been? You've been taking the Devil's food! My cooking's not good enough for you, goddammit?!?" As a slammed door muffled her screams, I heard her shouting, "How many times have I told you not to eat that stuff, those gifts from the malignant one?!?"[13]

Soon another adolescent, Mara, came loping down the trail with a palm oil–streaked face, happily sucking on some hard candy. When Tatiane, Mara's mother and the self-described lover of an infamous police detective, emerged from her patio and saw her daughter, she screamed, "That's right. Eating with the devil. You're gonna be *his* tonight!" Later that afternoon a Rocinha grandmother explained, as she swatted her preteen grandson about the face and neck, "Those things, those Candomblé offerings, they make the children sick. All that oil and coconut milk! I don't eat that stuff, that devil's food!!"

This condemnation of one of Brazil's most influential religions and the basic ingredients for what has been celebrated, especially since the 1970s, as typically Bahian cuisine, was enunciated by a woman I had seen preparing and eating *moqueca de peixe*, a fish stew made from dendê palm oil, coconut milk, cilantro, garlic, onion, and tomatoes. While it is by no means uncommon, anywhere in the world, for people's everyday habits and their representations of those habits to clash, the gap between the ways people in the Rocinha talked about food and the ways they actually prepare and eat their meals is intriguing. Mothers and grandmothers who produced delicious dishes by mixing palm oil and coconut milk argued publicly that such concoctions were both immoral and unhealthy. And Tatiane suggested that her teenage daughter would pay for the food she had eaten with sexual favors, thus highlighting issues of reciprocity and sexual mores in relation to discussions of Satan that closely resembled dominant Pentecostal discourse about the evils of foods associated with Candomblé.[14]

The fact that Rocinha mothers spoke explicitly of the state, of greedy "madames" who appropriated the work and culture of their domestic servants, and of officials who they believed were trying to corrupt children through the distribution of caruru, suggests the extent to which Pentecostal languages may permit the enunciation of alternative versions of Brazilianness. Put another way, in 1999, a group of Pelourinho residents who rarely associate themselves closely with any religious denomination, decried the state's attempt to "folklorize" them and confiscate their homes. These same people often wove in-depth analyses of the importance of Afro-Brazilian culture into Bahian political projects of the 1990s, arguing that their everyday habits were being used by the state to attract *gringos* (foreigners) and people from southern Brazil.[15] And on Saints Cosmas' and Damian's day, residents who for the most part did not consider themselves Protestants employed a language of Pentecostal denunciations of Candomblé to express their displeasure with the upper class and state-sanctioned distributors of a meal that had become more a public performance of Bahianness than an expression of neighborhood solidarity.

When I spoke to the wealthy women distributing caruru to Pelourinho children, they demonstrated little knowledge of Candomblé as a religion. I do not interpret their lack of expertise as a way of deflecting an ethnographer's queries about a religion whose practitioners often prefer to shield many of their beliefs and activities from outsiders. Their answers seemed to demonstrate a bewildered amusement at the fact that a foreigner would ask pointed questions about practices that this group of middle-class Bahians interpreted as more about being Bahian than about communication with or veneration of the orixás. A good example of this viewpoint, expressed in the context of debates about the propriety of Protestant attacks on the orixás, is a newspaper article written by Manoel Jorge e Silva Neto, a professor of constitutional law in Bahia. According to Silva Neto,

attacks by certain Evangelical churches against Candomblé . . . merit censure by Bahian society in general and an energetic reaction from the authorities. Due to the incontrovertible fact that Afro-Bahian religions are linked to the history of the Black race, these incidents indicate . . . a veiled racism as well as a creeping violence among fundamentalist Protestants . . . *the aggressions are also an offense against our cultural rights, since Afro-Bahian religious manifestations long ago stopped being issues of faith and became an integral part of the Brazilian people's cultural heritage* (emphasis my own).[16]

The claim that Candomblé no longer belongs to its believers alone, but to the nation, points to the importance of analyzing the genesis and meanings of Protestant attacks not solely as expressions of a latent racism on the part of Protestants, but as part of a wider dialogue about race, national identity, and citizenship which may or may not include examples of racism.

Bira, a nondenominational Pentecostal who commutes daily between his home in the working-class suburb of Ilha Amarela and the downtown Rocinha, once explained to me the importance of resisting the foods offered in celebration of Saint Cosmas and Damian. He argued that Candomblé worshippers insist on distributing food because, by eating these gifts, the consumer recognizes or validates the request made to the orixás. Food sacrificed in special places by Candomblé believers, as well as sacred dishes consumed by guests, friends, and the public at Candomblé ceremonies, ties those people together and to the gods (Bastide 2000:43–46). For Bira, the problem with "Afro-Bahian cults" is that participants believe that by sacrificing they will in turn receive something from the rest of the world and from God.

According to Bira, in Candomblé, as in Roman Catholicism, the consumption of offerings is a subterfuge to induce the public to confirm the pact made between an individual and the orixás. Thus, eating food associated with Candomblé is a form of witnessing or participation in networks of reciprocity that makes viable the contract at the root of such offerings. However, according to Bira, religion should address truth, not people's earthly desires. And such truth is appreciated through the word of God, by ethical care of the self, and by "abnegation" rather than "the worship of saints and the spilling of blood [through animal sacrifice]" designed to support individuals' worldly machinations. Bira's concerns about reciprocity and recognition point to ways in which conversion can reshape social structures by encouraging withdrawal from reciprocal practices basic to community solidarity.

Pentecostalism tends to disrupt exchanges of food, alcohol, and labor and thus reconfigures social bonds. Similarly, over the last ten years, as a part of the Pelourinho's ongoing "restoration," the Bahian state and the Pelourinho's primarily Afro-descendent, working-class residents have negotiated daily the combination of habits and personages consecrated as paradigmatically Bahian.[17] By spurning a type of paradigmatically Bahian food offered by the heritage bureaucracy and by the local bourgeoisie, Pelourinho residents, some of whom struggled to obtain the highest possible indemnifications even as their neighbors fought to remain in the neighborhood, seem to have rejected the state's offerings in a highly selective manner. Yet in light of Bira's commentary on food and reciprocity, and Rocinha residents' condemnations of the dishes IPAC offered their children, complaints about culinary mixtures appear as critiques of the intense tutelage imposed by a state that grooms its landscapes and its people to represent national essences. I turn now to these essences and their treatment in the languages of Pentecostalism so influential in the Pelourinho today.

Folklore Comes to Life

In keeping with its status as a self-conscious representation of the nation's origins, a variety of social movements, cultural expressions, and political discourses arose in the Pelourinho of the 1990s. Yet the neighborhood's Pentecostals are for the most part a somewhat atypical group of Bahian religious practitioners. The majority, as is true of a significant portion of neighborhood residents, have served time in prison. Most began to study the Bible for the first time while incarcerated. Additionally, a central group of these Pentecostals, influenced by the Assembly of God, the neo-Pentecostal Brazilian Universal Church of the Kingdom of God, and Jamaican Rastafarianism, cultivate dreadlocks and link themselves to what they describe as Jamaican "roots" reggae.

Roots reggae is a widespread phenomenon in Salvador. Yet its Christian adepts, due to their long hair and association with marijuana, sometimes have difficulty articulating with the city's mainstream congregations (da Cunha

1993). When visiting established churches, many Pelourinho Pentecostals face exorcism by pastors who claim that their unkempt appearances denote affinities with the Devil. Despite such rejections, and in part because they appropriate and reconfigure the languages of more established neo-Pentecostal congregations, Pelourinho Protestants have made significant inroads among Salvador's more politicized Afro-descendent youth. It is not uncommon for young adults to be invited to read from the Bible during Pelourinho reggae concerts, cultural events, political discussions, or domino games. The weekly concerts held in the Rocinha section of the Pelourinho and dominated by discussions of sin and salvation are packed with working-class youths from the periphery, university students, and foreign visitors. The messages put forth often involve the condemnation of Candomblé, of salient archetypes related to nationalist ideologies of mixture, and of specific state policies as they relate to the neighborhood's reconstruction.

One of the neighborhood groups most involved in analysis of the Pelourinho reforms in the mid-1990s was the Christian reggae band called Bem Aventurados ("The Blessed"). A majority of the Bem Aventurados were either the children of Pelourinho prostitutes or young men and women who moved to the Pelourinho as so-called street children after abandoning or being abandoned by their families. They have formed an NGO called "S.O.S. Children of the Historical Center" and, in a process not unlike IPAC's recuperation of the Pelourinho, they have forged new community genealogies through their particular reinterpretations of Bahian heritage. Rather than street children (*pivetes*), or "the children of prostitutes," common slurs in Bahia, the members of the band are now the "Children of the Historical Center," and thus of national history. In this way a language of philanthropy, heritage renewal, and the state's ongoing interventions in the reckoning of kinship becomes a way of enunciating identities created alongside, but not exactly in accordance with, the state. One of the most salient languages in which the Children of the Historical Center participate is that of nationalist folklore. A telling example of how the Bem Aventurados–Children of the Historical Center appropriate and rework nationalist efforts in the Pelourinho is their 1997 song, "The Buzz That Comes from a Cup" ("Lombra do Copo").

"The Buzz That Comes from a Cup" is a popular Pelourinho expression that highlights the tense process of crafting national culture around the reconstruction of Salvador's Historical Center. The words refer to the plastic mineral water cups employed by crack cocaine smokers in Salvador, a group whose presence in the Pelourinho was encouraged in the mid-1990s by the state's policy of vacating buildings and paying indemnifications to residents. The song is also renowned for its chorus, "Saci, saci, saci / é uma paranóia," or "Saci, saci, saci / it's a paranoia," a play on Pelourinho slang for crack abusers, known as "sacis," and the high that accompanies use of the drug, something dubbed a "paranóia." The word *saci* is especially significant, as it refers to the *saci pererê*, a term used throughout Brazil to refer to a mythological folkloric figure.

The saci pererê is an impish, black, pipe-smoking trickster said to hop about on one foot, confounding and stealing from everyone he encounters. Canonized early in the twentieth century by the writer Monteiro Lobato, the saci remains something of a marginalized outsider in the pantheon of Brazilian tricksters. Unlike the well-known fictional archetype Macunaíma, a "black" Indian who became brown by washing off a bit of his color in the influential 1927 novel of the same name, the saci lies somewhere beyond the nation. He is a black, semihuman, childlike, and disabled being said to inhabit forests and liminal areas. But in the Pelourinho of the 1990s, the saci stands as a crack abuser. By traversing and hence establishing the line between civilization and barbarism, the difficult-to-pin-down saci helps to distinguish the wild, overwhelmingly black and Native Brazilian antecedents of the modern nation from those modern, "brown" figures located securely within the recuperative story of racial democracy.

When the Bem Aventurados sang "Lombra do Copo" in the Pelourinho of the mid-1990s, hundreds of young crack abusers would scream, "Check it out. It's the Believers. The saci's coming!" They would bounce in front of the stage, cheering and holding aloft the plastic mineral water cups they use to smoke cocaine. As the song's author told me, he intended "Lombra do Copo" as an indictment of capitalist relations and the use of blinding drugs in the Pelourinho and as a critique of "Babylon's system," in which children not living with their families were relegated to the gutter. The song was usually sung by a former Pelourinho resident I will call Gula (the same man whose indignation at a London cocktail party opened this chapter) while a boney band member I will call Jorginho jumped about the audience, animating the lyrics with a mineral water cup and lighter as he pretended to smoke crack. The performance was so realistic that first-time, non−crack using concertgoers would often intervene, grabbing Jorginho, who bobbed and weaved, flicking his lighter and acting out the part of a deranged saci, as his bandmates sang,

Ai vem um saci, ci, ci, ci, ci	Uh oh, here comes a saci-si-si-si-si
É um saci, pererê	It's a saci pererê
É um saci, ci, ci, ci, ci	It's a saci-si-si-si-si
É um saci, pererê	It's a saci pererê
É uma paranóia	It's a paranoia
Essa lombra do copo	This buzz that comes from a cup

É uma paranóia	It's a paranoia
Essa onda do copo	This problematic habit in a cup
É uma paranóia	It's a paranoia
Podem beber cerveja, whiskey, Campari,	You can drink beer, whiskey, Campari,
cravo, cravinho com jatobá	cloves and jatobá bark liquor.
Gabriela, cravo e canela	Gabriela, cloves and cinnamon
É a onda do copo	It's the problematic habit in a cup
É uma paranóia	It's a paranoia
Essa lombra do copo . . .	That buzz that comes from a cup . . .
A-A-anónimo	A-A-anonymous
A-A-anónimo	A-A-anonymous
Não querem mais	They don't want any more
"Papãe: anónimo"	"Father: Anonymous"
"Papãe: anónimo"	"Father: Anonymous"
Não querem mais	They don't want any more
Não fumem agua mineral	Don't smoke mineral water
Que ela faz, muito mau . . .	Because it really does, a lot of damage . . .
É um saci, ci ci ci ci	It's a saci-si-si-si-si
Um saci pererê	A saci pererê
Pode beber cerveja, whiskey, cachaça, Campari, Gabriela, cravo e canela	You can drink whiskey, cane liquor and Campari, Gabriela, cloves and cinnamon liqueur
acchlachlululululullac-yu-yu!"	(sound of vomiting)
É uma paranóia	It's a paranoia
Blublublubub	blublublubub (sound of vomiting)
É uma paranóia	It's a paranoia
Blublublblbub	blublublblbub

Although clearer in Portuguese than in my translation, "Lombra do Copo" relies on a series of couplings. These include *lombra* and *onda*. "Lombra" refers to the state of being stoned, while "onda" describes the waves present, for example, in water. Bahians also employ onda to denote a general form of problematic, dangerous, or unexpectedly complicated activity. A bank robbery, a fight, or a dispute with a government official might all be characterized as "ondas." The minor substitution of the Portuguese *lombra* with *onda* in an otherwise identical phrase changes the translation of "That buzz that comes from a cup" to "This problematic habit in a cup," thus carrying the listener from the good times of being high or drunk to a concern for, or a desire to alter, habitual actions. Here social drinking, a staple of the exchanges that, like Saint Cosmas' and Damian's caruru, root working-class identity in reciprocity, is interpreted by Pentecostals as an addiction rather than a source of community. The song's chorus intones, "It's a paranoia," and the lead singer pretends to gag as he doubles over and screams "acchlachlulululullac-yu-yu!" Yet he vomits not just because he has drunk too much alcohol, but because of the nature of his drinks.

Tellingly, the final cocktail named in "Lombra do Copo" before the singer violently expels the poisonous mixture is the "Gabriela, Cravo e Canela," or "Gabriela, Clove and Cinnamon." A sweet brown concoction of raw sugarcane alcohol, honey, cloves, and cinnamon currently served in Pelourinho bars, the "Gabriela" is named after the protagonist of *Gabriela, Cloves and Cinnamon*, by Jorge Amado. Until his death in 2001, Amado was the Bahia's most famous novelist and chronicler of Pelourinho rogues and heroes, populizer of portraits of lusty mulatas, and a friend and supporter of the Pelourinho's patriarch, Antônio Carlos Magalhães.

Gabriela, Cloves and Cinnamon tells the story of a beautiful young woman —famous for cooking skills and sexual prowess that enthrall an entire city— who flees Bahia's interior only to become the lover, wife, and, when she cannot adapt to the demands of the bourgeois public sphere, the domestic servant of an immigrant café owner. The Bem Aventurados thus fill their cup with a mixed drink–fictional character metonymic of the imagined domestic scenes and the racial and gender politics the state strives to support through the Pelourinho's reconstruction. Their rejection of the cup is not an unreflective Protestant indictment, in favor of abstinence, of alcohol in general. Rather, in a specific critique of Bahian sociality the song becomes increasingly precise as it moves from "beer, whiskey" to "Campari" and on to three different markedly Bahian and Pelourinho aperitifs, "cloves [alcohol], cloves and jatobá bark [alcohol] / Gabriela, cloves and cinnamon [alcohol]." Beer and whiskey are found throughout the Americas, while Campari is produced under license in Brazil and assumed by the song's author to be Brazilian. Jatobá and Gabriela, however, are even more particularly Bahian spirits, made from the agricultural commodities cultivated and cut for export in the state's interior. In the Pelourinho they are associated with tradition and usually served from hardwood kegs, or plastic jugs masquerading as wooden barrels. They are even a staple of the state's tourist advertisements for the Pelourinho Historical Center.

By attacking mixed drinks canonized as Bahian, the Bem Aventurados assail an imagined Bahia and the ways Bahian identity and sociality are materialized and made public in the Pelourinho today. They do more than criticize an abstract Bahian identity. They undercut the very sign vehicles—in this case, alcoholic cocktails and the curling white smoke of crack cocaine— that carry the nationalist essences reworked, consumed, and thus embodied by both the state bureaucrats interviewing Pelourinho residents and the crowds dancing and singing on the Pelourinho's restored plazas. They prob-

lematize the embodied attachments promoted by the state in public figures
and in folkloric delicacies like the "Gabriela" that are based on, or seem to
emanate from, a private sphere of interracial mixture celebrated by both the
state and many of its citizens.

The alternating couplets and folkloric subject matter of "Lombra do
Copo" recall a nursery rhyme or children's song. Indeed, the saci is famous
as a character in the storybooks that have helped make national identity real
to millions of Brazilian children. The saci does so not by celebrating a mis-
cegenated national identity, but by symbolizing the savage whose very exclusion gives life to the official narrative of mixture as a story of salvation.
An official story of mixture requires apparently "pure" originary figures
away from which regenerative mixtures move. Thus the saci is not simply a
racialized drug abuser stigmatized in the present, but a black Brazilian folkloric figure whose problematic relationship to a nation defined in part
against him is reworked in "Lombra do Copo."

For example, as the Bem Aventurados sing "Uh oh, here comes a saci-si-
si-si-si / It's a saci pererê / It's a saci-si-si-si-si / It's a saci pererê," they crouch
down and whisper—as if afraid, as if sneaking up on someone—so as to indicate the fear and alterity they associate with the saci. On the other hand,
the sweet, brown, beautiful Gabriela appears repeatedly in today's Pelourinho as the epitome of a purportedly redemptive mixture made public and
enacted by her sexual availability and cooking skills. Like "Black Eva,"
whose cooking in 1927 led Manuel Bandeira to highlight the possibilities of
Afro-Bahian regeneration through creative mixture and the domestic habits
on which such hybridity relies, Gabriela is located in the Pelourinho's Brazilian future, not its African past. Nonetheless, a critical dilemma faced by
the modern state that invests in tradition while plotting its future is how to
"discipline the very forces that were necessary to its own emergence, but
that now threaten its newfound authority" (Herzfeld 1997:115). In the Pentecostal hymn "Lombra do Copo" the association of Gabriela and the saci
confounds a state-sanctioned movement away from the African and toward
a hybrid Brazilian brownness even as it speaks in new ways of salvation and
regeneration, precisely the goals of early-twentieth-century racial democracy and the late-twentieth-century reconstruction of the Pelourinho.

"Lombra do Copo" emerges as part and parcel of the heritage zone's purportedly redemptive reforms of architecture and Bahian humanity. Not a
distant point of origin or a primitive survival, the saci is a present-day ap-
parition who lives up to his folkloric fame. He allows IPAC to associate the
neighborhood's residents with racialized alterity and thus justify the state's
interventions. Yet the saci also returns in the Bem Aventurados' music in
unstable shapes that trouble those reforms. And Gabriela—who appears as
both an alcoholic drink and an attractive woman, each to be consumed by

ideally male, middle-class Pelourinho revelers who have turned out to be overwhelmingly Afro-Bahian and working class—is rejected by the Bem Aventurados as a form of pollution. This exorcism of a female figure may demonstrate a certain born-again Christian misogyny. But the rejection of the female figure may also have more to do with the ways in which Gabriela has been, quite literally, forced down the throats of a Bahian public as the epitome of feminine beauty, sociality, and national identity.

The Bem Aventurados' lyrics, like their neighbors' culinary habits, show how Pentecostalism, as a set of beliefs and practices that enable the alteration of domestic habits so important to the packaging of "Bahian culture," may play an important role in reshaping the archetypes productive of Brazilian national identity. These symbols, which today include the mulatta, the trickster, and the market woman referenced in Freyre's poetry, are in certain ways a response to a now-muted elite embarrassment over Afro-Bahian practices. They have been transformed over the course of the twentieth century into national attributes in a complex operation that has relied on and supported ideologies of miscegenation. Yet what is really novel today is that the rejection of such ideologies of hybridity is enunciated by people configured as embarrassing to the nation due in great part to their religious affiliations. In other words, Pentecostals occupy a structural position somewhat analogous to that filled in the early twentieth century by the Candomblé practitioners they attack today.

Unlike Candomblé's priests, priestesses, and adherents in the first decades of the twentieth century, Pentecostals today do not face legal sanction.[18] Yet they remain a painful secret resolutely shut out of the tourist brochures, celebratory monographs, state-funded dance troupes, and public celebrations of Afro-Bahian religiosity so important to Brazil's identity and political economy today. After all, what tourist would travel to tropical Bahia so as to listen to a group of stolid moralists dressed in cast-off fashions from the North American Midwest? Nonetheless new types of Pentecostals, such as the relatively exotic Pelourinho Rastafarian / Pentecostal community, have produced religious manifestations that have begun to attract foreigners and the attention of Bahian intellectuals. Yet these people still call on their audiences to raise their hands and praise the Lord and, if one raises one's hands high and earnestly enough, to come by and to read the Bible and prepare for the rebirth thought to accompany Christian baptism.

The bureaucratic management of national history in the Pelourinho has much in common with the Pentecostal language through which residents criticize their state institutions. If I have argued here that the saci critiqued by the Bem Aventurados emerges from the valorizations of folklore and nationalist history in the restored Pelourinho, in the following section I outline some of the overlaps between Pentecostal practice and state-directed attention to the past and Bahian culture. From this perspective Pelourinho Pentecostalism appears not just as a criticism of a state fundamentally invested in the myth of racial democracy, but as one result or correlate of the late-twentieth-century manipulation of hybridity in the service of a Brazilian identity that was once embarrassing and is today celebrated. Whether or not IPAC bureaucrats and Pentecostals will come to agree on the fundaments of their national community is still unclear. But it is apparent that Pentecostalism and IPAC's management of national history and culture draw on one another in ways that suggest how new types of Afro-Bahian religions may come to define Brazilianness in the coming decades.

The Multiple Voices of Cultural Heritage Planning

By the mid-1970s, IPAC's sociological questionnaires, soup kitchens, medical posts, and handicrafts education projects made a group of working-class Afro-Brazilians familiar with at least one office of the Brazilian state. Likewise, as the Pelourinho came to serve as a laboratory for a modernizing Bahian social science, intellectuals and elites continued to know themselves in a manner akin to Manuel Bandeira and Godofredo Filho of the 1920s. They identified as Bahians and Brazilians by means of a focus on sex and domesticity, masculine leisure, and their coconstruction with Pelourinho residents of an array of explicitly national habits. But even as Bahia's bourgeoisie leaned upon the crystallizations and enactments of national character so much a part of the Pelourinho project of the 1970s and 1980s, neighborhood residents became increasingly attuned to the power of ethnography. According to researchers who worked in IPAC at the time, inhabitants frequently appropriated their state heritage bureaucrats' sociological categories so as to describe themselves.

The familiarity between Pelourinho residents and the social scientific apparatus increased in the 1990s as architects measured the buildings they would restore and sociologists and anthropologists sought to maintain accurate censuses in preparation for the payment of indemnifications. Of the approximately 1,300 families residing in the Pelourinho in 1992, only about 200 have managed to remain in the neighborhood in the face of the IPAC's gentrification efforts. Those who remain have frequently done so by claiming social scientist status or by using IPAC's techniques against the institution. People keep field notes, maintain dossiers or archives, and produce questionnaires so as to present arguments about themselves and their neighbors when facing the heritage bureaucracy in conflicts over their homes.

The tight bonds between state and citizen resulting from IPAC's more than thirty-year effort to define the Pelourinho's population do more than unite a populace and a bureaucracy in shared techniques for calculating those qualities thought to define an insider and outsider. They return to-day to haunt a state invested in creating stable categories of hybrid identity around its historical center. For example, the musicians who perform "Lom-bra do Copo" delight in wordplay that pokes fun at the IPAC bureaucracy. For example, they alter the word philanthropy by substituting the slang term *pilantra*, or scoundrel, for the proper root of the Portuguese *filantropia* (phi-lanthropy). And they use the word *pilantropia*, akin to "misanthropy," when talking of IPAC and its indemnification of Pelourinho residents. Further-more, by slurring the prefix in "historians" (*historiadores*), they transform the word into "storytellers" (*estoriadores*), who produce accounts with uncertain truth values. In this way the Bem Aventurados create neologisms that sug-gest IPAC is a corrupt, self-interested helping hand rather than a beneficent caretaker. And they do so at a historical juncture reminiscent of an early-twentieth-century moment in which Candomblé practitioners moved from the status of embarrassing outsiders to absolutely essential sources of national identity.

While it would be incorrect to identify social scientific research as the source of Pelourinho Pentecostalism, the two moral discourses demonstrate substantial affinities that suggest the extent to which Pentecostal challenges to established notions of Bahianness both transform and reinforce dominant versions of Brazilian nationhood. For example, when the Bem Aventurados sing or, during reflective moments, discuss certain verses of "Lombra do Copo," they frequently alter their voices or draw an imaginary box with their hands. For this reason I have placed the phrase "Father: Anonymous" in quotations in my transcription of their lyrics, marking it as an instance of reported speech based on residents' appropriations of fragments of IPAC questionnaires and indemnification documents.

By framing the creation of a category of identity that arises alongside and in tension with a sociological questionnaire administered by IPAC, the Bem Aventurados indicate through verbal and corporeal gestures that they are quoting or redeploying a technology of state control. They stack or graft multiple perspectives and identities onto one another in a rhetorical opera-tion similar to that of an IPAC social scientist administering questionnaires to neighborhood residents being prepared to represent what UNESCO calls "Living Human Ancestors." In this way they ironize that bureaucracy's im-perfect objectification of their own everyday habits.

Even as Pelourinho Pentecostals and IPAC share an interest in private habits, personal redemption, and a language of social science, they also move together to produce a feeling of Brazilianness. For example, the cry, "Father: Anonymous" refers not just to the Bem Aventurados' own family situations or to their attempts to carve a symbolic paternity out of the history made material in the Pelourinho. Instead, the intonational shifts around the sarcastic quotation of an IPAC interviewer and interview schedule suggest some of the ways that Christian reggae expresses and makes concrete the Bem Aventurados' recognition of their reliance on the historical center for their own identities. After all, their community organization is called "Children of the Historical Center." Nonetheless, the Pentecostal appropriation of the language of heritage reveals a desire to alter the social structures by which IPAC seeks to construct them as objects, but not subjects, of national history.

Jorginho, who plays the part of the saci in the Bem Aventurados' rendition of "Lombra do Copo," claimed in 1998, "When IPAC comes looking for us with their tools of the devil, slandering us with incessant questions about 'Father: Anonymous,' we cry out to the Lord Jesus Christ for salvation and mercy for ourselves and for the godless bureaucrats, ventriloquized [*teleguiados*] by ACM [Governor Antônio Carlos Magalhães], who know not their sins!" Here Jorginho counterposes the Christian God to IPAC bureaucrats in an everyday interaction in which he quotes a song that both infiltrates and attacks the symbols of the state. At the same time, he ascribes multiple meanings to and invents disparate origins for the categories of social scientific analysis intended to eradicate his problematic habits from the Bahian cradle of Brazil. In other words, Jorginho, like the song "Lombra do Copo," inhabits a folkloric universe made possible by the Pelourinho but, in his view, ruled ultimately by a redemptive force far more powerful than his Governor or IPAC.

To point out that religion may both support and trace the limits of state power is not surprising. Yet Protestant protests against Candomblé reveal an ongoing reformulation of the archetypes that make up the modern Brazilian national imaginary. To shy away from this revelation, or to attribute Protestant denunciations of Candomblé to racism or to some sort of disability that conditions people to become Pentecostals, is to shut out, rather than formulate, sociological explanations. Instead, I have struggled to suggest how Afro-Bahian Pentecostalism and Afro-Bahian Candomblé might come to share goals, languages, and even structural positions in the construction of the Brazilian nation. Although the vehemence of Pentecostal critiques of Candomblé make this project problematic, the novel types of Pentecostalism emergent in the Pelourinho of the 1990s suggest the importance, and the feasibility, of considering these two types of Afro-Bahian religiosity alongside the state's attempts to domesticate a people and promote a comforting myth of shared essence.

The overlaps between Pentecostal religious and IPAC social scientific discourses have not yet been recognized by either side as examples of affinities or shared political projects. Instead, during the Pelourinho's restoration the Bem Aventurados and IPAC have struggled for control of the historical center's space and representations of Bahian culture. Neither the practitioners of Candomblé nor the Pelourinho Pentecostals have recognized any sort of shared project.[19] On the contrary, the disputes and vicious struggles emanating from the divergences between Candomblé and Pentecostalism are the point of departure for the present chapter. And in analyzing this contradictory opening I have worked to describe how Pentecostalism, and its novel forms arising in the restored Bahian birthplace of Brazilian tradition, stands perched on the brink of official commemoration. This already palpable shift has taken place even as Bahia's politicians and culture managers, invested in a myth of racial democracy, deny Pelourinho Pentecostalism's political salience as a type of working-class, Afro-Brazilian religiosity. This underscores the extent to which the nation's embarrassing features may over time become enshrined as secure cultural traits actively cultivated by the state.

Late-twentieth-century Bahia suggests not so much an agreement between state and citizen, but the very shiftiness of that which embarrasses and that which is celebrated. Rather than a sedimented condition of cultural intimacy in which enemies may find an unexpected common ground in their recognition of troubling habits, the rise of Pentecostalism as a source of Afro-Bahian critique in the 1990s highlights a moment in which to be Brazilian may soon derive in part from the recognition of a type of religiosity still configured by influential commentators as alien to the tropics. It is with this contemporary transition that I conclude. In doing so, I take up the challenge, or at least question the wisdom, of imagining the future of Brazil as what Gilberto Freyre described in 1926 as a forward-moving miscegenation.

Conclusion: National Icons and a "Cool Fact"

Scholars of and in Latin America have struggled recently to explain a contradictory moment in which nation-states face significant stresses to their salience and reach but are not in imminent danger of disappearing or seeing their influence drastically curtailed (Matory 2001; Warren 2002). Nonetheless, in Brazil, the most emblematic example of the development of a narrative of cultural and racial mixture that has helped maintain "oppositional politics within the flow of history with a 'big h'" (Hale 1997:572) is a recent series of popular and government initiatives that have focused attention on racial discrimination, the politics of culture, and the obfuscatory role of racial democracy in national life (Guimarães 2001; Hanchard 1999). In this light, I have argued that Pentecostal attacks on Candomblé that at first glance appear to be little more than racist attempts to claim space for a new type of religion provide important working-class commentaries on the racialized bases of belonging in the Brazilian nation-state.

If in 1926 Gilberto Freyre celebrated miscegenation upon the tables of

Bahian market women, at the end of the twentieth century new discussions of food, private essences, and the vehicles through which they appear to be made public have come to occupy intellectuals and Pelourinho residents. Freyre was involved in a valorization of his national culture, a process whose legacy in Bahia includes the recuperation of Candomblé as a prototypically Brazilian expression. Yet in Bahia today substantial numbers of working-class youth, Candomblé practitioners, and intellectuals reject the longstanding ideology of racial democracy. This is the context in which Pentecostals, and especially practitioners of Born Again Christian reggae—the Bem Aventurados drew an average of just under one thousand people to their Friday night concerts during the summer of 2003 —have come to play an important role in discussions of Brazilian identities. The Pentecostal critique of Candomblé and racial democracy seems to have altered the pantheon of national archetypes recognized by most Brazilians and discussed in this chapter. These include, among others, the saci, the sexualized mulatta, Afro-Bahian market women and Candomblé practitioners (baianas), and the patriarchal slaveholding family associated with racial fusion.

Recently, a member of the Brazilian Internet chat group "Massivereggae" sent out a message requesting a copy of "that Rastaman doll thing." She described the figure as that "funny picture of the Rastaman," one familiar to Bahians as a result of, among other media, IPAC-produced color maps of the Pelourinho and the logo celebrating Salvador's nationally diffused Summer Musicfest.[20] Some list members responded by sending the woman a file that contained the desired illustration. But one participant, a college student in São Paulo, responded with the following message that I have translated but left as punctuated by its author.

HaHaHaHa . . .

Let me just tell you a funny thing about these little dollies . . . yesterday I had a class at the university in Social Sciences and the teacher was talking about society and tribes and stuff like that . . . culture . . . and her class is nothing but slides . . . and in the one about music she showed the very same picture that Cris sent of the two rastas, one who I think is playing percussion and the other the cowbells HaHaHah . . . pretty cool . . . what a coincidence . . .

Good vibrations gang, see you later
     And sorry about a not very important email that's not very interesting, but that demonstrates a cool fact . . . kisses.[21]

Perhaps I am reading too much into the email correspondence, or misinterpreting her fascination with "little dollies" (which somehow brings to mind Manuel Bandeira's much earlier titillation with Afro-Bahian women). Nonetheless, this southern Brazilian woman's nervous yet excited description of folkloric Rastafarian figures playing the drums and cowbells so typical not of reggae, but of Brazilian samba music, draws attention to the rise of the male Rastafarian as a symbol of a folkloric Brazil in which new forms of Protestantism may come to support the Brazilian nation.[22] The pervasive showcasing of Pelourinho Rastafarians—most of whom are at least loosely associated with the Pentecostal Protestants of the Rocinha—on television, in magazines and tourist guides, and in performative genres such as carnival parades supports my suspicion. The figure of the "holy" Rastafarian is also important to the clientelistic entourages that follow and pay a self-consciously hypocritical homage to Antônio Carlos Magalhães as he parades about the historical center on periodic visits designed to steep his public persona in the aura of Afro-Bahian authenticity. Such legitimacy, drawn from public signs of an Afro-Brazilianness dependent upon the state's reworking of private life, is similar to that Magalhães has previously sought to cultivate through ties to Candomblé temples and to the restored spaces of the Pelourinho and its residents' homes.

Thus it seems that, as longstanding narratives of national identity have come under fire from a variety of quarters, the state has responded with technologies of heritage reconstruction that appear to mesh unexpectedly with some of the myriad Pentecostal faiths popular among Bahians today. It is important to avoid shutting out the messages enunciated by millions of Brazilians in the language of Pentecostalism. However uncomfortable they may make the observer who finds in Candomblé a symbol of centuries of Afro-Brazilian struggle and creativity, and however jarringly they may clash with established ideas of what a Brazilian, and particularly an Afro-Bahian, is and should be during Brazil's post-1985 redemocratization, it is worthwhile to remember that rueful self-recognitions are often, in fact, painfully rueful. And like the college student from São Paulo, one may feel unease when approaching the habits and beliefs of the people who now attack Candomblé and other cultural forms that have been canonized as distinctively Brazilian and valorized by nationalist discourse, social science, and Afro-Brazilian political movements.

Some, like the student's professor (if I am reading her remarks correctly), may express this unease through words like "primitive" and "tribelike." Others will try to block these trespasses onto the established terrain of Brazilian studies. It is critical to remember, however, that attempts to suppress such embarrassments are now, and have been since Candomblé was redeemed from its embarrassing state, a critical mode through which the Brazilian nation-state is imagined as a community. It is also important to consider creative research programs that explore the relationships between Candomblé and Protestantism in ways that, as I have not done here, include the viewpoints of Candomblé believers. Such projects might underscore the extent to which Candomblé, as an imaginative strategy implemented by Afro-

Bahians since their arrival in Brazil, has become a contradictory basis of Bahian governance. They might also portend the extent to which Afro-Brazilians may be able to modify creatively Pentecostal Protestantism as part of their ongoing reconfiguration of Brazilian political life.

Notes

1. Andrew Canessa (2000) addresses Evangelical protest against the Bolivian national imaginary. There is also an emergent literature on the subject of Pentecostal critiques of Afro-Brazilian religion in Rio de Janeiro, especially as concerns Umbanda. Works include Luiz Eduardo Soares, "A Guerra dos Pentecostais Contra o Afro-Brasileiro," *Comunicações do ISER* 44(12): 43–50; Sanchis (1994), and Birman (1996). With the exception of Serra (2003) I am not yet aware of similar literatures about Candomblé and Bahia, usually understood in Brazil and among Brazilianists as sites of more "traditional" values than Rio de Janeiro.

2. Overwhelmingly black, usually working class, consistently preaching fire and brimstone while attacking the most sacred symbols of the nation, dressed in ill-fitting secondhand clothes that recall and may originate in rural areas of the United States, and confusingly attached to a transnational Protestantism sometimes associated with North America, Salvador's Pentecostals appear so threatening to established notions of Brazilianness that Frei Leonard Boff, one of the Brazilian founders of liberation philosophy, recently claimed in Salvador that Pentecostal Churches attack Candomblé due to their ignorance. See José Bonfim, "O diálogo contra a intolerância," *A Tarde*, May 6, 2003.

3. Brazil's IPHAN, or Instituto do Patrimônio Histórico e Artístico Nacional (Institute for National Artistic and Historical Patrimony), was founded in 1937 as the Serviço de Proteção Histórico e Artístico Nacional. For a helpful history of SPHAN in English see Williams 2001.

4. All translations from Portuguese, unless otherwise noted, are my own. This January 14, 1927, letter has been published in Mário de Andrade et al. (2000:332).

5. The fact that Manuel Bandeira, his interlocutor, Mário de Andrade, Gilberto Freyre, and Godofredo Filho were all active in the early years of the Brazilian national heritage bureaucracy (SPHAN, later IPHAN) is significant to contemporary concerns over the production of public culture. Heritage, or patrimony, is typically understood as an ensemble of popular manifestations and natural wonders set off from everyday life by public ritual and government registry. As a type of collective property held in the name of a people and a national future, heritage is an extremely salient form of public culture critical to state sovereignty and development schemes today. Ethnographic examination of the definition, packaging, and uses of national patrimonies is critical to understanding the terms by which global master narratives are put together today. For important recent discussions of national patrimony and the heritage industry, see especially Ferry 2002, Handler 1985, Price 1998, and, for Brazil, Williams 2001.

6. Manuel Bandeira in Tavares (1961:131).

7. "Bahia" is frequently used today—and was more frequently employed in Freyre's time—to refer to the city of Salvador.

8. For an example of the importance of food to the myth of racial democracy, see Gilberto Freyre's *Manifesto Regionalista* (1996), originally produced in 1926 as part of a regionalist cultural and literary movement. Six of the Manifesto's twenty items revolve around food.

9. For examples of recent debates about the enduring impact of racial democracy, see especially Fry (2000). For a contrasting viewpoint on issues of mixture and racial essentialisms today see Goldstein (1999).

10. Nor can I do justice to how Candomblé is oftentimes presented in Bahia today as not at all about syncretism, but about African survivals.

11. Expedito Filho, "'Não vou desistir': Entrevista com Antônio Carlos Magalhães," *Veja*, June 3, 1998.

12. http://www.unesco.org/culture/heritage/intangible/treasures/html_eng/index_en.shtml. See Collins (2003) for a genealogy of the idea of "living human treasures" that suggests that in Bahia the people canonized as examples of Bahian culture are not so much the producers of a craft tradition, as UNESCO's language suggests, as they are embodiments of a rooted Afro-Bahianness important to the state. UNESCO's guidelines allow for such latitude; they explicitly say that each national state will establish its own criteria for defining its treasures. For recent analyses of culture and intellectual property see also Brown (1998) and, on UNESCO's Living Human Treasures program, Nas (2002).

13. I translate the Portuguese "o maligno" as "the malignant one." The invocation of the *maligno* is a specifically Pentecostal reference to the devil, rarely used by Bahian Catholics today.

14. And that also recalls the reciprocal relations that gird the power and functions of Candomblé. This correlation between Candomblé and Pentecostal conceptualizations of reciprocity suggests something of the extent to which Brazilian Pentecostalism is made possible and draws on idioms from Candomblé. I thank Jocélio Teles dos Santos for insisting on this point.

15. The word *gringo* is often used in Bahia to refer to anyone from outside the state or with a "white" complexion.

16. Manoel Jorge e Silva Neto, "Intolerância religiosa" *A Tarde*, October 21, 2001.

17. It is important to note that residents are not necessarily objecting to an abstract national imaginary based on miscegenation, as Canessa (2000) argues for fundamentalist Christians and indigenous groups in Bolivia. From such a perspective, "hybridity" serves as a relatively ahistorical and abstract explanation for contemporary essentialisms, rather than a specific problem that arises as a state seeks to instantiate sanctioned forms of public culture in spite of evidence that people's actual practices diverge substantially from such representations.

18. In fact, the Pentecostal electorate makes up an important base of support for Antônio Carlos Magalhães' political coalition.

19. Candomblé practitioners have instead brought suit in Brazilian courts against Protestant pastors. In a recent volume edited by Rafael Soares de Oliveira (2003), Ordep Serra, a Bahian anthropologist and student of Candomblé, points out the extent to which Candomblé represents a reckoning of African roots that goes beyond and presents itself as anterior to the nation. Unlike Serra, who insightfully demonstrates how practitioners of Candomblé often reject an ideology of hybridity or syn-

cretism, in the present chapter I am more concerned with the uses made of Candomblé by the Bahian state. Although Serra's knowledge of the practices and beliefs of the Candomblé community is an important contribution to the current religious debate, the experiences of Pelourinho Pentecostals suggest that there is much more to the current dispute than issues of "intolerance."

20. If many Bahian homes today feature portraits of "traditional" characters such as fishermen or *baiana* market women, it is increasingly common to see young middle-class automobile owners who have affixed a bumper sticker depicting the Rastafarian symbol of the Summer Musicfest.

21. The message appeared in September 2002 on the Brazilian Internet discussion forum "Massivereggae."

22. This has already begun to happen in national politics. In Bahia, Antônio Carlos Magalhães' political coalition draws substantial electoral support from political parties associated with Pentecostal churches. The Bem Aventurados, meanwhile, have come to support a Pentecostal member of the Universal Church of the Reign of God (IURD) in his struggle to become a city councilman.

References Cited

Andrade, Mário de, Manuel Bandeira, and Marcos Antônio de Morães. 2000. *Correspondência: Mário de Andrade & Manuel Bandeira*. São Paulo: EDUSP.

Bastide, Roger. 2000. *O candomblé da Bahia: Rito nagô*. Translated by M. I. Pereira de Queiroz. São Paulo: Companhia das Letras.

Birman, Patrícia. 1996. "Cultos de possessão e pentecostalismo no Brasil: passagens." *Religião e Sociedade* 17, no. 1–2.

Birman, Patrícia, and David Lehmann. 1999. "Religion and the Media in a Battle for Ideological Hegemony: The Universal Church of the Kingdom of God and TV Globo in Brazil." *Bulletin of Latin American Research* 18, no. 2: 145–164.

Brown, Michael. 1998. "Can Culture Be Copyrighted?" *Current Anthropology* 39, no. 2: 193–223.

Burdick, John. 1998. *Blessed Anastacia: Women, Race and Popular Christianity in Brazil*. New York: Routledge.

———. 2001. "Pentecostalismo e identidade negra no Brasil: mistura impossível?" Pp. 185–212 in *Raça Como Retórica: A Construção da Diferença*, eds. Yvonne Maggie and Claudia Barcellos Rezende. Rio de Janeiro: Civilização Brasileira.

Canessa, Andrew. 2000. "Contesting Hybridity: Evangelistas and Kataristas in Highland Bolivia." *Journal of Latin American Studies* 32: 115–144.

Chesnut, R. Andrew. 1997. *Born Again in Brazil: The Pentecostal Boom and the Pathogens of Poverty*. New Brunswick, N.J.: Rutgers University Press.

Collins, John. 2003. "The Revolt of the Saints: Popular Memory, Urban Space, and National Heritage in the Twilight of Brazilian 'Racial Democracy.'" Ph.D. Dissertation, Department of Anthropology, University of Michigan.

da Cunha, Olívia Maria Gomes. 1993. "Fazendo a 'Coisa Certa': Reggae, rastas e pentecostais em Salvador." *Revista Brasileira de Ciências Sociais* 8, no. 23: 120–137.

Douglas, Mary. 1966. *Purity and Danger: An Analysis of Concepts of Pollution and Taboo*. London: Routledge and Kegan Paul.

Ferry, Elizabeth. 2002. "Inalienable Commodities: The Production and Circulation of Silver and Patrimony in a Mexican Mining Cooperative." *Cultural Anthropology* 17, no. 3: 331–358.

Freyre, Gilberto. 1926/1996. *Manifesto Regionalista*. Recife: Fundação Joaquim Nabuco.

———. 1933/1946. The Masters and the Slaves, trans. Samuel Putnam. New York: Knopf, 1946.

Fry, Peter. 2000. "Politics, Nationality, and the Meanings of 'Race' in Brazil." *Daedelus* 129, no. 2: 83–118.

Gaudenzi, Paulo. 1999. *Operário do Turismo: Retalhos de Idéias e Pensamentos*. Salvador: Omar G. Editora.

Goldstein, Donna. 1999. "'Interracial' Sex and Racial Democracy in Brazil: Twin Concepts." *American Anthropologist* 101, no. 3: 563–578.

Guimarães, Antônio Sérgio. 2001. "The Misadventures of Nonracialism in Brazil." In *Beyond Racism: Race and Inequality in Brazil, South Africa, and the United States*, eds. C. Hamilton, L. Huntley, N. Alexander, A. S. Guimarães, and W. James. Boulder, Colo.: Lynn Rienner.

Hale, Charles. 1997. "Cultural Politics of Identity in Latin America." *Annual Review of Anthropology* 26: 567–590.

Hanchard, Michael. 1999. "Introduction." Pp. 1–26 in *Racial Politics in Contemporary Brazil*, ed. M. Hanchard. Durham, N.C.: Duke University Press.

Handler, Richard. 1985. "On Having a Culture: Nationalism and the Preservation of Quebec's Patrimoine" in *Objects and Others: Essays in Museums and Material Culture*. Madison: University of Wisconsin Press.

Herzfeld, Michael. 1997. *Cultural Intimacy: Social Poetics in the Nation-State*. New York: Routledge.

Leach, Edmund. 1972. "Anthropological Aspects of Language: Animal Categories and Verbal Abuse." Pp. 206–220 in *Reader in Comparative Religion: An Anthropological Approach*, eds. W. Lessa and E. Vogt. New York: Harper & Row.

Matory, J. Lorand. 2001. "The 'Cult of Nations' and the Ritualization of Their Purity." *South Atlantic Quarterly* 100, no. 1: 171–214.

Nas, Peter. 2002. "Masterpieces of Oral and Intangible Culture." *Current Anthropology* 43, no. 1: 139–147.

Price, Richard. 1998. *The Convict and the Colonel*. Boston: Beacon Press.

Rappaport, Roy. 1967. *Pigs for the Ancestors: Ritual in the Ecology of a New Guinea People*. New Haven, Conn.: Yale University Press.

Sanchis, Pierre. 1994. "O repto pentecostal à cultura 'católico-brasileira.'" In *Nem anjos, nem demonios*. Petropolis: Editora Vozes.

Sansi, Roger. 2001. "Arte publica, religião e iconoclastia na Bahia: O caso dos orixás do Dique de Tororo." Paper presented at the X Meeting of Social Scientists of the North and Northeast Regions, Salvador, BA, Brazil.

Serra, Ordep. 2003. "O candomblé e a intolerância religiosa." In *Candomblé: diálogos fraternos contra a intolerância religiosa*, ed. Rafael Soares de Oliveira. Rio de Janeiro: DP&A Editora/Koinona, pp. 53–70.

Skurski, Julie. 1996. "The Ambiguities of Authenticity in Latin America: Doña Bárbara and the Construction of National Identity." In *Becoming National: A Reader*, eds. G. Eley and R. Suny. New York: Oxford University Press.

Soares de Oliveira, Rafael, ed. 2003. *Candomblé: diálogos fraternos contra a intolerância religiosa*. Rio de Janeiro: DP & A Editora/Koinona.

Sommer, Doris. 1991. *Foundational Fictions: The National Romances of Latin America*. Berkeley: University of California Press.

Stepan, Nancy. 1991. *"The Hour of Eugenics": Race, Gender and Nation in Latin America*. Ithaca, N.Y.: Cornell University Press.

Tavares, Odorico. 1961. *Bahia: Imagens da terra e do povo*. Rio de Janeiro: Civilização Brasileira.

Teles dos Santos, Jocélio. 2000. "A cultura no poder e o poder da cultura: A construção da disputa simbólica da herança cultural negra no Brasil." Ph.D. Dissertation, Universidade de São Paulo.

Verger, Pierre. 1998. *Notas sobre o culto aos orixás e voduns*. São Paulo: EDUSP.

Warren, Kay. 2002. "Toward an Anthropology of Fragments, Instabilities, and Incomplete Transitions." In *Ethnography in Unstable Places: Everyday Lives in Contexts of Dramatic Politicial Change*, eds. C. Greenhouse, E. Mertz, and K. Warren. Durham, N.C.: Duke University Press.

Williams, Daryle. 2001. *Culture Wars in Brazil: The First Vargas Regime, 1930–1945*. Durham, N.C.: Duke University Press.

Zukin, Sharon. 1991. *Landscapes of Power: From Detroit to Disney World*. Berkeley: University of California Press.

PART FOUR

Fault Lines

CHAPTER 8

Intimacy and Corruption in Thailand's Age of Transparency

Rosalind Morris

Language and Politics

It is often said of politicians in Thailand that their language is sweet but vacuous. When people say of a politician that his mouth is sweet, "*paak waan*," they mean also that his words are without meaning, "*mai mii khwaammai.*" The irony is encrypted but in a way that everyone knows how to decipher. This suggestion, that politicians speak in a language that is either mellifluous or furious, but that signifies nothing, makes of the politician an odd kind of figure. He or she (but mostly he) is someone who has language, even beautiful language, but a language that has no relationship to the world. It does not represent. It is, in fact, inadequate to the task with which the politician in an electoral democracy is charged: namely, representation. How can an elected person voice the concerns of the voters or represent their interests when his tongue bears a language that won't signify? Although this might be dismissed as cynicism and a mere fatigue with bad politicians (their nepotistic appointments, their not infrequent dallying with mafia bosses, prostitutes, and drug smugglers), in Bangkok, and in many outlying regions, empty speech is not merely a characteristic of some (bad) politicians. It is believed to define the politician as such. The politician is someone who speaks nonsense, sweetly. If, indeed, a politician is thought to be virtuous or worthy of praise, it is because he has transcended the category of politics, the business of the metropole (*kaan muang*). Ask any taxi driver, or noodle vendor, or cell-phone toting, Web-browsing entrepreneur.

One might say that the ennui of the middle classes and the working masses manifests itself as a belief that the politician is something like a bad medium: someone who possesses the instrument of communication but who does not know how to make it function. At the same time, the politician may be said to resemble a mendacious medium, one who knows that he does not possess the technologies of mediation and who lies about it with enormous deftness. In other words, he is a fake. If the latter is revealed, then the politician will be dismissed, vilified as immoral, and accused of abusing power. Such sentiments do get articulated in everyday conversations about politicians in Thailand, but more often than not, politics itself is construed as a field in which distortion and exaggeration correlate with political discourse, but not necessarily the limit of its efficacy. Indeed, if the politician is someone who can be likened to a bad medium—and here medium must be understood to mean both the medium of communication (in the sense that the radio or the television is a medium) and that which transmits other powers—this is not because a politician functioning as a medium is itself bad, or even that mediation is bad, even when hypostatized. There is no recourse here to an ethics of presence, or a demand for direct participatory democracy. Rather, the dismissal of the politician on the grounds that he is like a bad medium is linked to a simultaneous commitment to the technology of mediation itself, to mediation as a good. This is why, on the one hand, a politician can be indicted because his speech is dislocated from the truth of the world, exceeding the content of the message, and, on the other hand, why the ideal of political behavior is "transparent communication." It is this language of transparency that interests us here.

Transparency, *khwaam prongsai*, is perhaps the most ubiquitous term of political discourse in Thailand today. No article about politics, no statement by a politician, no commentary on the postcrisis (1997 and after[1]) era seems to lack this term. This is true regardless of the venue in which political reform is being discussed. From such right-wing business magazines as *Matichon* to such major investigative dailies as *Thairath*, from such corporate mouthpieces as *Phujatkaan* to the tabloids, such as *Siamrath*, to say nothing of the major English dailies, the *Bangkok Post* and *The Nation*, all seem weighted by the demand for, or complaints about the absence of, transparency.

But what does "transparency" mean here? And what are its effects? In the era of liberalization, transparency translates the idiom of accountancy into that of politics. It is somehow associated with an ethics of sincerity, at least from the perspective of the IMF and the World Bank, to say nothing of those corporate institutions through which IMF policy has been implemented in Thailand—the foreign banks that have been able to purchase local lending institutions in order for the Thai government to be able to write off its nonperforming loans. The demand for transparency is thought to compel the performance of a certain honesty, and this honesty (or at least its performance), is thought to secure the possibility of smooth exchange relations in turn. It is perhaps not incidental that transparency is most desired in a context where translation is most at risk. At a time when foreign financial institutions are attempting to enter and to participate in the Thai economy in ways that were previously prohibited by law, the stakes in translation are especially high. Insofar as *performances* of transparency also signal the possibility of secrets elsewhere, one of its consequences is the creation of new kinds of intimacy, such that the assertion of transparency works to produce a bond that would have previously been produced through the sharing of otherwise occulted knowledge. In other words, the performative logic of transparency both mimics and transforms (translates) an older practice of intimacy. One of the questions that needs to be asked, then, concerns the ways in which the power of secrecy is, itself, secreted back into the logic of transparency. As we shall see, it is increasingly created through the ritual of disclosure, an act of transgression that offers to the viewer the sense that he or she is having a private knowledge (an intimacy) confirmed rather than repudiated.

As a discourse and an ideal, transparency acts here as a supplement, a kind of substitutional guarantee for what cannot be assumed in the transactions between persons and institutions from vastly different linguistic and social contexts.[2] But we are getting ahead of ourselves. Let us pause to consider the movement of language through which transparency has entered Thai.[3] When, in fact, does the term appear? With what developments is it associated?

Let me say it bluntly. "Transparency" emerges where "class" disappears. I cannot begin to cite the immense number of examples that would legitimate such a claim but, in brief, wherever the discussion of social inequality was once explained by reference to the structural inequities inherent in the *sakdina* system[4] or capitalism, it has been replaced by a rhetoric of transparency and corruption. Indeed, a history of "radicalism" in Thailand would divide the twentieth century and the first part of the twenty-first century into three periods: the first, dating from the early 1920s to the late 1930s, the second from the end of World War II to 1976, the third from the mid-1980s to the present. The first period would begin with the movement for constitutionalism initiated during the years of King Rama VI and ironically performed by his court.[5] It would end with the protosocialism of Pridi Banomyong, who headed the first government following the coup of 1932, but was exiled (Vichit Na Pombhejera 1979). The second period was led by many members from the first, including, most notably, Jit Poumisak, the author of *The Real Face of Thai Feudalism Today* (1957/1987). It includes both the overt revolutionary project of the Communist Party of Thailand and the slightly less antimonarchist alliance of students and the Farmworkers Union. The communists, farmers, and students were in open armed conflict with the military regime from 1968, and some Thai historians refer to this period as one of civil war. However, it was the alliance between students and farmworkers that succeeded briefly in ousting the military regime from power and, between 1973 and 1976, actually dominated the national government in Thailand. Their bloody suppression by a military junta can be said to have ushered in a third period: the present. This has been dominated by the NGO movement, various kinds of Buddhist reform (both progressive and conservative), and internationally affiliated proponents of civil society and human rights. Its occasional interruption by sporadic efforts to reinstitute militarism (as in the coup of 1991 and the attempted suppression of democracy activists in 1992) has not led to a major redirection of the neoliberal trend.

Telescoped as it is, this three-part history might, however, be reschematized as a binary history, the defeat of the left in 1976 constituting a definitive rupture in the possible future history of class-based radicalism in Thailand. The mark of that more profound rupture is to be found in the shifting terms within which a critique of the state has been articulated. Where once the language of social analysis was cast in terms of relative ownership over the means of production, it is now spoken in the idiom of corruption and transparency. It is almost inconceivable today to imagine a newspaper editorial holding the ruling and the wealthy classes responsible for the failures of the economy, the poverty of the working class, or the weakness of the nation. What one does encounter, at least in the popular press, is, by contrast, a consistent, almost homogeneous discourse in which social and economic ills are read as the function of nontransparency, which is to say the failure of representation. The profundity of this simple lexical difference is almost impossible to overestimate. This is because the lexical change also indexes a radical transformation in how the social is conceived. Its most dramatic element consists of an inversion of the presumptive cause-and-effect relations within the social field, what we might term a temporal reversal.

The failure of transparency, the bad representation, not only betrays the truth after the fact; it causes other kinds of failure. An incomplete highway construction project, for example, can be *explained* as resulting from nontransparency (as occurred in 1997). Voter fraud is *caused* by nontransparency (as was said to be the case in recent elections). Diminished exports are said to arise from a nontransparent economy. And no wonder. Transparency is, after all, supposed to effect positive changes. The IMF, for example, demands it as a condition of aid, and it is said to prevent the accumulation of nonperforming loans by local lending institutions. The "Truth" of transparency is, in other words, a performative one. It has its own time. It institutes what it names, coming both before and after that which it calls into being.

If, however, it often seems that critics would tolerate the most egregious sins by politicians were they simply confessed in advance, it is not simply Truth that is demanded in and by the discourses of transparency. It is, rather, the truth of a nation at a particular moment in its history, and in the history of the nation's absorption by global capital. But there is another dimension to be considered here. At stake is not only what happens inside Thailand, but what its image is when seen from afar. The anticipation of this being seen generates an enormous amount of reflexivity within Thailand (what Herzfeld [1997] identifies as the core of "cultural intimacy"), and such reflexivity inevitably produces a discourse upon the specific forms currently dominating the national polity, including the organization of the public and private, and of the family in relation to the nation. Bearing in mind the fact that the visual economy within which a drive to transparency takes place is highly mediated by this sense of being looked at from afar, and given that the sense of such scrutiny heightens a desire for new forms of intimacy that can take place within the halo of mediatic light, we will now want to consider the specific trajectories of transparency's discourse within Thailand, by way of example.

The Media Man

Our example is the case of Thaksin Shinawatra, the telecommunications tycoon who founded the Thai Rak Thai party, which won the largest share of seats in the national election of 2001. Following the elections of January 6, Thaksin's party forged an alliance with two other rightist parties, New Aspiration, led by former prime minister, General Chawalit Yonchaiyudh, and Chart Thai, led by Banharn Silpa-acha, a former government minister. Both of Thaksin's alliance partners had strong media ties. Banharn founded the Bangkok daily, *Baan Muang*, and Chawalit was closely associated with the founding of the Bangkok paper, *Naew Na*. Banharn and Chawalit represent a new generation of politicians who relate to the media not merely as that which is to be repressed or censored, but as a site of knowledge production and positive political force. Though they are innovators relative to their predecessors, it is Thaksin who incarnates the ascendancy of the digital era. His hugely successful Shin Corp (formerly Shinawatra Computer and Communication Public Company Limited) dominates all of telecommunications in Thailand, including wireless telecommunication, computers, satellite and multichannel television distribution.[6] The magnitude of its wealth is perhaps best indicated by Shin Corp's market capitalization, which in 1999 was estimated at more than fifty-seven billion baht.

The rise of the media tycoon in Thailand's political universe was foreshadowed in 1992 by the spectacle of cell-phone carrying protestors demanding the institution of an electoral system that would be, endlessly, on call to them.[7] That protest, famous around the globe for the sophistication of its media strategies, marked the end of the state's capacity to determine the content and reach of the print and television media. With virtual links to the major metropolitan centers, residents of Bangkok and Chiang Mai were able to transfer their own ethical positionality to those elsewhere, putting the world "on call" in anticipation of Thai history's violent recurrence. When the army did attack, its assault was transmitted and therefore witnessed, witnessed and therefore transmitted, in a complex circuit of specular exchanges. It was not that the protestors staged their own violation so much as they rendered the protest a *mise-en-scène* in which everything that occurred would be visible, on stage instead of backstage. This was achieved not through a visual enframement of the event, but through the establishment of a dispersed network of those who could receive messages from Bangkok. Indeed, protest organizers in Chiang Mai captured this quality perfectly when they introduced themselves to their supporters as telematic agents. "We will be your media," they intoned under brilliant spotlights from the backs of flatbed trucks.

All evidence suggests that cell phones played a crucial role in the organization of democracy protests, and in maintaining contact between local protestors and international media bodies during the military blackout on local television and print media following the assault on protestors.[8] It was estimated that more than two hundred thousand calls a day were made with cellular telephones from Sanam Luang, the park where the major rallies took place in Bangkok. Often dismissed for their middle-classness, the cell-phone radicals of 1992 enacted that movement by which the media has become the primary site of political relations in the modern world. As Pasuk Phongphaichit and Chris Baker have observed for Thailand more generally, the years after 1976 have seen a steady increase in the "importance of public media as a platform for communication with civil society, and as a focus of conflict between state and people" (Pasuk Phongphaichit and Baker 1995: 370). What changed in the late 1990s was the demand for a figure through which this ascendancy could be represented. That figure was Thaksin Shinawatra, a Sino-Thai businessman bearing the name of the first monarch of the Bangkok Era.

Thaksin's phenomenal success as CEO of Thailand's largest telecommunications company, and his rhetorically sharp opposition to the Democrat government's willing participation in IMF-sponsored liberalization schemes following the crash of 1997, made him a mesmerizing leader. His extravagant wealth, legible in a Buddhist society as evidence of merit, ensured that the structural necessity for a figure of media capital would be meaningful in local terms. And from the moment of his party's inception, Thailand was swept with Thaksin fever. Although we are now familiar with such larger-than-life political figures—the list includes Canada's Pierre Trudeau, the Italian Silvio Berlusconi, and Americans John F. Kennedy, Ronald Reagan, and, of course, Bill Clinton—they were virtually unheard of prior to television's era, and Thailand had certainly never experienced a comparable concentration of media-based authority in a nonmonarchical politician prior to Thaksin's emergence. Thaksin was not merely dependent on the media, he was capable of transmitting the power of that medium, and of appearing to possess power over it.

Partly, the success of Thaksin is to be explained by the extravagance of his promises. Among other commitments, Thaksin offered to pay one million baht to every village in Thailand, as part of a debt-relief program for farmers. Accusations that this amounted to vote buying had no capacity to mitigate the desire that such promises generated on the rural peripheries, where landlessness, underemployment, and the effects of environmental destruction are most acutely felt. Critics pointed out that such temporary stays of indebtedness would not address causal factors. Pots of money would not, they said, compensate for lack of title to land, aid in competition with large-scale agribusiness, improve softening economic conditions in the nations that typically import Thai commodities, improve poor agricultural techniques, or increase diminished soil productivity. But such criticisms fell largely on deaf ears.

What ultimately threatened to interrupt Thaksin's march to the prime ministership was the determination, made by the National Commission to Counter Corruption, that Thaksin had illegally concealed assets totaling more than six hundred million baht (something more than fourteen million dollars). These had been transferred in the form of shares to members of his household. If, however, fourteen million dollars seems rather a lot to deposit into the accounts of a driver, a maid, and assorted domestic workers, consider the fact that Thaksin *did* declare more than twenty-five billion baht (about six hundred million dollars) of his own assets. Although most of his wealth was disclosed, eight of the nine Commission members claimed that the rest was concealed for reasons of tax evasion. More damning than this possible effort to thwart the eye of the state, however, was the Commission's insinuation that Thaksin's primary intent was simply to mislead the Commission and to demonstrate his capacity to do so. "We consider Mr. Thaksin intended to hide those shares," said one of the commissioners.[9] One might observe here that innocence for Thaksin would consist in his being a "bad medium," but that guilt would entail his appearance as a malevolent one.

Thaksin himself claimed that he was merely ignorant of which assets had to be declared, that he wrongly interpreted the law (on the unfortunate advice of an Assets Management advisor), and that no malice or ill intention had informed his actions. It had not occurred to him, for example, that his wife's shares, transferred to domestic servants, would have to be declared along with his own. It is not clear in what sense these shares were transferred, though it seems they were placed *in trust* on the tacit understanding that they would be returned at some later date. Uncertainty about the na-

ture of the transfer—if it was a gift or a bribe, an act of generosity or calculated exchange—only incited more scrutiny by the press, to the extent that
Thaksin's domestic sphere became the most brutally lit but least clearly understood scene of the election. Thaksin's household became the object of a
grand media spectacle, but perhaps because the household is precisely that
which is said to lie behind and at the origin of the social, this scrutiny could
only display the fact of the family. Corruption, if it could be attributed to
Thaksin, would, by definition, have meant the subjection of his family to
corporate and therefore public logic (that of self-interest). Yet the media and
the public seemed unsure as to whether Thaksin had treated his family like
a business, or whether he had treated his employees like a family. If the former, he would be found guilty by the Counter Corruption Commission. If
the latter, he would be not only innocent, but virtuous. The mere appearance of his actions did not disclose which of these truths might lie behind
his deeds, and this ambiguity only heightened anxiety about a possible incommensurability between the fact of visibility and the fact of transparency.

Under new Thai law, holders of public office are not permitted to hold
more than 5 percent of the shares in a publicly traded company. By definition, Thaksin's power rendered him vulnerable to charges of corruption. This
could have been mitigated by disclosure, but according to the Counter Corruption Commission, Thaksin did not claim ownership of his own wealth.
Independently of the fact that he may have hidden his wealth (instead of simply not disclosing it), it is the failure of disclosure, rather than the extent of
his wealth, that made him subject to surveillance, and which then unleashed
the spectacle of the private domain. The case was adjudicated by the Constitutional Court, and the judgment itself became the subject of a report by
a working panel of the National Commission to Counter Corruption. In the
end, Thaksin escaped the guilty finding by one vote, in a process that was
widely criticized for its departure from precedent, particularly with regard
to the kinds of witnesses called and the degree to which they were subject
to cross-examination. Criticism of the findings appeared in many of the major media venues, and *Matichon* newspaper actually published the NCCC
report. The *Bangkok Post*, for its part, asked pointedly, "Why was Thaksin
made an exception?"[10] In the *Post*'s Sunday editorial, Thongbai Thongpao
noted again the NCCC panel's finding that Thaksin claimed ignorance of
what was in the public domain (his servants had appeared on a Stock Exchange of Thailand list of the nation's wealthiest individuals). The editorial
closed by lamenting the lack of disclosure on the part of the Court, which remained shrouded in "mystery," having failed to include crucial evidence, the
exclusion of which might have been read as a lack of belief in their veracity.

The displacement of anxiety about disclosure did not settle the matter of

Thaksin's culpability. Even as the sign of failed transparency slid from one political site to another (from prime ministerial candidate to Constitutional Court), Thaksin's image began to work as the paradoxical figure of that displacement. On several issues, he would later be accused of overvaluing personal diplomacy and of conducting in secret negotiations that ought to have been open (with Burma, for example). The Thai king used the occasion of his birthday address to chastise the prime minister for arrogance and a failure to restore economic stability, in the course of which he suggested that Thaksin had engaged in a policy of dissimulation, pretending to have confidence in economic recovery while secretly admitting to the difficulty of the task. The king himself suggested that the problems could be better faced with a more open, face-to-face strategy. At the same time, he expressed worry about Thailand's national image, about the possibility that all these accusations of corruption might reflect poorly on the kingdom's future economic prospects.

Had the Constitutional Court found him guilty, Thaksin would not only have lost his office, he would have been barred from politics for five years. In the anticipation of a judgment, he promised to assume the prime ministership on an interim basis, saying he was obliged to work for the nation for as much time as he was permitted. Such service is the essence of grace, he said. Even as he promised graciousness, however, Thaksin invoked something else. Shortly thereafter, he responded to a CCC statement by suggesting that an attempt to conceal assets was like "dying to make fun of the cemetery." It is an odd remark, this invocation of death at the moment when Thaksin faced his own political disappearance. How could death ridicule the cemetery, the institution in which it is at home, of which it is a part? In what sense is concealment that which belongs in the Counter Corruption Commission? In what sense does it constitute the ground of the Commission? Perhaps Thaksin was prophesying the subsequent revelation that the Election Commission, a related body charged with the observation of electoral processes and the revelation of corruption, was itself guilty of failed transparency, a number of its own members having taken bribes from those it was supposed to prosecute.[11] But the relevance of his statement lies elsewhere. Independently of his prophetic abilities, Thaksin's remark bespeaks the intimacy between legality and illegality at this point in Thai history. He is aware that corruption is that which it is defined to be under law. The performative constitution of corruption by law—as a violation of the law's letter—is something to which even he is subject, and which banishes precisely the question of origins and structural causality. This law works in the realm of appearances, of what can be seen and what can be hidden. What matters now in Thailand is that everything be visible, and more: that the processes of making visible, of moving things from the domain of the secret into that of the public, themselves be revealed, unfurled in the brilliant light of the media's perpetual day.

The intimacy that is so ironically observed by Thaksin is not restricted to the relation between law and illegality. As we shall see, it also operates in the relations between private and public. But it is not without risk. As with any intimacy, an excess threatens to collapse the identities of the parties who would otherwise be intimates. The law that is too intimate with its other, even in the interest of criminality's prevention, collapses inward, and becomes that convivial monstrosity that Achille Mbembe (2001) has described for the postcolonial state in Africa. In Thailand, the extrajudicial killing of drug traffickers and the briefly floated possibility of government drug sales (aimed at the usurpation of mafia power) exhibit many of the same characteristics. The state identifies with its opponents (drug traffickers and producers) in order to defeat them. As James Siegel has described for Indonesia, this act of identification is born of a desire to partake of the criminal's power, but in the process, that power comes to be imagined as a force in excess of the criminal or the state, as something that precedes it and exceeds it. So, both sides take refuge in a notion of technology that will allow them to capture that power and transmit it. Guns, cameras, techniques of detection and disguise all fall under this category. As do the media in general.

Siegel's (1998) point for Indonesia is that criminality has replaced ghosts as a category of recurrence in the place of death, and that it signals the nationalization of death. He means to understand the New Order regime of Indonesia as one in which the state can, in the interest of assuaging something called trauma, systematically murder the people. Criminality for him is the means by which the upper classes and the urban world intrude on the rural peasantry in ways that cannot be resisted or known in advance and that always threaten to occur again, violently. In traditional Java, says Siegel, ghosts could be exorcised or placated, and were, in any case, local beings with no real animus against individuals. Criminals, on the other hand, can come from anywhere, and no one knows how to deal with them. Hence, they justify the omnipresence of the state. We are not talking about ghosts, despite Thaksin's reference to the cemetery. But we are talking about a new kind of relation between the ruling class and the rest of the nation. And we are talking about the means by which the state legitimates its invasion of domains that were previously beyond its purview, even as it destroys oppositions that were previously beyond its control. If the veil behind which this occurs is the call for national or indeed cultural intimacy, as expressed, for example, in the king's spectral invocation of foreign observers and the conservative press's general concern about how the IMF or other foreign economic players will view the state of politics in Thailand, then this call must also be recognized for the violence it does to those who have no control over the means of (po-litical) representation, which today means control over the media.

Not a Family Business

Prior to and during the January 6, 2001, elections—the first ever in Thailand to use a bicameral system—there were accusations of vote buying, of vote nullification, violence, and intimidation against voters. These accusations were made against party members and the gangs they employed. In addition, the Election Commission itself was accused of accepting bribes and permitting party candidates to give gifts in excess. It was also accused of setting up poll stations with inadequate light, so as to create confusion. Lack of transparency was cited by villagers throughout the nation, and petitions against various candidates and their parties led to the nullification of several electoral results, to the extent that new polls were undertaken in sixty-two constituencies.

In the logic of petitioners' remarks, it is a lack of transparency, sometimes literalized in the image of shaded polling stations wherein people lose their capacity to choose knowingly, that generates the conditions in which widespread fraud can take place. Because the voters cannot see what they are doing, they cannot know how to make that gesture required of every citizen in an electoral democracy: namely, the ceding of the right to future decision making (at least until such time as another election is called). For in Thailand, as in other "liberal democratic formations," the franchise consists precisely in choosing a representative who will, in the future, make decisions on one's behalf. That is to say, political representation means the transfer of self-representation to another. It is an act of surrender, a temporary relinquishment of sovereignty to the state in a manner that produces the state as sovereign. It is a gift of sorts.

Normally, of course, a gift is something that a "powerful" person bestows upon a less powerful person. It is, indeed, a performative means of generating such power. As Mauss has told us, the gift is that which cannot be refused; or at least the refusal of that gift cancels the social relation that would have made the giving possible and meaningful in the first place. The gift also puts the recipient in a position of indebtedness vis-à-vis the giver. In places where gift giving is an elaborated social institution, such as Thailand, electoral processes often find themselves at odds with the demand for giving and the demand to be compensated for the rescinding of one's sovereignty—this despite the fact that true gifts are not supposed to be calculated in terms of return and that one is not supposed to admit to wanting a gift. This is why party gifts of such items as farm supplies and motorcycles, when distributed during campaigns, are so troubling for the Election Commission.

One of the great anxieties in the Thai electoral system is that gifts will be confused with exchanges, that the violence of the giver will be used to force the recipient into a position of debt and, therefore, will nullify his capacity to choose a candidate autonomously. At issue is the time and location of the choice to cede sovereignty. For if, as Mauss says, the only power and sovereignty available to the recipient of a gift is refusal, then acceptance means that he or she has already ceded that authority whose later surrender is required in the electoral process itself. Here, gifting is not so much vote buying (though it is also called this) as the short circuiting of a temporality that is considered proper to elections. It is a preempting of surrender. In the aftermath of such gifts, there are not sovereign citizen-subjects at the polling station. There are instead what we might call partial individuals, people who have become attached and dependent upon those with the power to give. Of course, the assumption of the Election Commission is that people accept gifts not out of a willing surrender to the giver, but out of need—which is itself an obviator of any real free will. The poor farmer accepts powdered milk with the Thai Rak Thai party's imprimatur because he is desperate, not because he chooses to do so. His surrender is therefore not one. It is the illusion of a willing choice, the simulacrum of a vote, and one that is out of place. But in this simulacral order, there can be nothing but confusion—about what is real and true, and who should perform the function of representation. No wonder that the polling stations seem poorly illuminated, and that confusion reigns among people who no longer feel like citizens, but who resemble members of a crowd moving randomly.

This image, the simple everydayness of which threatens to betray its profundity, does not merely imply a critique of the physical setting in which voting takes place. Nor is it merely a tacit attack on the inequities that make rural elections a matter of such basic service as electricity—though both of these are present. More than this, it indexes a confusion about the very status of the term transparency, whose ubiquity has failed to secure a change in the ways in which rural people are represented. It indexes a collapse of linguistic domains, domains that are also originally from different sociocultural milieus. For the promise of insight in Theravada Buddhist contexts is not reducible to that adherence to the law's letter that transparency entails in a Western context. Yet in the aftermath of a global convergence, what Thongchai Winichakul (1994) would have us understand as a false correspondence, the two terms intersect each other, and confusion reigns. The villager is left asking, how can there be proper representation when there is only darkness? How can there be transparency when there is no visibility? Sometimes, of course, what is most visible is least apprehended, as in Poe's famous purloined letter. In the case of Thaksin Shinawatra, revelation seems to incite suspicion, and that which is revealed discloses nothing about the intention that generated actions. Thaksin admits to transferring his shares.[12] But this says nothing, in and of itself. The question that accrues to him is therefore the question that accrues to every image in the space of the mass media. What does it mean? What is the nature of its truth? One has appearances, and one has resemblances, and one needs a technique to decipher differences.

In fact, when disseminated in the glow of the media, Thaksin's gestures seem to confuse gifting and buying, voluntary surrender and coerced submission, legality and illegality. The site at which these confusions take place is that of the household, and the point at which they condense themselves is on the thin line between the family and the domestic staff. Such a confusion is multiplied when the household becomes a spectacle in the public domain. When Thaksin transferred six hundred million baht to his domestic workers to "protect his family" (from the possibility that their wealth would be confiscated if his business failed), he implicitly enacted two assumptions. First, he assumed that his household, and not merely his family, constituted a domain of privacy that, while subject to him, is nonetheless not his property. Here, he resuscitated the encrypted etymological history of the word "family" (*khrop khrua*), which in Thai literally means "people of the hearth." Second, he assumed that the extent that his private life, including that of his immediate family, was subject to scrutiny by the state did not include his domestic staff. He hoped, intentionally or not, consciously or not, that the resemblance *but* difference between domestic workers and family would conceal assets. The domestic staff looks like a family but is not one. At least not in the postsakdina era, when the legal equality of all persons is presumed, and the possibility of satisfying one's debts by placing one's family members in debt bondage has been eliminated.

In Thaksin's case, the resemblance between domestic workers and family, and the substitution of one by the other, was to effect a disappearance. This would be the disappearance of money, yes, but it would also be the disappearance of a difference between family and labor, between the world of gifting and the world of the salariat. The workers who received the shares would have returned them later, just as the recipient of a gift would return it later. Here, one must note, what is being given is not the shares, or not merely the shares. It is the trust that allows a maid to safeguard millions of baht. This trust is to be reciprocated, and shares will be the instrument of its transfer. Once it is no longer possible to know, for certain, where the line that differentiates family and labor is to be found, attention shifts to the site of vanishing. People ask, "where did the money go?" But not, "what allows money to disappear in this way?" This is because there is a space into which money and the difference between those one loves and those one employs have both disappeared.

Something else disappears into this space, and it is the opposition that one might have expected the poor to feel in relation to this extraordinarily wealthy man. For in press coverage and in everyday discussions of Thaksin at the time, he never appeared as a representative of media capitalism. He was not construed as a class enemy of the people, and few people paused to remark that the acquisition of such enormous wealth must presume that some people were laboring for less. Instead, he was pictured as a fabulously successful family man, one with whom common persons might feel sympathy, with whom indeed they might identify. After the CCC made its decision, many people assumed that Thaksin's political party would actually gain seats, on the basis of a sympathy vote.[13] Common people said they could imagine themselves being harassed by the state, could believe that their wealth would be tracked down and expropriated. That they did not have servants to whom they could transfer assets, or assets to transfer, did not seem to mitigate this strong tendency to imagine themselves in the place of the most economically powerful man in the country. This is what Michael Herzfeld (1997) would describe as true "cultural intimacy": a kind of common sociality born of possible shame.

Such commonality covers over the obvious social inequities that sustain and are sustained at the politico-economic level, and one might easily invoke a notion of ideology here, where the ideology of cultural intimacy or indeed cultural belonging works in the service of a particular class. In fact, the social chasm between classes makes the desire to identify even more powerful. Thaksin's power and success, and his no-nonsense approach to solving the nation's fiscal problems, made many believe that, were they to be in that position, they might also act as he did. In this reading, his authority is not based on a structural relation in which the less fortunate are dependent; it is rather simply a function of his successful instrumentalization of the opportunities that are supposedly available to all members of the Thai nation. This is why, despite his nearly absurd transcendence of middle-class social and economic means, Thaksin is a figure of the middle classes. He appears to be them, they appear to be the nation, and he represents to them what they imagine they would represent to themselves.

The fact that Thaksin can stand as such a potent figure of identification for people who do not and cannot ever achieve his status, rests on his capacity to effect the collapse of differences: between family and employees, between the ruling class and the ruled. They collapse into the category of culture, with each remarked as a different location on a terrain that is miraculously flattened by the possibility of reciprocity. One might reverse this formulation to say that Thaksin succeeds as the figure of identification to the extent that he can represent the possibility of cross-class communication. If he can not only achieve but also represent the communication between classes, if he can effect the imaginative traversal of social difference so as to generate the (false) appearance of unity, power is his. That he achieves this through the deployment of money in the form of a gift, which produces debt and gratitude both, does not mitigate the fact that the fantasy of reciprocity and the imaginative movement across difference structures such relationships and indeed makes them thinkable.

In essence, then, he must perform in his person the function of the mass media, producing connections between unrelated things and allowing for the phantasmatic movement between places for those who are otherwise mired in poverty and rooted in local communities where migration is always literal, and where the necessity for such movement is appropriated by the imaginative representation of such movement (labor migration and related forms of travel) as the journey of desire rather than the drag of need. Thaksin's movement, recall, is that of social verticality. For working people in Thailand, movement more often than not means simply taking the highway to Bangkok for more of the same. It is banal and rarely a source of wealth, but it is enormously rich as the ground on which the idea of vertical movement can be fantasized.

Now, then, we are beginning to understand how and why Thaksin, the media mogul, is the ideal figure for a world in which the media is the "platform of the political," and the technology of mediation is itself the message. The middle class can assume domination over the social world only when in-between-ness is itself the goal, which is to say, only when structural contradiction has been relinquished in the interest of "mediation." The corollary of this is, of course, an obsession with technologies of mediation. One sees this, in Thailand as elsewhere, in the proliferation of cell phones, Internet cafes, cable television, and the digitization of public spaces. While these are, still, mainly urban phenomena, their ubiquity in cities like Bangkok and Chiang Mai, as well as smaller regional centers, is hard to overstate. And in rural areas, urbanity is virtually identified with the state of "being wired," which is to say, connected to elsewhere. This obsession generates a chain of proliferating institutions and metainstitutions devoted to the surveillance of representation and disclosure. There is, in Thailand, the NCCC, the Constitutional Court, the Graft Commission, the Election Commission, Pollwatch, and various coalitions devoted to precisely this scrutiny. The observation and regulation of communication, in the broadest sense of that word, becomes all the more necessary as the lines and sites of communication multiply. And as politicians buy newspapers, and media tycoons enter politics, we have the image of an increasingly involuted series of lines producing an increasingly totalized network.

Of these lines one can say, simply, that they function or they do not, and even when they do not, the network itself seems to be able to assume new forms. The question concerning information technology, as Heidegger

(1977) posed it and Kittler (1990) so brilliantly answered, can only ever be one of functional success, never of good or evil, beauty or baseness. Nonetheless there is relative proximity and privileged access to the network, and the fact of the network does not explain such proximity. Today, the idiom of the successful functioning of the network is transparency, which offers itself as a corrective to the accumulation or the containment of access—to power and information, if not knowledge. And the rituals of disclosure often appear as the extension of a privileged connection, or a protected connection. In a mass-mediated world, there will be connection or not. Opposition has no place here, except as a demand for inclusion. Indeed, one has the theatre of "cleansing by publicity," as McLuhan put it, and the public sentimentality of a world in which there is no real privacy, only the possibility of connection in a sliding chain of signifiers between a patriarch, his family, his staff, and a nation in thrall to the possibility of being what they are not, namely one nation: *chart Thai*. Obtruding into the fantasy of a unity that is without absolute difference (a fantasy that allows for the fantasy of reciprocity), are nodes of real opacity, privacy of a sort that cannot be violated, if only the kind of privacy that pertains to property. And here, one notes, Thaksin is a man who can claim extraordinary privacy.

There are, of course, pockets where that bypassing of radical social change has not yet assumed a naturalized form. The Assembly of the Poor, left academics, scattered trade unions, and radical NGOs continue to press for more thorough social change. Recently, they succeeded in halting WTO talks in Thailand, and following the crash of 1997 they persuaded George Soros to abandon his scheduled visit to Bangkok. But these communities and gestures have lost the power they had twenty-five years ago. To the extent that socialism has any force, it is a nostalgic one, a spectral one.

Some months ago, while in Bangkok, I spoke to a young artist whose installation on water and its disappearance was showing at the art gallery of the Chulalongkorn University library. In passing, I used the expression chart Thai, meaning the Thai nation, to speak about issues of development and democratization. He corrected me, reminding me that "chart Thai" is a term of the ruling class. It has nothing to do with us, he said. "We" are "the people." He used the term, *prachaachon*, the now outdated trace of a vanished movement, the voice of the past. It was as though a ghost had entered the room. A few weeks later, Thaksin would respond to his accusers by saying the concealment of wealth before the Counter Corruption Commission would be like dying to mock the cemetery. Ridiculing the NCCC, Thaksin might just as well have ridiculed the specter: the specter of that plurality evoked in a "we" (*rao*). But such a mockery would also be his undoing, for the performative force of such an utterance, of saying "we," cannot be relinquished by any politician in any endeavor, however compromised, to establish democratic rule. Indeed, as Benedict Anderson (1991) observed in his incisive history of modern nationalism,[14] the mass media are the scene for producing and codifying "we" formations, for generating that strange spectrality that binds people of diverse places to a single temporality. Nonetheless, the "we" to which Thaksin referred is not identical to that of the artist's outdated fantasy. And partly for this reason, he could never have succeeded simply by invoking cultural intimacy. The mediatized image of the nation exceeds the diversity of its actuality, a fact that appears most viscerally when individuals ask each other to protect a secret together, to share in something that outsiders may not enter. The specter to which the artist referred was nostalgically unitary, but limited by class; Thaksin's invocation, by contrast, could only ever be provisional, promissory, or, more precisely, speculative. It could be banished by a single refusal. In both cases, the expression, "We the people" is translated, ghosted, by other histories in nations far from Thailand, inscribed at the beginning of a trajectory that is not, properly speaking, Thai. It is nonetheless ambivalently inscribed in that country's future. It is ghostly, but not dead. Perhaps, then, mocking the cemetery is precisely what progressive politics in Thailand must continue to do—without irony.

Notes

1. By postcrisis, I am referring specifically to the crash of Southeast Asian economies beginning in 1997, the primary index of which was the devaluation of the Thai baht, and the subsequent collapse of lending institutions in that country and throughout the region. This crisis itself is usually attributed to the rise and burden of nonperforming loans, originating in lending practices that were not grounded in the assessment of collateral assets, and in a speculation-driven inflation of real estate values. However, the precipitating factor is also associated with currency speculation, and especially that of Western speculators such as George Soros (who was repeatedly named in local accounts of the events, both in Thailand and in Malaysia). Another salient factor was the devaluation of Chinese currency. In the aftermath of the crash, the consolidation of financial and other banking companies, and the implementation of IMF loan policies, led to the substantial redistribution of Thai financial power, the consolidation of banking institutions and authority, and the displacement of some Thai family-based corporations by transnational corporations.

2. I am using the term supplement here in the sense given that term by Jacques Derrida (1976), to designate something that seems to be added belatedly but which reveals a constitutive lack in the original (text). This lack is not something that is fully compensated for by the supplement, however; rather the supplement is part of a potentially limitless chain of signifying marks whose terminus cannot be known in advance.

3. This kind of historical analysis might well be termed the history of lexicalization insofar as it would account for the movement of a term from its origin in one language, and its historically particular discourses, into another. In its fullness, such

a history would have to account for the precise ways in which the movement of terms is facilitated first by what is a false correspondence between them. In this case, *khwaam prongsai* and *transparency* appear to share the same referents, but this is only when their meanings are abstracted and dislocated from the chains of association within which they function locally. The harnessing, therefore, of a term associated with Buddhist insight to a practice associated with accountancy and neoliberalism needs to be understood as a function of mistranslation and lexicalization as much as the mere migration of a term. For an example of this kind of historical analysis, see Thongchai Winichakul's (1994) brilliant reading of Thai modernity's birth in the false correspondence between astronomy and astrology.

4. In the critical work of Marxists such as Jit Poumisak, sakdina, the system for demarcating social status during the Ayutthyan and early Bangkok periods, is often translated as feudalism, but others have remarked that in Thailand, where labor was always more scarce than was land, this translation is inadequate. See, for instance, Akin Rabibhadana (1969) and Jit Poumisak (1957/1987).

5. The best account of Vajiravudh's reign remains that of Walter Vella (1979). It is usefully supplemented, however, by Scot Barmé (1993).

6. Satellite transponders accounted for 64 percent of 1999 revenues; advertising and media, 20 percent; information technology, 10 percent; mobile phones and pagers, 4 percent; and other, 2 percent. In 1999, Shin Corp's market capitalization was estimated at 57,565,200,000 baht, or US$1,354,509,156.

7. I have written about this moment elsewhere (see Morris 1998).

8. A comparable trend was visible in the Philippines, during protests against the Estrada government, where the use of text messaging functions on cellular phones made the silent communication of political messages and protest instructions possible.

9. "Thaksin case expected to be referred to court: Defense unsound, say inquiry sources." *Bangkok Post*, December 9, 2000.

10. "Why Was Thaksin Made an Exception?" by Thongbak Tongpao, *Bangkok Post* Internet edition, January 6, 2002.

11. "Democracy Groups Lash Poll Watchdog," by Anjira Assavananda. *Bangkok Post* Internet edition, January 22, 2001.

12. There is some reason to doubt this. Thaksin is reported to have denied this as well, saying he merely placed them under the control of nominees. The point was mentioned in the NCCC's critical report about the Constitutional Court's finding, as counterevidence vis-à-vis Thaksin's repeated efforts to explain his share transfer.

13. "Ruling fails to dampen support: Thaksin bags sympathy vote," by Wut Non-tharit. *Bangkok Post* Internet edition, January 2, 2001.

14. See also Anderson (1998).

References Cited

Akin Rabibhadana. 1969. *The Organization of Thai Society in the Early Bangkok Period, 1782–1873*. Ithaca: Cornell University, Department of Asian Studies, Southeast Asia Program, Data Paper No. 74.

Anderson, Benedict. 1991. *Imagined Communities: Reflections on the Origin and Spread of Nationalism*. London: Verso.

———. 1998. *The Spectre of Comparisons: Nationalism, Southeast Asia, and the World.* London: Verso.

Barmé, Scot. 1993. *Luang Wichit Wathakan and the Creation of a Thai Identity.* Singapore: Institute of Southeast Asian Studies.

Derrida, Jacques. 1976. *Of Grammatology.* Translated by Gayatri Chakravorty Spivak. Baltimore: Johns Hopkins University Press.

Heidegger, Martin. 1977. *The Question Concerning Technology, and Other Essays.* Translated and with an introduction by William Lovitt. New York: Garland.

Herzfeld, Michael. 1997. Cultural Intimacy: Social Politics in the Nation-State. New York: Routledge, 1997.

Jit Poumisak. 1957/1987. *Chomna sakdina thai nai patchuban.* Translated as *Thai Radical Discourse/The Real Face of Thai Feudalism Today* by Craig J. Reynolds. Ithaca, N.Y.: Southeast Asia Program, Cornell University.

Kittler, Friedrich. 1990. *Discourse Networks 1800/1900.* Translated by Michael Metteer, with Chris Cullens. Stanford, Calif.: Stanford University Press.

Mbembe, Achille. 2001. *On the Postcolony.* Berkeley: University of California Press.

Morris, Rosalind. 1998. "Surviving Pleasure at the Periphery: Chiang Mai and the Photographies of Political Trauma in Thailand, 1976–1992." *Public Culture* 10, no. 2: 341–370.

Pasuk Phongphaichit, and Chris Baker. 1995. *Thailand: Economy and Politics.* London: Oxford University Press.

Siegel, James T. 1998. *A New Criminal Type in Jakarta.* Durham, N.C.: Duke University Press.

Thongchai Winichakul. 1994. *Siam Mapped: A History of the Geo-Body of a Nation.* Honolulu: University of Hawaii Press.

Vella, Walter. 1979. *Chaiyo! King Vajiravudh and the Development of Thai Nationalism.* Honolulu: University of Hawaii Press.

Vichit Na Pombhejera. 1979. *Pridi Banomyong and the Making of Thailand's Modern History.* Bangkok.

CHAPTER 9

Monolithic Intentionality, Belonging, and the Production of State Paranoia

A VIEW THROUGH STASI ONTO THE LATE GDR

Andreas Glaeser

THIS PAPER SETS out to explain an institutionalized form of distrust that permeated most of public life in the former German Democratic Republic (GDR). Pitting individuals against collectivities, especially citizens against the state, members against the party, and workers against their work collective, it manifested itself as a highly indexical suspicion that radiated from the center of the party-state to its periphery. To trigger it, no empirical proof was needed, and anybody could be affected by it, irrespective of previous behavior and actual intentions. Due to this particular gestalt and its blatant phenotypical similarity to a well-known characterological disorder, I call it *state paranoia*.[1]

Paying close attention to the processes that produced state paranoia in the GDR is a fruitful enterprise because it reminds us that corporate groups can be based on ultimately self-defeating ideologies, practices, and institutionalizations of belonging. The case of the GDR (and the other Soviet-style socialisms around the world) is particularly fascinating because it encapsulates a veritable paradox of intentional community formation. The more the GDR leadership attempted to manufacture and control the collectivity's co-

I am grateful for an interdisciplinary collective research grant provided by the Division of Social Sciences of the University of Chicago, which has supported the research underpinning this paper. Many thanks go to Andrew Shryock not only for undertaking this project in the first place, but also for providing very useful and encouraging feedback and particularly for helping me smooth out my English, which even after a decade in the Anglophone world still bears the apparently indelible mark of my mother tongue. I would like to extend my gratitude to Michael Herzfeld, Sally Falk Moore, Dominic Boyer, Michael Biggs, Friedrich Katz, Robin Wagner-Pacifici, and Fowzia Khan for comments on earlier drafts of this paper.

hesion on the basis of the collective affirmation of a set of designated goals, the more the collectivity as a whole lost its capacity to develop politically actionable understandings of its own relations to a wider context. At the same time the leadership undermined the very solidarity that it hoped to stipulate.

In many ways this paradox of intentional community formation corresponds to the paradoxes of rational planning and design James Scott has analyzed in *Seeing Like a State* (1998). The connection between intentional community formation and rational planning lies in the reification of particular representations that have historically undergirded both processes. In both cases, reification obfuscates the knowledge that representations are, ontologically speaking, operating in a realm different from what they represent. Reification makes us forget that representations are but aspectual translations of the represented, and as such they necessitate selection, simplification, and reduction. Through this obfuscation they in fact assume the character of a fetish: a political one in the case of state paranoia and a cognitive one in the cases of failed rational design Scott discusses. What the confusion of concept and world is to rational planning, the confusion of a unitary goal, belief, or habitus with actual solidarity, intimacy, and trust is to the political realm. In both cases an aspectual translation is identified with the totality while knowledge of an underlying plurality is repressed.

As guidelines for action, both schemes ultimately fail, producing a kind of "return of the repressed." Yet the reason for failure lies not in reduction itself, a move that is ultimately necessary, both in the cognitive and in the social realm[2]; instead, it lies in the fetishization of the aspects represented. This move involves a denial that comes in various forms, all of which are part and parcel of what phenomenologists (such as Schütz and Luckmann 1984) have called "the natural attitude." Most absolutely, there is the denial that reduction is involved at all. This is the naïve positivistic illusion that representation and the represented are *essentially* identical: the formula is taken for the law of nature; the king is taken for the state tout court. Somewhat less absolutely, the existence of reduction in aspectual translation (and thus the ontological gap) is acknowledged but deemed irrelevant. When a reduction is seen as "right," the fact that it might quickly become problematic and in need of adjustment is denied. Finally, there may be either a dread of disagreement or a longing for harmony. In this case it is denied that genuine plurality of perspectives entailing substantive controversy is likely to be the best way to check which kinds of reduction are more suitable or acceptable. These denials are often features of formal political ideologies, but as phenomenologists have shown time and again (such as Goffman 1967), much of everyday interaction can be characterized in this way as well.

At the heart of the matter, then, is the tension between representations of a totality and an empirical reality that threatens to explode them due to the sheer complexity of lived life, its unruliness, its refusal to conform to representation. Such tensions play a significant role in the construction of in-group solidarity, of in-group presentation to the outside world as well as the determination of who belongs and who does not.[3] I have once before characterized a related phenomenon as the practice and fear of "synecdochical mischief." I have defined synecdochical mischief as someone's readiness to discredit a whole by virtue of discrediting any of its parts (Glaeser 2000: 261). In many social contexts, the practice of synecdochical mischief is taken to constitute outside status. Inside status is by contrast constituted by the (mostly imputed) ability to criticize parts without drawing the value of the whole into doubt. The displayed fear or practice of synecdochical mischief is thus a useful way of marking perceived boundaries of belonging. As such, the absence of the fear of synecdochical mischief lies at the root of what Michael Herzfeld (1997) has described as cultural intimacy; that is, the ability of group members to identify over their putative shortcomings, which, however, are omitted regularly in the self-presentations of groups to the outside world. I will show in particular how a prevalent fear of synecdochical mischief in the GDR undermined the emergence of a cultural intimacy that could include knowledge about reduction in representation and openly accept its precariousness, thus allowing for the emergence of a lively public sphere.

Through its focus on the tension between the representation of a totality and an experiential reality that tends to undermine it, this study can also be read as a contribution to a theory of totalitarianism. However, it is a theory of totalitarianism that takes a decisive turn away from typological concerns toward an empirical investigation of social processes: specifically, the fetishizations of representation that become organizing principles for regimes of belonging. These fetishizations occur in a wide variety of social settings; they are not exclusive properties of states labeled as totalitarian.[4]

By calling the phenomenon state paranoia, I borrow a term from psychopathology. Since such borrowings can produce a host of misunderstandings in social analysis, it is important to note up front what kind of explanation I will put forward in this essay. I will not try to link state paranoia in the late GDR to the personality of its leadership, although this explanatory move had considerable currency in everyday socialist discourses. As such it was a particular instance of a widespread socialist cultural form, which might be called the "personalization of perceived problems." In keeping with this cultural form, the blame for the GDR's ossification was typically placed on the shoulders of an "aging and increasingly rigid leadership," while hopes for change were pegged to a "biological solution." However, as I will show in what follows, besides overplaying the importance of individuals at the expense of institutions, personalization as a cultural form is more a part of the production of state paranoia than a suitable framework for its explanation.[5] Sometimes Western academics also engage in an explanatory move in which the personality characteristics of dictators are seen to shape emergent institutions (see Bullock 1993). The problem with this approach is that its explanatory purchase is limited to the rare moments in which individuals have the extraordinary power to shape emerging institutions. The late GDR hardly belongs in this category. What I propose instead is to look at state paranoia as a fully institutionalized form that is largely independent of the personality characteristics of those who enact it. Neither political leaders nor their functionaries have to be personally paranoid while enacting state paranoia.[6]

After turning away from psychopathology, there remain two possible sociological routes toward explaining state paranoia in the GDR. They mirror the two ways in which it can be thought of as having been socially constructed. The first explanation is genetic. To travel this route, one would have to trace state paranoia and the process of its institutionalization back in time, a task that would require an excellent GDR and Soviet historian with something of an ethnographic bent. The second route, which I will travel here, is a more modest investigation of the reproduction of state paranoia in the GDR during the 1980s. The social arena in which I will analyze the (re)-production of state paranoia is the attempt by Stasi (the secret police) to control critical statements about the GDR in general and the peace and civil rights movement in Berlin in particular.[7] Stasi is an especially revealing window through which to view the reproduction of state paranoia because Stasi was subject to this kind of paranoia and served as its key executor outside the party. I thus show in this essay that the secret police were not the source of pervasive distrust—not its cause, but only its symptom.

Expressions of State Paranoia in the GDR During the 1980s

There were primarily two distinct but complementary means by which the party in the GDR tried to influence the population. Both were aimed at the consciousness and emotional life of every GDR citizen. First, a well-oiled propaganda apparatus orchestrated socialist proselytization through a variety of communication channels: the educational sector, from day care to the Academy of Sciences; the mass media, both electronic and print; mass membership organizations representing a wide range of pastimes; large and small public rituals punctuating the socialist calendar, from weekly party meetings, biannual Central Committee gatherings, annual May Day parades, and Day of the Republic celebrations to local and national elections every four years and party congresses every five years; and finally, public performances of an artistic, folkloric, or otherwise entertaining kind. To a certain extent, this effort at proselytization reflects the party's confidence in its own ability

to make strong arguments for its chosen path, as well as its trust in the readiness of the population to accept its line of reasoning. Yet the sheer magnitude of the proselytization effort, with its enormous redundancies, already
betrayed an anxiety about failure that was compensated by what appeared to
many to be an enormous drive to do more of the same. Thus, the latest decisions and proclamations passed by the plenary session of the central committee were not only reported in the daily news, they were made the focus
of discussions in party group meetings where their correct interpretation was
taught; over time, they were used in countless public speeches by minor and
major party figures, and ultimately they were cross-referenced in economic
progress reports, masters and doctoral theses, and so on.

Second, an equally enormous security apparatus imposed multiple restrictions on access to information (including education), contact (including
movement and association), and goods (including employment). This security apparatus was a complement to propaganda. It dealt with cases in which
proselytization efforts did not yield the desired effect, where the internal-
ization of socialist ideology was imperfect, half-hearted, or did not succeed
at all. The scale and scope of the security apparatus betray the pervasiveness
and intensity of state paranoia. They express the party's often-unwarranted
fear that exposure to information not filtered and contacts not mediated by
the party would necessarily turn a person into a lost case for socialism.

The security apparatus tried to prevent the social formation of understandings that might challenge the party's position. It included a comprehensive system of censorship; far-reaching travel restrictions (especially to
capitalist countries) and even more severe contact limitations for state and
party functionaries; tight, strictly enforced rules of governmental information flow; and numerous security routines at the workplace and in public
buildings. The centerpiece of the security apparatus was Stasi, a large, bu-
reaucratically organized secret police organization with roughly ninety-one
thousand full-time employees. Following in the footsteps of Lenin's *Cheka*
(the acronym of the first Soviet secret police), Stasi understood itself as "the
sword and shield of the party." While arguably the most famous division of
Stasi ran the GDR's foreign espionage services, by far the larger part of Stasi
was concerned with internal security issues, which were grouped under the
heading "counterespionage" (*Abwehr*).[8]

Internal security was organized around "object" responsibilities. Every official organization in the GDR, including all government bureaucracies, with
the sole exception of the party (and arguably Stasi itself), was assigned to a
Stasi unit responsible for its security. By and large, local branches of larger organizations were assigned to local branches of Stasi, regional branches were
assigned to regional branches of Stasi, and national headquarters were assigned directly to the ministry in Berlin. Privately formed (and therefore un-

official) groups—which, given the state's monopoly on organizing people, should not even have existed—were dealt with in the official organizational context in which they emerged or to which they should have belonged. Independent rock groups, for example, were put under surveillance by the department responsible for youth; oppositional scientists were investigated in the context of the institutions in which they worked.

Stasi units looked after the security of "objects" assigned to them in both public and secret ways. Stasi officers maintained open contacts with their object, serving as official point persons for object leaders, who were supposed to report any "unusual occurrences." Officers also recruited a network of secret informants who participated in the life of the "object." Informants and officers met regularly in secret apartments. Originally, the idea was that every "object," as an integral part of the socialist party-state, was vulnerable to enemies, who might place spies or saboteurs in the organization to disrupt the favorable development of socialism. Activities deemed detrimental to the aims of the party-state were supposed to be discovered in *statu nascendi* and effectively thwarted before they could cause damage. Thus, Stasi's efforts were geared toward preventive intervention.

Stasi's task as "sword and shield of the party" was to identify all enemies of party and state. Stasi's own handbook of definitions describes enemies as "persons who alone or in groups intentionally develop attitudes and ideas which are alien to the essence of socialism and who try to realize their attitudes and ideas in their behavior by creating events or conditions which endanger or damage socialist society as a whole or in any of its parts" (Suckut 1996:121). The arch-images of the enemy were the spy who supplied capitalist secret service agencies with crucial information and the saboteur who, on these agencies' behest, intended to destroy goods or impede processes that were considered essential to the development of socialism. Increasingly, the good most vulnerable to tampering was thought to be "unity between party and people," and the image of the saboteur changed from someone derailing trains or blowing up factories to someone who committed ideological sabotage by spreading negative judgments about the party, socialism, or the GDR. Stasi even developed its own technical term to denote this new form of sabotage, *Politisch-ideologische Diversion* (political-ideological sabotage), or PID for short, which was thought to aim at "the decomposition of socialist consciousness . . . and the impediment or prevention of its development [and] at the undermining of the trust of wide circles of the population in the policies of the communist parties in socialist countries" (Suckut 1996:303).

Leads for finding such enemies were mostly supplied by secret informants, either during the direct investigation of unusual occurrences (accidents, graffiti, the appearance of flyers, a case of flight, unusual voting behavior), or during routine meetings. For this reason, secret informants were the very backbone of Stasi operations, and countless Stasi documents, including the major guidelines governing the work of Stasi with secret informants, call them "the main weapon in its struggle with the enemy." At the end, Stasi had about 108,000 registered secret informants of various kinds. Work with these informants was supported by thirty-three thousand people who were willing to supply their apartments or to work as couriers, and by another thirty-three thousand informants with whom Stasi maintained a less-structured relationship (Müller-Enbergs 1996:59).[9]

The remainder of this section will explore state paranoia in three variations. The first pertains to Stasi attempts to control all kinds of associations, especially those pursuing a political agenda. The second shows how Stasi tried to buttress the efficacy of propaganda while following up on anything the party might understand as a disturbance of its efforts. The third set of examples shows instances of distrust within Stasi's own ranks.

Civil Rights Activists and Stasi in Berlin's Prenzlauer Berg

Berlin's peace and civil rights movement centered on Prenzlauer Berg, which, despite its name suggesting a far higher elevation, is a minor hill directly north of the historical city center. It is also the geographical heart of the district with the same name. Like most of what is called Berlin today, Prenzlauer Berg was only settled in the late nineteenth century. Neoclassical and neobaroque facades adorned buildings with spacious apartments originally designed to house the aspiring petit bourgeoisie of the Wilhelmenian Empire. Hidden behind these stuccoed claims to propriety, however, lay highly compact structures built around cul-de-sac chains of inner courtyards that provided a mere mockery of open space, air, and light for craft shops and the much smaller dwellings of the working class. These structures, front and back, survived the air raids of World War II comparatively unscathed; the whims of Yalta flung them into the Soviet sphere of interest. Questionable policy choices made against the backdrop of a chronic shortage economy, coupled, perhaps, with an ideological dislike for the socio-spatial origins of the Prenzlauer Berg neighborhood, led to the total neglect of these buildings in favor of the socialist panel-style settlements that mushroomed on the ashes of war-torn districts and the sandy fields of Berlin's outskirts.

By the beginning of the 1980s, Prenzlauer Berg's pretty facades had yielded to the acidic fumes of bituminous coal-fired ovens, and many a backyard wing had become uninhabitable. For want of running hot water and central heating, the area had been almost completely abandoned by anybody with serious career stakes in the GDR. Offering cheap rents for large rooms in a central location, along with faint reminiscences of another time, Prenzlauer

Berg became instead the favored transitional space of East Berlin's emerging artistic, literary, and political scene, which tried to organize and live independently of party and state. By the late 1980s, Prenzlauer Berg was synonymous with this scene. Adventurous Western tour buses began to include it in their sight-seeing rounds of East Berlin to provide their clients with two tangible reasons why communism should go: its economic ineptness and its inability to accept the public expression of opinions and lifestyles in contradiction to the official, state-sponsored ideological norm.

Beginning in the late 1970s, people moved to Prenzlauer Berg or began to frequent its scene in search for a place of belonging. They had often run afoul of one socialist institution or another, with high schools, universities, and the military topping the list. This confrontation did not necessarily take the form of an overtly political disagreement. Instead, it often had roots in lifestyle or moral choices that contrasted, in ways everyone could see, with characteristics of what was taken to be a "good socialist personality." Such expressions of individuality could be as seemingly innocuous as flaunting a preference for long hair, jeans, and rock music in front of an overzealous schoolteacher. Or it could be more directly defiant; for instance, refusing to back down after being told not to invite a particular author for a public reading in a youth club. In the Prenzlauer Berg scene, people willing to try out a semipublic life beyond the state's predesignated categories and organizations were sure to find others who were already forcibly marginalized either because they were already formally expelled from socialist institutions (school, university, work) or because they preferred active self-marginalization in anticipation of such an expulsion.

Not all circles of the Prenzlauer Berg scene dealt in the same way with their marginalization. And not everybody participating in the scene was marginalized to the same extent. Some were still involved in mainstream careers, while others had abandoned all hope of employment befitting their level of education. Instead they centered their lives on the activities of the circles to which they belonged. On the one hand, important parts of the artistic scene remained self-consciously apolitical, "neither espousing nor opposing the state but rather trying to live without it," as Sascha Anderson, one of Stasi's key informants and a key figure of the arts scene (see also Borneman 1998), famously put it. On the other hand, circles crystallizing around issues such as peace and environmental protection—to the degree that they did not stay within the narrow perimeter of Protestant parish work—became more political as they sought a wider audience, faced more controversial issues (especially human rights), and developed novel, increasingly countrywide and international contacts (Poppe et al. 1995; Rüddenklau 1992; Neubert 1998). Although these politicized circles did in fact criticize real existing socialism, the general thrust of their actions was directed toward reform of the GDR. By and large, their stance remained clearly prosocialist and anti-capitalist (see Gehrke and Rüddenklau 1999). They did not try to topple the regime, but tried to involve the regime in an open, public dialogue about what they felt were burning issues that called for change.

For many Stasi officers Prenzlauer Berg was the deviant space par excellence. One of them said, for example: "you really had to be a particular way to want to live in these decrepit buildings." In the imagination of many officers, the area and the people fit hand in glove. They describe the hardcore activist groups not only as having been profoundly unsocialist—that is, ideologically aberrant—but as having been unable to pursue ordinary careers, as unkempt, sexually promiscuous, and even perverse. Identified as outsiders by Stasi, these activists and nonconformists were seen as easy recruits for foreign secret service agencies, which were thought to be organizing discontented citizens of the GDR into an internal opposition guided by the West.

Thus, Prenzlauer Berg became a favored terrain for the operations of secret informants and agents of Stasi. Throughout the 1980s Stasi busily followed up on any hint of independent group activity (irrespective of its size and purpose, public or private appearance) if it challenged publicly espoused ideology in any conceivable sense. The overtly apolitical artistic scene was as much an object of Stasi's investigations as the emerging civil rights movement. Relatively open women's discussion groups and closed philosophy circles were scrutinized as much as persons staging literary readings in private apartments or the meetings of people concerned about nuclear disarmament or the environment within and outside the protective umbrella of the Protestant church. As soon as it learned about a new group that had or might develop "negative-inimical" intentions, Stasi began to investigate with the help of its network of secret informants. It tried to find out who the leaders and participants were, how often and where they met, what they did, what kind of ideas were exchanged among them, and, most important, whether they planned actions that could in any way disturb the party-state. As soon as Stasi had collected enough evidence indicating that the group might engage in activities that could constitute a crime according to the penal code of the GDR (regular contacts with Westerners were completely sufficient in this regard), it actively tried to infiltrate it with secret informants. As a next step, the groups were not only investigated but Stasi made efforts to contain them: possible recruits were intimidated or lured away, collective actions were thwarted if politically feasible. If Stasi could find enough usable evidence to begin trial procedures, it did. If the evidence was insufficient or not usable (for example, because its use would have compromised a secret informant) or a trial seemed politically undesirable, Stasi began to undertake measures that would accomplish a "decomposition" [10] of the group through the instigation of jealousies of all kinds (including sexual ones), by trying to emphasize disagreement, by sowing distrust and destroying credibility, by organizing failures both for the group and its individual members. Again, secret informants played a major role in trying to get members to withdraw in despair, or rage, or with acute feelings of indignation. At the end, a significant number of the members of these groups were indeed secret informants.[11] At meetings, up to half of all those in attendance were often secret informants of various Stasi units.[12] Stasi even managed to plant informants in the inner circles of these groups, although they seldom belonged to the innermost hard core, the leaders most active in initiating, planning, and executing group actions.

Stasi's attempts to control the peace and civil rights movements are examples of state paranoia for the following reasons. Although Stasi constantly suspected that the members of these groups were working at the behest of Western secret services—for genuine internal opposition was, given the GDR's state of socialist development, unthinkable—Stasi never found any proof of such links.[13] Since the activists were assumed to be "inspired" and "guided" from abroad, Stasi never came to assess the motives of the members of these groups in a realistic way, continuing to insist on their antisocialist stance in spite of ample evidence to the contrary.

Moreover, up until 1989, activist and opposition groups generated very little echo among the general public. To some degree this was due to Stasi's intimidation of potentially interested participants and its success at depriving the groups of access to a wider public within the GDR. Fast-rising membership numbers in the fall of 1989, when it became obvious that the regime was no longer in control of the situation, clearly demonstrate this. Nonetheless, the public appeal of the groups remained rather limited if it is considered that the groups did in part reach a wider GDR audience via Western media, which were followed by the majority of the GDR population. This assessment is further corroborated by the truly devastating election results for civil rights groups in the first free GDR-wide elections of March 18, 1990.[14] It seems fair to say, therefore, that these groups did not pose a serious danger to the GDR regime. Yet Stasi never really produced a thoroughgoing analysis of their potential security impact. It kept pouring resources into controlling them, in amounts far beyond what was needed, and the high degree of redundancy in the information Stasi produced clearly shows this.

Controlling a Wider Public

The complementarity of propaganda and secret police was not limited only to cases where Stasi propaganda had failed to persuade; it was also visible in

Stasi's efforts to do whatever was politically feasible[15] to "secure" the efficacy of propaganda in the first place. This work involved actions aiming to ensure that the party's monopoly over sources of information was maintained to the largest possible extent. After all efforts failed to prevent the population of the GDR from receiving Western electronic mass media,[16] Stasi concentrated its effort to maintain party control over print media, education, public events, and, perhaps most important, over associations and personal contacts. Accordingly, Stasi cracked down on samizdat publications, the private importing of print media from abroad, private day care initiatives, and readings and performances staged by private persons. Stasi also investigated noncompliance with quasi-mandatory participation in mass events such as May Day parades and elections.

The "undisturbed course" of mass events was afforded great importance in Stasi work. This is reflected in the annual planning documents of Stasi, which, for purposes of resource management and motivation, centered on "social highlights" of national, regional, and local significance. It is also reflected in the room given to mass events in the biannual security briefings of the minister, which shed interesting light on the reasons why Stasi engaged in such work. Erich Mielke's argument about the particular vulnerability and need for protection of mass events took the following path: since mass events are demonstrations of the overwhelming unity between party and people, which is in itself proof of the enormous vitality of socialism, they attract the wrath of the class enemy who would with all means like to disturb these events (1984a). Such disturbances were thought to come in two distinct forms: as classical sabotage, for example, the derailing of trains transporting performers scheduled to appear at the event, the poisoning of food for participants, and so on; and as ideological sabotage, which might entail chanting, unfolding banners, or distributing pamphlets containing party-critical slogans that suggested the unity between party and people was not in fact as tight as media reporting on these events proclaimed.

To prevent what it considered sabotage, Stasi undertook an enormous range of measures. All performers in mass events had to be announced to Stasi beforehand by the organizers so security checks could be run on each and every one of them.[17] Anyone considered a potential risk—for example, because they were known to harbor party-critical attitudes, or because they maintained relations with such people—had to stay home. The network of secret informants was used to find out whether independent groups had plans to stage actions at events. Even if no actions were planned, it frequently happened that persons with ties to independent groups were kept under control during mass events, which meant their employers were prompted to keep them busy; in addition, key figures were put under surveillance and were, if deemed necessary, placed under house arrest or were temporarily detained on other pretexts. Moreover, Stasi inspected the technical condition of lo-comotives, railroad cars, and buses used to transport participants, as well as technical equipment used during the event. One officer commented: "just imagine, Honecker (the general secretary) would have grabbed the micro-phone and—silence!" Stasi also double-checked railroad schedules, secured key intersections in the traffic flow to and from events, and inspected the food and lodging of participants. The officers in charge of participating groups accompanied them, using secret informants throughout the event to learn of unusual occurrences as fast as possible. Other officers were strategi-cally positioned throughout the audience. Once I asked the officer in the ministry in Berlin who was responsible for coordinating the security of mass events whether he had ever encountered any form of sabotage. His answer was: "not really." There once was poisoned food, which had been stored in-correctly, but it could not be proven that someone had done it on purpose; another time, buses were misdirected and the participants did not show up in time, and again no conclusive evidence for sabotage was detected. The bombardment of buses with water bottles or the firing of an air rifle at the audience from a nearby apartment could be traced to disgruntled youths with no ulterior political motives. Alas, he said, efforts to control such events were increasing drastically during his tenure in the ministry.

Elections (more accurately, party candidate list approvals) in the GDR were a significant propaganda event. Not only were they used to rally the entire adult population in support of the regime, but also to communicate to each and every citizen that the party enjoyed a nearly perfect approval rating. Stasi was involved in the preparation of elections in the sense that I have just out-lined, and it also busied itself afterward with the scrutiny of undesired elec-tion behavior: nonvoting and no-voting. Erich Mielke (1984a), minister of state security since 1957, opened his May 1984 security briefing with re-gional and division heads with a celebration of the success of the party in the preceding local elections. He took the near-perfect approval rate not only to indicate the overwhelming trust of the population in the party and its lead-ership, but also as a token of patriotic love for the GDR. Yet, he continued his lecture, the 1 percent of naysayers and nonvoters had to be of grave con-cern for Stasi. He exhorted his subordinates to follow up on every single clue that would help them identify these "negative forces" and fathom their mo-tives. Worse, he continued, one could not be completely sure about "aye sayers" either, since overt approval might simply be used to disguise secret hostile thoughts. Mielke also showed great concern for regime-critical graf-fiti and flyers that had shown up during the elections in cities throughout the GDR: five occasions in Leipzig, three in Dresden, and three in Berlin. In the face of these "attacks on the socialist social order," Mielke called on his men to strengthen their efforts at "who-is-who reconnaissance," the Stasi term for dividing the population into progressive and reactionary forces, into friends and foes. This task too was supposed to be accomplished with the help of Stasi's network of secret informants.

Party Discipline

What looks at first like the party-state's severe distrust of the general population reveals itself, after closer inspection of the organizational cultures of Stasi and the party, as a generalized distrust radiating from top to bottom of the party-state and from center to periphery. The only person who seems to have been reasonably safe from doubt was the general secretary of the party himself, since he personally epitomized the collective intentionality expressed in the latest party line.[18] All other state or party functionaries, including full-time members of Stasi, were under constant scrutiny to ascertain what they thought about the GDR and socialism and whether their actions were in accord with the latest decrees of the party.[19] Apart from private conversations among friends, any serious critique launched in an official context doubting the wisdom of the party or any of its policies could have very serious consequences, including cancellation of membership in Stasi and the party.

Lieutenant Colonel Arnold Meyer, who joined Stasi as an eighteen year old in 1956, faced in January 1989, after thirty-three years of service, the serious prospect of being dismissed from Stasi and the party because he had dared to say in a party meeting that the party's media policies were inadequate. He was immediately reminded that the party's media policies were based on decisions of the central committee and the politburo and were therefore binding; thus, his comments violated the party discipline he swore to abide by once he joined. Following well-rehearsed patterns of accusation, Meyer was also asked how he could judge himself smarter than the party. A party trial was initiated wherein he would have faced the alternative of either recanting or being dismissed from the party. Apart from privately showing their sympathy, colleagues could not jump publicly to his defense without endangering themselves. Ultimately Meyer was saved by intervention from above and got away with a less-than-formal recantation. My point is that even a well-regarded, seasoned Stasi officer with decades of loyal work to his credit was instantaneously faced with severe suspicion as soon as he publicly veered from the official party line.

Not only did the party try to minimize the population's exposure to ideas and people critical of socialism and the GDR, the party also expected its own members to consciously avoid such contacts or exposures. Strict abstention from media, commodities, and persons originating in the West and avoidance of explicitly nonsocialist groups (for example, religious communities) was a touchstone of party loyalty. Accordingly, Stasi officers had to ask permission to marry a particular person, since partners were thought to pose security risks that needed to be officially assessed. One officer had fallen in love with a functionary of the communist youth movement who, according to his descriptions, was a fully committed socialist. Alas, the security check revealed that his partner's brother had once made an ill-fated excursion to West Berlin, where he apparently tried to sign up with the French Foreign Legion before returning to East Berlin (without having become a bearer of the *képi blanc*). The planned marriage had to be cancelled. Another officer's mother-in-law hailed from what later was to become West Germany. Most of her relatives still lived in the West, and she desired to visit them regularly. Stasi officers had to register any travels of their close kin to capitalist countries. Consequently, the officer in question was constantly urged to convince his mother-in-law to abstain from traveling to West Germany. Since the old lady would not budge, he finally had to consent to put her name on the blacklist of persons whose travel was restricted.

Distrust radiating from center to periphery was also a pervasive feature of Stasi's organizational culture. Almost all officers I have spoken to describe a dour culture of blame. Failures of any kind were inevitably attributed to the imperfect execution of orders, ordinance guidelines, and party directives. Since subordinates were thus seen to be more prone to failure, particularly important kinds of activities had to be concentrated at the top. Most notably, the analytical assessment of particular cases and the interpretation of their significance in a wider context were thought to be the prerogative of higher levels, while lower-level personnel were charged with assembling "pure facts." Since this interpretation/fact gathering division of labor was perfectly indexical, even Stasi reports written at higher levels remained oddly devoid of analytical assessment.

Why then were critical citizens, in spite of their statements to the contrary, considered antisocialist? Why did public rituals require a vast array of security measures, when "inimical" incidents of any kind were extremely rare? Why were scattered cases of graffiti, or an extremely low number of no-voters and nonvoters, considered dangerous? And why could seasoned party members and long-serving officers of Stasi so quickly become objects of party suspicion? In the following sections I will argue that the answer to these questions lies in a related interplay of cultural forms, institutions, and practices.

Monolithic Intentionality, Truth, and Agency

The GDR's pervasive concern with the commitment of its citizens to socialism must be understood as a consequence of the historical introduction and the continuing practice of socialism as an ultimately intentional, consciousness-driven social transformation. This quality of Eastern European socialism is first visible in the fact that it was not a form of social organization that emerged locally; rather, it was consciously introduced in an attempt to completely redesign societies in the Soviet sphere of interest based on Soviet institutional blueprints. More important, however, the intentionality of East European socialism is visible in the continuing practice of comprehensive central planning in all parts and at all levels of society. Even the secret police, for example, operated on a central plan. Instruction manuals for party propagandists reveal that officials believed the proper working of the system could be achieved only if the party's intentions were absolutely unequivocal and unimpeded by internal controversy. It was assumed that the system could function only if nearly everyone was willing to realize the intentions of the party as completely as possible. In other words, socialism would succeed to the degree that it created a monolithic collective intentionality. Thus, the party had two main tasks. Internally it had to avoid schisms, and externally it had to convince everyone to internalize the collective intentionality embodied in the decrees of the party. Since these decrees were thought to reflect both the objective laws of social organization and the movement of history as discovered by the science of dialectical materialism, reason should dictate their adoption;[20] resistance, by the same token, could best be explained by some quirky subjectivism, or worse, as the consequence of a bourgeois (and thus inimical) class position. The party's decrees were thus dignified as truth or, as a much quoted and later much reviled song had it: "the party is always right" (Judt 1998:47).

Since the objective laws of society and its development had revealed history to be class warfare in which the forces of progress, now identified with socialism, do battle with the forces of reaction, now identified with capitalism, and since the successful establishment of socialism in Eastern Europe had awoken the jealousies and rage of the capitalist class enemy, the GDR had to face directly an ever more dangerous, ever more unpredictable foe. Mielke (1984b) describes the severity of these threats in the following words:

In the context of his crusade, the enemy uses all his political, military, economic and ideological means to intensify his fight against socialism and to damage socialism in every conceivable way. He will try to cause phenomena of economic destabilization, he will undermine, weaken and destroy the foundations of socialist societies, he will try to develop an internal opposition . . . and he will try to dissolve the unity and the oneness of the socialist community.

The theory of an ever-intensifying class warfare led to the postulation of a Manichaean duality presented as a zero-sum game: what helps socialism harms capitalism and vice versa. The acute understanding of a severe, persisting threat fueled constant calls for uncompromising unity. Every non-alignment with the party was turned into an alignment with the enemy. The logic of duality was always rigorously "us or them"—*tertium non datur!*[21]

Party members in particular were beholden to what was cherished as party discipline. The statutes of the party obliged every member "to preserve the unity and the purity of the party . . . to actively realize the party decrees . . . [and to] support socialist consciousness building in all citizens" (Schröder 1998:688–692). This principle is furthermore enshrined in the very concept of democratic centralism in which "all decisions of higher party groups are binding for lower ones, . . . [and] every individual has to submit in a disciplined way to the decisions of the majority." Ultimately, all citizens of the GDR were expected to become rational by internalizing the intentionality of the party, by replacing subjectivity with objectivity. Self-objectification was thought to be accomplished by regular and sustained participation in the party's propaganda efforts. The continuous, diligent study of the Marxist-Leninist classics[22] and the continuing flow of party documents, as well as constant deliberation on what both meant for everyday work situations, was supposed to provide the cognitive tools. "What do we try to accomplish with 'FDJ-program-GDR-40?'" was the rhetorical question at the opening to a yearlong cycle of ideological studies in the communist youth movement, in which all members participated. "The continuing realization of the decisions of the XIth party congress" was the first answer (FDJ 1988). Reflecting a deep belief in the powers of (Durkheimian) effervescence, participation in public rituals, from party meetings to Day of the Republic celebrations, was thought to provide the emotional energy for the successful individual appropriation of collective intentionality.

For Stasi officers this meant they were asked to "digest" not only the various party directives, but also interpretations of these directives given by the minister of Stasi. In the annual report of the SED party group in division XX, which was responsible for controlling what Stasi called "the political underground," the first party secretary is quoted thus:

It has to be the explicit task of every party organization, to make use especially of the fundamental political directives of the comrade minister for any further ideological work and to mobilize all collectives and all employees for the realization of the political-operative tasks at hand (MfS-SED-KL 1985:2).

The report continues to explain that it is precisely through ideological work aimed at aligning everyone with the collective intentionality of the party that the Stasi unit in question will be able to take on its "ever growing responsibility."

The direct identification of the intentions of the party with the objectivity of history had two major consequences. First, it implied that if the intentionality of the party was perfectly realized, indeed monolithic, the intended state would come true quasi-automatically. Seen this way, the key to success for socialism was to make people believe. Within this consciousness-driven model of social transformation, it was perfectly rational to go to extraordinary efforts and to spend considerable resources for proselytization.

By the same token it was rational to focus the security apparatus on maintaining the party's influence on the consciousness of the people.[23] Second, the identification between party intentionality and objective truth had consequences for the party's understanding of self-efficacy. The party assumed that it had the *agency* to realize its intentions. It believed that comprehensive planning and comprehensive control were in fact possible. Mielke's exhortation of his men to investigate the motives of *every* nonvoter or naysayer, his demand to know the various social contexts of the GDR so well as to enable Stasi to address *each* and *every* case, are good illustrations of this overextension. Although Stasi was itself arguably the most prodigally endowed political police in the world, and although Stasi's net of secret informants was comprehensive by any historical standards, Mielke's demands on his men, much like the party congresses' encompassing development programs, have an almost eerie, phantasmagoric character. There are no realistic circumstances under which they could ever have been fulfilled.[24]

Belief in the party's efficacy to produce a monolithic revolutionary intentionality manifests itself not only in the language of the major party documents, but in virtually all official communications. Stasi's official language is a case in point. There is, for example, a prodigal use of what might be called the *continuous positive*, where today everything is asserted to be more than what it was yesterday: the officers become "ever more vigilant," their class perspective becomes "ever more defined," the use of resources is "ever more efficient," and the "early recognition of the enemy is ever more successful." Maybe the most surprising aspect of such communications is that there was never any need to make the slightest effort to provide evidence for actual growth in vigilance, class consciousness, efficiency, or effectiveness. The continuous positive is a consequence not of empirical investigation but of deduction from theory believed to be absolutely true.

Moreover, official language, internal and external communications, supported monolithic intentionality through a *totalizing language* of complete mobilization. "Every member" had to participate in the latest measure, "all means and methods" had to be used to defeat the enemy, "every effort" was to be made to realize the targets set by the last party congress, "every enemy" had to be identified. As Mielke (1984b) put it: "Nobody shall be allowed to escape the influence of this society."

The thrust of socialism's monolithic intentionality was also manifest in the belief that the future was completely transparent, a belief that was extended, in public speeches, both to large-scale events and to happenings that, in retrospect, can only be described as minor occurrences.[25] Social events that were said to depend on the voluntary actions of participants were treated, at the same time, as if their outcomes were known beforehand, leaving no doubt that they would indeed materialize. In other words, monolithic intentionality, once achieved, was assumed to be self-realizing. Here, again, Mielke's lectures at the biannual security briefings are very instructive. Mielke (1984a) anticipated the results of a countrywide youth festival scheduled to take place in several weeks' time. Not only would it be an "impressive and powerful demonstration of capabilities" but "500,000 members of the FDJ [youth movement] will again demonstrate their loyalty to the party of the working class and will offer proof of their readiness to contribute to the consolidation, strengthening and defense of socialism." Mielke implies in his speech that Stasi's role in "securing the festival" is to guarantee that the achievement of these results will not be endangered by planning mishaps or by machinations of the enemy. "Securing" an event came increasingly to mean that Stasi was to insure that intentions matched outcomes. And this was indeed a role Stasi played in the GDR, not only by making sure a youth festival proceeded according to plan, but also by helping the economy to stay on plan or research institutes meet their deadlines.

The coupling of monolithic intentionality with an equally imposing understanding of self-efficacy, by way of insight into absolute truth, raised thorny questions about apparent failures. It is not surprising that GDR officials, as guardians of truth, had great trouble admitting to failures at all. The propaganda apparatus celebrated success stories and hushed up or remained completely silent about problems, lest the party's connection to absolute truth, and therefore its intentionality and agency, be cast into doubt. When failures or problems could no longer be suppressed, they were stereotypically explained in one of two ways, both of which focused on the consciousness of individual people while protecting the integrity of the party by silencing questions about the system. The personalization of failure was practiced in benevolent and malevolent fashion. The former insisted on what one might call ideological negligence. A problem's occurrence meant that the party's intentionality had been imperfectly internalized due to underdeveloped socialist consciousness. In security briefings and other speeches Mielke (1984a, 1986, 1988) points out time and again that if all his orders had been followed, if all the party documents had been studied correctly, Stasi successes would have been much higher. He says, for example:

If we are again and again surprised by spectacular occurrences, or by the flight of important persons [i.e., by failures of control—A.G.], then the cause for these surprises is that we have allowed mistakes to happen, that we did not discover weak points in time or that we have done nothing to get rid of them (Mielke 1986).

The consequence for Mielke was that orders and party documents must be studied ever more intensively because there is nothing better for a good socialist than to "steel his ideological consciousness," which will in turn provide sure guidance in difficult situations.

The more malevolent interpretation of failure, by contrast, points to an opposing intentionality, to the machinations of the class enemy, as the root cause. No doubt true accidents may occur, but as Mielke points out:

One has to investigate whether there are possible hints of the clandestine production of such occurrences [accidents], where the causes and motives lie in the neglect or in the incorrect or not timely reaction to the development of sources of danger (1984b:122−3).

Mielke asserts that enemies like to hide behind what might be accidents only in name. In keeping with the cult of secrecy surrounding failures, Stasi had to decide what kind of failure it was: a true accident, lacking consciousness (which includes all cases of neglect), or outright sabotage. Whether it was a fire in a factory, the crash of an airplane, or the derailment of a train, Stasi appeared on the scene, using its methods, especially its widespread network of secret informants, to find out.

The Ethics of Absolute Finality and the Moral Basis of Hierarchy

So far I have shown how self-objectification was thought to be rational because it was deemed to be true; that is, historically necessary. Yet personal submission to collective intentionality was also justified because it was believed to be the only sure route to the ultimate moral good, a classless and therefore just human society.[26] Self-objectification was rational because it was done in the pursuit of a common moral purpose. From this understanding followed a conception of socialist morality that I would call an "ethics of absolute finality" in which whatever furthered the realization of party intentionality was morally desirable and good; whatever impeded it was bad. Since all legitimation works by suggesting an association with the good, the right, the beautiful, or the true, it is not surprising that virtually all Stasi documents took pains to demonstrate how Stasi work was in keeping with the ethics of absolute finality. Studies of Stasi's own university were framed as contributions to the fulfillment of the latest party decrees; annual planning documents enumerate ways in which they resonate with the pronouncements of the last plenary session of the central committee. By the same token, praise for individuals or organizations was first and foremost recognition of their contribution to the realization of collective intentionality. Organizations were lauded for "plan overfulfillment"; individuals were commended for helping realize the directives of the Xth party congress.

In conjunction with the Manichaeism of an ever-intensifying class war, the ethics of absolute finality yielded a convenient precept, a socialist categorical imperative, if you will. It was often simply stated as: "be always partial!" or "show a firm class standpoint!" These slogans could be translated to mean "always act in such a way that the proletariat is maximally supported in its struggle with the bourgeoisie—and the best way to do that is to realize collective intentionality." The moral worth of actions undertaken in the class struggle could be measured by the following procedure: "ask yourself who (we or they) benefits from this action and no action can be right where they benefit and we lose." A good communist and, above all, a good *chekist* —that is, a good member of a socialist secret police organization—is someone who has a firm class standpoint, someone who has practiced, and is therefore always ready to take, the perspective of the party (and hence the proletariat).[27]

Group boundaries are always moral boundaries. The distinction between insiders and outsiders involves de facto a distinction between who is worthy of solidarity and who is not, who belongs and who does not. The ethics of absolute finality divided the inhabitants of the GDR into two camps: friends, who at least in practice supported collective intentionality, and foes, in Stasi jargon "negative-inimical forces," who were thought to undermine it. To determine who belongs where, to decide "who is who" (*wer ist wer?*), was Stasi's task (Gill and Schröter 1991:295–345). Stasi constructed between the two categories a gray area of people whose consciousness was "unclear," "unsteady," "unsolidified," and who might already have said or done something that brought them into conflict with monolithic intentionality. These were people whose attitudes against socialism had not yet hardened and thus had to be treated differently from enemies. According to Mielke (1984b):

In our *chekist* work we have had the experience that many sympathizers and fellow travelers of oppositional groups are people who have for various reasons temporarily come under the spell of internal and external enemies. . . . With the help of prudent ideological influence and in collaboration with state and social organizations we have to make every effort to bring them back to positions which are in accordance with society or which are at least loyal.

The friends of socialism were not conceived as homogeneous. Mielke distinguishes between "in accordance with society," meaning in enthusiastic support of collective intentionality, and "loyal," meaning at least implicitly pro-GDR (rather than explicitly pro-FRG—the Federal Republic of Germany in the West). The degree to which collective intentionality was internalized, the degree to which a firm class position was exhibited in action, distributed belonging unevenly along a spectrum from center to periphery. In the true spirit of democratic centralism, those higher up were thought to be superior precisely because they were "politically more mature" and thus better equipped to understand what realizing collective intentionality in a given situation really meant. Hierarchy was thought to have a moral underpinning, all the more so in the GDR, where the leadership generation had, in the understanding of many younger people, proven their integrity by fighting the Nazi dictatorship.

The presumed moral basis of hierarchy meant that election to higher positions, which in the beginning of the GDR allowed for competition, degenerated into a self-recruitment of elites legitimized by acclamation from below. Those higher up were supposed to have better judgment and, because of their political maturity, they would know best who a suitable candidate was. Party members openly rebelled against this practice only when the leadership proved absolutely clueless about how to address the crisis of the Fall of 1989, when socialism began to disintegrate rather fast. The moral underpinnings of hierarchy also make clear why Stasi's organizational life was characterized by such a dour culture of blame: since a weak class position was one of the acknowledged causes of failure, and since such weakness was more characteristic of the bottom than the top, blame was deflected downward.

The model of belonging that emerges has the following gestalt. Belonging is made by living one's life in accordance with the ethics of absolute finality. The self-objectification such a life requires can be more or less perfect, which implies that people's *objective* support for socialism does vary by degree. Consequently, belonging was not seen as a state reached once and for all, but as a hard-won achievement that needed to be constantly reattained because the intentionality of the party, and the contexts in which it could be realized, were constantly on the move. Belonging was always problematic. Those higher up, who were held responsible by their own superiors for the successful education of those below, not only supported practices that furthered the self-objectification of subordinates, they also demanded tokens of successful alignment, which they could display to their superiors. These tokens came to function as indicators of the state of the socialist project at a particular level in the hierarchy. Hence Mielke could hail the election results of the Socialist Unity Party as proof of the electorate's commitment to their socialist fatherland, the GDR.

Everybody with career stakes in the GDR had a vital interest in producing tokens of their absorption of collective intentionality and their dedication to the ethics of absolute finality. Life in the GDR was therefore awash in proclamations of commitment, in ostentatious displays of knowledge about party documents, their significance and usefulness. In this context it was particularly troublesome that intentions could be feigned. With any demonstration of intentions, the nagging question became: "are they true?" Again, that Mielke (1984a) worried not only about nonvoters and naysayers but about the value of the aye votes, reveals one of the fundamental tensions of socialism.

Because key intentions proved very hard, if not impossible, to realize, this model of belonging produced consequences that are not difficult to understand. The tendency to step up proselytization efforts led to situations in which even party members felt annoyed by what appeared to be empty talk. The drive to find more ways to make people prove they were in synch with collective intentionality was experienced by many as a proliferation of vacuous submission rituals. Stasi was seen as the only agency that could effectively separate wheat from chaff, true displays of intention from false ones, and Mielke (1984a) ultimately went so far as to order his men to investigate the motives of everyone. Accordingly, Stasi moved to the center of social truth practices in the GDR, assuming responsibility for telling the leadership, in "atmospheric reports," how people in the GDR really thought; not only members of the opposition, but the population at large. What was at work here can be described (with only slight exaggeration) as a secret police model of truth.

Synecdochical Mischief and Cultural Intimacy

One aspect of state paranoia in the GDR that needs further exploration is the fact that the party-state tended to overread critical statements about any of its policies as negative (if not inimical) actions. To shed light on this issue, I asked Stasi officers why they believed that the members of civil rights groups were, contrary to their stated convictions and intentions, involved in a ploy to end socialism. Throughout their answers, one argumentative pattern predominates.[28] By questioning decrees of the party or criticizing parts of the socialist system, I was told, the activists contributed to a weakening of the system as a whole. By introducing doubts, civil rights activists inevitably played into the hands of the class enemy, who used any sign of internal disunity to try to shatter the system. Since this would clearly be the result if their action succeeded, activists had to be considered foreign (directed) agents.[29] Had the activists appreciated the necessity of absolute, unwavering unity behind the party leadership in times of intensifying class warfare, they would have put aside their individualistic concerns in the service of the system's survival. Thus, in the eyes of Stasi officers, the civil rights activists were practicing "synecdochical mischief" (see also Glaeser 2000), the critique of a part to discredit the whole, or vice versa, a discrediting of the whole to devalue some or all of its parts. In this sense, the activists' concerns with peace, the environment, or human rights were but strategic choices to undermine socialism (see Mielke 1984b). By zeroing in on the critique of particular party policies, while discounting the anticapitalist, prosocialist commitments of the opposition, Stasi officers were themselves practicing synecdochical mischief, for the fear of its practice by others.

Moreover, the attribution of a totalizing, ultimately destructive intention to movement members was justified in the eyes of the officers, because the activists used Western media, and thus agents of the enemy, to transport their messages. Of course, the officers did not see that this use of Western media was itself the direct result of their own practice of synecdochical mischief. Western media were important to the activists because they provided some protection and because they were the only means by which to reach a wider audience in the GDR itself. What Stasi officers saw, however, was activists discrediting the GDR in the West, possibly triggering further sanctions, and undermining public trust in the GDR and its leadership.

The key activists suffered greatly from the imputation of synecdochical mischief because, unlike many other East Germans, they did not want to leave the country. They wanted to stay and reform what they considered their home. This awareness and fear of being the object of the state's synecdochical mischief led to harsh controversies among the activists about their position toward citizens who applied for permission to leave the country. For most of them, it was clear: these people had made a radical decision to reject the GDR as a whole, and it was precisely this kind of total rejection that they wanted to distance themselves from.

Of course, members of the party, even high-ranking ones, and Stasi officers could themselves become objects of the state's fear and practice of synecdochical mischief. Every public critique of the regime implied lax class consciousness, if not inimical motives. Critique immediately put belonging at stake. In a ritual called "critique and self-critique," the party-state provided a tool for critics to recant publicly. Critics were invariably accused of putting their own subjective interests and views of the world ahead of the objective understanding of the collective. Critics, it was argued, had put themselves in opposition to the collectivity. The potential loss of belonging involved was existentially threatening. As one Stasi officer put it: "what should I have done? The party was my life, and I just couldn't imagine a life outside it."

The reality of state paranoia in the GDR placed formidable limits on the development of "cultural intimacy," which Herzfeld defines as "the recognition of those aspects of cultural identity that are considered a source of external embarrassment but that nevertheless provide insiders with their assurance of common sociality" (1997:3). The instances of cultural intimacy Herzfeld analyzes cast it as a kind of counterdiscourse of belonging in which common, insider knowledge about a society's dirty linen actually predisposes people to identify with it in spite of its shortcomings. Discourses of cultural intimacy stand in a tense yet complementary relationship to the official self-images of a community because they at once undermine untenable official claims while offering ultimately stabilizing alternative identifications. Thus, despite what might appear to be their defiant tone, discourses of cultural intimacy can serve rather conservative purposes, especially when they are reduced to a few cute cultural stereotypes: the stingy Swabian, the obedient Prussian, the exuberant Bavarian. What I take to be at the heart of cultural intimacy in the widest sense, however, is the common assumption that all members share an unquestionable identification with the whole, even if they criticize or ridicule parts of it. This understanding of cultural intimacy captures a wider range of phenomena than what Herzfeld originally had in mind. Intimacy presumes a domain of open but sheltered vulnerability, and what I am describing goes beyond self-reflexive knowledge of a group's "flaws" (and the solidarity they can create) to encompass any openness to systematic doubt, critique, or playful questioning (including the use of humor, irony, and even satire). Nevertheless, I will continue to use the term cultural intimacy because, given its allusion to background understandings of the "I know that you know that I know" variety, the concept is aptly named.

Bounded by freedom from synecdochical mischief, cultural intimacy designates a particular form of belonging, which is an important precondition for finding solutions to controversial problems within a group. Cultural intimacy in this sense is a necessary, if not quite sufficient, condition for the emergence of a dialogic public sphere. It is easily broken by the vicious dynamic of synecdochical mischief, the very fear of which can create the practice, which often prompts repayment in kind. In other words, once synecdochical mischief has become endemic, extraordinary measures of trust building are needed to overcome it. In the GDR, party and state developed an acute fear of synecdochical mischief as a consequence of their failures to achieve a monolithic collective intentionality. This fear triggered attribution of synecdochical mischief to those who seemed to hinder the realization of this intentionality; and the attribution eventually triggered its practice by many opposition members, who toward the end of the 1980s began to conclude that socialism could not be reformed after all. The state's own paranoia fed a self-radicalization of the opposition.

Cultural intimacy itself can be divided, pertaining to some domains but not others. In the GDR it emerged to a limited extent in the David-versus-Goliath metaphors that were used to celebrate the smaller, less complicated nature of GDR products in comparison to those produced in the FRG. Yet the party's ideological fixation on monolithic intentionality, combined with democratic centralism, prevented the emergence of cultural intimacy in matters political, even within the ranks of the party. Consequently, dialogue could not emerge in the public sphere; it was confined to the shelter of personal friendships. Even discussions among the highest cadres of Stasi, in the central committee (Modrow 1994; Uschner 1993) and in the politburo (see also Schabowski 1991), eventually lost all vestiges of dialogue, succumbing to the same proclamations of loyalty that filled the rest of public space. Although we cannot know for sure, I doubt whether genuine dialogue survived within even the innermost leadership dyads of the GDR; for instance, in general secretary Erich Honecker's relationships with Günter Mittag, the politburo member in charge of the economy, and Erich Mielke, member of the politburo and head of Stasi.

The loss of cultural intimacy shines through rhetorical practices that defined a distinct socialist lingo: the numerous references to authority in the form of party decrees, speeches of the general secretary, the Marxist-Leninist classics, and laws and regulations (in that order); the incessant celebration of success, the relativization or outright silence about failure. Given the suspicion that surrounded all dissent, it is not surprising that next to nobody gave extemporaneous public speeches, not the general secretary, not the politburo members, not even Mielke, who within the innermost circle of his generals read for hours from prepared manuscripts. Public life in the GDR was in the grip of state paranoia.

Certain historical contexts and types of ideologies are more conducive to the generation of synecdochical mischief, and thus to the production or destruction of cultural intimacies, than others. Socialism, with its reliance on a consciousness-driven model of social transformation, must confront the fact that before people became socialists they believed in something else; they had another way of understanding the world. If success is predicated on total commitment to the new way, failures will inevitably raise doubts about the degree or purity of the new commitment. The converted socialist is in this sense even more vulnerable to suspicion than the converted adherent to a salvation religion, who is in the comparatively lucky position of not being held accountable for the success of planned social changes. Socialism also has the problem of beginning its work by facing an enemy within. And again, if the development of socialism does not proceed smoothly, certain questions will linger: has the enemy been defeated for good, and has its defeat created only superficially subdued sentiments of revenge? Nationalism is in a much nicer situation insofar as its greatest potential enemies will be situated outside the community. Finally, it has to be considered that socialism in Eastern Europe was not brought about by internal revolutions, supported by the masses, but was a gift of Soviet tanks to local revolutionaries who, deep in their hearts, must have understood that the initial and—as periodic upheavals seemed to demonstrate—the continuing, critical support for their regimes came from outside.

Conclusions

I have introduced state paranoia as an institutionalized *form* of distrust. Although public life in the former GDR was rife with state paranoia, I do not want to suggest that all of social life in the GDR was beset by distrust, nor do I believe that socialist societies were characterized overall by lower levels of trust than capitalist societies, as Cold War rhetoric wanted us to believe. It must be remembered that no matter how deep-seated distrust of others might be, control can never be comprehensive. Successful social interaction involves at least minimal trust, and it follows that social life everywhere entails different forms of trust and distrust. Thus, a meaningful use of these terms requires specificity. Speaking of state paranoia, it is useful to distinguish who distrusts whom (source), about what (object), why or in what regard (target), and under what particular circumstances (context). The source of distrust was the real or imagined dissident who was weakening the resolve and thus the revolutionary fervor of the party. The particular object of distrust was the quality of the consciousness of individuals and, hence, their reliability as members of socialist collectives. The target of distrust—and of course in retrospect this is ironic—shifted in the course of the development of the GDR from fears about the survival of socialism to concerns about its smooth functioning.

I have analyzed the reproduction of state paranoia from the perspective of those who enacted it. My argument is based on interviews with Stasi officers and Stasi documents, but a comparison with materials generated by the politburo and the central committee reveals a similar picture. The people who enacted the system did not believe all the facts they were presented with, nor did they support every policy the regime favored. They did, however, believe deeply in the logic of the arguments, practices, and institutions I discuss in this essay. They believed in the value of the socialist project as a whole. Their commitment belies a popular Western discourse on socialism, which attributes cynicism to the enactors of the system. Often enough, scholars follow the same path of reasoning by attributing the suppressive characteristics of the system to the immoral (material or power) motives of its functionaries.

This argument founders not necessarily in detail (for of course there was cynical behavior) but at large, because it makes misleading assumptions about how community and belonging were constructed in socialism. The very fear that tokens of belonging were possibly faked and the immense efforts socialist institutions undertook to tell true from false are much less expressions of ruthlessly self-interested behavior and much more the outcome of the interlocking ideologies and practices I have described here in detail. Just as paranoid institutional forms can be enacted by perfectly "healthy" human beings, so can cynical institutional responses be produced by basically well-meaning individuals who work in these institutions.[30]

State paranoia prevented the emergence of a public sphere in which critical ideas about the system could be freely exchanged and alternative understandings of socialism or individual policies could be debated. Consequently, socialism closed itself to a vital source of internal renewal. Even worse, state paranoia was self-amplifying. In immediate reaction to inevitable mismatches between intentions and outcomes, state paranoia led to more centralization, more and more tightly controlled propaganda, a continuing increase in security measures, and so on. The key to understanding the enormous growth of Stasi (see also Gieseke 2000:551–557) during the history of the GDR lies precisely in this feedback cycle. In 1955, when the GDR resumed responsibility for its internal security from the Soviet Union, Stasi had 16,344 employees; at the end of its existence, Stasi counted 91,015 heads on its payroll. During this period, the number of spies caught in East Germany, the number of identifiable acts of sabotage, and even graffiti and pamphlets directed against the party (at least until late 1989) all declined sharply.[31] The irony of history in this case is that Stasi officers, though hired to protect socialism, probably contributed to its downfall by helping to enact state paranoia in the GDR.

Effective intimacy requires the cultivation of some form of pluralism. Ironically, it was the acceptance of pluralism and the emergence of cultural intimacy within the GDR's opposition movements that protected them from secret police tactics intended to undermine their sociality by spreading rumors about who thought what about whom, or who might or might not be a Stasi informant. Tragically, I would argue, the celebration of pluralism and a strong insistence on the right to differ have prevented many GDR opposition members from becoming successful politicians in the election machines of West Germany's established political parties. Successful political organization requires symbolic and social representation and hence the voluntary acceptance of reductions; this, too, is a significant aspect of cultural intimacy. The opposition members who took such pains to create a sphere of intimacy for themselves found themselves outside it within the parties they joined. The construction of public spaces characterized by cultural intimacy has two sides: (1) a self-understood abstention from attempts to undermine the whole by attacking its parts and (2) the negotiation of a relative comfort with the reductions entailed by relevant symbolic and social representations. A complex maneuver indeed.

Notes

1. The *Diagnostic and Statistical Manual of Mental Disorders: Fourth Edition*, better known as *DSM-IV*, defines paranoid personality disorder as "a pervasive distrust and suspiciousness of others such that their motives are interpreted as malevolent" (American Psychiatric Association 1994:637). Diagnostic criteria include, for example, the assumption of ill-intention even where there is no indication of it; unfounded doubts about the loyalty of friends or associates; unwillingness to confide in others;

reading hidden meanings into benign remarks. All of these, as will become apparent throughout the paper, are characteristic of state paranoia as well.

2. On the problematic conceptualization of political representation on the basis of a close identification between the represented and their representative agents, see Pitkin 1967, Dahl 1989, and more recently, Young 2000.

3. And it is precisely here, as Andrew Shryock shows so forcefully in his contributions to this volume, where the practice of ethnography has to wrestle with related issues. After all, ethnography is often written and even more often taken to represent the life of a particular group of people in a totalizing fashion and the ethnographer herself is that ambiguous figure striving to be an insider, while remaining, by profession, an outsider.

4. The literature on totalitarianism is mostly concerned with defining it as a historically new state form (Arendt 1958; Friedrich 1954; Friedrich and Brzezinski 1965; for a recent overview see Jesse 1999). Thus much of the debate centers on how much and at which times the various fascisms and communisms can be properly seen as totalitarian. It is precisely this concentration on a phenomenology of state forms that juxtaposes totalitarianism to others that has made the literature an apt means of propaganda. A preoccupation with state form, as well as the historical orientation of the literature toward the Holocaust and the Stalinist purges, has also prevented the use of Arendt's (1958) often brilliant insights about the use of symbolic forms for a critical analysis of political processes in Western democracies. A first step in this direction was taken by Goffman (1972).

5. It is interesting to see how, among many former party members, learning to think in terms of institutional failures emerged slowly only in the late 1980s, taking firm root for most only after the final fall of the old regime. A fascinating account of how a reform-minded socialist slowly comes to recognize that personalization must give way to a systems critique is Wolf 1999. Party members who saw the inability of personalization to explain failure were systematically driven underground. On SED reformers, see Land and Possekel 1998; Rauh 1991.

6. Nevertheless, while I do want to argue that the enactment of state paranoia involves feelings of fear (and fear-anger cycles), I will use the term "paranoia" purely descriptively without invoking intrapsychic processes to explain it.

7. This paper is based on interviews with twenty-five Stasi officers, twelve peace and civil rights movement activists, and three secret informants, as well as extensive archival research at the Stasi document center, the Matthias Domaschk archive, and the federal archives in Berlin. The original research is supplemented by a host of secondary materials, such as published interviews, memoirs, and biographies of former secret informants, Stasi officers, members of the central committee, the politburo, and their staff.

8. In 1989, only about 3,800 employees belonged to the *HV A*, the foreign espionage service. For a distribution of employees over various departments, see BStU 1996; for employee statistics over time, see Gieseke 2000. It is difficult to estimate how many Stasi officers were directly involved in efforts to control oppositional political thought. Responsibility and support for this task was not lodged in any single department.

9. Including the ninety-one thousand full-time members of Stasi, and given the fact that informants were regularly retired, it can be roughly estimated that by the end of the 1980s about 5 percent of the adult population of the GDR was working or had worked directly for the secret police. For purposes of comparison, it is interesting that about 19 percent of the adult population of the GDR were card-carrying members of the party (Schröder 1998:393).

10. See especially the guidelines on operative procedures (Gill and Schröter 1991: 346–413, especially 389ff).

11. Since it was illegal to constitute groups not sanctioned by the state, groups considered themselves more as open networks. Membership, which was never formally defined (in spite of some attempts to do so), came in a set of concentric circles determined by degree of participation: regularity of attendance, participation in group actions, initiation and leadership planning, and execution of group actions.

12. During my research I came across a presentation given by a leading member of the peace and civil rights movements who was talking to a group composed entirely of informants!

13. The suspicion that there could not be any real opposition is nicely reflected in linguistic practices such as the use of "so-called" or of inverted commas in connection with "opposition."

14. In total, the civil rights groups gained only 5 percent of the vote (see Schröder 1998:365), a number that might have to be corrected slightly upward because some former opposition members had thrown in their lot with the large Western parties. Some voters might have been drawn to these parties as a result.

15. What was politically feasible is not identical with what Stasi could or would have done if allowed free reign. For example, in curtailing samizdat publications the international political context had to be taken into consideration. Thus, Stasi tried to deal a devastating blow to the important samizdat paper *Grenzfall*, which was edited and produced by members of the "Initiative for Peace and Human Rights," only after Honecker had come back from his state visit to West Germany.

16. Efforts ranged from clumsy actions such as "operation Ochenskopf," in which antennas on GDR roofs were turned away from Western radio and TV transmitters, to actual jamming efforts; mechanical limitations on frequency dials were tried alongside regulatory means such as introducing the French color television system SECAM in the GDR, which was incompatible with West Germany's PAL system.

17. In the simplest case the check consisted of a screening of records. Depending on security needs, however, such checks could also include investigations undertaken by secret informants, neighborhood beat patrol officers of the People's Police, or Stasi officers in the guise of city employees. See the guidelines on "security checks," the so-called 1/82, and guidelines on operative person checks, the so-called 1/81 (Gill and Schröter 1991:295–345).

18. Apparently at the beginning of the 1980s the slogan disseminated by party schools was to consider the general secretary "the embodiment of the total social subject" (Schabowski 1991:119)

19. Several of my interview partners have faced party trials as a result of such behavior.

20. This point is constantly emphasized in proselytizing work and is the central

tenet of Marxist-Leninist textbooks. A good example (because it is widely spread) is: "Marxism has uncovered the fundamental laws of the development of society. Thus it elevated history to the status of a true science, which can exactly explain both the character of any given social order as well as the development from one such order to another" (Kuusinen et al. 1960:8–9). Starting from the foundation of the classics, it was the party's task to provide the correct interpretation of any particular historical situation (see Central Committee of the CPSU 1951, especially conclusions). In his book, Dominic Boyer (2003) calls this particular interpretative prerogative of the party "hermeneutic power."

21. It is particularly this aspect of a demand for total alignment that demands a radical differentiation into "friend and foe," that Hannah Arendt (1958) has called terror and sees as the constitutive characteristic of totalitarian rule. Alas, Arendt pays much less attention to what this means for totalitarian models of belonging, which I discuss later in the chapter.

22. Of course the canon was never fixed. Stalin's works were no longer consulted after the XX party congress of the CPSU. The works of Marx, Engels, and Lenin were read very selectively and were often reduced to particular quotations, depending on what portions seemed relevant to support a particular party line. Since participation in propaganda work was already time-consuming, especially for party members, even the highly motivated rarely extended their reading of the classics beyond selections used in meetings or classroom settings.

23. Mampel (1996) has spoken of Stasi as an "ideology police," which is a slight misnomer. The object of Stasi policing was not ideology per se—that was the party's prerogative—but more precisely the party's influence on the consciousness of the people.

24. Proclaiming unattainable goals was a tradition in socialism, and it was practiced at all levels. Ulbricht wanted to "overtake [West Germany] without catching up with it." Honecker proclaimed the "unity of social and economic policies."

25. Arguably this is another unmarxian tenet of Soviet style socialism. "The marxist science of social development does not only enable us to find our way among the complicated social contradictions but to predict the course of events and the direction in which historical progress will proceed" (Kuusinen et al. 1960).

26. Socialism thus proclaimed a seductive unity of rationality, eliminating the possible tensions between the true and the good by aligning them through the discovery and the practical pursuit of the only path to a just social order. Socialist rationality is, in Weber's lingo, substantive not procedural, a fact that has direct consequence for the understanding of law.

27. Although the party made wide use of the notion of "tactical retreat" by engaging in practical deals with the class enemy, this move could be easily justified only from the top down; it was virtually indefensible from the bottom up.

28. The same argument was used against Robert Havemann, a communist but also the GDR's leading critic in the 1960s and 1970s, and against Rolf Biermann, a singer and poet, also a communist, whose forced exile in 1976 lead to a public outcry in the GDR.

29. Several officers pointed out that in the end it didn't matter if they were directly hired by Western secret services. What mattered was that their actions pro-

duced precisely the kind of effect Western services would have produced if in fact they had hired them.

30. In a similar vein, Herzfeld (1992) tries to show how perfectly affable human beings enact a system of bureaucratic indifference.

31. This assessment is based on the memory of Stasi officers, who all confirm this decline.

References Cited

"SAPMO-BArch" refers to "Stiftung Archiv der Parteien und Massenorganisationen der ehemaligen Deutschen Demokratischen Republik im Bundesarchiv," a partial holding of the German Federal Archives, Berlin office. "BStU" refers to the Archive of the "Bundesbeauftragte für das Stasiunterlagengesetz," the Stasi document center in Berlin FDJ. 1988. Referat für die Beratungen mit Propagandisten zum Auftakt des Studienjahres der FDJ 1988/89. BArch, 5.329.

LITERATURE AND PUBLISHED SOURCES

American Psychiatric Association. 1994. *Diagnostic and Statistical Manual for Mental Disorders*, 4th ed. Washington, D.C.: American Psychiatric Association.

Arendt, Hannah. 1958. *The Origins of Totalitarianism*. New York: Meridian Books.

Borneman, John. 1998. *Subversions of International Order: Studies in the Political Anthropology of Cultures*. Albany: State University of New York Press.

BsTU (Der Bundesbeauftragte für die Unterlagen des Staatssicherheitsdienstes der ehemaligen Deutschen Demokratischen Republik). 1996. *Die Organisationsstruktur des Ministeriums für Staatssicherheit 1989*, in the publication series: *Anatomie der Staatssicherheit: Geschichte, Struktur Methoden*. Berlin: BSTU.

Boyer, Dominic. 2003. "Censorship as a Vocation: The Institutions, Practices and Cultural Logic of Media Control in the German Democratic Republic." In *Comparative Studies in Society and History* 45, no. 3.

Bullock, Alan. 1993. *Hitler and Stalin: Parallel Lives*. New York: Vintage.

Central Committee of the Communist Party of the Soviet Union (B). 1951. *The History of the Communist Party of the Soviet Union (B): Short Course*. Moscow: Foreign Languages Publication House.

Dahl, Robert. 1989. *Democracy and Its Critics*. New Haven, Conn.: Yale University Press.

Friedrich, Carl Joachim, ed. 1954. *Totalitarianism: Proceedings of a Conference Held at the American Academy of Arts and Sciences, March 1953*. Cambridge, Mass.: Harvard University Press.

Friedrich, Carl Joachim, and Zbigniew Brzezinski. 1965. *Totalitarian Dictatorship and Autocracy*. Cambridge, Mass.: Harvard University Press.

Gehrke, Bernd, and Wolfgang Rüddenklau, eds. 1999. *Das war doch nicht unsere Alternative: DDR Oppositionelle zehn Jahre nach der Wende*. Münster: Westfälisches Dampfboot.

Gieseke, Jens. 2000. *Die hauptamtlichen Mitarbeiter der Staatssicherheit: Personalstruktur und Lebenswelt 1950–1989/90*. Berlin: Ch. Links.

Gill, David, and Ulrich Schröter. 1991. *Das Ministerium für Staatssicherheit: Anatomie des Mielke-Imperiums*. Berlin: Rowohlt-Berlin.

Glaeser, Andreas. 2000. *Divided in Unity: Identity, Germany and the Berlin Police*. Chicago: University of Chicago Press.

Goffman, Irving. 1967. *Interaction Ritual: Essays in Face-to-Face Behavior*. Garden City, N.Y.: Anchor Books.

———. 1972. *Asylums: Essays on the Social Situation of Mental Patients and Other Essays*. New York: Doubleday.

Herzfeld, Michael. 1992. *The Social Production of Indifference: Exploring the Symbolic Roots of Western Bureaucracy*. New York: Berg.

———. 1997. *Cultural Intimacy: Social Poetics in the Nation-State*. London: Routlege.

Jesse, Eckhard. 1999. *Totalitarismus im 20. Jahrhundert: Eine Bilanz der internationalen Forschung*. Baden-Baden: Nomos.

Judt, Matthias, ed. 1998. *DDR-Geschichte in Dokumenten*. Berlin: Ch. Links.

Kuusinen, Otto Wille, et al. 1960. *Grundlagen des Marxismus-Leninismus: Lehrbuch*. Berlin: Dietz.

Land, Rainer and Ralf Possekel. 1998. *Fremde Welten: Die gegensätzliche Deutung der DDR durch SED-Reformer und Bürgerbewegung in den 8oer Jahren*. Berlin: Ch. Links.

Mampel, Siegfried. 1996. *Das Ministerium für Staatssicherheit der ehemaligen DDR als Ideologiepolizei: Zur Bedeutung einer Heilslehre als Mittel zum Griff auf das Bewußtsein auf das Totalitarismusmodell*. Berlin: Duncker & Humblot.

Modrow, Hans, ed. 1994. *Das große Haus: Insider berichten aus dem ZK der SED*. Berlin: edition ost.

Müller-Enbergs, Helmut. 1996. *Inoffizielle Mitarbeiter des Ministeriums für Staatssicherheit: Richtlinien und Durchführungsbestimmungen*, 2nd edition. Berlin: Ch. Links.

Neubert, Ehrhart. 1998. *Geschichte der Opposition in der DDR 1949–1989*. Berlin: Ch. Links.

Pitkin, Hanna Fenichel. 1967. *The Concept of Representation*. Berkeley: University of California Press.

Poppe, Ulrike, Rainer Eckert, and Ilko-Sascha Kowalczuk, eds. 1995. *Zwischen Anpassung und Selbstbehauptung: Formen des Widerstandes und der Opposition in der DDR*. Berlin: Ch. Links.

Rauh, Hans-Christoph, ed. 1991. *Gefesselter Widerspruch: Die Affaire um Peter Ruben*. Berlin: Dietz.

Rüddenklau, Wolfgang. 1992. *Störenfried: DDR-Opposition 1986–89*. Berlin: Basis-Druck.

Schabowski, Günter. 1991. *Der Absturz*. Berlin: Rowohlt-Berlin.

Schröder, Klaus. 1998. *Der SED-Staat: Geschichte und Strukturen der DDR*. Munich: Landeszentrale für politische Bildungsarbeit.

Schütz, Alfred, and Thomas Luckmann. 1984. *Die Strukturen der Lebenswelt*, vol. 1. Frankfurt: Suhrkamp.

Scott, James. 1998. *Seeing Like a State: How Certain Schemes to Improve the Human Condition Have Failed*. New Haven, Conn.: Yale University Press.

Suckut, Siegfried. 1996. *Das Wörterbuch der Staatssicherheit: Definitionen zur "politisch-operativen Arbeit,"* 2nd edition. Berlin: Ch. Links.

Uschner, Manfred. 1993. *Die zweite Etage: Funktionsweise eines Machtapparates.* Berlin: Dietz.

Wolf, Markus. 1999. *Im eignen Auftrag: Erkenntnisse und Einsichten.* Berlin: Schwarzkopf & Schwarzkopf.

Young, Iris Marion. 2000. *Inclusion and Democracy.* Oxford: Oxford University Press.

UNPUBLISHED DOCUMENTS

Mielke, Erich. 1984a. Referat des Ministers at the "Dienstkonferenz" on 11 May 1984 (Presentation of the minister, biannual security briefing with divisional and district heads.) Berlin: Matthias Domaschk Archiv, cassette (without call number).

———. 1984b. "Probleme der Feindtätigkeit und die Aufgaben zum Schutz unserer sozialistischen Staats- und Gesellschaftsordnung." Presentation given at "Parteischule Kleinmachnow." Berlin: SAPMO-BArch, Dy 30/IV 2/2.039.

———. 1986. Referat des Ministers at the "Dienstkonferenz" on 6 October 1986 (Presentation of the minister, biannual security briefing with divisional and district heads.) Berlin: Matthias Domaschk Archiv, cassette (without call number).

———. 1988. Referat des Ministers at the "Dienstkonferenz" on 5 September 1988 (Presentation of the Minister, biannual security briefing with divisional and district heads.) Berlin: Matthias Domaschk Archiv, cassette (without call number).

MfS-SED-KL. 1985. Jahresbericht der SED Kreisleitung im MfS 1984, BStU-MfS-SED-KL 5150.

PART FIVE

Overly Familiar

CHAPTER 10

In the Double Remoteness of Arab Detroit

REFLECTIONS ON ETHNOGRAPHY, CULTURE WORK, AND THE INTIMATE DISCIPLINES OF AMERICANIZATION

Andrew Shryock

Report from the War Zone: August 2003

Nearly two years have passed since I wrote the introduction to this volume. During that time, the Arab and Muslim populations of Detroit have been transformed into a domestic front in the Bush administration's War on Terror. The suburb of Dearborn, home to the Ford Motor Company and to thirty thousand Arab residents, was the first American city to have its own office of Homeland Security. No government official has said it explicitly, but Arab Detroit is now a zone of threat, and its inhabitants have good reason to feel threatened by the contradictory messages they have received from officialdom and society at large. The first months after the 9/11 attacks were a time of hate crimes and intimidation, but a desire to "understand" Arabs and Muslims flourished in America. Initial attempts to "reach out" to anyone who might suffer from scapegoating suggested, for some observers, that a solid decade of pluralist conditioning had finally paid off. "At this moment," poet Khaled Mattawa wrote, "as Arab and Muslim Americans are being inducted into a kind of collective citizenship ceremony, I find it encouraging that in its time of crisis America has opted for its multiracial, multilingual, multicultural face" (2002:160).

I would like to thank Sally Howell, Amaney Jammal, Ramez Abdelfattah, Nabeel Abraham, Michael Herzfeld, and Hashim Al-Tawil for helpful criticisms of this essay. The views I express are not necessarily theirs, nor are they responsible for errors in the text. The Center for Advanced Study in the Behavioral Sciences, through funding provided by the Andrew W. Mellon Foundation (Grant # 29800639), supported me generously during the time in which this essay was written.

Such language now seems strangely optimistic. The USA Patriot Act and subsequent policy decisions made by the Department of Justice, Homeland Security, and the Department of the Treasury have created an atmosphere in which Arabs and Muslims can be treated as a special population to whom certain legal protections and civil rights no longer apply.[1] Hundreds of un-named, uncharged detainees languish in prisons across the United States, while hundreds more have been summarily deported. Arabs and Muslims living in America, whether they are resident aliens, out of status, or full-fledged citizens, are now routinely exposed to mass interrogations, back-ground checks, and special surveillance. In Detroit, where the local offices of the FBI have doubled in size since the 9/11 attacks, one of the largest fed-eral investigations in U.S. history has resulted in the conviction of two Arab immigrants (and the acquittal of two more) accused of running a terrorist "sleeper cell" out of their shabby apartment in Dearborn. Nationally, the mass-mediated structures of public opinion, especially those that materialize on cable news networks, in the wide circulation press, and on talk radio have performed well as a conduit for the anti-Arab, anti-Muslim views espoused by a complex network of conservative think tanks, pro-Israeli pundits, U.S. (and other) government spokespeople, and retired military and State De-partment officials. It is ironic, and more than a bit depressing, to learn (from pollsters) that Muslim Americans enjoy a higher "approval rating" today than they did before the 9/11 attacks.[2] Apparently, they have never been re-garded more fondly.

As Arabs in Detroit struggle to secure their position in a multicultural pub-lic sphere that compels them (but does not always allow them) to identify with other Americans as Americans, they must also confront new disconti-nuities in their own zones of cultural intimacy. The spaces in which Arab Americans identify with each other *as Arabs* are being pried open, moni-tored, compulsively Americanized, or driven further into realms of stigma. Preexisting divisions within the community (between Christians and Mus-lims, between new immigrants and long-established ethnics) have been ex-acerbated in predictable ways, but profiling and selective government pene-tration of Arab Detroit's gray and black markets—a world of sharp business, tax evasion, smuggling, forgery, identification fraud, and other crimes that proliferate among immigrant populations located on the margins of the U.S. political economy—have put Arab community leaders in awkward posi-tions. Not only have they been forced to admit that such crimes do occur among Arab immigrants; they feel compelled to stress that similar crimes oc-cur among Asian and Latino communities as well and that, however serious this pattern of infractions might be, it is not the same as terrorism.

"It's hard," Muna Bakir,[3] a prominent activist, told me. "The whole cli-mate has changed. The community is really taking a beating. We are being marginalized. We could lose everything we've built here."

Loyalty, Doubt, and Identification

Accurate and earnest though it was, Muna's comment perplexed me. I have worked closely with Muna's group for many years, and friends employed there provide me with a steady stream of news about the organization. I regularly visit their Web site, which announces the organization's accomplishments in the grand, adulatory tones appropriate to the genre. By all (public) accounts, Muna Bakir's group is weathering the 9/11 "climate" quite well, as are several of Arab Detroit's religious and ethnic associations, which have received an impressive array of official commendations, awards for service, positive media attention, and substantial infusions of public and private funds. I remember listening, with mixed emotions of pride and embarrassment, as a Muslim cleric told a delegation of visitors to his Dearborn mosque: "I would say that we have seen, in this congregation, more positive developments after September 11 than negative ones. People have never been so eager to learn about Islam. We cannot meet the demand for lectures and workshops. This is a good thing that has come from a very bad situation." These words came in response to a question about harassment and profiling, which the cleric acknowledged were daunting problems. His upbeat conclusion, however, is a refrain I hear often among Arabs in Detroit. It is partly a refusal to cower, but it is also a testament to the adaptability with which many mosques and secular community groups have responded to the crisis.

All of this suggests that it is prudent to distinguish between "the community," which is "taking a beating," and certain Muslim and Arab American organizations that represent "the community," which are clearly succeeding and being rewarded for valuable work. The Arab/Muslim population of Detroit has long been a site of extreme marginality (where beatings are administered) and confident mainstreaming (where beatings stop and magnanimous gestures of incorporation and fellow feeling are perfectly in order). Moreover, these acts of inclusion and exclusion occur simultaneously in "the community," almost as functions of each other, and this simultaneity has representational effects that are still poorly understood. Arab Detroit, with a population of roughly two hundred thousand, is large; it is over a century old; it is composed mostly of Lebanese, Iraqis, Yemenis, and Palestinians, roughly half of them Christian; many Arabs in Detroit are affluent and politically influential; many are poor, illiterate in English, and trapped in unskilled, low-pay jobs; the majority are (or think they are) members of the American middle class.[4] This broad range of lifestyles, national backgrounds, and levels of assimilation has made the Detroit Arab community hard to represent, both intellectually and politically. It is not simply an American ethnic community; parts of it make sense only in relation to the Yemeni highlands or the Lebanese countryside. Nor is Arab Detroit an integral part of the Arab world; the city is home, for instance, to thousands of Arabs who cannot speak Arabic and have never traveled to the Middle East.

A community of this complexity is not held together by simple acts of cooperation between Arab "insiders," who organize and speak for it, and non-Arab "outsiders," who recognize and fund it. To materialize at all, Arab Detroit must conform to an elaborate set of assumptions about identity that are shared among persons both external and internal to "the community." Such conformity and sharing must be encouraged; they are expected; they are made public through specific kinds of representational effort, which I will call "culture work"; and their genuineness, as forms of identification, is often a matter of speculation. In Arab Detroit, identification and doubt (about being Arab, about being American) are never far from view. The profiling and harassment that followed the 9/11 attacks were merely amplified versions of the suspicion routinely directed at Arabs in the United States. The exaggerated display of American flags by Arabs in Detroit—on clothes, skin, cars, homes, storefront windows, and places of worship (Shryock 2002)—was part of a heightened desire, familiar among immigrants of manifold sorts, to "belong" or (failing that) to be sheltered from the brute consequences of not belonging. The forms of "culture work" I will explore in this essay are more complex than the talismanic display of patriotic symbols, but the same impulses animate them.

When acts of identification with the state are believed to be insincere or insufficient—a situation Andreas Glaeser examines in his contribution to this volume—their public display tends to reinforce patterns of political anxiety that resemble paranoia. In times of war, these patterns take on a brazen clarity and are later regretted, but I would insist that paranoia has long been a defining feature of the relationship between the United States and its Arab Muslim immigrants, who are typically assumed to be anti-American if they identify with, or merely resemble, Arabs and Muslims who live abroad. I would develop this claim further, however, by suggesting that fears of Arab/Muslim Otherness (and a pressing need to allay them) have become the defining feature of "culture work" commissioned and endorsed by Arab community leaders in Detroit. The unfortunate result has been that "Americanization," for Arab Muslims, consists of incessant attempts to prove that "we are people just like you," while experiences drawn from the shared social frameworks of everyday life—whether these are Arab, American, Arab American, Muslim, or all of them together—respond, in a clear voice, "no, you are not like us, and we are not like you."

The Conditions of Culture Work

The problem of stigmatized difference is the backdrop against which I have done much of my own "culture work" in Arab Detroit. Since 1987, I have served as a curator for museum exhibits, authored and edited teaching materials for use in elementary schools, helped produce a documentary film, written and consulted on grants for community groups, arranged public lectures, and participated in dozens of seminars for teachers, church leaders and laypeople, law enforcement agencies, hospital workers, businesspeople, and others who serve, administer, trade with, protect, and struggle to "understand" Detroit's Arab populations.[5] This activity, which has never been isomorphic with my work as a scholar, belongs to a larger, forthrightly political agenda. I engage in "culture work" as part of a broad coalition of people who, by means of artistic representation and cultural education, try to insure that Arabs and Arab Americans are included, on favorable terms, in American public life. Demolishing stereotypes and replacing ignorance with useful knowledge are important tasks, but there is very little about "culture work" that evokes the romance of resistance, or the rush of frontline, march-and-chant activism. The target of "culture work" is almost always an established institution that solicits and participates willingly in this activity, from which it hopes to derive tangible rewards: a more flexible and sensitive workforce, improved community relations, or a better hold on ethnic niche markets. The fact that funding for culture work in Arab Detroit comes largely from the U.S. government, private foundations, and corporate sponsors is essential to any understanding of why it succeeds and what it is meant to accomplish.

In the 1980s, Arabs in Detroit were still routinely excluded from pluralist discourses and public diversity displays; initial attempts to break into these formats met with stiff resistance. The cultural programming and project grants put forward by Arab American groups had to be of the highest quality, and even the most conventionally folkloric events—an exhibit of Palestinian embroidery, say, or a performance by a Yemeni dance troupe—were tainted, in the minds of funders, by their association with Arabs, Islam, and political conflict in the Middle East. In a fascinating analysis of aesthetic politics in Detroit, Sally Howell (2000) recounts the (in)delicate arrangements whereby the first Palestinian Intifada and the Gulf War served as contexts in which funding for Arab American cultural programs could be justified, by private foundations and government agencies, as part of a larger agenda of "understanding Arabs, Muslims, and the Middle East." The Oslo Peace Accords of 1993, Howell argues, made Arab Americans a target of funding for major cultural foundations (the National Endowment for the Humanities, the National Endowment for the Arts, the Lila Wallace Fund, and others) that had once scrupulously avoided Arab American groups. Indeed, mainstream institutions of all kinds suddenly vied to bring American Arabs and Muslims into their funding agendas as evidence of a more general "peace dividend" and as proof that relations between Jews and Arabs in America (and, by extension, between Israel and its Arab neighbors) could be "normalized."

By the mid-1990s, the inclusion of Arabs and Muslims in the larger project of Americanization was a *fait accompli* in Detroit, in part because Arafat
and Rabin shook hands on the White House lawn, in part because the city's
Arabs, once an uneasy alliance of assimilated, old-line Syrian immigrants,
new refugees and labor migrants from Lebanon, Palestine, and Yemen, and
an insular cohort of Iraqi Catholics, had created public institutions—and a
thriving network of private, family-owned businesses—that the larger society could no longer afford to ignore. In Detroit, Arab Americans have secured their place in the distribution of public and private funds set aside for
cultural programming in ethnoracial communities. The money comes easily now, and it flows in direct proportion to levels of violent conflict in the
Middle East. Detroit's leading Arab American organizations have never been
more generously funded than they are today, in the middle of America's
"War on Terror." ACCESS, the Arab Community Center for Economic
and Social Services, located in Dearborn, received over $4 million in grants
and gifts in the months following the September 11 attacks, most of it ear-
marked for educational and cultural programs. Ford, DaimlerChrysler, and
the Mott, Kellogg, and Kresge foundations are prominent among its ben-
efactors. "I'm happy this money is pouring in," a veteran of culture work
told me.

The community really needs it. It's a vote of confidence. But I know that's only half
the story. I mean, when this kind of money suddenly becomes available, after something horrible like September 11, it's a blessing and a curse. It means you're about to
take a hit. This money will soften the blow. Maybe. It'll help the community handle
the major shit that's about to go down. People are scared. I see these million dollar
checks coming in from everywhere and I think, man! They're actually paying Arab
organizations to "sensitize" the FBI; we're running workshops now for the same
people who are cracking down on the community. It's weird as hell, quite frankly.
Part of me thinks . . . well, part of me *knows*, this is all a way of maintaining "homeland security" and keeping things in order. There *is* incredible potential here to develop new cultural resources people can use to educate, and the need for that is really urgent. Basically, you've got to get to work and not be all freaked out about the
big picture. Or else you'll be totally paralyzed.

In the latest regimen of culture work, knowledge about Arabs and Muslims will be contorted, yet again, to fit the framework of political danger—
of "major shit"—in which it is displayed. The flood of financial support is
simultaneously a tool, a burden, and a potential liability. Gifts to ACCESS,
for instance, augment an annual budget that already stood at $8 million. This
concentration of resources has caused a great deal of jealousy and suspicion
in Detroit, which is nothing new for ACCESS. Similarly, the support Arab
Americans are now receiving from mainstream institutions fuels resentment
among other "communities of color" and, more conspicuously, among anti-

Arab racists who, as Abraham (1994) has argued, are firmly entrenched in mainstream institutions of all sorts. Again, this situation intensifies a structural paranoia that beset Arab Detroit even before the September 11 attacks: every financial gift or show of solidarity enhances the fear that things could go irreversibly wrong at any moment; indeed, it is high levels of support, activists repeatedly tell me, that will embolden enemies of the Arab community to act. In this tense setting, new powers of mass mediation, and calls to display Arab Detroit to an ever-expanding (and potentially less sympathetic) audience, are creating a pervasive mood of vulnerability in which the boundaries of what can be shown and seen are being shifted toward more comfortably American terrain.

Magical Manipulation and Self-Conscious Display

As I began, in the mid-1990s, to think critically about Arab American identity formation, I unwisely projected my own sensibility (that of a culture worker who is also an anthropologist) onto the entire enterprise of representational politics, calling it "self-conscious cultural display." By use of this phrase I meant to describe a cultural enterprise that produces signs of identity oriented toward audiences who do not necessarily share that identity. The signs themselves—whether they are poems, dresses, life histories, or songs—are often made to be (or become) mass-mediated artifacts. As Özyürek's earlier analysis of Republic Day exhibits in Turkey suggests, it is wrong to assume that explicit cultural display is intelligible only in relation to what it consciously intends to convey, that all motives for display are equally alert to themselves, or that audiences for these displays are as self-conscious as the people who produce them. Even elaborately orchestrated cultural events send messages that were unexpected. Who would have guessed that what non-Arabs would "learn" at the ethnic street fair is "Arabs don't know how to stand in line"? Who foresaw that the reporter covering the Arab American photography exhibit would discover talent, yes, but also how hard it is to interview a Yemeni female without her brother's permission?

It was not until I began to publish on the topic, however, that I realized how firmly culture workers believe that the self-consciousness of public cultural display should be treated as a secret, a "trick of the trade." When I wrote about how Arab characters in a documentary film were selected and juxtaposed (1998), or how cultural programs were framed and pitched to funding agencies (2000), the indignant response (among fellow culture workers) helped me see just how closely public cultural display resembles stage magic. To be convincing and effective, it must obscure its own means of production. Kelly Askew has already shown us that Hollywood filmmakers invest heavily in their own artifice, in "movie magic," which is essential to creating "surface realism." Reality effects, in film and other media, play on preconceived notions and the viewer's useful ignorance of how things "really are." We can tell ourselves that movies are "not real," but we also know that movies are part of everyday life, and others might assume they are real. As a result, films can be more or less "accurate," more or less "fair" in their portrayal of social worlds that we know intimately, but others can not.

The desire to "see through" mass-mediated images to an underlying reality (if only a reality of production) is intensified, not diminished, by "media literacy"—by knowledge of how the seemingly real is artificially produced—and this explains the growing popularity of products that explain how a museum exhibit, movie, book, or music video was made. The same desire, however, makes it difficult to discuss how images of purportedly *real* social worlds, *real* people and places, are crafted in ways meant to enhance their impact or appeal. The links between surface realism and the (un)real are especially hard to analyze when image making is done *on behalf of* stigmatized groups whose "reality" has already been adversely shaped by others. In my introduction to this volume, I showed briefly how writing a simple museum text about Arab American families involves radical elisions (and second guessing and placating language) that cannot be displayed as such—they would immediately disqualify the text in the eyes of most readers—even though these representational games are what makes the writing of such texts possible. When the accuracy of (socially constructed) images is at stake, taking note of artifice at all can undermine one of culture work's most vital resources: the power of "authenticity," a quality of the real that, despite all evidence of stagecraft, is located (or is thought to exist) beyond the reach of magical manipulation.

Our Business/Everybody's Business

The argument I am trying to make places the self-conscious and the taken for granted in an uneasy relationship, and I should perhaps simplify matters by politicizing them in a more immediate way. As practice and politics, culture work is most effective when people are oblivious to the manner in which key terms—Arab, American, community, mainstream, culture, heritage—are built into the very grammar of identity discourse and made to appear natural. As levels of "reflexivity" increase (that is, as people become more aware of how their identities are *always being made* and are not simply "out there"), the political efficacy of key terms is no longer guaranteed. When basic concepts like "Arab" and "American" are understood to be zones of dispute and social control, the activists who rely on these naturalized key terms to unify and mobilize a constituency are suddenly required to expend valuable political capital in arguments over what identity labels mean and

how they should be applied.[6] In turn, culture workers who use identity labels to organize the materials they display are handicapped when "outsiders"
can suddenly argue that the labels belong not to an ethnic community defined by a cultural heritage, but only to a unifying, mobilizing effort that
makes use of cultural materials in order to attain socioeconomic privileges
or access to power. When "identity" and "politics" are portrayed as self-
conscious aspects of each other, both are diminished. Their advocates are
said, always dismissively, to be "pushing an agenda," which is the political
equivalent of "magical manipulation."

   This delegitimation effect has its origins in the moral politics characteristic of modern nation-states, wherein "the" community, "its" culture, and
"its" leadership are seen to be in proper alignment only when they are bound
to each other by an authentic sameness that produces loyalty. As Benedict
Anderson so famously put it, "regardless of the actual inequality and exploitation that may prevail in each, the nation is always conceived as a deep,
horizontal comradeship" (1991:7). Ethnoracial and other marked communities in the United States can be accurately described as miniaturized, minoritized nation-states, and they must imagine themselves in constant relation to the supersized, majoritized national community of which they are
part. Devout nationalists tend to reject Anderson's claim that the nation-state
is a social construction of recent origin whose unity is dependent on acts of
the imagination. In parallel (and predictable) fashion, the most committed
advocates of ethnoracial politics are dismissive of attempts to scrutinize the
invented, formulaic, and politicized aspects of the identities they endorse,
even when this scrutiny is aimed at unsettling the structures of advantage
that prevent cultural solidarities and political movements of a less predictable type.

   Among scholars who study nation-states and their internal Others, it is
now standard fare to insist that majority and minority cultures are, at the
very least, second-order representations. Each must be made and mediated
on a mass scale. They must be defined, internally managed, and externally
projected in certain ways (not others), and entire cohorts of professionals do
this work for a living.[7] Insofar as "communities," to invoke Anderson's terminology once again, are limited in membership and sovereign, this maintenance work is likely to be construed as "our own business." Germans
should not write the textbooks used in Spanish schools; Canadians should
not conduct the U.S. census; Malaysians should not represent Cambodians
at the United Nations. The same logic applies, but with a peculiar twist, to
ethnic communities in the United States (and in many other nation-states).
The maintenance and development of the Arab American community in
Detroit is, for Arabs, "our own business." Yet these activities are also part of
a larger, nation-building project, which is "everybody's business." The re-

sult is an awkward, elaborate domain of limits within public spheres, internal sovereignties within shared contours of citizenship, mainstreams within margins, and lines of trespass within structures of inclusion. As I began to think and write about Arab Detroit as a socially constructed space, I encountered barriers to ethnographic representation that were also openings to more general insights about representational politics; whenever I passed through these thresholds, I alienated myself from the activists who were once my closest allies.

Our Business/Everybody's Business . . . Nobody's Business

The publication of *Arab Detroit: From Margin to Mainstream* (Abraham and Shryock 2000) was a happy event for me. The book was reviewed warmly in the Arab American press, and readers in Detroit were eager to acquire copies of it. Border's Books & Music in Dearborn could barely keep *Arab Detroit* in stock; copies were repeatedly stolen from local libraries. It appeared on the "must read" and "gift idea" lists of Detroit's mainstream newspapers and magazines; the Historical Society of Michigan honored it with an Award of Merit; public readings were well attended. Amid this positive response, I began to hear rumblings of dissatisfaction, most of them emanating from the upper ranks of the Arab American organizations. Nabeel Abraham and I had portrayed several of these groups as "mainstreaming" in the book, and the nature of our argument apparently upset key leaders. We argued that the success of organizations like ACCESS, ACC (Arab American and Chaldean Council), ADC (American Arab Anti-Discrimination Committee), and the American Arab Chamber of Commerce was predicated on their ability to render Arab identities conformable to a larger, Americanizing rhetoric of national inclusion, thereby gaining a place for Arabs in spaces (and funding domains) set aside for minority representation.

Because "identity" and "community" are ideas used—by political interests of diverse sorts—to manage America's "special populations," it is vitally important for immigrant and ethnic organizations to secure a controlling interest in this management strategy by constructing an Americanized "identity" that can stand for the "community" in question. To assume a shape the larger society can recognize, Abraham and I argued,

a group must be distinguishable from the mainstream in some ways but essentially like it in others; it must have a definite size and shape (in relation to the national mainstream); it must have a general experience (or at least a memory) of struggle and disadvantage; and, most important, it must possess a history, a collective biography, that it tells the larger society. These attributes of community do not arise naturally out of the populations they describe. Instead, they must be actively produced, distributed, and consumed by individuals who are heavily invested in the community as a resource (Shryock and Abraham 2000:41).

This formula for belonging is not the only one available to Arabs, Arab Americans, or Americans at large. To understand its purpose and appeal, one must pay close attention to how "the mainstream" figures as both an object of desire (we must somehow enter it) and a site of rejection (we are being kept out of it). When identity formation is geared toward entering and altering the American mainstream—as opposed to keeping a safe distance from it—a sensibility emerges in which "our culture" is divided into "good" and "bad" parts, into things that are "useful" or "inappropriate" to the mainstreaming project. This bifurcation of cultural materials, Abraham and I suggested, is the moral equivalent of "assimilation" in our times. Arab Americans (and others) are oddly unwilling to see this process as evidence of a continued insistence that "foreigners" become "like us," and this is why the process works so well. It is the medium in which "our business" (making an ethnic community) and "everybody's business" (making a national community) merge. It is the medium in which self-conscious cultural display merges with a politics of authenticity. By showing how activists, scholars, and culture workers had, in effect, "created" a compelling identity for Arabs in Detroit by means of scholarly writing, media representation, cultural education, and political networking, Abraham and I had fashioned a social constructivist argument that some people could read only as an accusation that Arab American identity was the product of "magical manipulation." This was not what we had in mind, but scholarship about Arab Detroit has traditionally been construed as a kind of political advocacy, not as an attempt to situate Arab American-ness within larger contexts of identity formation or cultural display. Critics of *Arab Detroit* have a very clear understanding of what research in the community should (and should not) be about.

Shortly after it was published, a prominent activist told me that *Arab Detroit* could be used against ACCESS *because* it explains how that organization has built and institutionalized an Arab ethnic constituency in Michigan (1) by promoting one set of historical and identity narratives (while ignoring others) and (2) by promoting the claim that Arab Detroit has over 250,000 inhabitants—actually, community leaders now say 370,000—when its population might be under 150,000. I responded that, by showing how these things are done, the book would in all likelihood enhance the reputation of ACCESS as a successful and politically effective agency. I also noted that ACCESS policies are a matter of public record, and that exaggerating a group's headcount and crafting its collective story to fit American tastes are standard operating procedure in ethnic politics. Nonetheless, the idea that all of this is "confidential" and must be concealed from outsiders is common among culture workers and activists, who must compete with other special

constituencies for access to limited resources. The use of numbers and narratives to elicit financial support gives each a strategic value, even when the
representational strategies employed by community groups are generic and
available to anyone.

Another critic argued that public support for Detroit's Arab American
organizations is strong precisely because Arabs are seen as alien and at risk.
Mainstreaming, he argued, is a strategy that addresses both perceptions effectively. It is simply a case of "showing your best face." Besides, "we're not
doing anything other groups don't do." I agreed. Other groups do this, which
is why Abraham and I could not pretend that Arab Americans do not. There
is nothing inherently wrong with "showing your best face," I continued, but
the tactic assumes you know what an ugly face looks like and why; it also suggests that mainstream standards dictate what is ugly about Arabness, with the
result that some Arabs, especially newly arrived immigrants, will be deemed
"ugly" when, in fact, they are simply different. Another critic noted that
new immigrants are the people Arab organizations want to help: "we're trying to get people settled here; we're trying to get them the things they need
to live here, and you don't talk about that. You give the impression that we're
a bunch of cynical operators who cook the numbers, but you don't talk about
the really important thing, which is helping some people who really need
our help." I had confused "public relations" with the *realpolitik* of running
multimillion-dollar human service agencies and this, in her opinion, was un-
wise and irresponsible.

In several encounters of this type, I have noticed that my critics do not
doubt, even for an instant, that they speak on behalf of the Arab community
as a whole. For all the positive response *Arab Detroit* has enjoyed, these critics are convinced that it is harmful to "the community," or could be harmful if the wrong people read it. The latter claim, designed to suppress scholarship that might be of use to political opponents, shows rather nicely what
"both sides" hope to control. At stake is (1) the ability to sustain public institutions that provide social and legal services, job training, health care, and
English language instruction to newly arrived Arab immigrants and (2) the
ability to create and publicly display identities that solidify political constituencies, business networks, and ethnic niche markets that benefit Arab
Detroit's emergent (and old line) bourgeoisie. These two capacities reinforce each other, but only when they conform to the dominant patterns of
"masked assimilation" through which ethnoracial and other minority groups
are recognized and managed as "special populations" within the American
mainstream.

By arguing that Arab Detroit is a space in which ethnic inclusion and cultural exclusion overlap and constitute each other, Abraham and I went to
the heart of what is most contestable, and most important, to people who
are heavily invested in creating Arab Detroit and brokering its interactions

with the "larger society." It is the *integration* of American and Arab things—not their difference or, even less, their opposition—that matters most to this group. They assume the existing structures of integration are extremely fragile, when all evidence suggests these are solidly in place and (for the community's mainstreaming institutions) are actually growing stronger, even coercive, under duress. They also assume that structures of integration are based on a kind of equality, on respect for difference, when all evidence suggests that integration can be accomplished only when Arab Otherness is naturalized, normalized, muted, consigned to another time, or linked to a place and way of life that the immigrant, or the immigrant ancestor, has left behind (Shryock and Abraham 2000:17).

In the remainder of this essay, I will try to make sense of this predicament, which I believe is related to Arab and American intimacies that, because they pull in different directions, produce an unconventional, highly mutable identity space. In a geographic sense, Arab Detroit exists at a remove from "Arab homelands," yet it is situated within a "larger society" that is not Arab and, in ways too numerous to count, is anti-Arab. The phrases "at a remove" and "situated within" correspond to spatial as well as social dispositions, and both can be used to constitute Arab Detroit as a "remote area," which does not mean, necessarily, that it is a marginal place; attempts to mainstream Arab Detroit have been successful, but only when they perpetuate the community's status as an opportunity zone that needs to be hooked up to the master grid, through recognition and investment. To understand why ethnoracial and immigrant communities are so often defined by the quality of remoteness (in space and time, as a feature of persons, as an attribute of social forms and events), it is helpful to recall Edwin Ardener's observation: "remoteness," he argued, is "a condition not related to periphery, but to the fact that certain peripheries are by definition not properly linked to the dominant zone" (1989:223). Arab Detroit is doubly remote. When it is "properly linked" to one dominant zone, this connection triggers feelings of impropriety in relation to another. It creates new terrain on which "Arab-as-Other and Arab-as-American converge, scrutinize and assess each other, conceal and appeal to each other, and sometimes look away from each other in shame" (Shryock and Abraham 2000:24).

Double Remoteness

Ardener developed his notion of "remoteness" through reference to a set of examples drawn from Cameroon and the Scottish Isles. In the following sketches, I do the same for Arab Detroit, but I have been careful to double the evidence of remoteness. Just as the Bahia described earlier in this volume by James Matory and John Collins is remote in relation both to Brazil's dominant sociopolitical zones and to an imagined African source of origin,

Arab Detroit is remote in relation both to the Arab world and to American society at large. Signs of "improper linkage" to dominant American zones appear in plain text, whereas remoteness from dominant Arab zones is suggested by italics. The numbered observations, with minor rewordings, are from Ardener's essay (1989:218–220).

1.   REMOTE AREAS ARE FULL OF STRANGERS.   A van of businesspeople cruises slowly down Dix Avenue in Dearborn. They are staring hard, taking everything in: the Arabic lettering on the storefronts, the long robes worn by men, the head scarves and face veils worn by women, the green, onion-shaped dome of the mosque. Cameras are drawn; shutters click. Young boys wave eagerly as they run alongside the van; adults stare back or discreetly turn aside. They've seen it all before. *Yesterday, the van was loaded with Arab men with cameras. They wore the same look of curiosity on their faces. Who were they? Some say "professors from Algeria," others say "mayors from Egypt."* The TV news crews descend on Detroit like a plague of locusts whenever anything goes wrong in the Middle East; they park in front of mosques to gather "man in the street" interviews. *Al-Jazeera and other Arabic networks dispatch reporters as well, who send home images of Detroit, exotic outpost of the Arab world. How odd that so many of the people interviewed speak Arabic with an accent. They are Arabs, aren't they?* Ed Bradley and his crew from *60 Minutes* are spotted wandering the streets of Dearborn with local Arab leaders as guides. *The local social service agency has a new employee in the _____ office. Who is she? They say she's from Palestine, but no one knows her family. There is talk.* Another group of researchers wants to do an opinion survey in the community; at least that's what they say; God knows what they're really up to.

2.   REMOTE AREAS ARE FULL OF INNOVATORS.   He's not local, but he's certainly an insider. In just a few years, he turned Dearborn's Arab American business community into a high- profile lobby; he and his circle of (mostly Lebanese) confidants throw their weight around with mayors, congressmen, diplomats, and CEOs. *Daughter of a well-known politician, she wanted to be a party leader and public intellectual in her home country, but seeing the glass ceiling for women, she packed her bags and headed for Detroit, where she has enjoyed a successful career as an activist.* She has not a drop of Arab blood, but she raised millions of dollars to support Arab cultural programs in Detroit, *and she relied heavily on the help of _____, a painter from Iraq who has carved out a lucrative niche for his work among immigrant and ethnic Arabs who want to buy art that reminds them of the homeland.* A relationship of convenience, meanwhile, has been worked out between _____, a non-Arab ethnic marketer who wants to run advertising campaigns in Arab Detroit, and _____, *who represents an Arab company that wants to sell products to Arab Americans while, on the side, he headhunts for bilingual American Arabs who want to work for affiliated companies in the Gulf states.*

3. REMOTE AREAS ARE FULL OF RUINS OF THE PAST. *The Beit Hanina Social Club, where immigrants from the West Bank village of Beit Hanina once held their weddings, funeral visitations, and political meetings, has been languishing in a state of benign neglect for years. Its sign continues to shed letters. Last time I checked, it was the "_ e__ Hanina Social Clu_."* Most of the club's members have moved to Cleveland, where they are opening small businesses. Recently, Yemenis bought the building. Nearby, a mural, funded by an Arab social service agency, stood vandalized until it was finally painted over. The lettering for Arabian Village, a failed development scheme backed by the city and local Arab businesses, fades and flakes a few blocks down the street. *Everywhere one turns, there are signs of heritage and tradition: the restaurants are decorated with old guns and swords (or new ones made to look old), with antique coffee grinders and pots, with sepia-toned photographs of Bedouin in tents. The newest mosques are built to Ottoman and Mogul specifications. Maids of honor at upper-class Arab weddings dress like harem girls from A Thousand and One Nights.* The working-class Arab and Chaldean neighborhoods are built amid the residue of Polish, Italian, and Jewish neighborhoods; Arab-owned liquor stores and groceries proliferate in the disintegrating fringes of Detroit's urban economy; the newest Yemeni and Iraqi immigrants toil as unskilled labor in broken-down factories so old there is now talk of turning them into museums.

4. REMOTE AREAS ARE FULL OF RUBBISH. Literally and figuratively. The immigrant receiving areas of Dearborn's Southend and Detroit's Seven Mile are described by journalists and activists alike as "gritty," "run down," and "poor," and they are. But they are also filled with other kinds of "dirt," with "matter out of place." *The visiting professor from Lebanon cannot help but inform me that the people of Dearborn are "not of the best type. They are villagers of peasant background. If you travel to Beirut, you will see a much more impressive society and culture."* The media people and the tourists all want the same pictures, the men in robes and headscarves on Dix Avenue, the Iraqi women in their black, full-body cloaks, the Arabic speakers and the Arabic lettering on their storefronts. Arab leaders complain: "We are not all Muslims. We do not all live in Dearborn. Most of us look and act just like you." *The physician, just arrived from Egypt, is shocked by the way her Arab American nieces and nephews behave. They do not speak Arabic well, which is bad enough, but they also seem to have no manners. "I will not watch my daughter grow up a slut. When she is old enough, I will send her home to live with my family, who will teach her to be a decent girl."*

5. REMOTE AREAS ARE IN CONSTANT CONTACT WITH THE WORLD. *As I drive through the Southend with the delegation from the university, I notice that almost every house is adorned with a satellite dish.* _____ watches the *al-Jazeera* satellite station every night with his mother; the next day he goes to work at Oakwood Hospital, where he is joined by his Arab and non-Arab coworkers; he attends

softball practice with them later in the afternoon. *The _____'s call their family in Amman almost every other day; they read the* Detroit Free Press *as well as Web versions of the* Jordan Times *and* al-Rai; *they vacation in a rented house in the hills of Ajlun, in northern Jordan, every July.* After one year in the Dearborn Public Schools, the Lebanese immigrant kids next door speak only English to each other; they are addicted to *Rugrats. Bilqis does her Yemeni homework after she studies for the spelling test she will take tomorrow in her school in Dearborn; right now, she is completing the textbook exercises for sixth grade Arabic; next year, she will return with her older sister to her home village of Mawar; several of her aunts, who also attended school in Dearborn, will help her keep up her English; she will need it. As soon as she marries her first cousin—who is currently working in Dubai—she will return with him to Dearborn to finish high school and start a family.*

6.-7.   REMOTE AREAS ARE FILLED WITH ENTREPRENEURS; THEY ATTRACT INCOMERS AND ECCENTRICS WHO ARE DRAWN TO THE POSSIBILITY OF EXPERI-ENCING, DOING, OR BEING SOMETHING NEW.   *According to the American Arab Chamber of Commerce, there are 5,000 Arab-owned businesses in Greater Detroit, most of which are gas stations, liquor stores, and grocery stores owned by immigrants.* Less obvious is the fact that many of the most successful culture workers and activists are also newcomers and incomers. *Some arrive from dominant Arab zones and use their cultural capital to stake out leadership positions in the community*; others come from "white America," where they grew up as "halfies" and "washouts." After rediscovering their Arabness in college, they move to De-troit to live in the community. Others are non–Arab spouses and lovers who devote their energies to Arab American causes. *A handful are scholars, Arab and non-Arab, whose interest in Arab Detroit was first piqued by an interest in the Middle East*, ethnicity, transnationalism, *or family ties to the Arab world.* Detroit's Arab American organizations are filled with "bridge" people like these, who serve as gatekeepers and cultural guides. There are also odder forms of doubled re-moteness: the white middle-class women who provide the "Arabic dance" at community events; *the immigrant Arab men who take up golf, usually playing in large groups of similar national and religious background, as proof that they have ar-rived in the America of country clubs and inside deals.* No large community event is complete without one or two "identity extroverts," who dress up in idio-syncratic versions of "traditional costume" and offer unsolicited testimonials (too long or too earnest or both) chronicling epic struggles against stigma and persecution. The possessive phrase "my people" is beloved of these types. *Equally peculiar are the elitist, progressive Arab immigrants (usually but not invari-ably Christian) who crusade against anti-Arab stereotypes while privately despising Arab immigrants and Arab ethnics, disdaining most expressions of Arab popular and elite culture, and taking up hobbies associated, in Arab circles, with Western tastes: clas-sical piano and jazz are safe bets, but conspicuous affection for dogs is another. Until the Arab world is respectably modern, members of this crowd would request that you kindly look away.*

8.   IN REMOTE AREAS THE SAME SET DO EVERYTHING.   Check the morning papers; watch the nightly news; read the latest studies: the same names appear over and over again. Arab Detroit, circa 2003, is represented by Imad Hamad, director of the local chapter of the American Arab Anti-Discrimination Committee (ADC), Nasser Beydoun, director of the American Arab Chamber of Commerce, Ismael Ahmed, director of ACCESS, Imam Hassan Qazwini, leader of the Islamic Center of America, Osama Siblani, editor of the *Arab American News*, Ahmad Chebbani, board chairman of the American Arab Chamber of Commerce, Hassan Jaber, deputy director of ACCESS, Radwan Khoury and Haifa Fakhouri, both of the Arab American and Chaldean Council (ACC), and several others. If news must be gathered; if initiatives are planned; if overtures to the community must be made (by the FBI, General Motors, or the Arab League); if an international conference must be organized; if mayors or congressmen would like to travel to the Arab world—these are the individuals whose involvement will be solicited. Their allies and operatives, who are placed at nearly every level of organized political life in greater Detroit, can be relied upon to do the necessary work.

The reader will note a lack of italics in the final sketch. This is because "the set who do everything" in Arab Detroit, as their titles suggest, do everything in relation to the endless, exacting work of Americanization. They build "proper links" between Detroit's Arab populations and the dominant American zone, and their engagements with dominant Arab zones are calculated, in nearly every case, to bolster lobbying and organizational agendas that will enable Arabs (in the United States and abroad) to gain access to the privileges that define membership in the American mainstream, a space of "arrival" that is always somewhat mythical and, in the blunt experience of being excluded from it, always palpably real. Not all forms of difference and identification are equally matched. Arab Detroit, as a lived reality, is a dense overlap of things Arab and American, *but it is in America*; that is one reason why Arabs have chosen, for over a century, to settle in Detroit. The persistence of double remoteness—and the vitality of transnational ties—cannot overwhelm the pressure to adapt and cater to the moral challenges posed by the more dominant of the two dominant zones. Meeting those challenges seems to require that the bewildering complexity (and the disturbing in between-ness) of Arab Detroit be subjected to the unifying discipline known, in the euphemistic identity talk of our time, as "celebrating diversity."

Identity/Identity 2

Perhaps the best way to discuss this problem is to present two ways of talking, each a kind of "social fact" for Arabs in Detroit. The first is a pervasive, multicultural rhetoric. It is familiar in most Western nation-states, and it is spreading to other regions of the world as a feature of the global economic, political, and cultural initiatives sponsored by G8 countries. In his earlier essay on Spain, Richard Maddox called this discourse "cosmopolitan liberalism," associating it with "current preoccupations with tolerance, pluralism, and multiculturalism in liberal societies." Gerd Baumann, whose ethnography is based in a multiethnic, working-class suburb of London, speaks more generally of "the dominant discourse," which he identifies as the ruling genre for "the representation, descriptive as well as political, of people singled out as ethnic minorities" (1996:188). Arabs in Detroit, when they speak local dialects of this global language of identity, produce utterances like the ones that appear in an attractive, glossy flyer called *Understanding Arab Americans, the Arab World & Islam*, which was distributed by the ACCESS Cultural Arts Program as part of its post-9/11 educational push.

As befits its genre, the flyer is concise and promotional. It begins with a brief account of Arab immigration to the United States, when it started and why it continues; next, it catalogs some of the internal diversity of the Arab American community, which includes people who are Christian and Muslim, racially mixed, native and foreign born, able and not able to speak Arabic, from different socioeconomic classes, and (this is an unusual addition) women who are stay-at-home mothers and women in "all kinds of professions." A thumbnail sketch of the Arab world, its population and member states, is followed by a series of necessary disclaimers: the Middle East is not uniformly Arab; not all Arabs are Muslims and not all Muslims are Arabs; Islam is a religion of peace, and "there is absolutely nothing about Arab or Muslim culture that condones or encourages violence." The flyer ends with an appeal to protect the political rights of Arab Americans, who face "stereotyping, discriminatory treatment, and civil rights violations," even though they "have become a vital part of American society." Lest respect for Arabs as human beings is not enough inducement to treat them decently (and usually it is not), the flyer reminds us that new antiterrorism laws, "which have legitimized ethnic and racial profiling for Arab Americans, present a threat to all of our civil rights and liberties."

The presentation is fluid and congenial throughout: exactly the effect one wants in writing such material. In less than two thousand words, arranged on six panels, among seven photographs and five boxes of factoids, the flyer artfully condenses information that, in the ACCESS Museum of Arab Cultures, is conveyed in two large exhibit spaces and a guidebook twenty pages long. The motifs that organize *Understanding Arab Americans*, though dedicated to Arab American subjects, are applicable to almost any immigrant group: "This is why we came (to America); this is who we are (in America); this is where we came from." The template for such representations works as a unifying format, which explains the heavy use of such normalizing phrases as "like other ethnic groups," "as is the case for other immigrants," and "for all of us." Things that make the group stand out in a negative way are distanced or problematized: "not all of us are x," "this bad thing, though associated with x, is not part of x culture." Things that make the group stand out in positive ways (suggesting bigness, historical precedent, or success) are fronted; hence, the following factoids: "The first Arabs are thought to have come to the United States with Spanish explorers in the fifteenth century"; "In 2000 it was estimated that there were five million Arab Americans, 60–65% Christians and 35–40% Muslims"; and "Overall, Arab Americans have a relatively high level of education. Sixty-three percent of all Arab Americans ages twenty-five and over have been to college."

Narratives about Latinos or Asian Americans are made of similar stuff; even the anachronistic historical claims and inflated population figures are recurrent and would seem to be mandatory. The point is to set a "foreign" identity within an American context that, diversity aside, makes all groups comparable and should, ideally, make all of them equal (despite any singular accomplishments or supposed failings that make them unique). This model of national belonging is utterly hegemonic. It is widely understood, and this makes it an effective vehicle for the mass mediation of minoritized identities. Though it might initially seem counterintuitive, a moment's reflection is enough to suggest that when diversity is displayed against national backdrops, it is shown in order to demarcate a larger sphere of sameness and sharing. This logic is reproduced, on a subnational scale, in the following statement about Arab American "identity," which appears in the flyer.

IDENTITY

Despite their diversity, Arab Americans have much in common. They feel bound by shared history, values, and culture. They trace their roots to the same region of the world. They speak Arabic—or their parents and grandparents did.

People's identity is rather complex and every one of us has multiple identities. Arab Americans are no different. While the majority of people who come from an Arab country identify themselves as Arab Americans, some can also identify themselves in terms of their country of origin: Syrian Americans or Yemeni Americans, or in terms of their religion, as Muslim Americans or Jewish Americans. On the other hand, some, who trace their ancestry to an ethnic minority in the Arab world, such as Chaldeans from Iraq, might identify themselves as Chaldean Americans, or Iraqi Americans, rather than Arab Americans.

Like most other groups in this country, many second and third generation Arab Americans have married outside their ethnic group and may identify themselves as

Americans. Although they might know a few Arabic words, or continue to eat Arabic food, they would mostly identify with mainstream American culture.

At the same time, many second and third generation Arab Americans whose parents felt the pressure to assimilate are reclaiming their Arab American heritage. This is reflected in their art, literature, and theater, and in the many national institutions they have built to address the needs and concerns of Arab Americans.

Again, little is said about Arabs that could not be said, with minor terminological shifting, of most other ethnic groups. We do learn, however, that "Arab American culture" is not the same as "mainstream American culture," although Arabs clearly can enter the mainstream. We learn that Arab Americans are "no different" from other Americans; they even have their own minority groups, like Chaldeans, who have special identities. It is possible, though, to marry out of the Arab group and become something marked only as "American," and this zone is not portrayed as "ethnic." It is also implied that first-generation Arab immigrants are somehow closer to ancestral Arabness than second- and third-generation Arabs; newcomers are not described as marrying outside the group (although they do) nor are they described as identifying as "American" (although they do). Interestingly, "pressure to assimilate" is located in the past. Also, we see that, having gone mainstream, one can "reclaim" the Arab heritage, largely because of a blood tie (however diminished it might be as a result of exogamy). We are also told that ethnic organizations and the cultural arts are vital features of this return to identity, which tells us perhaps the most important thing: reclamation ethnicity is a kind of public, expressive culture, a social construction, yet one rooted in the "biological fact" of shared blood.

What I find most intriguing about the text is its voicing. Who is talking, and to whom? The author could be anyone—that, in a sense, is the whole point—but s/he is authorized to speak for and about Arab Americans by Arab Americans (and by five mainstream cultural foundations, dutifully acknowledged on the back flap). The person addressed by the flyer is assumed to be part of a larger, ethnically unmarked audience that is American *as a matter of fact, not public assertion*. The message the reader is meant to receive is that Arabs can belong to the category "American ethnic group" and are therefore entitled to respect; the correctness of the message is signaled by its unflinchingly positive, supportive tone. All this being said, it is also true that the "identity space" created by the text is not one in which real people would care to live their lives, even if they could. Identity spaces made for others to see are not places in which people can relax or "be themselves." Instead, their appeal is based in the fact that they do not allow "outsiders"— the Americans who are unmarked and everywhere—to see the things about us that are distinctive and, alas, a bit harder to handle. Insofar as official discourses of identity make us all alike, they mark off, rather neatly, the nuanced interiority of the everyday worlds in which Arab Americans (like the rest of us) actually live.

A knock on the front door will alter the comportment of everyone in the house, if the house is a home. Informal identity spaces, where all of us spend a good deal of time, are filled with things outsiders would not understand and do not need to see. For exactly this reason, however, intimate spaces are filled with things that, if outsiders are to be made "at home," they must inevitably be shown. This terrain extends behind and beneath contexts of self-conscious cultural display; it is produced by them, and responds to them, in much the way a shadow records the movement of a spotlight. Anyone familiar with Arab Detroit will understand that the text called "Identity" was written as part of, and in response to, other ways of knowing "the community." The following text, call it Identity 2, is a shadow of the first. It would never be approved for mass distribution in a promotional flyer; having written such material over the years, I know the rules. I also realize that one can never be fully "at home" in Arab Detroit without knowing the following script and, more important, knowing why it cannot be the official script.

IDENTITY 2

The label "Arab American" is an umbrella term of recent origin. Before the 1967 Arab-Israeli War, Arab Americans were more likely to identify with their nation or region of origin, or with their religious sect. These "older" ways of associating are still more important than "Arab American-ness" in determining where people live, whom they socialize with, the organizations they join, and whom they marry. People who immigrated from Syria and Lebanon a century ago might not identify as Arab at all, and many Arabic-speaking minorities from the Middle East—Chaldeans, Maronites, Assyrians, Kurds, Armenians, Copts, Jews, and Berbers—are reluctant to describe themselves as Arab and sometimes harbor strong anti-Arab sentiments. Even among people who avidly embrace Arab American identity, its meaning is hotly contested; there is little agreement on what it means to belong to this group or how it should be represented to a larger, non-Arab audience.

Not all Arabs in the United States consider America the object of their primary political or cultural identification. Some have strong ties to their homeland and want to return there in future; others have never been to the Arab world but are heavily involved in political and cultural activities that connect them to Arabs abroad. There are Arab Americans who know little about the places their parents or grandparents came from. They do not consider these places their "homelands," and they are not fond of "Arab culture," which they see as backward and strange. Because all of these people might identify as Arab Americans in certain situations, it is difficult to find a shared framework in which individuals can identify as American and Arab simultaneously. People argue about what these terms signify. A willingness to engage in this ongoing struggle of definitions, both as an Arab and as an American, is what best defines Arab American identity.

Being Arab in America does not always mean being ethnic. Newly arrived Arab immigrants do not know how to be "ethnic"; they must learn this as part of becoming American. Being Arab in America does not always mean being an immigrant, either. Arabs born in the United States and those who have lived here a long time tend to describe themselves as "ethnic" or "White" or "American" or "of color"; often, they resent the implication that they are "from somewhere else." Ethnic identities, which produce "hyphenated" Americans, are not the same as transnational Arab and Muslim identities. The U.S. government supports "legitimate," domestically oriented Arab/Muslim groups even as it tries to shut down Arab/Muslim organizations that send money and personnel abroad to support political movements whose goals are in conflict with U.S. policy. Many Arab Americans feel excluded from mainstream politics in the United States, which is strongly pro-Israel. They believe they are portrayed, generically, as cultural enemies whose global networks should be broken up, or made illegal, and whose local organizations should be rewarded only if their commitment to Americanization is not in doubt. To make matters more complex, every prominent Arab American organization is opposed by other Arab American organizations, who claim it is corrupt or that it misrepresents "the community."

Though pluralism and tolerance are widely endorsed in the United States, many aspects of Arab and Muslim identities are stigmatized within even the most inclusive brands of multiculturalism. Arabs are associated with sexism, religious fanaticism, terrorism, opposition to democracy, and aversion to individual freedoms. Their large, cohesive families, of which they tend to be proud, are seen by most Americans as patriarchal and stifling. Marriage between close relatives and a protective attitude toward female members of the family, seen by many Arabs as evidence of moral superiority, carry negative connotations in the American middle class, a population that includes many Arab Americans. As a result, much of Arab American domestic life (especially that which prevails among newly arrived immigrants) must be sheltered from public view if members of the community are to achieve mainstream inclusion.

These trends pose serious obstacles to effective Arab American participation in multicultural politics. Still, Arab Americans, like other immigrant and ethnic groups, are willing to contribute to, and benefit from, an American-style politics of inclusion. That is why most of this text cannot appear on a museum wall, or in a glossy flyer, even though there are situations in which Arab Americans might want you to know what is said here. Oddly enough, they will say most of it to you themselves once you know them, and they know you.

What casts this text as a shadow? Why is this knowledge often central to the writings of scholars who study Arab Americans, yet strategically ignored when Arab American activists and their scholarly allies collaborate to "advance" or "promote" Arab American causes through public cultural display? The problem is general. Academics at work in "special populations" that are not Arab (and are not even ethnic or immigrant) will recognize many of the patterns described in Identity 2; often, multiethnic and multiracial coalitions are held together by this invisible glue. Unlike malicious stereotypes—"Islam is a violent religion" or "Arabs hate women"—the observations made in Identity 2 are shared, sometimes urgently, with "outsiders" who engage with the group on a personal level, and the terms of revelation are usually less delicate than those offered by me. If ethnic and racial communities so often have semiofficial "spokespeople," it is because journalists (and almost anyone else who cares to) can gain access to Identity 2 discourses all too easily; "ordinary" people tend to speak them fluently, and without reservation.[8]

Identity 2 is a shadow and not a deflecting surface for very good reasons. As a narrative, it is too complicated, too multiple, too aware of diversity and conflict within the community it describes. It would be totally ineffective as a unifying public statement. Identity 2 is also three times longer than Identity (hereafter "Identity 1"). In the world of identity politics, shadows tend to be larger than the representational objects that cast them. If Identity 2 fixates on nuances that take more time and space to explain carefully, this is because Identity 1 is intentionally small, angled to deflect, and placed so as to protect (by shading) a large area of sensitive terrain. Identity 1 is parsimonious; it is designed for non-Arabs, who are assumed to have negative impressions of the group. Identity 1 counters this negativity by inviting the unidentified reader/viewer to imagine Arabs as Americans, not Others. Identity 2, less impoverished but still generic, belongs to a body of information that might be called "inside moves." It is *for* insiders, of course, but it is also a means by which "outsiders" can be remade as (or prove they already are) "acquaintances," potentially friend or foe, but no longer a passerby in the American public square. This is why, in culture work aimed at non-Arabs, Identity 2 is often confined to the medium of speech, or is buried in a list of "suggested readings." In "real life"—the "suggested readings" seldom belong to this zone—competence in Identity 2 discourse is acquired through personal interaction. Ability to engage with and reproduce Identity 2 is what constitutes Arab American selves (and the Arab American community) as something more than public fronts.

A Stranger Truth

In contemporary nation-states, where mass mediation is the dominant form of community representation, Identity 2 belongs to an elaborate array of experiences and bodies of knowledge that animate, and must be systematically removed from, the images of "special populations" that circulate in our most polite and public spheres, where "stranger sociability"—a mode of interaction oriented toward what we have in common with large cohorts of people we will never know personally—is the default mode of citizenship and a preferred form of mutual recognition (Warner 2002 : 58–59). The idea that ethnoracial and immigrant minorities, no matter how culturally peculiar, can be represented in ways that are inclusive and generally inoffensive, is compelling to many Americans, especially Americans who identify as (or with) ethnoracial and immigrant minorities. Yet Identity 2 discourses acknowledge in-group differences, even stigmatized differences. To escape the cosmetic standardizations of Identity 1, speakers of Identity 2 (or 3 or 4 or *n*) routinely link what is "human" and "real" about their lives to what might, in mixed company, seem most alien or embarrassing. When one no longer wants to be a complete stranger, the temptation to speak Identity 2 "in front of the foreigners" (*gudam al-ajanib*) can be overwhelming. Individuals who live in exaggerated states of doubled remoteness—never quite Arab enough, and always unconventionally American—are likely to cross the line in public ways that, in their attention to the everyday and interpersonal, are oddly reminiscent of what ethnography used to be (and, in its popular and accessible forms, still is).

The confessional, coming-of-age memoir is a common venue for these "outings," which are also invitations to enter. The ethnic memoir, like ethnic fiction in general, tends to fixate on the cultural distance that separates an (almost always) immigrant household from the "American culture" that prevails just outside. The Arab American "halfie," in keeping with the genre, will tell "us" about the challenge of growing up under the thumb of her Jordanian immigrant dad (Abu-Jaber 1990); the Yemeni American will tell how her aunts from "back home" did not believe she, brought up in Detroit, could really be a virgin and recommended chicken blood for her wedding night (Alwujude 2000); the Palestinian American will recount how he learned, when his school teachers giggled, that most American boys (circa 1960) were not circumcised at age 5, at a celebration attended by guests from the home village, and that he should never tell an "outsider" such things again (Abraham 2000). In the end, however, the memoirist does tell "us" such things, artfully and movingly. "We," the faceless reading public, are now as much "their" imagined community as "we," non-Arabs and nonkin, were once complete strangers to whom "such things" (the hard stuff of cultural difference) should never be divulged. Now, through its introduction to the public sphere, cultural difference becomes the stuff of which an expanded sense of common sociality might be built.

As an ethnographer, I face a similar predicament. I am not Arab, but I have lived and worked with Arabs for so long that I am "wise" to their sensitivities and cultural styles—"wise" in the sense Erving Goffman (1963) intended; I have been taken in provisionally and carry, in certain contexts, a "courtesy stigma"—which compels me, like the memoirist, to tell tales that prove just how inside and outside I am (and "you" are). The habit is well established; my interactions with Arabs and Arab Americans are an endless acting out and overcoming of my own state of doubled remoteness, which mirrors their own. As a result, I share with certain Arab American writers a strong distaste for Identity 1, which we see as a muzzle, not a protective shield. "It makes me sad in a way," writes Arab American novelist, Diana Abu-Jaber,

that people do feel this kind of tense fearfulness about the way that they and their culture are written about. . . . Arab Americans have been so maltreated by the media, their image has been so dark, that I think there's a real anxiety about the artistic representations [by Arab Americans] that are out there. "Is this just going to make us look worse? You're exposing us, you're making us even more vulnerable. What we need to do is be quiet, we need to close ranks. We need to really control what's being said about us" . . . It's an instinct to try to hide if you're feeling like you're under attack, to be quiet. And you learn that, unfortunately, what looks like the easy way is often a really bad choice. If you silence yourself, if you try to be good, if you try to be polite, or toe a party line, you end up paying for that in the long run (Shalal-Esa 2002:6).

Silence is not the only alternative. It is not even the preferred strategy. In Arab Detroit, the response to attack has been to confidently, vigorously disseminate Identity 1, expanding the public forums and formats that enable it to thrive. Because evidence of "double remoteness" is abundant; because alternative models of Arabness, Americanness, and Arab Americanness are flourishing in Detroit's multicultural contact zones; and because some Arab Americans would like "you" and certain sectors of their community to remain completely strange to each other—for all these reasons, Identity 1 must become more streamlined than ever, more positive, and more conspicuously American(ized). As its distinctively Arab cultural content bleeds away, Identity 1 must be held in place by real institutional muscle.

Downsizing

The reader who wonders why I lavished so much commentary on a six-panel brochure called *Understanding Arab Americans, the Arab World & Islam* should realize that proof of "real institutional muscle" often comes in glossy little packages like these. The flyer in question is part of a $15 million ACCESS fundraising campaign led by the CEOs of Detroit Edison and Comerica International, big energy and banking interests who would never risk a penny on a people or a cause that was difficult to endorse, hard to sell, or bad for their corporate image. The undeniable "thinness" of the information conveyed in the ACCESS flyer is not a result solely of the need to fold it, or mail it to thousands of people. The same leanness is found in diverse media of multicultural display, and it is best understood, to use Andreas Glaeser's term, as a "reduction" that facilitates representation. Thus, in museum exhibits, what the "visitor" can know about Arab American immigration history, work, politics, religion, or family life must be garnered from less than three hundred words of explanatory text per topic, plus photo captions; the richly illustrated pamphlet or brochure is assigned to the difficult task of educating people about Islam; when people "learn about Arab culture" at the Dearborn International Arab Festival, this usually means they bought and ate some falafel, hummus, or shish kabob, heard Arabic music, perhaps had their fortune read in a coffee cup, or had henna applied to their hand. Indeed, a respectable level of cultural competence (and a State Board of Education–certified "continuing education unit") can be gained by attending a seven-hour seminar at ACCESS, during which lectures and films —each less than fifty minutes long—flesh out the brochures, handbooks, supplements, flyers, and museum displays, with lunch catered by a local Middle Eastern restaurant, and a guided tour of a local mosque and business district.

Lest anyone think I am belittling this activity, I should point out that I have taken part in it for many years. I have raised money to support it, and I have helped produce a good deal of the material that circulates in these venues. It is important work, not only because the imagery and information are worth disseminating, but because programming of this kind is one way in which Arab Americans can assert and find evidence of their value as a community. Not having an abbreviated, publicly respectable identity of this kind to show others is tantamount, in today's America, to political invisibility, and Arab Americans know, better than most of us, what it is like to live without the minimal dignity Identity 1 can provide.[9] The work of cultural representation begins to trouble me, however, when "value as a community" is subordinated to the logic of public relations and ethnic marketing. In a textbook case of neoliberal transition, Arab Detroit in the late 1990s witnessed the growth of a robust, sales-inflected approach to culture work, just as public sector funding for cultural arts programming was shrinking and the Lebanese and Chaldean business communities, like the economy at large, were booming. The newest forms of cultural "education," which grow out of these tandem developments, are oriented toward the conspicuous display of group success, which is portrayed as an outcome of Americanization.

"For maximum benefit," writes Ahmed Chebbani, publisher of *Arabica*, a Dearborn-based culture and business magazine,

ethnic groups, such as Arab Americans, eventually strive to assimilate into mainstream America. Census and demographic studies have pinpointed the qualities of Arab Americans that give them a decided edge when they accomplish that goal: youth, high educational achievement, extraordinary self-motivation and self-empowerment, strong work ethic and entrepreneurial spirit, business ownership, and economic affluence (1999:8).

All of this is said in relation to a cultural zone that is not Arab, but could include Arab Americans. Movement toward that zone will be rewarded (or is already proof of success); movement away, we can only assume, is proof of failure, or lack of motivation. Later in the same issue of *Arabica*, Ismael Ahmed, executive director of ACCESS, alludes to recent demographic studies that place the Arab American population at three million. The conclusion he draws from these findings has the comparative, boast-and-brag flavor that is the diagnostic sign of "model minority" packaging.

When you add these numbers to some of the other data on Arab Americans, their potential as a political and an economic force in this country becomes quite apparent. Arab Americans are the second most educated population in the United States and have the most millionaires per capita. If it were not for the large number of new low-income immigrants who arrive in urban centers each year, we also would have the highest per capita income in the country. Add to that the fact that 70% of the Arab American population is concentrated in less than a dozen states and in several key industries, and you have to ask why the marketers and politicians aren't lining up (1999:48).

Another question, perhaps equally important, is *where* these politicians and marketers might go to stand in line, and *what* they are waiting to do. The answer is so obvious it need not be stated: they should be queuing up to bestow money, recognition, support, special terms, respect, and other acts of legitimation on "the set who do everything" and the institutions they control. Culture work and public display, because they accommodate advertising, are a prime target for these gifts, which, in a new trend, arrive now in the form of mass-mediated culture work done on behalf of the Arab American community by others.

In the year 2000, the *Detroit Free Press* published a booklet—again, the quality of slimness returns—called *100 Questions and Answers about Arab Americans*. Only sixteen pages long, the booklet was compiled in consultation with sixteen activists and scholars and six major Arab American organizations. Though ostensibly designed as an educational aid for journalists who work for the *Free Press* and other Knight Ridder newspapers, it is more reasonable to conclude that the booklet—pure Identity 1 throughout, reluctant to address hard issues, and prepared in a series that includes booklets on Asian Americans and Native Americans—is a savvy gesture of goodwill toward the Arab American community. As the editor of the project acknowledges, the *Free Press* is "published in the city with the nation's most concentrated Arab American population," and Tony Ridder, CEO of Knight Ridder, tells the reader he is "honored" to publish the booklet, which will help his papers "serve" Arab Americans better. The booklet now appears on dozens of Web sites around the world, most of them run by or for Arab Americans, and each time the booklet is downloaded or clicked on, the *Detroit Free Press* and Knight Ridder have benefited from free advertising in a niche market that includes millions of Arab Americans, their businesses and political associations, and a growing market of Arabs overseas who want to keep up with events in Detroit.[10]

It is not cynical to draw such conclusions. Politicians and marketers (not to mention "the press") cannot engage directly with "the Arab American community"; they, more than most of us, know that ethnic constituencies and markets are organized and represented by interest groups. What marketers and politicians receive in return for attending to these groups—again, one hardly needs to spell this out—is votes (or political influence) and customers (or market share). These are the practical materials of which "proper links" to the dominant American zone are built. In the correct usage of the academy, the statehouse, and the boardroom, new immigrants are no longer "assimilated" or "melted down"; they are "incorporated," a term that captures the political and commercial logic of Americanization perfectly.

The idea that "cultural diversity" is bolstered by this process—that "assimilation" is no longer expected in exchange for incorporation—is a useful illusion. In fact, a fairly specific kind of cultural production, lean and derivative, is required if the incorporation of Arab Americans (or any other "special population") is to be symbolically expressed on a mass scale. Habermas astutely characterized this activity as "publicity, staged for show or manipulation, with the help of which the groups participating in the exercise and balancing of power strive to create a plebiscitary-follower mentality on the part of a mediated public" (1989:247). In Arab Detroit, the effort of showing and manipulating is made in relation to "the mainstream," a gilded domain whose allure is inseparable from the dominance of the social classes who administer it and the cultural styles assumed to flourish there.

Internal Discipline

The American mainstream is no longer exclusively (or literally) white; nor is it necessarily Christian. It is no accident, however, that most Arab immigrants, who grew up watching American TV in their home countries, think otherwise. In the popular street dialects of Arab Detroit, "American" usually means "non-Arab"; it can also mean "a white person." In Jordan and Yemen, where I have done ethnographic fieldwork, American citizens who are not white, or not Christian, are seldom considered "real Americans." Jews are not. Blacks and Asians are not. Certainly Arabs are not. In the United States, by contrast, many people (Arabs among them) now believe that essential, exclusive links between "American culture," whiteness, and Christianity are based on racialized models of citizenship that are outdated and immoral. There are other, more acceptable ways of assessing who belongs and who is inadmissible.

In an op-ed piece written by Jim Zogby (2001), head of the Arab American Institute, a Washington-based advocacy group, the scrutiny aimed at

Arab Americans by journalists after the 9/11 attacks provides an opportunity to (re)assert the Americanness of Arabs in America. Note what counts here as evidence of "diversity."

Arab Americans are being discovered, or should I say being rediscovered, by the same papers and networks that have discovered us twice before in just the past decade. As I speak to those assigned to do the story, they discover yet again the diversity of my community. The fact that we are not a new ethnic group in America (we've been here for 120 years). That most Arab Americans are not Muslims (in fact, only 20% are). That most Arab Americans are not recent immigrants (in fact, almost 80% are born in the U.S.). And that many Arab Americans have achieved prominence and acceptance in America (two proud Arab Americans, Spencer Abraham and Mitch Daniels, serve in President Bush's cabinet, and Donna Shalala served in Bill Clinton's cabinet).

The numbers, proportions, and terminology are all debatable, but Zogby's narrative is flawless in its ability to map the terrain of Otherness in which many Arab Americans, especially those in Detroit, now live. The Arab community Zogby does not speak to (and would encourage his readers not to dwell on) is new, Muslim, born overseas, unknown, unaccepted, accented, culturally peculiar, and politically untouchable. In Arab Detroit, people who belong to this zone of Otherness are called, by fellow Arabs, "boaters," and there is an elaborate body of lore associated with their looks and ways. As a public identity, "Arab American" can never include the "boater" as an acceptable role model, although "boaters" can be posed as figures of fun, tricksters, victims of discrimination, objects of nostalgia, or a gauge of one's acquaintance with, and attitudes toward, all things Arab. I am always shocked by the contempt Arab Americans can show toward "boaters" with whom they do not share a national or village background. The Lebanese who came to Dearborn as refugees in the 1970s, and were denounced as "savages" by their Italian and Polish neighbors, now complain about "dirty" Iraqi Shi'a who are running down property values. When the "boaters" are your own parents, or your own spouse, the humiliation they sometimes cause you is tempered by affection. Still, there is a tendency to keep "boaters" off stage, unless they appear as tokens of authenticity. The "boater" makes bread at the ethnic restaurant, and is eagerly photographed; she does not give the public lecture about gender and family among Muslims in America. Boaters are like those "silly" Egyptian musical comedies that, as Walter Armbrust has noted, Egyptian intellectuals might love to watch but are ashamed to screen at the foreign film festivals, where EuroAmerican standards are dominant.

America stigmatizes Arabs, but it is Arab Americans who stigmatize "boaters," by linking them to the past or to the homeland—"they're backward," "they do things the old country way"—and by constituting Americanness as a quality of superiority "boaters" do not yet have, but will gradually acquire. If, to invoke Ahmed Chebbani's formula, Arabs assimilate to the American mainstream, they will by definition possess values and a standard of living that are "middle class" and probably better. They will be, as Ahmed and Zogby assure us, highly educated, highly salaried, and highly placed in government and the estimation of their fellow Americans. Most new immigrant communities in North America have a slang term similar to "boater," and this is because the concept is a powerful tool of internal group discipline, highly effective for carving out a delicate, always relational, and commonsensical measure of how "Americanized" someone is (or is not), and where and why it should matter. In all this evaluation, one is never required to stop being Arab, or Mexican, or Korean, or Bangladeshi—remember, Identity 1 and even Identity 2 will facilitate very public and very private versions of these categories—but one does begin, rather quickly, to participate in the strategic reductions of Otherness that transform new immigrants into ethnic Americans who enter mass-mediated publics in the guise of *100 Questions and Answers* and, most important of all, feel proud when they do.

Conclusion: Ethnography in the Totalized Network

The mainstream is a zone of accomplishment, especially for immigrants, but it is also construed as a zone of freedom, where "homeland culture"—especially the peculiar, incorrigible kind that marks the "boater"—would appear to fall away, or be reduced to a nonthreatening, empowering substrate commonly known as "heritage" or "identity." The voice of our times insists that all of us should have, and *do* have, an "identity" that can be expressed publicly as a "heritage." Our heritage should fit us well. It should look good on us, and it should be the heritage of our choice. We should embrace it and be proud to display it, if that is our inclination. Heritage is not the only outfit we can wear, of course; it should not prevent us from blending in. We should be careful to respect the heritage of others, if they have indeed chosen it freely and did not have it forced on them by ignorance, or by others. Some people, especially those who carry stigmata, of color or difference or poverty or political threat, cannot freely choose who they are, or what we make of them, and they do suffer for it. This is why the "American mainstream" is a destination worth traveling to.

Children acquire cultural things in the way they acquire a spoken language, through social interaction, but American children learn about "heritage" in more formal ways, most of which belong to a collective ritual called school. I speak from direct experience, having devised lesson plans that elementary and secondary school teachers can use to educate their students about Arabs and Arab Americans. Most teachers want "heritage" to enter their classroom on friendly terms, as it should. Heritage goes to school, so to speak, in the form of distinctive foods, storytelling, music and dance, costume, traditional art forms (which can easily become craft projects), learning basic phrases— or your name—in a different language, religion (but tread lightly here), family life, holidays, famous people who belong(ed) to the culture, and the contributions they have made to "civilization" or "America." This is an effective teaching regime, consistent with how "identity" and "community" are self-consciously displayed in the adult world of secular, middle-class America today.

We are dealing, yet again, with a kind of formatting. It is used to structure and discipline both the learner and what is learned. The assumption behind the heritage format—which is how most Americans now acquire their fluency in Identity 1—is that diversity is good (when it can be appropriately standardized) and that appreciating heritage in this way will make us more tolerant and accepting of each other; in turn, we will be able to live with and protect the rights of people who are different. I am fairly sure the theory is wrong; it is partly false consciousness, partly misdiagnosis, and partly moral smugness of a kind common to the American bourgeoisie. Still, given a nasty set of rival ideologies, and what I judge to be the good intentions of people who want to celebrate diversity, I continue to endorse the theory as a kind of "civil religion," even as I try, through my writing and teaching, to develop alternative understandings of how cultural differences might be constructed, of how both the understandings and the differences have changed over time and might be made to change in the future. This volume has been one aspect of that work, which many ethnographers and anthropologists share.

But recent events in Arab Detroit have made me question my practical commitment to the manufacture of Identity 1. As a "protective shield," it has proven too flimsy, whereas its disciplinary powers, wielded against Arabs and Muslims by the larger society, seem too great. The cultural education programs Arab Americans are running across the nation are command performances: "Be American! Show us you are not a threat! Help us understand you! Tell us you belong!" The efflorescence of Identity 1, the desire to prove and reward its dominance, has increased the capacity of Arab American organizations to serve and manage new immigrants, and it has enabled leaders (Arab and non-Arab) to put forward boldly Americanizing agendas. One can no longer distinguish in all this the difference between fear, political opportunism, and heartfelt support for the Arab American community and the institutions it has built. A cascade of conformist discipline is pouring down on Arab Detroit, and its primary target is a double remoteness many Arab Americans themselves want desperately to exchange for a cultural heritage that enables them to feel a common sociality, and a reciprocal one, with "the American mainstream."

Which prompts me to add a final proposition to Edwin Ardener's account of "remote areas":

9.   IN REMOTE AREAS, ALL MESSAGES FROM THE DOMINANT ZONE ACCENTU-
ATE THE REMOTENESS OF THE RECEIVER.   November 2002. George and Laura
Bush extend Ramadan greetings to Muslims in America and abroad: "Islam
is a peace-loving faith that is practiced by more than one billion people, including millions of American Muslims. These proud citizens contribute to
the diversity that makes our country strong, and the United States is grateful for the friendship and support of many Muslim Nations that are vital
partners in the global coalition to fight against terrorism." On the same day,
the American Arab Anti-Discrimination Committee requests that all Muslims currently held in U.S. jails and military prisons receive proper accom-
modation for fasting during the holy month. ADC and the Arab American
Institute ask the White House for guidance on Ramadan charitable contributions. No one wants to have their property confiscated, their accounts
frozen. No one wants to face detention or deportation because they gave
money to the wrong people. AAI also announces, on its Web site, that
70 percent of all forty Arab American candidates were successful nationwide
in the November 5 mid-term elections. Ismael Ahmed, Democratic candidate for Regent of the University of Michigan, was not one of them. A Republican activist ran a smear campaign against him, claiming Ahmed was a
supporter of "Islamic terror groups." A public letter of support for Ahmed
signed by Jewish members of Michigan's Democratic congressional delegation came too late to kill the rumor. Meanwhile, Imad Hamad, head of Detroit's ADC chapter, voted for the first time; after seven years of legal challenges, and threats of deportation, he finally became a citizen in 2002. His
swearing-in ceremony was attended by FBI officials, who praised Hamad for
his cooperation in recent months. Two days later, over thirty Arab American
activists from across the nation convened at ACCESS to discuss plans for a
$9 million National Arab American Museum and Cultural Center. The mu-
seum, first of its kind in the country, will be designed and built by Jack
Rouse Associates, an exhibit production firm that specializes in trade shows,
theme parks, and zoos. The museum's focus will be placed squarely on Arabs
in America, not on ties to the Arab world, a separation that troubles some
people involved in the project, even as it thrills others. "This is the great divorce," one observer noted. "They're going to replace two thousand years
of culture with Casey Kasem's Top Forty Arab Americans." "It's time for us
to define who we are where we are, which is in America," said another.
"This is my home. I'm not foreign. We've got over a hundred years of history in this country. People need to hear that now more than ever."

Arab Americans in Detroit are feeling a highly concentrated version of pressures now felt everywhere. Rosalind Morris, writing of transparency and corruption in Thailand, called our attention to the "totalized network," a set of cultural forms held together by the global spread of capitalist economies and nation-state politics. The totalized network, she argues, turns political opposition into appeals for inclusion; it turns the problem of cultural difference into demands for the recognition of "fantasy" cultures, reduced, streamlined, interchangeable, amenable to the tastes and consumer appetites of the middle classes that dominate the "social imaginary" of the modern state and (perhaps even more so) its transnational extensions. I would add that totalized networks are never closed. As they envelop a social space and (re)configure its links to other cultural locations, these networks create a heightened sense of what they cannot hold. Communities take shape around this incompatible and impolitic material, which they protect, suppress, reproduce, hold apart, and entrust to others as evidence of belonging. In an age of mass-mediated cultural display, this problematic (and privileged) material constitutes the internal remoteness of all publicly recognized identities.

Ethnographers, it seems to me, have no heroic ability to escape "totalized networks," just as writers of ethnic memoir and fiction do not. Neither genre would be conceivable without these larger grids against which similarity and difference are perceived. Still, as the essays in this volume demonstrate, ethnographers routinely find themselves at home in social settings that resist the formulaic, functionalized renderings of "identity" that predominate in mass-mediated publics. The internal remoteness of public identities, like the double remoteness of Arab Detroit, is a sociospatial quality that determines how identity politics can be played. Writing about how this quality is produced, why it is important to people, and the points at which it animates and is insulated from public display—these ethnographic agendas are oddly effective in their ability to destabilize totalized networks (analytically at least) by countering systemic "reductions" with strategic "increases" in cultural content the networks cannot hold. This maneuver thwarts mandatory cultural standardizations not by showing the odd and exotic (which are products of standardization) but by showing how mainstreaming works and what it is working on. My experience in Arab Detroit has taught me that ethnography of this kind can be alienating and difficult. It has also convinced me that work grounded in cultural intimacy is indispensable to the study of public culture and its politics.

Notes

1. For excellent reviews of "official" and "unofficial" U.S. policy and their effects on Arab Americans after 9/11, see Cainkar (2002) and Hassan (2002). Howell

and Shryock (2003) cover similar terrain, but focus primarily on developments in Detroit.

2. On September 11, 2002, the *San Jose Mercury News* ran a story entitled "U.S. Muslims Held in Higher Regard" (p. 18a), announcing results of a new Knight Ridder poll in which 58 percent of Americans claimed to have "favorable feelings" toward Muslim Americans. Only 45 percent expressed such feelings in March of 2001.

3. A pseudonym.

4. Kim Schopmeyer's (2000) demographic portrait of Arab Detroit, the best to date, quantifies these observations.

5. I did most of this work in collaboration with the Cultural Arts Program at ACCESS. For detailed accounts of "culture work" in Arab Detroit in the 1990s, see essays by Shryock (1998, 2000) and Howell (2000, 2000a).

6. Nadine Naber (2000) gives an excellent overview of the problems inherent in defining Arab American identity.

7. Arlene Davila's *Latinos Inc.* (2001) is a fascinating exploration of how a specific class of professionals—namely, ethnic niche marketers—"make" ethnoracial identities in the United States.

8. Gerd Baumann coins the term "demotic discourse" (a nondominant, low register of identity talk) to explain the qualities of Identity 2. His account of what constitutes "dominant discourse" sums up perfectly the features Identity 2 lacks: "its conceptual make-up should be economical, not to say simple; its communicative resources border on monopoly; it should be flexible of application, and should allow for the greatest ideological plasticity; finally, it should lend itself to established institutional purposes" (1996:22).

9. Suad Joseph (1999) offers an incisive analysis of the political and intellectual means by which Arabs are excluded from American pluralist thought.

10. The booklet is available on the *Detroit Free Press* Web site, http://www.freep .com/jobspage/arabs.

References Cited

Abraham, Nabeel. 1994. "Anti-Arab Racism and Violence in the United States." Pp. 155–214 in *The Development of Arab American Identity*, ed. Ernest McCarus. Ann Arbor: University of Michigan Press.
———. 2000. "To Palestine and Back." Pp. 425–462 in *Arab Detroit: From Margin to Mainstream*, eds. Nabeel Abraham and Andrew Shryock. Detroit: Wayne State University Press.
Abraham, Nabeel, and Andrew Shryock, eds. 2000. *Arab Detroit: From Margin to Mainstream*. Detroit: Wayne State University Press.
Abu-Jaber, Diana. 1990. "In the First Generation." *Seattle Review* 13, no. 1: 11–19.
ACCESS Cultural Arts Program. 2002. *Understanding Arab Americans, the Arab World & Islam*. Dearborn, Mich.: ACCESS.
Ahmed, Ismael. 1999. "Here Comes the Undercount." *Arabica* 1: 48.
Alwujude, Shams. 2000. "Daughter of America." Pp. 381–390 in *Arab Detroit: From Margin to Mainstream*, eds. Nabeel Abraham and Andrew Shryock. Detroit: Wayne State University Press.

Anderson, Benedict. 1991. *Imagined Communities: Reflections on the Origin and Spread of Nationalism*. London: Verso.
Ardener, Edwin. 1989. "Remote Areas." In *The Voice of Prophecy and Other Essays*, ed. Malcolm Chapman. New York: Basil Blackwell.
Baumann, Gerd. 1996. *Contesting Culture: Discourses of Identity in Multi-ethnic London*. Cambridge: Cambridge University Press.
Cainkar, Louise. 2002. "No Longer Invisible: Arab and Muslim Exclusion after September 11." *Middle East Report* 224. Available at http://www.merip.org/mer/mer224/224_cainkar.html.
Chebbani, Ahmed. 1999. Publisher's Letter. *Arabica* 1: 8.
Davila, Arlene. 2001. *Latinos, Inc.: The Marketing and Making of a People*. Berkeley: University of California Press.
Detroit Free Press. 2000. "100 Questions and Answers about Arab Americans." Detroit: Knight Ridder.
Goffman, Erving. 1963. *Stigma: Notes on the Management of Spoiled Identity*. Englewood Cliffs, N.J.: Prentice-Hall.
Habermas, Jürgen. 1989. *The Structural Transformation of the Public Sphere: An Inquiry into a Category of Bourgeois Society*. Cambridge: Massachusetts Institute of Technology Press.
Hassan, Salah D. 2002. "Arabs, Race, and the Post–September 11 National Security State." *Middle East Report* 224. Available at http://www.merip.org/mer/mer224/224_hassan.html.
Howell, Sally. 2000. "Cultural Interventions: Arab American Aesthetics between the Transnational and the Ethnic." *Diaspora* 9, no. 1: 59–82.
———. 2000a. "The Art and Artistry of Arab Detroit: Changing Traditions in a New World." Pp. 487–513 in *Arab Detroit: From Margin to Mainstream*, eds. Nabeel Abraham and Andrew Shryock. Detroit: Wayne State University Press.
Howell, Sally, and Andrew Shryock. 2003. "Cracking Down on Diaspora: Arab Detroit and America's War on Terror." *Anthropological Quarterly* 76, no. 3: 443–462.
Joseph, Suad. 1999. "Against the Grain of the Nation—The Arab-." Pp. 257–271 in *Arabs in America: Building a New Future*, ed. Michael Suleiman. Philadelphia: Temple University Press.
Mattawa, Khaled. 2002. "Assimilation and Resistance in Arab Detroit." *Michigan Quarterly Review* 41, no. 1: 155–161.
Naber, Nadine. 2000. "Ambiguous Insiders: An Investigation of Arab American Invisibility." *Journal of Ethnic and Racial Studies* 23, no. 1: 37–61.
Schopmeyer, Kim. 2000. "A Demographic Portrait of Arab Detroit." Pp. 61–92 in *Arab Detroit: From Margin to Mainstream*, eds. Nabeel Abraham and Andrew Shryock. Detroit: Wayne State University Press.
Shalal-Esa, Andrea. 2002. "Diana Abu-Jaber on Speaking in the Face of Silence." *Al Jadid* 8, no. 39: 4–9.
Shryock, Andrew. 1998. "Mainstreaming Arabs: Film Making as Image Making." Pp. 165–188 in *Tales from Arab Detroit. Visual Anthropology* 10, no. 2–4.
———. 2000. "Public Culture in Arab Detroit: Creating Arab/American Identities in a Transnational Domain." Pp. 32–60 in *Mass Mediations: New Approaches to*

Popular Culture in the Middle East and Beyond, ed. Walter Armbrust. Berkeley: University of California Press.

————. 2002. "New Images of Arab Detroit: Seeing Otherness and Identity through the Lens of September 11." *American Anthropologist* 104: 917–922.

Shryock, Andrew, and Nabeel Abraham. 2000. "On Margins and Mainstreams." Pp. 15–35 in *Arab Detroit: From Margin to Mainstream*, eds. Nabeel Abraham and Andrew Shryock. Detroit: Wayne State University Press.

Warner, Michael. 2002. "Publics and Counterpublics." *Public Culture* 14, no. 1: 49–90.

Zogby, James. 2001. *"Rediscovering" Arab Americans*. Available at http://www.aaiusa.org/wwatch/111201.htm.

Afterword

CHAPTER 11

Intimating Culture

LOCAL CONTEXTS AND INTERNATIONAL POWER

Michael Herzfeld

AS AN ANTHROPOLOGICAL concept, intimacy is paradigmatically deceptive. It looks easy to understand: we all know about intimacy. But *cultural* intimacy, specifically, is not so easily encompassed. It appears to be a contradiction in terms, compounded of both social closeness and collective formality. The idea that cultures might have less-than-ideal aspects and that cultures also often seem to betray on the inside what they claim about themselves on the outside is acutely disturbing, because it contradicts the prevalent, statist model according to which culture is an austerely formal, permanent property. *We* may be intimate with each other; *it*, surely, cannot be a source of intimacy.

And yet it is. We, after all, make and remake it; it is not just our heritage but our plaything, not just our glory but also all the recognizable messiness that somehow makes life together something for which we are prepared to fight. It bears familiar stains that recall amusing but perhaps also awkward or embarrassing moments. Official discourse would have no meaning for ordinary people were it not for the constant need to deny the improprieties in which citizens are constantly and predictably involved—from influence-peddling in a world newly enamored of political transparency to prejudice in a world newly calibrated to ideas of cultural diversity.

Anthropologists have long conducted ethnography in socially intimate spaces, and others have objected that their scale of operation is irrelevant to

This chapter emerged from a complex textual conversation, deftly refereed with firm hand and sharp wit by Andrew Shryock, in which an earlier version seems to have provoked substantial rewriting of the other papers, in turn leading me to reformulate the focus on key challenges as well as residual ambiguities. This fast-paced intellectual play is here collapsed into the synchronic still capture of the final shot, which I nevertheless hope will expose some of the conceptual intimacies of our mutual mediation.

world affairs. But that is a false contrast. On the one hand, national polities both encapsulate local and familistic forms of identity and yet also draw their primary imagery from these. On the other hand, as Walter Armbrust notes here, the "thickness" of ethnographic description depends on also acknowledging those larger discursive universes in which everyday experience is embedded and from which social actors draw legitimacy; it is in this sense above all that intimacy is culturally mass mediated. We cannot understand local perceptions of larger events without directly knowing their media sources (Herzfeld 1992). This is not a choice between text and texture but a recognition of their necessary complementarity, without which ethnography—as Armbrust ironically observes—degenerates into "sound bites" lacking both depth (local detail) and resonance (echoes of encompassing discursive worlds). By overcoming that deficiency, on the other hand, ethnography can reciprocally, and radically, reorient views of world affairs currently too dependent on ill-considered regurgitations of popular prejudice recast as expertise—on, in short, sound bites.

This mutual centrality of localized ethnography and the analysis of encompassing cultural arenas is one of several points I wish to emphasize here. It should be considered in tandem with the evidence for a globally powerful hierarchy of cultural value; ethnography both reflects the effects of that hierarchy and, through the intimate critiques and eccentric perspectives vouchsafed to ethnographers, permits the development of an ethically responsible critique of global hegemonies. These concerns provide a context for probing the elusive nature and definition of cultural intimacy itself; the historical volatility of its content; its self-justification in terms of nostalgia for an elusive golden past that is the very antithesis of historical experience; and the implications of these insights for the practical ethics and obligations of anthropology itself. As these points are interdependent, and as they variously concern different parts of the several chapters of this book, I shall no more address them in sequence than I intend to treat each author's contribution separately. Instead, while acknowledging the rich intertextuality of all the contributions and their themes, I simply want to alert the reader at the outset to the recurrence of these key points throughout the ensuing discussion.

Having said that, I will now immediately but temporarily contradict myself by starting from the first of these generic issues. The reason is strategic: the mutual dependence of intimate ethnography and encompassing structures of power has consequences at once both methodological and epistemological, and it lies at the heart of our collective enterprise in this volume. Conceptually a simple point, it poses serious operational challenges in practice. These authors, however, have managed to transcend the traditional local grounding of ethnography without abandoning it, showing—against the convenient escapism of those who would prefer to avoid ethnography and its ethical and practical challenges altogether—that intimate ethnography and the analysis of mass media richly illuminate each other's implications for the understanding of cultural identities and dynamics.

They have been able to identify intimate encounters on many larger stages, by tracing cultural intimacy through multiple recastings of domestic tensions as public culture. They have mostly chosen to emphasize the public modeling of intimacy rather than the privacy of the reciprocal ramifications of such representational practices in daily life. But their knowledge of the intimate zones of the social has reversed a besetting tendency to read public culture as supplying the totality of its own context. And they have shown that the old charges of parochial anecdotalism no longer apply, when ethnographers accompany millions of visitors to the Seville Fair, to the alleged Bahian birthplace of Candomblé, or to the cinematic worlds of mass exoticism, and when they read messages apparently intended to rally local masses to the defense of various ideological projects.

Fieldwork is a self-discomfiting practice that has always entailed the exploration of hidden territories, here extended into ostensibly more public and large-scale spaces in ways that intensify the focus on another of the issues I have raised, that of professional ethics. The embarrassments that arise in fieldwork, Kelly Askew reminds us, impose new burdens of responsibility and tact as we endeavor to teach our own societies about cultural difference without reducing it to exoticism. Indeed, she worries that terms like "cultural intimacy" may fail to convey these ethical burdens adequately. But intimacy implies responsibilities grounded in actual social experience, as opposed, for example, to the routinization of ethics by boards operating in terms of an "audit culture" (see Shore and Wright 2000). Despite its superficial resemblance to accounting, an audit-based ethics cannot secure ethical accountability precisely because it has legitimized the transfer of obligation from personal intimacy to impersonal procedure.

The obligations of intimacy pose difficult choices. An abstract notion of "harm to subjects" is no substitute for an awareness that multiple actors may be variously affected by our interventions, some of which are activist in intent and benevolent in effect.[1] As the "guest" of a country, as one metaphor of intimacy has it, does one stand up for one of its persecuted minorities or does one instead protect the state (since mistreatment of minorities is a major embarrassment in modern international politics) from the still more powerful forces of which one is, willy-nilly, a representative (Herzfeld 1997: 167)? Does one condemn the cultural management attempted in Hollywood films, as Askew asks, or does one try to work with and through them? All terms have their limitations; but "cultural intimacy" at least draws attention to the socially embedded consequentiality of tact and, especially, of its violation, and thus also to the personal, sometimes agonizing nature (as Askew herself shows) of the decisions that anthropologists face long beyond the completion of research.

Thus, to write something in good faith that others nevertheless take as a justification for genocide, persecution, or derision may reflect anything from poor judgment to an unavoidable accident of history. But not to rebut such an abuse of one's own reportage, and especially such a totalizing misrepresentation, is irresponsible precisely because it is a betrayal of the social intimacy that made the larger cultural analysis possible. It is, to expand Andreas Glaeser's useful expression, a synecdochical act of betrayal that is worse than mischievous. It is, indeed, particularly destructive in that it allows partial misrepresentation to legitimize overall annihilation—which is why Richard Maddox sees in the model of cultural intimacy, with its bodily and sexual overtones directly linked to racist theories about "miscegenation," the beginnings of a sound anthropological response to the horrors of genocide. The key here is to remember that cultural intimacy is not the public representation of domesticity, an often asexual idyll of harmony and cooperation, but the often raucous and disorderly experience of life in the concealed spaces of public culture. This is a distinction that all too easily escapes our attention.

Nation-states represent one major, if not the only, expansion of social to cultural intimacy; national sensitivity is a particularly powerful motivator of tact. Where the state is more abstractly ideological, such sensitivity, as Glaeser shows, can easily deteriorate into repression, so that its constant surveillance of everyday life inhibits the emergence of any recognizable sense of cultural intimacy at all. But national states, which often grow from weak and dependent beginnings, may also react sharply to criticism, particularly if they are embedded in a world order the rules and norms of which, promulgated by more powerful states, are alien to their citizens. It is both true and significant, as J. Lorand Matory argues here, that entities far larger than nation-states not only have their own zones of cultural intimacy but also generate the contexts in which the cultural intimacy of nations takes shape.

Most nation-states are nevertheless products of a peculiarly deliberate process of self-construction, as a result of which they often also have especially elaborate and analytically accessible ideologies of self-glorification, with correspondingly elaborate defenses of their collective intimacies. These ideologies, moreover, usually enjoy more popular support than do those of repressive systems such as that of the former German Democratic Republic described by Glaeser, precisely because they can carry a far greater load of dirty secrets—grounded in everyday experience—than can the Stalinist state's self-consuming purism. When nation-states become intolerant of minorities, they, too, begin instead to approach the paranoid condition that Glaeser describes. In general, however, they continue to command loyalty, so much so that repressive regimes often emphasize nationality rather than ideology as a means of maintaining stability.

My original formulation of cultural intimacy (Herzfeld 1997) was grounded in the specific case of Greek nationalism and its local refractions. Greece was an especially appropriate candidate for analysis in these terms, given the country's ambivalent relationship with the hegemonic model of Europe: Greece was at once the nominal ancestor of Europe and one of its most marginal components. The societies discussed here share many of Greece's historical vicissitudes. Turkey, for example, is the mirror image of Greece in the ambiguity of its relationship with "Europe."[2] Esra Özyürek's analysis of wedding rituals shows how that country's Western-leaning secularists must address both a resurgent tide of self-orientalization and antimilitaristic revisionism within their own ranks. Yet this constant glancing over the shoulder at the judgment of "Europe" suggests a global cultural hierarchy that has succeeded to the mantle (and also some of the weapons) of colonialism. These authors have in quite varied ways pushed the analysis of cultural intimacy toward a clearer recognition of such hegemonic entanglements, as indeed I have tried to do in my own work since publication of the original edition of *Cultural Intimacy*.[3]

Greece and Turkey do not stand alone in this regard. Brazil also provided an important early example in the way creolized architectural forms conveyed the tension between the European and the local (see Vlach 1984; see also Herzfeld 1987:119). To complicate such comparison, Spain, a former colonial power later thrown on hard times, is a complex mixture of internal cultural inequalities in which the question of whether such tongues as Catalan or Andalusian are dialects or languages is an index of relative political clout within a newly federated and ostensibly "diverse" system; it also provides interesting material for comparison in that official Spanish policy has gone in exactly the opposite direction of the Greeks' emphasis on ethnic unity and singularity (but see now Yiakoumaki 2002). The Arab world, although far more diverse in itself and hardly a unified field, was, like Greece, a *locus classicus* for the analysis of the linguistic phenomenon known as diglossia (Ferguson 1959)—the original inspiration and template for my coinage of "disemia." Here the referents are not primarily Europe and the Orient but Islamic pan-Arabism and localism, although these matters are also entwined with both an often-Eurocentric cosmopolitanism and Arab claims to have originated important aspects of European culture.

Thailand might not obviously fit this set. The notion of "Thainess" is grounded in a well-learned collective self-confidence. Like Greece, however, and for related political reasons, Thailand has for over a century and a half danced a complicated pas de deux with the Western powers whose version of cultural nationalism it agreed to imitate in key respects—including the development of an aggressively local sense of "heritage"—as the price of not being formally colonized (Herzfeld 2002). Rosalind Morris's observations about the ambiguities of whether the Thai prime minister's employees were his family or whether his family members were instead his employees illustrates nicely the slippage between private and public spaces that is key to the dynamics of cultural intimacy. "The things of the *oikos* [household] should not be seen in the *demos* [public weal]," so the Greek adage tells us (Herzfeld 1997:95, 167)—but which is which and why either should be a particularly privileged space for intimacy are questions to which the answers are surprisingly unpredictable.

What all these cases have in common is the way in which the ambiguities of the respective societies' relationship with Western culture underscore their problematic status in a globalized system of cultural value. This forces us to examine questions of cultural ambivalence as issues, not of definition (mixed or hybrid versus "pure" cultures), but of the power to define the good, the beautiful, and the important, and to say what constitutes the center in relation to which other things are marginal or mixed.[4] Ideals such as diversity, respect for local heritage, self-determination, and cultural citizenship are all well-intentioned concerns. They nevertheless risk becoming routinized within larger, global hierarchies of significance, much as the growing emphasis on auditing ethics risks surrendering ethical responsibility to an equally abstract set of routines. Moreover, because the oppressed populations of the world have discovered that identity discourse is one of the few tools they can use against hegemonic national structures, anthropologists are often justifiably reluctant to point out that trap (see, notably, Jackson 1995).

Their concern is to guard against breaches in the cultural intimacy of those who can least afford such an invasion. As Andrew Shryock points out in his introduction, however, it is precisely here that we might make principled and possibly unexpected decisions. Whatever we decide, the dilemmas are tough. The critique of officially benign policies that disguise persistent inequalities, for example, risks provoking a reversion to worse alternatives. Thus, the ideology of "cosmopolitan liberalism" that Maddox imputes to the Spanish authorities is certainly preferable to restoring the grim cultural and other tyrannies of the *franquista* era. But failure to point out its ironies, as Maddox does here, would leave intact the criteria by which the strong castigate and categorize the weak.

These essays show how easily conceding victory to tact can shade into a refusal to shoulder responsibility. Ethnography can speak truth to global power, because its focus on what Arthur Kleinman (1999:90) has usefully called "local worlds" reveals that cultures are not things, cannot be clearly defined, keep changing, and—for all these reasons—should not be reified as property in a manner that reduces them to playthings of the neoliberal economic order.[5] Today's anthropology is no longer willing to play that sycophantic role; its practitioners have too much respect for the people with whom they work. For that reason, they are also willing to face those people's criticisms of what they write; Shryock's essay on Arab Americans takes a particularly courageous step in that direction.[6]

Principled tactlessness may be ethically useful, because, in the reactions that it provokes as well as in the insights that it generates more directly, it can expose powerful hegemonies. In the discourse of foreign policy, world-dominant models of culture extend the logic of colonialism, through an often taken-for-granted ranking of allegedly typical traits—what I have called "the global hierarchy of value" (Herzfeld 2004) and what in a broadly similar vein Rosalind Morris here calls the "totalized network." Whether as Spanish cosmopolitan liberalism, Turkish modernist secularism, Thai "transparency," or a Hollywood director's desire to represent essential African culture honestly, the result is, broadly speaking, a powerful valorization of criteria identified as conforming to (or surpassing) Western ideals. Maddox takes the analysis to its home base: reading the European Union bureaucracy from Cris Shore's (2000) ethnographic revelations, he probes the behind-the-scenes cultural intimacy of the new Europe—gossip about the supposedly un-European activities without which many bureaucrats would not have been able to function in the European system at all.

The geopolitical aspect of cultural intimacy is crucial. Without it, we would not know *why* some cultural forms are devalued. By examining the historical and political conditions under which certain cultural ideals are considered noble and others less so, we contest the pernicious (but pervasive) notions that Western values are universally valid; that there are fixed cultural boundaries "out there"; and that these boundaries—running approximately from west to east and north to south—reproduce on the earth's surface the contours of a natural hierarchy of culture. Who decides that the musical comedies Egyptian intellectuals love to watch are lowbrow? Why are "boaters" embarrassing? Why are these, in fact, embarrassing questions, and whom do they embarrass?

Beyond the abstract model of culture-in-general lies an arbitrary hierarchy of cultures, one that is of largely European derivation and has lost little of its power in the postcolonial era. The echoes of Gobineau, for example, ring clear in the modern Brazil described by Matory. In Europe itself, for all the pious endorsements of diversity, there are still those who, even after the horrors of ethnic cleansing in the 1990s, would exclude Bosnia and Turkey from the EU because they "are Muslim" and "therefore" not European. In a gentler vein, what Maddox has identified as cosmopolitan liberalism in Spain has a larger reach throughout a continent at times desperately reaching to co-opt and sometimes to subvert the currently mandatory language of inclusiveness (Shore 2000:82), much as European Space Agency bureaucrats recuperate a rhetoric of "cooperation" from patterns of constant conflict (Zabusky 1995). The official Brazilian enthusiasm for hybridity and creative cultural mixing that Collins describes offers a precise parallel from the New World. Since hybridity, like cosmopolitanism and cultural diversity, represents threats to taxonomic order, states and other identity bureaucracies seek to control such anomalies by transforming the disorder they represent into new forms of order. The key task here is to historicize this constant reworking of ostensible absolutes—especially that of "order" itself.

What then emerges in the intimate spaces of conventional ethnographic practice has a strong public and global grip as well, so that our commentaries are far from inconsequential. They show *who* gets to define what is moral, acceptable, and appropriate. This is what Kelly Askew and Andrew Shryock mean when they point out that anthropologists' work is always potentially "applied." By the same token, some communities could be damaged by the exposure of their collective intimacies. But why is that information damaging at all? By what standards can the persistence of nonstandard religious forms, uncouth manners, or ethnic hybridity become a source of danger to a larger interest? And what happens when the powerful take over the discourse of difference—turning Candomblé into a national treasure or celebrating the diversity of Spanish identities, for example—to those whose local concerns have been expropriated in this way?

Ethnographers seek connections between daily life and larger cultural patterns as a matter of course. If the originality of this collection lies largely in its authors' having pushed ethnography out into the public space, we will now want to ask how this might reform the practice of ethnography in its more conventional settings as well. At the same time, it would be seductively easy to stretch the concept of cultural intimacy in the direction of intimacy *tout court*—a psychologistic reduction against which Glaeser, in particular, usefully warns. Personal experience is clearly the key to the kind of cultural knowledge discussed here. Walter Armbrust, for example, clearly has an insider's sense of what Egyptians "really" like in the cinema, and he skillfully shows us *how* he knows. He recounts what happens when Egyptian friends sense that he is about to put Egyptian cinema itself on stage and so expose their own cultural foibles; the split between self-presentation and the sources of casual pleasure emerges more or less identically in writing for a public and in dinner-table conversations in the presence of foreigners.

Tact remains at issue for many reasons, not the least of which is the practical consideration of friendship. We want to understand citizens' personal and collective perspectives, whether or not these emanate from state-controlled media, but we do not want to embarrass our friends. Only when citizens are excluded from the process of cultural defense, becoming its victims instead, does frontal critique seem more appropriate. Glaeser, for example, robustly dissects the appalling silliness of the fears that the Stasi implanted in the East German populace. Armbrust, on the other hand, among sophisticated friends, sympathetically but firmly contests their denials of musical films' significance in their lives. He does not reject the denials outright, but instead analyzes them, shifting critique away from simplistic endorsements of local assumptions about the suitability of particular genres for particular groups—a source, as he says, of the frequent inadequacy of media ethnography. He courageously lets us in on some of the more private conversations that reveal the shifting grounds of his Egyptian friends' reactions. This is the sort of ethnography of casual encounters that really does give the lie to received cultural pieties and, in so doing, reveals the international structures of value that still govern the lives of even the most powerful citizens.

It would be especially interesting to compare Armbrust's perceptive use of his own status as a knowledgeable foreigner with Purnima Mankekar's (1999) insights, arguably grounded in a paradoxically more ambivalent status as a fellow Indian, into the reception of television shows. Do Armbrust's Egyptian friends engage in a comparable commentary in their own intimate spaces, and are their comments similarly differentiated from what they tell him? One would expect that to be the case, because the presence of an outsider of virtually any degree provides the touchstone for the defense of the cultural intimacy revealed in these socially intimate spaces. Do the specific relationships among those discussing the films affect their assessments? Do husband and wife, for example, offer each other the same sorts of observations as colleagues at work? Do two brothers? Armbrust's skill as a writer of ethnography partly subsists in his ability to adumbrate such engagements while writing under the confining discipline of a single essay, but a further discussion of such details might yet expand our understanding of how people reconcile their defensive use of official discourse with their own lived experience.

In the same vein, Rosalind Morris's reading of Thai political "transparency" is convincing because it springs from direct personal experience, again skillfully conveyed through what one might call, with apologies to Clifford Geertz, "thick inscription."[7] But her account prompts yet further questions. First, is this a peculiarly Thai phenomenon? Morris wisely suggests that it is not entirely so, drawing parallels—increasingly heard in the Bangkok press as well—between Thailand's Thaksin and Italy's Berlusconi.[8] Such transnational comparisons are especially valuable because one of the most common defenses of cultural intimacies takes the form of arguing that "we" are not the only country to display some undesirable feature (or, alternatively, that "we" are uniquely qualified to know what is right). Such defensiveness is a response to the awareness of a larger international audience's potentially mocking interest. Morris's account supports her recognition of a "totalized network" of value, in which the language of political decency and even of transparency, with its overtones of a global morality, becomes a means both of concealing and of protecting some of the seamier realities of social and political life.

The parallel with Italy raises questions about the extent to which revelations of nontransparency are reproduced in—or themselves reproduce—the everyday forms of neighborhood gossip in Thailand, Italy, or many other countries. The fact that the Italian term *mafia* has wide currency in Thailand today is suggestive of insertion in some larger discursive universe.[9] To show convincingly how the "totalized network" achieves its effect, however, we must reciprocally pursue its ordinary realizations in everyday life; for many Italians, for example, *mafia* conveys a code of menacing courtesy in defense of certain supposedly traditional values at least as much as it does the organized violence usually understood by the term in English, and this is important for understanding how most Italians read the current national political scene.

Recognizing such connections entails a return to conventional sites of ethnographic analysis, but via a thoroughly postmodern awareness of hybridity and contingency; it is an acknowledgment of the *reciprocal* relevance of larger ideological structures and local forms of social interaction. When Morris writes that Thaksin's ability to induce middle-class Thais to identify with him "rests on his capacity to effect the collapse of differences: between family and employees, between the ruling class and the ruled . . . on a terrain that is miraculously flattened by the possibility of reciprocity," her argument presupposes evidence that is offstage here—the evidence that people actually do invoke Thaksin as a role model and do seek his leadership as a guarantee of their own imagined future successes. Thaksin's continuing popularity suggests that this conclusion is right on the mark. But what about those Thais who express distaste for his antics and would be horrified at the very suggestion that they wished to identify with him? His successes are embedded in a complex reality, to which ethnography must now return if it is to secure the imaginative insights of Morris's appealing analysis at an empirical level. Such a requirement springs from the realist transparency, so to speak, of anthropological method; and it also suggests new ways of examining in parallel the class and educational basis of the distaste that Berlusconi's many critics express for his policies and actions.

We can reorient this plea for localized ethnography in another way. To decide whether transparency is in fact a form of what Glaeser calls synecdochical mischief, we must determine how this rhetoric operates in the home, at the village council, in the schoolroom, and so on. What do ordinary people say about the language of campaigns? Do they mimic the media, or do the media mimic them? Do the media persuade, or simply confirm existing prior judgments? Morris, in a Baudrillardian parallel with my own "simulacra of sociality" promulgated by big companies like airlines (Herzfeld 1997:6–8), perceptively seizes on what she calls the "simulacrum of a vote." Is it so perceived by the local actors, and do they in turn reproduce these simulacra for their own, perhaps very different local purposes? Morris is able to convey the pervasiveness in everyday Thai life of the rhetoric of transparency, and acutely pinpoints the mutual dependence of legality and corruption at the very core of cultural intimacy.[10] In many societies, such connections are obscured by distinctions between formal and informal or official and popular; these discriminations, as Charles Stewart (1989) has demonstrated for the ecclesiastical-folk distinction in modern Greek religion, are themselves both expressions and instruments of a hegemonic cultural order, and an important task for ethnography is to trace their effects in everyday life. The dialectical tension thus revealed between public representations and the immediacy of local worlds calls for new ways of doing ethnography in old spaces; the fashionable stuff of representation has great currency in the no-longer-so-fashionable sites of traditional ethnography. We have been there, but we have not always done that. Refusing the challenge of rethinking local ethnography is a surrender to those same hegemonic forces that represent the local as unimportant and would have us follow suit.

By facing the defensiveness of elites and the real risks to subaltern others that lie in the exposure of culturally intimate spaces, these authors have bridged the complicated methodological gap between public culture and lived experience. Some very interesting and new results emerge. For example, when Shryock somewhat reluctantly—and thus all the more bravely—breaks his silence about the embarrassments of Arab self-representation in Detroit, he is opening up for critique the very hierarchy that forces his Arab American friends to feel so defensive in the first place. His self-aware breaching of the walls of their cultural intimacy is a critique of the cultural hierarchy that forced them to build and maintain those walls. In a classic form of hegemony, Arab Americans' apparent willingness to play the patriotic game generates accusations of duplicity from outside as much as from within the fractured ethnic community, in which any hope of unity must often subsist in precisely those aspects of their supposedly collective culture to which they cannot admit without serious risk—including, prominently, the fact of internal differentiation itself. They are induced to concur in an upsetting ideological process—what Shryock describes as "mainstreaming"—through which they can gain incremental advantages with no long-term assurance that these will last.

Shryock's determination to refuse complicity in their self-silencing parallels Matory's equally principled stance in refusing the stigma that some Afro-Brazilian leaders had been induced to accord homosexuality—a process, as he bluntly remarks, that "deserves explanation in itself." By asking *who* defines acceptable, polite, or "good" culture—by demanding to identify the forces that impinge on the ethnographic situation we are analyzing—we can also suggest how and why that risk should be faced. Often, the key agent here is the national state and its bureaucracy, the classic instance of a formal organization that cannot admit, but could not survive without, the socially unifying presence of informal relationships and disreputable knowledge.

Özyürek's deeply informed account of Turkish collective self-representations at weddings again illustrates the importance of knowing both the local practices and the context in which official values are produced and change. She shows how, in adapting a long tradition of familistic metaphors in Ottoman and Republican Turkish history (see Delaney 1995), state officials also actively encourage identification of the voluntaristic characteristics of civil marriage with a similarly voluntaristic reading of national identity. State officials actively refashion intimate social relations in order to recast the ideals of national culture. But Özyürek's perceptive move prompts a further question. Since we know that virtually all families have dirty linen, and that both the joys of shared intimacy that this creates as well as the attendant fear of exposure are significant factors in preserving these families' united fronts, does the adoption of new familistic metaphors allow Turkish citizens to extrapolate from their direct experiences of marriage and other rituals to a more saucy perception of what lies behind the austere face of state power? And does such intimate insight afford the state the same kind of loyalty that it does the family?

Özyürek writes of the shift from "paternalistic notions of intimacy" that "stress obedience and respect" to a new intimacy based on free choice. Yet if we concede that what the older state ideology projected was not intimacy at all, but its denial at the heart of the family, and if we may guess also that the ideals of obedience and respect were often defied in the truly intimate spaces of family life, then the real cultural intimacy of modern Turkey also rests on what we do *not* see in public ritual. The "intimacy" that Republican ideologues project is an idealistic representation of familial intimacy; it is not the lived social experience, at once disturbing and comforting, that constitutes the metonymic basis of cultural intimacy as such. The experiential reality of family life does not lie in this state-produced display of affection freely given, but at least partially in family quarrels and tensions that parallel the political friction and horse-trading about which the self-appointed military guardians of state political morality (as well as ordinary citizens) both complain and (in international settings) enjoin silence.

It also lies not in the suppression of paternalism, but in its persistence. As

Özyürek notes, Yapı Kredi Bank exhibit organizer Zafer Toprak, by reject-
ing slavish submission to the memory of Atatürk, implicitly recognizes this
persistence, which is dramatically sustained in the ceaseless drumbeat of visitors' invocations to their historic national "father." The old values have become embarrassing to the leaders of a country in which occidentalizing tendencies define a powerful modernity; they now constitute an important
element of the cultural intimacy of which they were once the very antithesis. Maddox describes a strikingly similar reversal in the transition from franquista to democratic Spain, with the increasingly secretive and embarrassing
persistence of a personalism that was well-established long before Franco
came to power and was common in Europe far beyond the borders of Spain,
but that today has come to be seen as incompatible with the ideals of Eurocentric liberalism.

The tantalizing hints of cultural intimacy thus transformed are no easier
to probe than were their predecessors. Where once men sought to hide the
shame of their women's presumed licentiousness, for example, it is persistent
patriarchy that Turks now experience as "embarrassing" (the term, significantly, is Özyürek's). Paternalism, formerly the public face of a society in
which displays of affection were seen as subversive of morality, masculinity,
and militarism, is now at odds with the conventions of the modernist state
morality. It would therefore be helpful to know more about the forms the
newly furtive patriarchy takes in daily social life, enriching Özyürek's probing dissection of state ritual through juxtaposition with the kind of analysis
of internal family discord that Panourgiá (1995), for example, has dared to
apply to modern urban Greece. Debates about morality, as much in the privacy of family homes as in public spaces, "are regularly a source of ideological and organizational change," as Matory remarks for the African diaspora
in this volume; it would be useful to be able to listen in ethnographically to
those conversations. Intimacy is always the space of the dirty linen; what
changes, to historicize Douglas's (1966) celebrated definition, is the composition of "dirt."

Özyürek has usefully introduced the term "collective familiarity" into
the discussion. But it is crucially important to distinguish—as Özyürek does
not—collective familiarity, a state-inspired simulacrum of social relations
(to invoke again that Baudrillardian trope), from cultural intimacy. Cultural
intimacy is not the same as the public representation of domestic intimacy;
it is the antithesis of the latter. True cultural intimacy is rarely acknowledged
by state actors. The latter rely instead on the *tacit* acceptance of moral inver-
sions as necessary to securing citizens' daily political participation and cooperation. In this regard, the premise of cultural intimacy reverses the public
character of Habermas's "bourgeois intimacy" altogether. The nineteenth-
century Greek state-sponsored folklorists who praised the idealized Greek

family as a repository of Western notions of affect were producing a bourgeois public image (see also Bakalaki 1994), but there is nothing to suggest
that most Greeks necessarily saw it as an accurate portrait. In the modernist
settings Özyürek describes for Turkey, again, such simulacra are the very antithesis of cultural intimacy; they generate an *ersatz* "intimacy" to which
neither politicians nor family members necessarily conform.

Indeed, Özyürek's telling observation that such familiarity was not always
in place before it was adopted for public display—that it did not always represent already-existing social experience—shows how and why an *absence* of
reciprocal conjugal affection and equality may now be a hallmark of cultural
intimacy. Coldness among family members was appropriate to the old Turkish reception room, but it is not formally appropriate to the modern living
room—both spaces, not of familial intimacy, but of domesticity on display.
As Özyürek demonstrates through her analysis of museum displays, it is the
agency of journalists and public intellectuals, as well as of political leaders, to
which we must attribute these changes.

Özyürek, like Maddox, has cleverly exposed the socially complex and
historically fast-paced deployment of artifice, much of it mass mediated,
through which a reversal of public morality emerged. Such work, which his-
toricizes the phenomenon of cultural intimacy far more effectively than appears in my initial attempt to formulate the concept, inspires me to suggest
an ethnographic parallel with recent changes in official Greek notions of
ethnicity. For Greek political leaders in the late 1990s, diversity suddenly became more respectable, although without entirely displacing the old exclu-
sivism (see, for example, Yiakoumaki 2002). Such an apparently profound
shift in attitude actually draws on older self-perceptions of Greek people as
generous and tolerant hosts, on the familiar device of staging spontaneity (although now under the guise of adaptability), and on the routinization of
"diversity" as a trope for "unity"—the paradox at the core of what Maddox
has identified as the "cosmopolitan liberalism" of the modern Spanish state
and the condescending reductionism that Askew discovered at the heart of
the film industry. None of this means that the new attitudes are a form of
insincerity; such a claim would clearly be an unjustifiable calumny. They are
nevertheless far less discontinuous with past defenses of cultural intimacy
than may at first appear to be the case. This insight is a particularly valuable
consequence of historicizing the model.

New attitudes always contain the histories of what they have displaced.
Suddenly, with accession to and active engagement in the European Union,
extremes of Turkish nationalism—once normative but now potentially embarrassing—have been transmuted, along with equally delegitimated models of patriarchal authority, from public norms into aspects of cultural intimacy. Similarly, in the Brazil of Collins's account, the strategic emergence of

sexual freedom as an expression and explanation of hybridity has displaced older norms of Catholic chastity and racial purity as the key source of cultural legitimacy. Matory shows, however, that, as a result, Afro-Brazilian efforts to sustain legitimacy in a hierarchy of value still nominally dominated by Eurocentric ideals now refocus on specific *kinds* of sexuality, and specifically on the suppression of homosexuality. The alternative, as we see among the Pentecostalists described by Collins, is to rebel against the newly dominant idiom of hybridity, whether as race, as ritual, or as food.

More ethnographic detail on what Collins here calls "historical shifts in the structures of intimacy" at the level of domestic practices, as well as on the forms of resistance to such changes in households and other private spaces, could only enrich these already persuasive accounts of the cultural intimacies thus transformed. Work of this kind helps to create critical distance from the occlusion of historical process and cultural contingency through "structural nostalgia"—the invocation of a supposedly always-recently lost world of reciprocity and respect (Herzfeld 1997:109–114). Structural nostalgia is an important defense of cultural intimacy; it allows social actors to "justify" present "flaws" as historical intrusions in the eternal essence of perfection. It conveniently obscures evidence suggesting that the moral order itself has changed—that what is now considered disreputable was once the moral ideal. Despite its relative absence from this collection, it thus serves as an important symbolic prop for cultural intimacy in many places, especially when it is coupled with the device of blaming foreign interference for present-day degeneracy.

Anthropology is now old enough as a scholarly practice for its exponents to be able to historicize their own entailment in the phenomena they study, framing structural nostalgia in terms of their own recorded perceptions. They can compare earlier forms of domesticity, recorded by their predecessors, with what is to be found in the field today, and show how once-dominant rural modes now function as benchmark stereotypes for self-consciously modernizing, urban elites (whether these people work on exhibits of national culture or on their own self-presentation). Özyürek's urban secularists, for example, take on new life when they are compared with the rustic images of Paul Stirling's *Turkish Village* (1965), which correspond to aspects of national culture the present-day secularists might prefer to suppress. Anthropologists must also not forget to investigate the experiential realities of modern domestic life; otherwise, comparison cannot reach beyond speculation, or beyond stereotypes embedded in modernist self-stereotypes and their associated images of the past and of remote regions.

While these essays largely rectify the historical deficiency of my original formulation, they necessitate a return to local worlds so that we can observe how these processes articulate with current social experience. In so doing,

we will more easily understand the extraordinary willingness of human beings to follow flags, ideologies, and collective names—symbols about which
they often express skepticism or disdain—at times even unto death. Above
all, we will begin to understand why they appear to acquiesce in those encompassing tyrannies of collective embarrassment that Australians, with a fine
sense of embodiment as well as of global hierarchy, call "cultural cringe." It
will become paradoxically clear that power operates globally only to the extent that it is able to pervade the intimate spaces of social life.

Anthropologists not only have arguably the most effective access to the
lived consequences of such contradictions, but also are in their own experiences a practical source of insight into the fluid realities of social life. Their
privileged but ethically charged involvement with at least some dimensions
of cultural intimacy, as Askew forcefully argues, demonstrates that cultures
are neither hermetically bounded nor mutually irreconcilable. In that context, cultural intimacy, too, constantly changes in its particular burdens of
embarrassment. The mass mediation of cultural forms has only served to amplify the cacophony and accentuate the cringe, generating new avenues of
inquiry. The goal is not to return to an old-fashioned, community-bounded
ethnography that simply reproduces the logic of case studies in support of
some formal theory. Instead, it is to capture the synergy generated by close
ethnographic encounters with the multiple zones of interaction between the
management and the impact of global political processes. From such encounters comes responsible, and responsive, social critique. In this context,
while some might disagree with our decisions or our practices, none could
accuse us of refusing the ethical accountability that intense, passionate, and
—above all—intimate engagement with social worlds entails.

Notes

   1. Institutionalized good intentions alone are an insufficient guarantee of enduring commitment; while anthropologists can be relatively proud of their discipline's
serious approach to ethical issues, my argument is that *no* formula can protect a con-
scientious individual from the moral imperative of addressing unintended consequences, but that all too often generic formulae—including both disciplinary self-
satisfaction and the automated alibis of human subjects declarations—do serve to
blunt the edge of ethical self-examination.
   2. In a comparable case, Kligman (1989:326–327n.4) applied the notion of "religious disemia" to Romania—a country split between Orthodox and Catholic religious factions but also tormented by an ambivalent relationship with Europe.
   3. See, especially, Herzfeld 2004; a new edition of *Cultural Intimacy* is also in
preparation as I write.
   4. Gupta's (1998) important discussion of the categories of "indigenous," "scien-

tific," and "hybrid" knowledge reveals a similarly global power dynamic in the politics of their significance.

5. Huntington's (1996) "clash of civilizations" argument represents a particularly disturbing instance of this construal of the culture concept, so deeply at odds with anthropological experience. For a discussion of the role of "possessive individualism" in the conceptualization of modern cultural heritage, see Handler 1985. For a sensitive overview of the dilemmas of cultural ownership, see Brown 1998. For a critical analysis of "heritage" (*moradok*) as an intrusive concept in Thailand, a country long locked in a complex engagement with Western models, see Askew 1996. For a useful discussion of the expansion of person-property relations to definitions of national territory, see Sutton 1997.

6. It was especially when anthropologists began studying Western (and more particularly European) societies that they had to confront the issue of what to do when "they read what we write" (Brettell 1993); this historical circumstance is revealing of where cultural power still lies.

7. As Morris shows, ordinary people co-opt the grand rhetorical tropes; in the local community politics I have studied in Thailand, two key terms that have been adopted in this way are "cooperation" and "participation" (the latter often, significantly, in its English form even in Thai speech).

8. See, for example, Bangkokian 2003 and Pana 2003. In Italy, where I have also done fieldwork, people worry about the image their prime minister gives their country; they are less inclined than Thais (or Greeks, for that matter) to defend national rather than local intimacies, yet the recent antics of their unusually nationalistic prime minister on an international (and especially European) stage may, ironically, have increased their sense of solidaristic embarrassment—a nice demonstration, if so, of the importance of cultural intimacy as a basis for national bonding. At the same time, admirers may experience politicians' tactlessness, not as embarrassing, but as reassuringly proud; during the 1990s, for example, many Greeks admired their then foreign minister, Theodoros Pangalos, for his outspoken sarcasm about, notably, the German political leadership of the time.

9. There is also a Thai expression (*phuu mii iththiphon*—literally, "people having influence") that invites comparison with the Italian *amici degli amici* ("friends of friends").

10. Morris's linkage of mediums with media moguls is inspired, in that it allows her to transcend the artificial and ethnocentric line between traditional forms of ritual and the technological wonders of modernity. Moguls, too, are fit subjects for ethnographic analysis.

References Cited

Askew, Marc. 1996. "The Rise of *Moradok* and the Decline of the *Yarn*: Heritage and Cultural Construction in Urban Bangkok." *Sojourn* 11, no. 2: 183–210.
Bakalaki, Alexandra. 1994. "Gender-Related Discourses and Representations of Cultural Specificity in Nineteenth-Century and Twentieth-Century Greece." *Journal of Modern Greek Studies* 12: 75–112.

Bangkokian. 2003. "Bangkokian: Thaksin and Silvio: Separated at Birth?" *The Nation* (Bangkok), 6 August 2003.
Brettell, Caroline B., ed. 1993. *When They Read What We Write: The Politics of Ethnography*. Westport, Conn.: Bergin & Garvey.
Brown, Michael F. 1998. "Can Culture Be Copyrighted? *Current Anthropology* 39: 193–222.
Delaney, Carole. 1995. "Father State, Motherland, and the Birth of Turkey." Pp. 177–199 in *Naturalizing Power: Essays in Feminist Cultural Analysis*, eds. Sylvia Yanagisako and Carole Delaney. New York: Routledge.
Douglas, Mary. 1966. *Purity and Danger: An Analysis of Concepts of Pollution and Taboo*. London: Routledge & Kegan Paul.
Ferguson, Charles A. 1959. "Diglossia." *Word* 15: 325–340.
Gupta, Akhil. 1998. *Postcolonial Developments: Agriculture in the Making of Modern India*. Durham, N.C.: Duke University Press.
Handler, Richard. 1985. "On Dialogue and Destructive Analysis: Problems in Narrating Nationalism and Ethnicity." *Journal of Anthropological Research* 41: 171–182.
Herzfeld, Michael. 1987. *Anthropology through the Looking-Glass: Critical Ethnography in the Margins of Europe*. Cambridge: Cambridge University Press.
———. 1992. "History in the Making: National and International Politics in a Rural Cretan Community." Pp. 93–122 in *Europe Observed*, eds. J. K. Campbell and João de Pina Cabral. London: Macmillan.
———. 1997. *Cultural Intimacy: Social Poetics in the Nation-State*. New York: Routledge.
———. 2002. "The Absent Presence: Discourses of Crypto-Colonialism." *South Atlantic Quarterly* 101: 899–926.
———. 2004. *The Body Impolitic: Artisans and Artifice in the Global Hierarchy of Value*. Chicago: University of Chicago Press.
Huntington, Samuel. 1996. *The Clash of Civilizations and the Remaking of World Order*. New York: Simon and Schuster.
Jackson, Jean E. 1995. "Culture, Genuine and Spurious: The Politics of Indianness in the Vaupés, Colombia." *American Ethnologist* 22: 3–27.
Kleinman, Arthur. 1999. "Bioethics and Beyond." *Daedalus* 128, no. 4: 69–97.
Kligman, Gail. 1989. *Căluş: Symbolic Transformation in Romanian Ritual*. Chicago: University of Chicago Press.
Mankekar, Purnima. 1999. *Screening Culture, Viewing Politics: An Ethnography of Television, Womanhood, and Nation in Postcolonial India*. Durham, N.C.: Duke University Press.
Pana Janviroj. 2003. "Berlusconi: Is He an Emperor in New Clothes?" *The Nation* (Bangkok), 12 February 2003.
Panourgiá, E. Neni K. 1995. *Fragments of Death, Fables of Identity: An Athenian Anthropography*. Madison: University of Wisconsin Press.
Shore, Cris. 2000. *Building Europe: The Cultural Politics of European Integration*. London and New York: Routledge.
Shore, Cris, and Susan Wright. 2000. "Coercive Accountability: The Rise of Audit Culture in Higher Education." Pp. 57–89 in *Audit Cultures: Anthropological Stud-*

ies in *Accountability, Ethics and the Academy*, ed. Marilyn Strathern. London: Routledge.

Stewart, Charles. 1989. "Hegemony or Rationality? The Position of the Supernatural in Modern Greece." *Journal of Modern Greek Studies* 7: 77–104.

Stirling, Paul. 1965. *Turkish Village*. New York: John Wiley & Sons.

Sutton, David E. 1997. "Local Names, Foreign Claims: Family Inheritance and National Heritage on a Greek Island." *American Ethnologist* 24: 415–437.

Vlach, John Michael. 1984. "The Brazilian House in Nigeria: The Emergence of a Twentieth-Century House Type." *Journal of American Folklore* 97: 3–23.

Yiakoumaki, Vassiliki. 2002. "'The Nation as Acquired Taste': On Greekness, Consumption of Food Heritage, and the Making of the New Europe." Ph.D. dissertation, Anthropology, New School University, New York.

Zabusky, Stacia E. 1995. *Launching Europe: An Ethnography of European Cooperation in Space Science*. Princeton, N.J.: Princeton University Press.

Index

.

The authorized representative in the EU for product safety and compliance is:
Mare Nostrum Group
B.V Doelen 72
4831 GR Breda
The Netherlands

www.ingramcontent.com/pod-product-compliance
Lightning Source LLC
Chambersburg PA
CBHW030636270326
41929CB00007B/103